NEW TECHNOLOGY AND INDUSTRIAL RELATIONS IN FLEET STREET

NEW TECHNOLOGY AND INDUSTRIAL RELATIONS IN FLEET STREET

RODERICK MARTIN

CLARENDON PRESS · OXFORD
1981

Oxford University Press, Walton Street, Oxford OX2 6DP

London Glasgow New York Toronto
Delhi Bombay Calcutta Madras Karachi
Kuala Lumpur Singapore Hong Kong Tokyo
Nairobi Dar es Salaam Cape Town
Melbourne Auckland

and associate companies in
Beirut Berlin Ibadan Mexico City

Published in the United States by
Oxford University Press, New York

British Library Cataloguing in Publication Data
Martin, Roderick
    New technology and industrial relations in Fleet Street.
    1.   Industrial relations — Great Britain
    2.   Newspaper publishing — Great Britain
    I.   Title
    331'.041'07941   HD6976.P9G6

    ISBN 0-19-827243-X

Typeset by Anne Joshua Associates, Oxford
Printed in Great Britain
at the University Press, Oxford
by Eric Buckley
Printer to the University

Preface

This book deals with new technology and industrial relations in Fleet Street between 1975 and the end of 1979; it was substantially written between December 1979 and August 1980. Whilst it was being written major changes continued in Fleet Street, especially at The Times, and an attempt has been made to comment briefly upon major developments taking place during the period of writing; however, the analysis is concerned primarily with the late 1970s and, although many of the features of the 1970s will continue in the 1980s, no attempt is made to predict future events. The story of new technology and industrial relations in Fleet Street is thus a continuing one. But the period 1975-9 constitutes a relatively clearly defined phase. In 1975 both management and unions believed that the industry was facing a major economic crisis, which required joint management–union action; in 1977 the industry experienced one of its best financial years ever; in 1980 both management and unions again believed that the industry was facing a major economic crisis. The period was thus one of crisis, revival, and further crisis. In 1975 major question marks hung over the future prospects of the two London evening newspapers, at least one national daily, and one national Sunday newspaper; in 1980 the two London evening newspapers merged, to form the *New Standard*; and one daily newspaper and one Sunday newspaper were up for sale.

Research into current industrial relations problems poses considerable intellectual and personal difficulties. It is difficult to maintain detachment and a sense of perspective, especially when researching into industries as controversial, and as prone to dramatization, as national newspapers. It is particularly difficult to maintain such detachment and the avoidance of appearing to adopt the perspectives of one 'side' or the other without losing the confidence of participants;

the following pages will provide some indication of the extent to which I have succeeded in maintaining the role of empathetic observer. To enable the reader to judge my own preconceptions, they are the hardly unconventional ones that British national newspapers are amongst the best in the world, that in order to maintain their position, politically, culturally, and economically, major changes in their methods of production will be required in the near future, that such changes must be negotiated rather than imposed, despite the time and resources such negotiations involve, and that such negotiations can, initially, be more appropriately conducted at industry than company level.

The project could not have been undertaken without the co-operation of many people in the industry, both in management and in trade unions; I am very grateful for their willingness to talk fully, and in confidence, to an outside observer about the industry and its problems. In my experience newspapers have usually been willing to acknowledge that freedom of information works both ways, involving newspapers themselves in providing information to outside observers. In the interests of confidentiality I must thank them collectively rather than individually for their time and interest; without them the study would have been impossible. Fortunately, the same rules of confidentiality do not apply to personal friends or in academic life, and I am happy to acknowledge my debt to Mr J. D. F. Jones, who originally suggested the idea of a research project on new technology in Fleet Street, to Mr Peter Baker, and to Mr Gerry Bowen-Thomas, of the Department for External Studies, University of Oxford, for assistance and encouragement. I am also very grateful to Mrs Stella Wood, the Fellows' Secretary, Trinity College, for typing successive drafts quickly and accurately in the limited time available.

Information from the public record is documented appropriately; information from confidential sources is not footnoted.

I am happy to acknowledge the financial assistance of the George Webb Medley Fund, of the University of Oxford, and, especially, of the Social Science Research Council.

Trinity College, Oxford.
9 November 1980

Contents

List of Figures

Abbreviations

ACAS	Advisory Conciliation and Arbitration Service
ACP	Association of Correctors of the Press
APEX	Association of Professional, Executive, Clerical and Computer Staffs
ASTMS	Association of Scientific, Technical, Management and Supervisory Staffs
ATV	Associated Television Company Ltd.
AUEW(E)	Amalgamated Union of Engineering Workers (Engineering Section)
BBC	British Broadcasting Corporation
BDM	Bienniel Delegate Meeting (of NGA)
BPIF	British Printing Industries Federation
COHSE	Confederation of Health Service Employees
CPSA	Civil and Public Services Association
EEC	European Economic Community
EETPU	Electrical, Electronic, Telecommunication and Plumbing Union
FFI	Finance for Industry
FOC	Father of the chapel
FT	Financial Times
G&MWU	General and Municipal Workers Union
GLCSA	Greater London Council Staff Association
IBA	Independent Broadcasting Authority
ICI	Imperial Chemical Industries Ltd.
ICL	International Computers Ltd.
IOJ	Institute of Journalists
IPC	International Publishing Corporation
IPCS	Institute of Professional Civil Servants
IRE	Industrial Relations Executive (of NPA)
ITU	International Typographical Union

JHC	Joint House Committee
JSC	Joint Standing Committee
LTS	London Typographical Society
MGN	Mirror Group Newspapers Ltd.
MOC	Mother of the chapel
NALGO	National and Local Government Officers Association
NAP	New Agreements Project
NATSOPA	National Society of Operative Printers, Graphical and Media Personnel
NATSOPA RIRMA	NATSOPA: Revisers, Ink and Roller Makers and Auxiliaries
NATSOPA TA&E	NATSOPA: Technical, Administrative, and Executive
NGA	National Graphical Association
NGA TAE	NGA: Telecommunications and Electronics
NPA	Newspaper Publishers Association
NS	Newspaper Society
NSES	National Society of Electrotypers and Stereotypers
NUJ	National Union of Journalists
NUPE	National Union of Public Employees
NUPT	National Union of Press Telegraphists
NUS	National Union of Students
NUWDAT	National Union of Wallcovering, Decorative and Allied Trades
PKTF	Printing and Kindred Trades Federation
PPITB	Printing and Publishing Industry Training Board
SLADE	Society of Lithographic Artists, Designers, Engravers, and Process Workers
SOGAT	Society of Graphical and Allied Trades
SOGAT LCB	SOGAT: London Central Branch
SOGAT MMB	SOGAT: Machine Branch
TA	Typographical Association
T&G	Transport and General Workers Union
TASS	Technical and Supervisory Section (of AUEW)
TNL	Times Newspapers Ltd.

TSSA	Transport Salaried Staffs Association
TTO	The Thomson Organisation
TUC	Trades Union Congress
TUC PIC	TUC: Printing Industries Committee
TWG	Thomson Withy Grove Ltd.
UCATT	Union of Construction, Allied Trades and Technicians
USDAW	Union of Shop, Distributive and Allied Workers

Acknowledgements

I am grateful to The Open University for permission to reproduce Fig. 1 from The Open University, Industrial Relations: A Post Experience Course, *Press, Papers, and Print: A Case Study in Industrial Relations in the National Newspaper Industry*, © 1976, The Open University Press; to Her Majesty's Stationery Office for permission to reproduce Figs. 2, 3, and 4 from The Advisory, Conciliation, and Arbitration Service, *Industrial Relations in the National Newspaper Industry*, Cmnd 6680; to The Financial Times Ltd. for permission to reproduce Figs. 5 and 7; and to Arthur Andersen & Co. for permission to reproduce Fig. 8.

Note.   Throughout, The Times and the FT (roman) refer to the companies, *The Times* and the *FT* to the newspapers.

Chapter 1

Introduction: Fleet Street in the 1970s

At the beginning of 1971 Fleet Street appeared to have successfully withstood the mass development of television. Although the ownership of television sets had increased from 4,651,000 in 1955 to over 15 million, and television had usurped the role of the press as the prime manipulator of public opinion in left-wing demonology, Fleet Street's economic and political position had not been undermined, and new technology appeared to have the potential for giving Fleet Street new security.[1] The combined circulation of daily newspapers was 10.41 per cent lower in 1971 than it had been a decade earlier (14,176,000 in 1971, compared with 15,823,000 in 1961), and the return on capital invested remained low; but Britain remained a newspaper-reading nation — only Japan and the Scandinavian countries had a higher circulation of national daily newspapers per thousand of the population.[2] The *News Chronicle* and the *Sunday Citizen* had closed, and the *Daily Sketch* was soon to do so; but the *Daily Herald's* resurrection as the *Sun* resulted in a financially successful newspaper, and *The Times* and the *Sunday Times* were expanding circulation, if at great promotional expense. The attention politicians devoted to the press indicated their belief in its power to determine the content of the political agenda, especially during election campaigns, if not to determine the electorate's attitudes towards items on the agenda. Fleet Street had substantially colonized television; the companies involved in publishing newspapers were major — indeed, the major shareholders in commercial television.[3] The political commentators who appeared on television were normally Fleet Street figures, and the BBC as well as the commercial television companies had long ago signed recognition agreements with the National Union of Journalists.[4] These very close economic and editorial links between television and Fleet Street served to strengthen the position of Fleet Street.

By 1975 the situation had apparently changed, and Fleet Street felt itself to be in a crisis, with newspaper proprietors announcing the imminent death of Fleet Street 'as we know it'. Percy Roberts, then deputy chairman and chief executive of Mirror Group Newspapers Ltd., commented in his verbal evidence to the Royal Commission on the Press in March 1976, 'without being emotional or hysterical about it, we really do regard this joint committee [the Joint Standing Committee, discussed in chapter 5 below] as the absolute last chance for the industry. If we do not get it right now — and I am talking about 12 months, not 2 years — then . . . we might as well all wrap up and go home, because there will not be an industry as we know it in five years if we go on behaving in the way we are.'[5] The Royal Commission's chairman, Professor O. R. (now Lord) Macgregor, agreed, adding that the Royal Commission's Interim Report had been written in the same frame of mind. The change over the five-year period was not due to any dramatic social or cultural revolution; the British public had not suddenly decided that newspapers were a luxury they could dispense with now that television provided immediate and dramatic coverage of news and current affairs, as well as entertainment. The change was due more to the way in which long-standing economic and industrial relations problems were working themselves out in the face of changes in printing technology, bringing to a head problems which had been endemic in Fleet Street at least since the abolition of newsprint rationing in 1955.

This introductory chapter is a general account of the economic, political, and technological conditions in Fleet Street between 1971 and 1975, which led to the belief in 1976 that a new phase was imminent. The following chapters examine particular aspects in detail, and trace subsequent events.

i

The finances of national newspapers were, and remain, notoriously weak. Between 1970 and 1975 the financial results of national newspapers moved from a trough in 1970 to a peak in 1972, to a deeper trough in 1974, although the timing of peaks and troughs differed for different categories of newspapers.[6] Table 1.1 summarizes overall financial results for the six-year period.

Table 1.1

Profits and losses of national and London evening newspapers
1970–1975 (£,000s)

	Qualities		Popular and London Evenings		
	Daily	Sunday	Daily and Evening	Sunday	Total
1970	(1718)	(612)	3067	3151	3888
1971	1273	(1127)	8392	2631	11169
1972	4356	381	7875	3132	15744
1973	1863	1003	(357)	1957	4466
1974	(1592)	(1163)	(716)	(604)	(4075)
1975	(3802)	(3000)	8117	3428	4743

Notes   (i)   Figures for 1970–3 are for companies' own financial years. Those for 1974 and 1975 are calendar years. The figures for 1975 are companies' own estimates.

(ii)   Profits and (losses) are before interest, related publishing activities, extraordinary items and taxation.

(iii)   The allocation of common costs between titles is according to the companies' own methods.

Source   Royal Commission on the Press, *Interim Report*, p. 99.

The substantial losses indicate that the industry's financial results were poor, but the significance of the overall results can be judged only in relation to the capital employed and to the performance of other sectors of manufacturing industry. Unfortunately, it is impossible to present evidence on capital employed: unlike the earlier EIU Report, the Royal Commission on the Press did not publish figures for capital invested — perhaps understandably so, as accurate and up-to-date figures for the capitalization of Fleet Street are difficult to establish, and depend heavily upon the valuation of 'goodwill'.[7] As a substitute, Table 1.2 shows trading profits expressed as a percentage of turnover.[8]

Table 1.2

Trading profits as a percentage of turnover
1970–1975 (£,000s)

	Qualities		Populars and London Evenings	
	Daily	Sunday	Daily and Evening	Sunday
1970	−3.9	−2.8	2.8	7.7
1971	2.5	−4.9	6.9	5.6
1972	7.1	1.3	5.8	6.2
1973	2.7	3.0	−0.2	3.6
1974	−2.2	−3.2	−0.4	−1.0
1975	−4.8	−8.1	4.0	5.0

Notes   On same basis as Table 1.1.

Source   Royal Commission on the Press, *Interim Report,* p. 37.

Expressing trading profits as a percentage of turnover makes comparison with the financial performance of other industries impossible, since comparable figures are not available, and the Royal Commission made no attempt to compare the industry's financial performance with that of other industries. However, the financial performance of the industry was undoubtedly significantly worse than that of other industrial and commercial sectors. Table 1.3 shows the rates of return on non-North Sea trading assets for industrial and commercial companies in the same period:[9]

Table 1.3

Rate of return on Non-North Sea trading assets:
industrial and commercial companies

	(i) Pre-tax historic cost	(ii) Pre-tax real
1970	14.4	8.7
1971	15.0	8.7
1972	15.8	8.6
1973	17.3	7.2
1974	17.1	4.0
1975	15.5	3.4

Source   *Bank of England Quarterly Bulletin,* December 1978, p. 516.

The industry as a whole performed badly in the 1970s, the quality newspapers performing especially badly. Over the six-year period 1970-5 the quality dailies made a total profit of £380,000, a negligible rate of return, and the quality Sundays a total loss of £4,518,000; the financially most successful quality newspaper, the *Financial Times*, did not of course publish on Sundays. In contrast, the popular newspapers made a profit over the same period, but not a substantial one: £26,378,000 for the dailies and London evenings, £13,695,000 for Sundays. All categories of newspapers made an overall loss in 1974, and the qualities continued to do so, at a higher level, in 1975. Despite falling circulation, the popular newspapers were able to return to profitability in 1975 through charging higher cover prices, although a major reason for this success was the good performance of the *Sun*, counterbalancing a continuing poor performance by the *Daily Express*.

Although the industry's economic performance was poor over all, some newspapers were more successful financially than others. Unfortunately, it is impossible to provide a satisfactory account of the financial position of individual newspapers. At the publishers' request, the Royal Commission did not publish financial data on individual companies, and full financial results are not available elsewhere.[10] Some newspapers are owned by 'close' companies, and only limited financial data are published: the *Guardian*, the *Daily Telegraph*, and the *Observer*. Other newspapers are wholly owned subsidiaries, or part of larger corporations whose financial results, even when published by industrial sector, include activities outside national newspapers: the *Daily Mail*, the *Daily Express*, the *Sun*, the *Daily Mirror*, *The Times*, and the *Financial Times*. The most successful newspaper company was Murdoch's News International Ltd., publishers of the *Sun* and the *News of the World*. Throughout the 1970s the company paid a significant dividend (a peak of 37½ per cent in 1970 and 1971, a low of 27½ per cent in 1973, when there was a change in the capital structure, and 1974).[11] In 1976 News Group Newspapers, the subsidiary for News International's national newspapers, made a pre-tax profit of £6.8m on a turnover of £74.1m, or 9.1 per cent, higher than the average rate achieved by any category of newspaper in the 1970s: since the total profit made by all popular newspapers in 1976 was only £7.56m, other popular newspapers must have done substantially worse.[12] The financial results of Associated Newspapers Group Ltd., publishers of the *Daily Mail* and the *Evening News*, were substantially better than those of Beaverbrook Newspapers Ltd., publishers of the *Daily Express* and the *Evening Standard*; ordinary dividends for the former varied between 26.0 per cent (in 1969-70, 1970-1, and 1971-2) and 16.204 per cent in 1973-4, compared with between 14 per cent (in 1969-70 and 1970-1) and 1.34 per cent (in 1973-4) — although of course the differences may have been due to different financial structures, as well as to differences in the profitability of activities outside Fleet Street.[13] The publishers of *The Times* and the *Daily Mirror* encountered serious financial problems during the period, whilst the *Financial Times* remained profitable throughout: their financial situations are discussed in detail in the chapters on events in those houses. There is no detailed information available on the finances of the *Daily Telegraph*, *Observer*, or *Guardian*, but the latter two papers both came near to closing, and remained financially insecure throughout the period.

The poor financial results of Fleet Street were due to a deterioration in both markets in which the industry operated — readership and advertising. All newspapers drew revenue from both the sale of newspapers, and from the sale of advertising, the proportion of revenue from each varying markedly between categories of newspaper: quality newspapers obtained a far higher proportion of their income from the sale of advertising, as Table 1.4, covering the period 1970-5, shows.[14] The revenues of the quality newspapers were thus more sensitive to changes in the advertising market than the revenues of the populars, whilst the revenues of the latter were more sensitive to circulation changes, although of course the two mutually influenced each other.

Even in 1975 the number of daily newspapers bought approached the number of households, and the number of Sunday newspapers bought comfortably exceeded the number of households: in 1975 there were just over 17 million house-

Table 1.4

Advertising revenue as a percentage of total revenue:
national and London evening newspapers 1970–1975

	Qualities		Populars and London Evenings	
	Daily	Sunday	Daily and Evening	Sundays
1970	69	73	31	38
1971	63	71	31	36
1972	67	72	34	36
1973	70	74	36	38
1974	65	71	32	34
1975	58	66	27	31

Source   Royal Commission on the Press, *Interim Report,* p. 99.

holds, whilst the combined circulation of daily newspapers
was 14,112,000 and that of Sunday newspapers 20,495,000.
But whilst the trend in population and in household formation was up, the trend in newspaper circulation was down.[15]
As Table 1.5 shows, the average daily circulation of popular
newspapers declined from 12,423,000 in 1970 to 11,962,000
in 1975, of quality papers from 2,271,000 to 2,150,000 over
the same period, and of Sunday newspapers from 23,491,000
to 20,495,000.[16]

The trend in circulation was not one of uniform decline;
the circulation of daily newspapers rose to a peak early in
1974, and that of Sunday newspapers to a peak in 1973.
The overall trend was demoralizing rather than disastrous:
the peak circulation was below the peak circulation in the
previous decade, and the lowest point in the trough was substantially lower. The drop in circulation between 1974 and
1975 was especially steep — and was to be followed by a
further fall in 1976. Quality newspapers were more affected
by the drop than popular ones; the circulation of quality
newspapers was 6.72 per cent lower in 1975 than in 1974,
that of popular newspapers 4.24 per cent (or 6.52 per cent
excluding the *Sun*). Despite an increase in the adult population,
the overall circulation of daily newspapers was 5.32 per cent
lower in 1975 than it had been in 1970, and that of Sunday

Table 1.5

Circulation of national newspapers 1970–1975:
average daily circulation (000s)

Popular Dailies	1970	1971	1972	1973	1974	1975
Daily Express	3563	3413	3341	3290	3154	2822
Daily Mail	1890	1798	1702	1730	1753	1726
Daily Mirror	4570	4384	4280	4292	4205	3968
Daily Sketch	785	—	—	—	—	—
Sun	1615	2293	2699	2966	3380	3446
Total	12423	11888	12022	12278	12492	11962
Quality Dailies						
Daily Telegraph	1409	1446	1434	1420	1406	1331
Guardian	304	332	339	346	359	319
Financial Times	170	170	188	195	195	181
Times	388	340	341	345	345	319
Total	2271	2288	2302	2306	2305	2150
Sundays						
Total	23491	22744	22091	22095	21876	20495

Source   Royal Commission on the Press, *Interim Report,* p. 92 (adapted).

newspapers 12.75 per cent lower. But the grounds for collective concern were more substantial than indicated by the overall circulation figures: the rate of overall decline in the circulation of daily newspapers was held in check only by the massive expansion in circulation of the *Sun*. Whereas the circulation of the *Sun* was 113 per cent higher in 1975 than it had been in 1970, the combined circulation of other daily newspapers was 18 per cent lower. As well as bringing in totally new newspaper readers, and providing a substitute for former readers of the *Daily Sketch,* the *Sun* was capturing readers from the *Daily Mirror*. The *Daily Express* and *The Times* sustained particularly serious losses in circulation over the quinquennium, although the latter's decline was partly the result of a change in management policy, restricting the efforts made to expand circulation at all costs which followed Thomson's acquisition of the newspaper in 1966.

The effects of declining circulation upon newspaper revenues were held in check by increasing cover prices. Between 1970 and the end of 1975 all newspapers increased their cover prices on at least six occasions, increasing them significantly faster than the rate of inflation, especially in 1974 and 1975. Between 1970 and 1975 the index of retail prices rose from 100 to 185; but the average cover price of daily newspapers rose from 100 to 229, and of Sunday newspapers from 100 to 236.[17] Historically, increases in cover price had not had a direct effect upon circulation: the demand for newspapers appeared to be perhaps surprisingly inelastic. However, the substantial and rapid increase in cover prices in 1974 and early 1975, both absolutely and relatively to general price levels, was associated with a marked decline in circulation, although this may have been due to an overall decline in disposable income during rapid inflation rather than to the increase in the price of newspapers *per se*. Owing to the effects of cover price increases, and the comparative resilience of circulation in the face of those increases, the significance of revenue from sales became greater for all newspapers, both popular and quality, than it had been five years earlier, although the contrast between quality and popular newspapers remained.

Changes in advertising revenues did not march *pari passu* with changes in circulation, although declining circulation obviously made it difficult for advertising managers to justify increased rates to advertisers. Advertising revenues were affected by the same factors as circulation levels, only more so. The share of the advertising market being won by newspapers was shrinking very gradually, over a long period: between 1960 and 1975 advertising expenditure in the national press declined by 0.7 per cent a year in real terms, an expansion of classified advertising failing to offset a decline in display advertising.[18] The development of commercial television significantly limited the market for display advertising in national newspapers, although the Royal Commission's studies could not reach a precise conclusion on the effects of television upon newspaper advertising revenues: nevertheless, the expansion of display advertising in national newspapers when commercial television was off the air in the summer of 1979 suggested that national newspapers and commercial television were direct competitors in this market.[19] Against a background of secular decline, advertising revenues were worryingly volatile: fluctuations in economic activity were reflected, in exaggerated form, in fluctuations in advertising revenues.

Between 1960 and 1974, the year to year changes in Gross Domestic Product in constant prices varied between +6% and +1%. Over the same period the year to year changes in expenditure on all advertising in constant prices varied between +12% and −10%; equivalent figures for display advertising were +8% and −11%, and for classified advertising +33% and −9%.[20]

Different types of advertisements were used by different customers, and were therefore affected by different features of the economic situation. Classified advertisements were used mainly for recruitment, and, especially in the *Sunday Times*, for houses and motor cars: the market for classified advertisements was therefore especially sensitive to the labour market. Since the *Financial Times* had relatively few classified advertisements it was protected from this trend, in contrast to *The Times* or the *Daily Telegraph*. On the other hand, display advertisements were primarily directed at consumer expenditure, or, in the case of financial advertisements, at the business world: they were therefore less affected by the state of labour demand, and more by company liquidity.

The volume of both display and classified advertising expanded between 1971 and 1973, only to contract in the following two years, display advertising falling below 1971 levels. Although the volume of display advertising was 3 per cent higher in the popular dailies in 1975 than it had been in 1971, it was 1 per cent lower in the quality dailies, 8 per cent lower in the Sunday populars, and 8 per cent lower in the Sunday qualities. Classified advertising was 10 per cent up in the popular dailies, 7 per cent up in the quality dailies, 28 per cent up in the popular Sundays, and 11 per cent up in the quality Sundays — but only in the popular Sundays, which contained relatively little classified advertising, was the 1975 level higher than the 1973 level. Changes in advertising volume had a much greater impact upon quality newspapers than upon popular newspapers, partly because a greater proportion of their revenue was derived from advertising, and partly because the gross contribution to profits was considerably greater: after deducting directly attributable costs advertising contributed an average of about 5p a copy profit.[21] One reason for the higher proportion of revenue derived from advertisements than from copy sales was simply that quality newspapers contained more column inches of advertisements, although not proportionately more than popular newspapers: the proportion of space devoted to advertisements varied surprisingly widely within the same category of newspaper. In the three sample weeks in 1965 and 1966 studied by the EIU team the average space devoted to advertisements varied between 49 per cent (*Daily Telegraph*) and 26.7 per cent (*Financial Times*) for quality newspapers, and 37.5 per cent (*Daily Express*) and 18.2 per cent (*Daily Sketch*) for popular newspapers: no similar analysis was published by the Macgregor Royal Commission.[22] A second reason was that quality newspapers could charge higher rates owing to their comparative efficiency in reaching readers in social groups A, B, C1 (managerial, professional, and administrative workers): predictably, quality newspapers had a very significantly higher proportion of such readers than popular newspapers. Whereas 51 per cent of *Times* readers and 52 per cent of *Financial Times* readers occupied higher or intermediate level administrative, professional, or managerial jobs, only 5 per cent of the readers of the *Daily Mirror* and 4 per cent of the readers of the *Sun* did so.[23] With their higher personal incomes, and control over organizational resources, members of social groups A, B, and C1 were of course especially attractive to advertisers. Advertising's greater contribution to the profitability of the qualities than to the populars was due more to the higher rates charged than to the greater absolute volume: owing to the cost of producing advertisements (both in newsprint and in labour) popular newspapers would have been in a weaker financial position if they had attempted to expand their advertising volumes to the level of the qualities. In 1975 costs abosorbed 100 per cent of advertising revenue in the popular dailies, and 115 per cent of revenue in the popular Sundays; even in 1973, a relatively good year, the relevant figures were 85 and 95 per cent. Comparable figures for quality newspapers were 65 and 70 per cent in 1975 and 55 and 60 per cent in 1973.[24]

Advertising rates did not rise as fast as might have been expected to compensate for increased costs of production or declining volumes − the initial reaction to both trends was to attempt to increase volume. This may have been a source of financial weakness, as Graham Cleverley concluded: 'Fleet Street doesn't suffer from a shortage of advertising: it suffers, desperately, from trying to carry far too much. To get it back to health it needs, perhaps more than anything else, much less advertising at a much higher price.'[25] He argued that newspapers with an excess of demand for their advertising should increase their rates, thereby obliging advertisers to shift to financially weaker newspapers, thus reverting to the more egalitarian situation prevailing during newsprint rationing. Since his book was written (mainly in 1973 although published in 1976), there have been substantial increases in advertising rates, which have served to improve considerably the financial situation of the newspapers involved, but which have not led to any major redistribution between newspapers, or between newspapers and other media. The market for advertising appears to be more segmented than Cleverley supposed.

In short, Fleet Street was suffering from a demoralizing long-term decline in the early 1970s, which appeared to accelerate sharply in 1974 and 1975. The trends were of two kinds − a long-term secular decline, upon which was superimposed an unusually severe cyclical down-turn: in essence, a microcosm of Britain's overall economic situation. Both types of trends affected both markets in which newspapers operated. Over a fifteen-year period, national newspapers were very slowly losing their appeal both to readers and to advertisers, as commercial television and local newspapers prospered. On top of this, the sharp rise in the rate of inflation in 1974 and 1975 resulted in a rapid decline in disposable income and the normal drop in newspaper circulation which accompanied this. The effects of declining disposable income were re-inforced by steeply rising cover prices. The financial effects of declining circulation were exacerbated, especially for the quality newspapers, by the advertising industry's usual volatile reaction to economic recession as firms cut back on advertising expenditure.

The effects of declining revenues were exacerbated by a rise in the cost of newsprint: the rise in the price of news-print brought to a head more rapidly the difficulties which would eventually have been produced by demand factors. The price of newsprint depended upon the quality, but Table 1.6 shows the sharp rise in the price of one widely used quality from 1973.[26]

Table 1.6

Price of newsprint 1970–5

	Price per tonne of 50gsm newsprint (£s)	Index 1970 = 100
1970	69.63	100
1971	73.08	105.0
1972	76.25	109.5
1973	88.60	127.2
1974	154.37	221.7
1975	165.19	237.2
1976	184.28	264.7

Source   Royal Commission on the Press: *Final Report*, p. 57.

The price of newsprint thus nearly doubled between 1973 and 1974. The rise was partly due to an increase in world demand and partly to the falling value of sterling. Since 1970 newspapers had come to rely upon Scandinavian and Canadian newsprint, which was cheaper than British; news-papers were thus left exposed when the value of sterling declined. The effect of the rise in newsprint prices depended upon the structure of production costs, with newsprint (and the relatively insignificant ink) accounting for 36 per cent of the costs for popular dailies, 34 per cent for the popular

Sundays, and 28 per cent of the costs of quality newspapers, whether daily or Sunday.[27] For all newspapers the increase was serious, but not debilitating: newsprint accounted for a lower proportion of total costs for most newspapers in 1975 than it had in 1960.[28] Moreover, the steep rise in the price of newsprint between 1974 and 1977 was followed by a period of stabilization and a slight drift downwards in the relative price of newsprint. The industrial relations and economic problems of Fleet Street, like those of New York newspapers, were due to more fundamental problems than the price of newsprint.[29]

In general terms, firms can react to a decline in their product market by attempting to stem the decline in demand directly (through increased marketing effort or reduced prices), by attempting to maintain existing levels of revenue despite lower demand (by reducing costs or increasing prices), or by diversifying into other products. Of course the strategies are not mutually exclusive. Each strategy can be followed either individually or in combination with other firms operating in the same product market. Fleet Street managements followed all strategies individually, and to a limited degree collectively: this book is an examination of one aspect of one strategy, the use of new technology to reduce costs. But brief comments are required on other approaches. Individual houses increased their marketing efforts, both for advertisements and for circulation, although mainly the former; increased marketing effort was an element, although small, in the increased costs of producing advertisements. But collective attempts to expand marketing efforts failed dismally, mainly owing to perceptions of the competitive pressures within the industry. The failure of the NPA to develop an effective marketing function was a major reason for Mirror Group Newspapers' disatisfaction with the NPA.[30] There has never been agreement between newspapers on the cover price of newspapers or on advertising charges (either on rates or on the very important discounts), even before the passage of the Resale Price Maintenance Act in 1964 made such agreements illegal. Individual newspapers structure their prices according to their perception of the market, attempting to gain a competitive advantage where possible. In general, newspaper manage-

ments delayed increasing prices and did not increase prices
by the full amount required when increases were made, until
1974-5, when the overall economic situation exacerbated the
effects of price increases which might have been accepted by
the market more easily had they been made earlier. This delay
was partly due to newspaper managements assessment of the
secular decline in the demand for newspapers, and advertising,
and partly to delays caused by the operation of the Price
Commission. Attempts to reduce costs involved attempting
to increase efficiency in the use of raw materials, especially
newsprint, and, more importantly, to reduce labour costs,
mainly through adopting new technology. There was relatively
little scope for reducing costs by improving efficiency in the
use of raw materials, and, as we have seen, the rapid rise in
the price of newsprint was a major factor in the increase in
the costs of production. The final strategy, diversification,
had already been followed extensively by newspaper proprietors before 1970: all companies publishing newspapers
also had interests in commercial television or radio or were
part of larger groups which also had interests in commercial
television.[31] Associated Newspapers owned shares in Southern
Television and London Broadcasting; Beaverbrook Newspapers owned shares in ATV; Mirror Group Newspapers also
owned shares in ATV; News International owned shares in
London Weekend Television, as did the *Daily Telegraph*;
Thomson owned shares in Scottish Television; Pearson
Longman, owners of the *Financial Times*, owned shares in
London Weekend Televsion; and even The Guardian and
Manchester Evening News Ltd. owned shares in Anglia
Television. By 1975 the financial position of all Fleet Street
newspapers was heavily reliant upon activities outside Fleet
Street.

ii

Relations between governments and the press in Britain are
inherently antagonistic; as (Sir) Ian Gilmour, then Opposition
spokesman on Defence and former editor of the *Spectator*,
commented in 1974, 'relations between Government and
Press should not be too close or too cosy.'[32] Politicians
depend upon the press as well as on television for establishing

a public image and for an immediate test of public reactions to their policies. But dependence does not make for charity: politicians believe that the press does not fully live up to its political role, trivializing fundamental issues and pursuing the private lives of public figures beyond the bounds of decency. In 1974 leading politicians of both parties were especially aggrieved by the press's activity in investigating the private lives of public figures, and the Press Council's alleged failure to provide adequate safeguards against the infringe- ment of editorial standards: Conservative leaders were particularly concerned about the press role in the 'Lambton affair', and Labour leaders, especially the then Prime Minister, Harold Wilson, by the treatment of Mrs Marcia Williams (Lady Falkender) and her alleged involvement in dubious land deals. The fundamental tension between politicians and the press based on the press's duty to expose and criticize government action was thus heightened by specific resent- ments against what were seen as unacceptable invasions of privacy and lax editorial standards. For their part, news- papers believed that politicians attempted to hide behind conventions of confidentiality, threatened or actual legal proceedings, the national interest, and in extreme instances the Official Secrets Act. The 'D' notice system remained a frequent source of frustration for journalists. Anxiety was heightened by what some termed the Prime Minister's 'para- noia' about journalistic standards.

Since this book is concerned with the press as an industry, and not with the press as 'an institution' — to use C. P. Scott's classic distinction — the merits of politicians' views of edi- torial standards or of journalists' views of politicians are not of direct concern, except in so far as they affect the major theme. However, in the mid 1970s the issues of editorial standards and economic performance were linked in the eyes of politicians, in two ways. Firstly, some politicians believed that economic difficulties led newspapers to lower their editorial standards in the pursuit of increased circulation; editorial standards were seen as threatened by the need to expand circulation at all costs.[33] The changes in the *Daily Mirror* designed to counter the success of the *Sun* were seen as an illustration of this trend. Secondly, possible solutions

to Fleet Street's economic difficulties could involve government action, either to facilitate action by the industry on its
own behalf or in a more direct role. It was hardly surprising
that political attitudes to Fleet Street's industrial performance
would be influenced by concern about editorial standards.

A broad spectrum of political attitudes towards the press
was revealed by the major Supply Day debate on the press in
May 1974, on the motion of the Conservative Opposition.[34]
Both Conservative and Labour speakers were critical of the
press, but the causes of concern and the intensity of feeling
differed considerably between the two major parties. Conservative speakers were primarily concerned with the economic difficulties of the industry, and with the press's treatment of national and personal affairs: but there was no
feeling that Fleet Street was fundamentally failing in any
way. Edward Heath's speech opening the debate was sanguine
– his opponents described it as 'complacent'. His attitude
towards journalistic standards was essentially untroubled:
the reporting of politicians' speeches was normally inaccurate,
but politicians could scarcely expect to be treated at their
own valuation. The major source of concern was Fleet
Street's economic situation, which required urgent action.
There were three reasons for the economic difficulties of the
press: the decline in advertising revenue, the increase in newsprint prices, and, most importantly, out-of-date machinery,
overmanning, and weak management. Nothing could be done
about the decline in advertising revenue or the increase in
newsprint prices, except to reduce the delays imposed by the
Price Commission in permitting allowable cost increases to
be reflected in higher prices. Similarly, the major responsibility for improving the industry's poor record on the use of
labour and technological change rested with the employers –
government financial assistance on the lines of the Dock
Labour Scheme was ruled out as too expensive. However, the
government should take the initiative in bringing employers
and unions together, and aim for a two-year programme to
introduce new technology and more realistic manning levels.
Subsequent Conservative speakers echoed Mr Heath's speech,
varying mainly in the extent to which blame for the industry's
economic difficulties was placed upon weak management,

stressed by Jonathan Aitken, or strong trade unions, stressed by (Sir) Ian Gilmour. For Conservative speakers there was nothing wrong with the press which could not be remedied by raising prices, cutting costs, and increasing the powers of the Press Council. Perhaps not surprisingly, the Conservative Party did not think it worth presenting evidence to the Royal Commission set up by the Labour government.

Labour speakers were considerably more worried about the basic structure of the industry: for many Labour MPs Fleet Street represented a particularly glaring example of the unacceptable face of capitalism. Peter Shore, the Secretary of State for Industry and as such responsible for the newspaper industry, replied to Mr Heath on behalf of the Government. The press was fundamentally biased against the Labour Party, failing to report accurately where Labour policies differed from those favoured by newspaper proprietors, for example on the Common Market and industrial relations. After the conversion of the *Daily Express*, no newspaper represented the views of opponents of the Common Market. Whereas the press 'bathed the wounds' of the Conservative Party when in government, it 'picked the scabs' of Labour governments, even when they followed policies favoured by the press (as over industrial relations in 1968–70). The public interest required variety in the press, but capitalist economic trends, towards concentration of ownership, were reducing variety. For the Prime Minister, resentment against anti-Labour bias was reinforced by deep personal bitterness against what he regarded as personal vindictiveness: he resented the press's treatment of the election campaign, and resented the treatment of Mrs Marcia Williams (Lady Falkender) even more. The journalists' pressure upon Mrs Williams over her alleged involvement with Shields and Millhench in dubious land deals was seen as characteristic of a corrupt press hounding an innocent public figure. Ioan Evans, the major proponent of the need for a Royal Commission, was especially critical of press treatment of the miners during the miners' strike. Labour speakers wished to reform Fleet Street radically, in order to foster the publication of a wider range of news-papers and journals of opinion, especially of course favourable to the Labour Party, if necessary by government action; 'the need for an intellectually independent press must surely be greater than the need for a financially free Press.' The precise means for increasing variety in the press varied. Eric Moonman, chairman of the Labour Newspaper Group, was the only speaker to present a detailed scheme during the debate: all newsprint should be centrally procured, and sold at subsidized prices to unprofitable journals of opinion.

The Labour Party shared the Conservative Party's concern over the economic position of the newspaper industry, and its viability as a continuing source of employment. The closure of the *Scottish Daily Express* in Glasgow in March 1974, with the loss of 1,800 jobs, was the first major employment crisis which faced Peter Shore at the Department of Industry; at the time of the debate he was considering whether to provide financial assistance to the *Scottish Daily News*, its proposed successor. The severe economic problems of the *Evening Standard*, also owned by Beaverbrook Newspapers, as well as the *Guardian* and the *Observer*, raised doubts about the ability of the industry to maintain existing employment levels. Nor was there any fundamental disagreement between Labour and Conservative speakers on the sources of the press's immediate economic problems — falling advertising revenues, increased newsprint costs, and high labour costs, although there was disagreement over the economic impact of restrictive practices and over-manning. However, Labour speakers saw the press's economic difficulties as inherent in the capitalist nature of press ownership: it was unrealistic to expect stable employment and diverse viewpoints from a privately owned press — newspaper proprietors owned newspapers to make money and to propagate their views. The future of the press 'cannot [therefore] . . . be determined by market forces, certainly not if that were to lead to an unacceptable reduction in the number of newspapers and a further concentration of press ownership.'

There was even stronger feeling about the condition of the press in the Labour Party outside Parliament. The working party document on the press, *The People and the Media*, which was published in July 1974 and became Labour Party policy when endorsed by the 1975 Conference, contained a complex scheme for removing press monopolies, increasing the variety of views available, and making the press more accountable both to workers in the industry and to the general public.[35] The proposals involved redistributing advertising revenue, and a differential newsprint subsidy. The redistribution of advertising revenue was designed to ensure that all newspapers would receive the same amount of advertising revenue per copy sold, thus removing the financial advantages of newspapers catering to affluent audiences. The differential newsprint subsidy was also designed to reduce the advantages of economies of scale enjoyed by large-circulation publications. In the longer term, the Party believed that the barriers to entry into newspaper publishing could be removed by the establishment of a National Printing Corporation, which would assume ownership of spare printing capacity and lease it to newspaper publishers, thus reducing the costs of entry. The tone of the Party Conference debate on the press in 1975 was highly critical: 'We must . . . use this crisis in the newspaper industry as the opportunity for a radical reform, to reestablish the finances of newspapers on a sound public service basis, and to open up the market for new newspapers.' Public funds should not be used simply to 'bail out the existing Tory newspapers by helping divest them of men they hired and no longer want.'[36]

The Labour Party's fundamental assumption was that Fleet Street's political bias and the absence of a national newspaper reflecting working-class interests were due to the structure of ownership and the operation of market principles. Since newspaper proprietors owned newspapers to propagate their views and to make money – in varying proportions – it was inevitable that privately owned newspapers would be responsive to the political views of their owners, even where they ran counter to the views of the journalists themselves, and would also respond to the sensitivities of the advertising market. The vaunted independence of the press was an illusion. However, the Labour Party was clearer about the iniquities of Fleet Street than it was about the desirability – and practicability – of alternative means to remedy them. The fundamental difficulty was the danger that government assistance might result in government discrimination between publications, and possibly ultimately in a form of censorship. Different members of the party viewed this danger differently. Maurice Edelman was opposed to any form of subsidy to the press because it would lead to a 'kept press'. Sidney Bedwell and Ioan Evans believed that the press was not independent, and would be liberated by government assistance.[37] The Labour Party's proposals attempted to avoid government discrimination by providing, in effect, for cross-subsidization within the industry and by administration at arm's length. The focus of the initial scheme reflected Labour beliefs about the desirability of variety and the representation of minorities, and the need to restrict the operation of the market. As precedents for government aid, without government domination, the Party could quote the government's favourable treatment of the industry through special postal rates, zero-rating for VAT, and extensive government advertising.

The Liberal Party was not greatly concerned about the state of the press. In the Supply Day debate Clement Freud expressed the view that he thought the Opposition ought to have more important issues to debate than Fleet Street, and Jo Grimond commented that the newspaper group in which he was involved, the Guardian and Manchester Evening News Trust Ltd., was not badly managed. The freedom of the press was not seen as depending upon the survival of all existing newspapers.[38] In so far as the Liberal Party regarded Fleet Street as a problem, it saw the solution in the application of the general Liberal principles of worker participation, trade-union reform, and the creation of a joint management–union body to discuss over-manning and working conditions, and the encouragement of new technology and more realistic manning levels.[39]

The differences in political attitudes towards Fleet Street's economic problems crystallized in the attitudes adopted towards the Royal Commission on the Press, set up by the Labour Government. The Royal Commission, together with its terms of reference and chairman, was announced on 2 May 1974 in reply to a question by Eric Moonman, the NGA-sponsored MP who was then chairman of the Labour Newspaper Group: Ioan Evans, the left-wing Labour MP for

Aberdare, had drawn attention to the need for a Royal Commission on the Press in the first week of the new Parliament.[40] The terms of reference of the Royal Commission, the third since 1945, were:

to inquire into the factors affecting the maintenance of the independence, diversity and editorial standards of newspapers and periodicals, and the public's freedom of choice of newspapers and periodicals, nationally, regionally, and locally, with particular reference to:
 (a) the economics of newspaper and periodical publishing and distribution;
 (b) the interaction of the newspaper and periodical interests held by the companies concerned with their other interests and holdings within and outside the communications industry;
 (c) management and labour practices and relations in the newspaper and periodical industry;
 (d) conditions and security of employment in the newspaper and periodical industry;
 (e) the distribution and concentration of ownership of the newspaper and periodical industry, and the adequacy of existing law in relations thereto;
 (f) the responsibilities, constitution and functioning of the Press Council;
and to make recommendations.[41]

It was simultaneously announced that Sir Morris Finer, formerly chairman of the Committee on One Parent Families (1969–74), would be chairman of the Commission.

The announcement of the Royal Commission was welcomed by most members of the Labour Party, inside and outside Parliament, although there was some criticism from both right- and left-wing members. Maurice Edelman believed that 'the origin of the Royal Commission lay in specific problems which are not related to the essential questions affecting the Press', and that the Commission had been 'rather hysterically promoted'; from a different perspective, the left-wing proposer of the resolution on *The People and the Media* at the 1975 Annual Conference believed that the Royal Commission was irrelevant — 'we have had enough Royal Commissions on this subject over the years.'[42] The announcement of the Commission was not welcomed by the Conservative Party, the Liberal Party, newspaper proprietors, journalists, or print unions. The Conservative Party believed that the problems of the industry were already well understood, and that urgent action was required along well-recognized lines. A limited inquiry into the economics of the industry might be helpful, but a full-scale Royal Commission was unnecessary and would be positively harmful if it delayed urgently needed action. The Liberal Party believed that the Commission was unnecessary. So did the newspaper industry. As the Commission itself commented, 'most newspapers, both editorially and at management level, were at best lukewarm and suspicious of the Government's motives in establishing the Commission. Of the unions in the industry, only the NUJ welcomed the Commission.'[43] And although the NUJ welcomed the Commission the *United Kingdom Press Gazette*, an important, if partial, organ of journalist opinion, did not.[44]

The Commission was designed to take a thorough look at the industry from the outside. The terms of reference were wider than the terms of reference of previous Royal Commissions on the Press, covering the relationship between the press and other interests where companies had interests outside newspapers. Newspaper owners included companies with very wide ramifications, like S. Pearson & Son Ltd., the major vehicle for Lord Cowdray's interests, and Thomson British Holdings Ltd., the major vehicle for Lord Thomson's interests, making the potential scope very wide. Since the Annan Commission on Broadcasting was set up almost simultaneously, a comprehensive examination of the mass media was set in train.[45] The membership of the Commission indicated the Government's commitment to an outside view, containing little representation from the industry — thus confirming the industry's scepticism about the value of the Commission. No member of the Commission had direct personal knowledge of management or production problems in the industry; there was no print technologist, despite the importance of new technology; there was no industrial accountant, despite allegations of inadequate financial controls in the industry; there was no industrialist with direct experience of a labour-intensive industry, despite the importance of labour costs.[46] In addition to the first chairman, Sir Morris Finer, Professor O. R. Macgregor, who became chairman on Sir Morris's death in 1975, had also been a member of the Committee on One Parent Families. Professor of Social Institutions at the University of London, he was an experienced member of public bodies, but had no experience, practical or academic, of industry. Baron Hunt was most widely known for his leadership of the British expedition to Everest in 1952-3, and although a very active public figure, he had no experience of industry. Eirlys Rhimen Roberts had been in the Information Division of the Treasury for several years, and was deputy director of the Consumers' Association at the time of her appointment to the Commission. Elizabeth Anderson was a freelance journalist and past president of the Church of Scotland Women's Guild. Malcolm Horsman was a director of the Bowater Corporation, and thus had immediate experience of one area of special concern to the Commission, newsprint and paper costs. David Basnett, the general secretary of the General and Municipal Workers Union, had of course wide experience of industrial relations, but none of newspapers or the printing industry. The only members of the Commission with direct experience of Fleet Street were Geoffrey Goodman and Paul Johnson. Geoffrey Goodman had worked as a journalist for several years, mainly on financially insecure newspapers (the *Manchester Guardian, News Chronicle*, and *Daily Herald*, as well as the *Sun* and the *Daily Mirror*), and was Harold Wilson's press advisor. Paul Johnson had been editor of the *New Statesman* between 1965 and 1970, and had written on a freelance basis for a number of newspapers. The commitment to an outside view was carried through to the professional advisory staff; the industrial relations advisor to the Commission was Mr (now Professor) S. Kessler of the City University, who had worked for the National Union of Mineworkers. Although direct personal experience of the industry concerned may not increase the wisdom of Royal Commission decisions, it provides legitimacy in the eyes of the industry concerned: the total absence of influential representatives of the industry on the Macgregor Royal Commission inevitably served to weaken it in the eyes of the national newspaper industry.

In summary, both the Conservative and Liberal Parties fundamentally accepted Fleet Street's own definition of its problems. The industry was suffering from management weakness, excessive trade-union power, and technological backwardness, exacerbated by market conditions. The remedy lay in reducing costs through the use of new technology and fewer workers, raising prices, and, for the Liberal Party, trade-union reform. But, over all, both parties believed that the British press was fundamentally sound, providing for the expression of a wide range of views, and successfully fulfilling its critical role as the Fourth Estate — 'the modern version of the separation of powers' (Sir Ian Gilmour). The Labour Party believed that there were more fundamental deficiencies in Fleet Street, where the application of market principles to the distribution of opinion and information was seen as limiting the range of free expression, and especially limiting the free expression of opinion favourable to the Labour Party. The problems of Fleet Street required more than a minor government diplomatic initiative to bring the two sides of the industry together to assist in resolving the industry's economic problems. The victory of the Labour Party in February 1974, after an election campaign in which all the press, except the *Daily Mirror*, had opposed the Labour Party, (and even the *Daily Mirror* had been doubted before the campaign), confirmed the Party's worst assessments of newspaper bias, and naturally meant that Fleet Street was no longer faced with a government willing to accept Fleet Street's definition of the press's problems.[47] Government interest in fundamental reform of the press could be expected. This was all the more likely in view of the employment consequences of the press's economic difficulties. The appointment of a Royal Commission, with wide terms of reference, was a judicious way for the Government to retain the reform of Fleet Street on the political agenda, whilst giving prior attention to more urgent problems elsewhere. The terms of reference appealed both to the industry, and to the Labour Party: the reference to the industry's economic problems and the special attention to be paid to industrial relations encouraged newspaper proprietors to accept the Commission as, at best, a stimulus to improve management–union relations, and at worst a harmless waste of time, whilst the reference to diversity, independence, and editorial standards met the Labour Party's feeling that radical action might be taken, if the Commission thought it desirable.

iii

In 1975 there was a general belief that 'something had to be done' about Fleet Street. Although the motives differed, both the industry and the Government believed that reform was needed to maintain the industry's economic health, regardless of opinions on political bias and journalistic standards. Major changes in printing technology pointed towards one possible solution, technological change, although proprietors and unions naturally disagreed on the extent to which technological changes would solve the industry's problems. Proprietors and some Conservative politicians believed that new technology was the complete solution to the industry's problems — hence Jonathan Aitken: 'this new technology could be the saviour of all our British newspapers, and with them most of the jobs in the industry.'[48] Union leaders were less enthusiastic about the contribution of new technology, and of course new technology in itself would make no contribution to answering Labour Party criticisms of Fleet Street's political bias. However, all agreed that new technology provided an opportunity — or a threat — to the industry. The third stimulus to change in Fleet Street was thus technological, the emergence of a new printing technology, based upon the computer, photocomposition, and web-offset printing, which provided the basis for restructuring newspaper production and ultimately for making substantial savings in labour costs.

Although important improvements had been made in the press room, with better and faster presses, and in publishing rooms, with counter-stackers and automatic binding and tying machines, the basic origination technology of newspaper production in Fleet Street had not changed between the late nineteenth century, when the linotype came into extensive use, and the mid 1970s.[49] Under the traditional system copy was sent from the editorial and advertising departments to the copy desk in the composing room. The copy desk acted as a routing service, sending body copy to the linotype area, and copy for headlines to the piece-case area. Illustrations were sent to the process department for block making, except where blocks were brought in from outside, as was normally the case with advertisements. All blocks were then mounted in the stereotyping department and sent to the composing room where all the type, headlines, and blocks were assembled in a heavy metal chase (frame) to make up a page forme. This basic relief system of printing was described as a 'hot-metal' system. Operators hit the linotype keys (or more accurately 'stroked' the keys, hence the term key-stroking) and a matrix for each letter fell from a magazine into an assembler. At this stage the operator carried out any necessary hyphenation. With the addition of fixed spaces and variable spacebands the operator 'justified' the line, i.e. set the line to a standard length and equalized space between words. He then injected molten lead into the recesses in the matrices making up the line, which created the slug or line of type. Copy for headlines or requiring special treatment was set by a compositor who assembled matrices by hand in a 'stick', which was then placed in a Ludlow machine for a line of type to be set, again by injecting hot metal into the recesses in the matrices. The lines of type were collated and proofed in a galley-proof press. These proofs were sent to the proof reader who corrected them and returned them to the relevant department for corrections to be set in hot metal. The corrected type was sent to a page-make-up area where it was assembled with blocks in a heavy metal chase (frame) on the 'stone'. The pages of metal type were then 'locked up' to make a page forme which comprised a mirror image of the page in metal. A moist art-paper flong was placed over the page and both were placed in a moulding press to create a mould. The mould was dried and trimmed before being placed in a stereo casting machine which forced hot metal into the mould to produce a semi-cylindrical printing plate. The plate was then mounted with others on the cylinder of a printing press in the machine room. A web or webs of paper had already been fed into the printing press from reels of paper situated underneath the press and, when the press was started, the plates, suitably inked, left a right-reading impression on the web or paper as it was drawn through the printing press. The webs of paper emerged from the printing press in collated form at a folder where the paper was folded and cut to produce printed copies in a continuous stream. From the machine room the paper moved to the publishing room where it was taken off the press, stacked, bundled, and tied, and loaded on vans for distribution. The production system is summarized in Fig. 1, which also conveniently summarizes union demarcation lines. The whole operation was complicated, fragmented, and labour intensive.

Important technological developments occurred from the late 1950s onwards which affected both the preparatory and the printing stages of the production process.[50] Changes in printing came first. The major change in printing was the introduction of the web-offset press, first used in Britain in 1957. Offset lithography involves the use of a smooth metal plate, on which only the printing areas have been made receptive to ink, as the printing surface. The plate is fitted round a cylinder, and as it revolves it picks up ink on the printing areas. 'The role is then transferred, usually by a second cylinder, on to the paper.'[51] Web simply refers to the use of continuous reels rather than sheets. The use of web-offset involves a totally different plate-making process from letter-press systems, reducing the demand for NGA(NSES) stereo-typers, but did not substantially change the organization of the machine room. Its great advantage over letter-press was the improved quality of reproduction of illustrations (both black and white and especially colour). However, although web-offset machines were widely introduced into provincial newspapers, they have not been introduced into Fleet Street, and are not likely to be so in the immediate future. This is due partly to the heavy investment Fleet Street made in rotary letter-press machines in the 1960s, which it would have been uneconomic to replace, and partly to the difficulty of removing a letter-press system and putting in a web-offset system while maintaining production, unless new premises were acquired. Moreover, the web-offset system generally produces higher paper wastage figures than the letter-press system. It was also believed that web-offset systems would have difficulty in coping with the very long runs and high

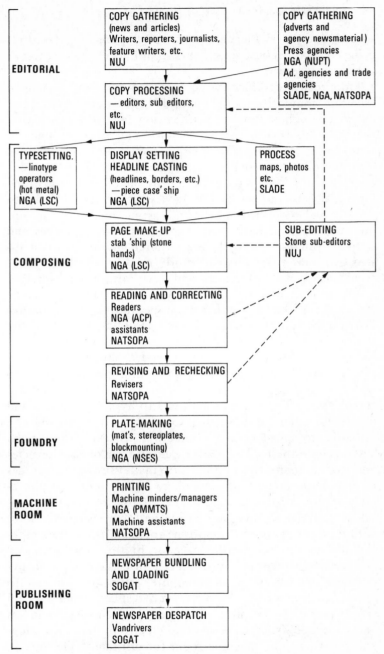

Fig. 1. The organization of production of a national newspaper (hot metal)
Source: The Open University, *Press, Papers, and Print*, p. 14.

speeds required in Fleet Street, although press manufacturers believed that web-offset presses could meet Fleet Street's production demands.

More relevant to Fleet Street was the rapid development of tape-fed composition in the mid 1950s, leading to computerized hyphenation and justification and the use of photocomposition. Instead of producing metal slugs or lines of type, operators using a keyboard based on the standard typewriter produced punched paper tape. This paper tape was then fed into a computer which hyphenated and justified lines and gave out an output tape which could be fed into suitably adapted hot metal line-casting machines or into phototypesetters. Early phototypesetters used matrices and optical systems to project the required images on to light-sensitive materials whereas more modern machines electronically digitize characters and have outputs in excess of 1,000 newspaper lines per minute. Page negatives are made by copying the assembled bromide output from phototypesetters, and the negative used to make a plate to be printed by the offset system. In newspapers using letterpress presses the negative is used to create a pattern plate from which a mould is made from a flong in a moulding press to be used subsequently for the casting of semi-cylindrical stereo plates. The use of computers to hyphenate words and justify lines, and the use of photocomposition, provide the potential to speed up the production process greatly. Such systems have the facility to accept input from outside agencies and from branch offices and thus to make use of other sources of data in-put. The new technology of computerized photocomposition as it developed in the 1970s provided the possibility of ultimately merging editorial and composing functions, with large reductions in composing-room staffs and the simplification of the production process. In the most advanced systems, copy can be keyed directly into the computer, by-passing the compositor, the computer can be programmed to permit page-make-up through visual display terminals, and whole pages can be photocomposed: in such systems plates can be made from camera photographs of page bromides and passed to the machine room for printing.[52] The precise system adopted depended upon the management strategy and the production system of the newspaper in question: the approaches adopted by the Financial Times, TNL, and MGN are examined in detail in chapters 6, 7 and 8.

iv

Three sets of environmental pressures — economic, political, and technological — were thus pushing Fleet Street towards a crisis in the mid 1970s, and towards a particular resolution of the crisis. Severe economic problems, an unsympathetic government, and the existence of a technology theoretically capable of transforming the system of production, made it likely that Fleet Street would take radical action to remedy its economic difficulties. The pressures could be responded to individually or collectively. On the one hand, the pressures operated differently on different types of newspapers, and even on different individual newspapers. The decline in the advertising market affected the quality newspapers disproportionately, whilst the rise in newsprint prices affected the popular newspapers disproportionately. The Labour Party's hostility towards the press was, at least partially, softened towards the *Daily Mirror*. The new technology offered the prospects of more substantial savings to the quality newspapers than to the populars, owing to the higher level of first-copy costs, and was therefore more attractive to them. Furthermore, competitive pressures had previously caused Fleet Street houses to act independently of each other: previous attempts at a collective approach to the industry's problems had failed, and, although managements and unions bargained collectively on an industry level, earnings for similar jobs varied widely between houses. There were thus grounds for anticipating that newspaper managements would react individually to the environmental pressures of the mid 1970s. On the other hand, economic, political, and technological changes affected all newspapers to some degree. Moreover, collective action would strengthen the hand of the industry in any discussions with the government, especially collective action in conjunction with the printing-industry unions. It would also increase the effectiveness of action designed to improve the industry's overall economic performance, especially in the advertising market. It was therefore likely that the industry would respond to the crisis of the mid 1970s as it had responded to previous crises, by collective lamentation and individual action. However, there were also grounds for believing that the industry might respond differently, by attempting a collective response to a particularly severe economic crisis. This book shows how the conflicting pressures towards individual and towards collective action interacted between 1975 and 1979. The industry's initial response to the crisis suggested that history would not repeat itself; subsequent events indicated all too clearly that it did.

Chapter 2

Industrial Relations in Fleet Street

In the previous chapter the economic and political environment Fleet Street faced in 1975, the basic technology of the production process, and the technological opportunities beginning to appear were outlined. The industry faced a major economic crisis, to which managements believed that the only effective solution was a substantial reduction in labour costs, preferably associated with the introduction of new technology. Fleet Street's economic difficulties made it necessary to reduce labour costs. New technology provided the means. Even in industries with weaker trade unions than the printing industry, reducing labour costs and introducing new technology would involve major initiatives in industrial relations; in Fleet Street, success required either securing union co-operation, or, preferably for management, re-asserting managerial authority, recovering control over the production process, and weakening trade-union power. Management's initial strategy in 1975 involved closer working relationships with national union officials, and the weakening of chapel power, for both managements and national officials believed that the unconstrained exercise of sectional bargaining posed a serious threat to the industry's economic position. The necessity for this strategy and the prospects for its success were both determined by the structure of industrial relations in the industry. This chapter is therefore an outline of industrial relations in the industry, beginning with the organization of industrial relations at management level, before turning, in section iv, to the major unions involved. Since the prospects for new technology depended especially heavily upon the reactions of the NGA and NATSOPA they are examined in detail in the subsequent chapters, 3 and 4: the NUJ's attitude towards new technolgy is discussed more briefly in the concluding chapter.

Management's conduct of industrial relations in Fleet

Street has been heavily criticized. Graham Cleverley, for example, in his book *The Fleet Street Disaster: A Case Study in Mismanagement*, accused management of incompetence, of being as myopic over industrial relations as they had been over economics, where they failed to ensure that increases in advertising produced adequate financial returns.[1] Incompetence was compounded by timidity and insecurity. Fleet Street managers recognized that they had lost control of the production process. But they naturally interpreted the sources of their industrial relations problems differently, as the result of excessive trade-union bargaining power, intransigence, and indiscipline. Trade-union bargaining power was seen as deriving from the unusually perishable character of the industry's product (making it impossible to catch up on lost production), tightly constrained production schedules, and a competitive market situation which made the maintenance of circulation at any price the first proprietorial priority. The effects of production and marketing constraints were reinforced by fragmented bargaining institutions, which encouraged competitive bargaining. As will be shown, the sources of management's difficulties lay in the structure of the industry and in its industrial relations; but management's conduct of negotiations over new technology increased the difficulties of an already difficult situation.

i

By comparison with engineering, or even with provincial newspapers, the national newspaper industry provided a favourable environment for the development of an effective industry-wide employers' organization. The number of companies in the industry was small, only nine. The senior management teams in each company were also small, well known to each other, and relatively similar in background and experience. The industry was geographically concentrated, within three-quarters of a mile of Holborn Circus. The companies shared important facilities, notably the distribution system. They also negotiated with the same unions – primarily the NGA, SLADE, NATSOPA, SOGAT, NUJ, AUEW, EETPU, and at house level, UCATT. Finally, the processes of production in each company were broadly similar. Nevertheless, the NPA was not an effective organization, especially in industrial relations; it was less effective as a negotiating body than the Newspaper Society in provincial newspapers, and less capable of providing expert advice for its member companies than, for example, the Engineering Employers' Federation. The NPA's weakness was evident in its failure to achieve an effectively centralized industrial relations policy and in its inadequate performance as a trade association and industry spokesman. Part of the explanation for the Association's ineffectiveness lay in its low level of funding; the Association lacked the staff to sustain effective operations. But the lack of resources was a symptom, as well as a cause, of weakness: had the Association been effective on a small scale its member companies would doubtless have been willing to allocate further resources. A more fundamental reason for the NPA's ineffectiveness lay in the member companies' mutual suspicions of each other and their reluctance to accept collective organization, despite successive reports on the industry which had stressed that collective organization was the most effective way for managements to regain control of industrial relations. The Joint Standing Committee approach to new technology represented an opportunity for the NPA to emerge as a major industrial relations force: the rejection of *Programme for Action* by print-union members destroyed the opportunity and exacerbated the already marked tendency to fragmentation in the industry.

The NPA was established as the Newspaper Proprietors' Association in 1906, when a group of London newspaper proprietors settled separately from their fellow members of the Master Printers' Association following the issuing of strike notices by the London Society of Compositors. The name was changed to Newspaper Publishers' Association in 1968. The NPA is both an employers' organization and a trade association.[2] Its formal objectives include the regulation of employer–employee relations, the exchange of views on matters of common interest, the presentation of evidence on behalf of the industry to outside bodies, the organization of joint action, and the provision of expert advice on distribution, advertising, marketing, training, administration, and finance. In practice the NPA's major roles have been in industrial relations and in distribution; on other matters, for example financial and commercial advice, the Association lacks the resources to match the expertise available to individual houses. Membership is open to all national newspapers with an agreed national minimum circulation. In 1975 membership included all the major publishing houses except MGN, whose relationship remained close and which continued to belong for commercial purposes, paying a proportionate subscription, together with the Society of Licensed Victuallers, as publishers of the *Morning Advertiser*; only the Morning Star Co-operative Society remained outside the Association, and it followed NPA practices on many issues. The nine companies employed 37,367 workers in 1975, including Glasgow and Plymouth MGN employees — although the numbers employed in any one week were probably higher, since the official PPITB figure defined 'employee' as anyone working two-thirds of a normal working week, which excluded an unknown number of casual casuals. In comparison, the thirty-one members of the Newspaper Society employed 42,338 workers in provincial daily and weekly newspapers.[3]

Figure 2 provides a simplified representation of the NPA's formal organization. The governing body of the Association is the NPA Council, consisting of representatives of each newspaper, usually the proprietor or chairman; the officers of the Council are the chairman (in 1975 this was Lord Goodman, who was succeeded in 1976 by Sir Richard Marsh) and the vice-chairman (from 1972 until 1979 this was Mr M. J. Hussey of Times Newspapers Ltd.). Council meets as required, and appoints an Executive Committee, consisting of the managing directors of the major companies, which meets monthly. Reporting to the Council is the Industrial Relations Executive, composed of the senior managers or directors responsible for industrial relations in the member companies, and normally chaired by the Director of the NPA (in 1975 this was Mr John Dixey, who was succeeded by Mr John Lepage in 1977): the IRE is the effective working arm of the NPA in industrial relations, responsible for the conduct of national negotiations, and meeting weekly. Reporting to the IRE is the London Labour Committee and

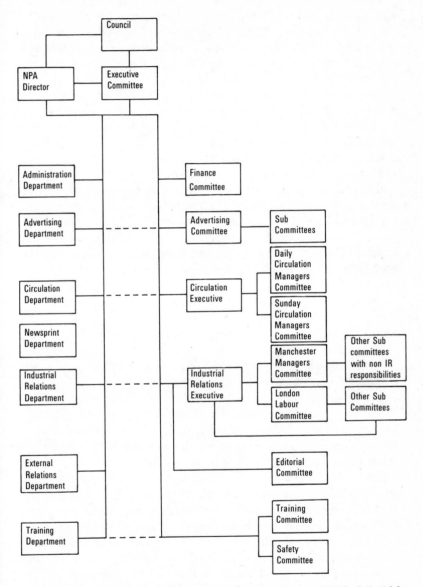

Fig. 2. The organization and structure of the NPA. *Source:* ACAS, *Industrial Relations in the National Newspaper Industry*, p. 268.

the Manchester Managers' Committee, responsible for the application of national agreements in their respective spheres. The London Labour Committee (or sub-committees thereof) consists of house representatives with industrial relations responsiblities; it meets the unions at branch or regional level to work out the details of national agreements and makes recommendations to the IRE. The NPA's industrial relations committees are serviced mainly by the NPA's two industrial relations advisers. The major 'associational' responsibility of the NPA is the joint distribution system, which is governed by the Daily Circulation Managers' Committee and the Sunday Circulation Managers' Committee, reporting to the Circulation Executive, which in turn reports to the Council.

The NPA's most prominent role has been in industrial relations. The Association is responsible for the conduct of the annual round of wage negotiations with the print unions, jointly and severally: negotiations are conducted by the Industrial Relations Executive. Attempting to maintain unity inevitably involved tailoring bargaining strategy to the financial resources of the weakest member — 'the lowest common denominator approach'. Hence industry-level agreements in the 1970s were not generous. Between 1 September 1969 and 1 April 1972, the longest period during which negotiations were not constrained by incomes policies, NPA rates rose as follows: 1 September 1969, 2 per cent of basic, plus consolidation of 11s. cost-of-living bonus; 1 July 1970, 5 per cent of basic; 1 July 1971, 5 per cent of basic or £1.12½p.; 1 January 1972, consolidation of 55p cost-of-living bonus; 1 April 1972, consolidation of 55p cost-of-living bonus. The NPA basic example, the SOGAT LCB rate, rose from £17.1.6p to £20.175p over a two-and-a-half year period, a rise of 18.16 per cent: over the same period basic rates for manual workers in manufacturing industry rose by 32 per cent.[4] Negotiating relatively low settlements might seem an obvious means of reducing pressure on the wage costs of individual companies. However, the effectiveness of this policy depended heavily upon the proportion of earnings determined at industry level. In Fleet Street this proportion was relatively low, and in the 1970s declined further. Table 2.1 shows the relationship between industry-level determined

Table 2.1

Average earnings as a percentage of National Minimum Rates

	1970	1971	1972	1975 (April)
Time-hands	233.81	243.39	234.27	312.76
Readers	221.63	236.36	223.17	291.44
Copyholders	231.34	254.83	236.6	309.72
Process workers	218.17	239.56	217.8	292.49
Machine managers	271.29	238.14	284.64	306.74
Brakehands	283.37	277.61	287.95	313.22
Publishing (outdoors)	252.76	278.58	260.87	299.73
Stereotypers	296.11	316.20	293.03	352.36
Engineers	258.22	n.a.	n.a.	310.53
Electricians	243.64	n.a.	n.a.	326.98

Source   ACAS, *Industrial Relations in the National Newspaper Industry*, p.256
(adapted).

minimum rates and average earnings in 1970, and the trend between 1970 and 1975.[5]

For all groups average earnings were more than double the industry rate, the average (unweighted) gap being 151.03 per cent; by 1975 the gap had grown to over three times the industry level for seven of the ten groups for whom data is available, and the average gap had increased to 211.60 per cent: the figures exclude linotype operators, for whom the minimum rate had no relevance.

The wide gap between average earnings and industry-level negotiated rates inevitably meant that the NPA exerted only limited influence upon earnings in Fleet Street. This reflected the wish of individual managements to maintain traditional proprietorial independence over earnings, and to respond as they thought fit to the bargaining power of their own chapels and to changes in their own patterns of work organization; it permitted a flexible approach to wages, making it possible — theoretically — to increase rewards only for those work groups that contributed directly to increases in productivity. However, in practice the flexibility only operated upwards, resulting in rapid increases in earnings through sectional bargaining. There was thus little pressure from unions to make industry-level negotiations more meaningful, because it was easier to obtain increases at house and chapel level. The reluctance of employers to attempt to centralize bargaining is more surprising, for more centralized bargaining would have reduced the ability of chapels and unions to pick off employers seriatim — as engineering employers recognized in the 1890s when they sought to centralize bargaining during their 'counter-offensive'.[6] Moreover, the marginal significance of industry-level negotiations, conducted by national union officials, naturally weakened the power of such officials over their members; power within the union was naturally influenced by ability to influence wage negotiations, and earnings 'drift' favoured chapel officials' power. The limited power of national officials, despite their formal authority, was to be of major importance in undermining the joint approach to the introduction of new technology.

In line with their 'minimalist' strategy, the NPA also followed a conservative policy on differentials and conditions. The NPA policy was to maintain existing differentials as far as possible. This policy was carried through successfully in the early 1970s, ACAS evidence showing that the major change in rankings on the basic rates in the period 1969–75 was the movement of the engineers and the electricians from joint-fifth to joint-first place in the table (although their data excluded linotype operators).[7] Both groups, especially the electricians, significantly increased both their relative rates and their relative earnings. However, neither group could be easily assimilated into printing-industry wage structures, and changes in their relative positions had 'fewer reverberations upon the structure of differentials than changes in the relative positions of other groups. The only other significant change in the period was the inevitable compression of differentials associated with flat rate rather than percentage increases in 1974 and 1975. On conditions, the NPA's policy was simply to refuse to concede any union preferential terms, a policy successfully maintained throughout the period 1970-5 — although journalists had always received better conditions of employment than had members of the production unions.

The NPA had, of course, long recognized the relative weakness of its bargaining role, and the central importance of house-level bargaining. In an attempt to establish at least the basis for a policy of co-ordination between member companies — given that collective action was unlikely — the House Claims Procedure was developed from December 1964. The NPA letter outlining the thinking behind the procedure stated: 'The NPA Council decided . . . to impose an obligation on all offices to report to the NPA all house claims which, if met, would result in additional payments or a reduction in working hours. This would provide the opportunity for collective discussion of the claims with particular reference to possible repercussive effects.'[8] The central record would, at the least, help to prevent individual houses from conceding claims based on misleading information about agreements elsewhere, and might provide useful arguments against claims. However, the House Claims Procedure had little effect and dropped into disuse. The development of comprehensive agreements from 1965 changed the character of chapel agreements — agreements were made step by step, and the registration of only the final agreements meant that important concessions had been made before the NPA became aware of them (although there was little the NPA was able to do with the information it did obtain). Additionally, managements did not always bother to report agreements. The House Claims Procedure thus provided a useful means of exchanging information, but not for NPA influence, much less control, over the terms of house agreements. And even the informational role had disadvantages. In view of the patchy coverage, information was not wholly reliable; and by legitimating inter-house comparisons the procedure widened the scope of 'coercive comparison', giving a further twist to earnings 'drift'.

The NPA's major 'associational' role was an organizer of the distribution system.[9] Since 1910 the NPA has negotiated distribution contracts with the railways and with the airlines on behalf of its members, although the members were individually responsible for arranging road transport as an alternative when they failed to meet deadlines. There was wide, but not universal, satisfaction in the industry with the NPA's handling of distribution. MGN criticized the system on the grounds that they paid a disproportionate share of its costs, which were determined on a circulation basis, without receiving an adequate service; they alleged that 'quality' newspapers, less sensitive to the need to supply newsagents for early-morning counter sales, and with circulations more heavily concentrated in the south-east, did not make a proportionate financial contribution, and did not always make sufficient effort to meet delivery deadlines.[10] Improving distribution in the West of England was a major reason for MGN's decision to print the *Daily Mirror* at the West of England Press in Plymouth. However, MGN's criticisms were not widely shared. The effective administration of the distribution system did not, however, increase the NPA's authority in industrial relations, primarily because the system was organized and financed separately from the NPA's other work, and there was no attempt to use the influence acquired through administering the distribution system to change the method of conducting industrial relations. When MGN withdrew from the NPA there was no move to exclude the company from the distribution system, although it would have been an obvious means of exerting pressure on the company to remain within the Association.

A second 'associational' role was the promotion of national newspapers as an industry, through industry-wide marketing campaigns directed at increasing both circulation and advertising revenue. However, although a marketing executive had been established in the late 1960s, relatively little effort was devoted to industry-level marketing; although the NPA Council agreed in 1973 to the appointment of a top-level marketing director, none was ever appointed, allegedly because of failure to agree on the level of salary to be paid. Similarly, it was suggested that the industry should establish a joint advertising bureau under the umbrella of the NPA to co-ordinate work with the advertising industry, possibly modelled upon the Evening Newspapers' Advertising Bureau set up by regional newspapers.[11] The proposal was favoured by representatives of the advertising industry. But no bureau was established; proprietors believed that any moves towards industry-level co-operation on advertising would lead to pressure for greater uniformity on rates and discounts, and thus reduce competition in the industry.

The final NPA role to be considered is that of political respresentation. According to its articles of association, the NPA's objectives include representation of the interests of the national newspaper industry before outside bodies, including political organizations. However, the Association found difficulty in fulfilling the role adequately, partly because of difficulty in drawing the boundary between the responsibilities of individual houses and the Association, and partly because of limited resources. This was illustrated by the NPA's relations with the Royal Commission. The Commission asked for written evidence from interested parties in 1974, immediately after its establishment, but as late as March 1976 the Commission complained that it was 'ignorant about the NPA, its organisation and functions . . . because we have had no written evidence from them, although we have sought it.' Written evidence was eventually received from the NPA in December 1976, dated July 1975.[12] The NPA chairman, Lord Goodman, commented on the difficulty the NPA experienced in drawing up its evidence, since the NPA's functions were only very limited.

. . . it is not easy [to present written evidence on behalf of the NPA] because as an Association we can only speak for the newspapers to a very limited extent and a very specialised extent. We do not speak on policy matters relating to the editorial content of the newspapers and other matters which are really of fundamental importance.[13]

Despite its lack of resources, especially for long-term planning, its preoccupation with immediate industrial relations problems, and its feeling that the Royal Commission was essentially irrelevant, the NPA's dilatory approach to the Royal Commission did little to improve the Association's public standing: if the employers' association was incapable of speaking on behalf of the industry, who was? MGN, the only house to present comprehensive evidence to the Royal Commission, stated that they would probably not have been able to present their evidence had they remained members of the NPA.[14]

Some of the NPA's difficulties stemmed simply from lack of resources, which remained small despite statements from

inside and outside the industry that the Association's resources ought to be increased. In 1972 the NPA employed
thirty-four staff in cramped Bouverie Street headquarters:
in 1976, after a brief drop, the number had increased to
thirty-five, in the same cramped quarters, at which level
it remained throughout the remainder of the 1970s. But the
numbers involved in commercial and industrial relations
affairs dropped, from ten in 1973 to six in 1976, significantly
fewer than those of the Newspaper Society, whose members
faced fewer economic and industrial relations problems:
the only areas in which staff increased between 1972 and
1976 were the Mail Order Fund, from none to four, and
Newsprint, from none to two.[15] The staff responsible for
industrial relations were hard pressed to provide an adequate
service for day-to-day fire fighting and the annual round of
wage negotiations, and were unable to devote time to considering the long-term problems of the industry. The Royal
Commission recommended that the NPA should appoint
'sufficient new staff to be able to make long term plans for
industrial relations in this period of technological change,'
but no new appointments were made to formulate a new
strategy.[16]

But lack of resources was not the major reason for the
NPA's weakness, especially in industrial relations. Employers'
associations can work effectively where their members believe
that their individual interests can best be served by granting
authority to a collective body, or where they combine to work
collectively through an industry-level association. Individual
interests must be regarded as similar or complementary. But
Fleet Street proprietors acted as if their interests conflicted
with each other, seeing their major competitors within, rather
than outside, the industry. This competitiveness was partly
proprietorial individualism: owners such as Rothermere and
Beaverbrook had been unwilling to limit their scope for
independent action voluntarily, especially where collective
action might lead to the disruption of production, and the
loss of circulation: their traditions had been carried on by
less colourful successors.[17] However, separatism was not
solely the result of proprietorial individualism. The emergence
of what Simon Jenkins has described as 'the new men' at the

top of newspaper managements in the 1970s did not lead to a willingness to combine to form an effective employers' organization.[18] MGN's withdrawal from the NPA indicated the attitudes of the least proprietorial house.[19] NUJ members at MGN took industrial action in support of a wages claim in November 1973: after initially agreeing to negotiate over the claim, the company changed its mind following pressure from the NPA, who were acting on advice from the Pay Board — negotiation over the claim was inconsistent with the then current incomes policy. The journalists thereupon struck. MGN management, believing that other companies were taking advantage of MGN's difficulties to increase their circulation, and that other houses had already settled with their own journalists on better terms than the NPA settlement they were being restricted to, withdrew from the NPA and settled above NPA levels. MGN's critical attitude towards the NPA was well known, and its competitive position was exceptionally vulnerable owing to the success of the *Sun*; but the company was willing to withdraw from the NPA without certain evidence of payment over the odds. Loyalty to the NPA was clearly not a powerful sentiment. The belief that each newspaper had distinctive interests, faced distinctive problems, and was in direct competition with other newspapers, was a commonplace assumption of newspaper managements, in proprietorial and non-proprietorial houses alike. From this perspective, serious involvement with the NPA represented, at best, a waste of valuable time, and at worst a serious barrier to effective local action to resolve local difficulties.

ii

Company autonomy limited the effectiveness of the NPA as an employers' organization, and the deficiencies of the NPA reinforced pre-existing trends to separatism. Similar pressures existed on the trade unions, as shown in detail below: the bargaining power of print trade unionists rested on their strategic importance in a tightly constrained production system, not upon numbers, and the greater part of production workers' earnings were determined by house-level negotiations. It is therefore hardly surprising that the major focus of management's industrial relations effort should be at house level. The organization of industrial relations at house level differed between houses, and is only meaningful in relation to the overall organization of specific newspapers: there are therefore few useful generalizations about the house-level organization of industrial relations. However, there were three major features common to all houses which importantly affected management's approach to the industrial relations consequences of technological change: first, the reliance upon experience within the printing industry and the lack of industrial experience outside printing; secondly, the close integration of industrial relations management with production management; and thirdly, the wide variation in the formal organization of industrial relations, despite basic similarities in the size of company, processes of production, and approach to industrial relations.

Managerial experience of industrial relations was almost wholly confined to the printing industry. Only two of the forty-one staff specifically concerned with industrial relations or personnel matters covered by the ACAS survey had worked for more than five years outside newspapers or printing, and thirty-two had never worked outside newspapers or printing at all.[20] Promotion was mainly in-house, from the craft chapels. The reliance upon managers experienced in the industry was even greater in production management. At the first level of management, overseer level, membership of the appropriate union was a precondition for employment and higher posts were usually filled from below, by recruitment of personnel with directly relevant experience. The restricted sphere of recruitment, together with the small size of the industry, inevitably exaggerated the importance of specific knowledge and experience, and of personality. Knowledge of particular house practices was useful, in view of the complex customs, practices, and agreements; but recruitment from a narrow range inevitably restricted awareness of new ideas and reduced critical appreciation of any new ideas that were adopted. In the late 1970s newspaper managements exhibited a technological gullibility which would have been less likely in an industry whose senior management had wider industrial and technological experience. The limiting effects of restricted recruitment were not alleviated by systematic career development or by the wide use of outside training courses. For example, the NPA-stimulated courses for newspaper managers at the University of Warwick did not succeed, and were stopped through lack of commitment by the industry.

As a matter of policy, the conduct of industrial relations was closely integrated into the responsibilities of production management, down to, and including, the overseer level. The number of levels between the Board and the overseer depended upon the size and number of titles in the house. But the organization of production management was basically simple: the overseers for each department (composing, reading, foundry, machine room, etc.) reported to the assistant production manager during the day, or to the night manager; the assistant production manager and the night manager reported to the production manager, who reported to the production director. The lines of communication between the shop floor and senior management were thus very short, resulting, according to critics, in undue involvement by senior management in the details of day-to-day shop-floor activity. The specialist industrial relations staff normally provided an advisory function for production management, although in newspapers, as in other industries, the line between advice and control is difficult to establish in practice: the negotiation of comprehensive agreements, involving greater formalization, was believed to have narrowed the scope for line-management initiative in industrial relations matters, further limiting the effective authority of overseers, already significantly curtailed by chapel power. However, the lacunae inevitably left by even the most elaborate comprehensive agreement, and the continuing need for *ad hoc* negotiations over special payments, work organization, and working conditions, especially at night time, ensured the continuation of an industrial relations role for overseers, despite comprehensive agreements. Integrating industrial relations into production management had considerable advantages, both in theory and in practice. However, it inevitably strengthened tendencies to conserve existing custom and practice: newspaper managers were no more likely than other managers to

repudiate the value of their accumulated experience, despite
its narrow range, and in any event lacked the time to stand
back and evaluate their traditional practices. Where specialist
industrial relations personnel or outside advisors outlined
new approaches, they could be dismissed as impractical and
showing lack of insight into the complexities of shop-floor
behaviour. At the same time, the narrow focus inevitably
meant that when senior management did adopt new methods,
under the pressure of external economic circumstances, production managers were ill equipped to evaluate them with
the necessary sympathetic scepticism, except within the
narrowest frame of reference. The result could be either strong
opposition, or uncritical acceptance — neither response
particularly appropriate to the situation.

Production management were confirmed in their scepticism
of the nostrums of industrial relations experts by their experience of comprehensive agreements. For managements,
the aims of comprehensive agreements were to reduce overtime working, to simplify payments systems by absorbing
diverse special payments into a single comprehensive rate,
and to reduce manning levels if possible.[21] For trade unions
the initial objective was to secure significant pay increases
during a period of incomes policy under the productivity
clause umbrella, although the majority of comprehensive
agreements were negotiated after 1970, outside the period
of incomes policy. Comprehensive agreements usually comprised an agreement with a specific chapel on the staffing
level required for a 'normal' edition, with specified pagination: extra payments were agreed for 'abnormalities' or
higher pagination. Any savings made by reduced manning
were divided in agreed proportions between management and
the chapel concerned, initially on the basis of an equal
division, and subsequently on terms more favourable to the
chapels. The long-term effects of comprehensive agreements
on earnings levels in Fleet Street are impossible to assess without extensive research into comparative earnings trends in
chapels with and without comprehensive agreements, and
even then the 'demonstration' effects of increases granted
under comprehensive agreements upon other chapels could
not be ignored. However, production management were often

critical of comprehensive agreements. Some of the criticisms concerned the failure to specify clearly enough the tasks covered by the agreement, leaving loose ends to be tied up by subsequent bargaining. This was especially likely with the very limited use made of systematic work measurement and job evaluation. More generally, the method adopted for dealing with variations in pagination proved to be inflationary. Pages in excess of agreed levels were paid for at the end of an agreed time period: in theory, pagination bonuses would fall when pagination fell, as in 1974. In practice, there was considerable pressure to maintain earnings when pagination fell and to increase earnings further when pagination improved. Moreover, as in other industries, the negotiation of comprehensive agreements encouraged further the already strong tendency in the industry towards a 'restrictive' approach to working arrangements. Finally, codifying and formalizing agreements increased their salience, and in the particular circumstances of Fleet Street, with sophisticated chapel bargaining, thereby increased the likelihood of further bargaining pressure. What began as a management attempt to link earnings directly to improvements in productivity frequently ended as a strategy for avoiding incomes policies and providing a consolidated platform for further increases in special payments.

Despite the similarities in production systems and background experience, the formal organization of industrial relations and the formal distribution of final authority differed between houses. According to the ACAS survey in 1975, board-level responsibility for industrial relations matters was carried by the managing director in one house, the managing director and the production director jointly in a second house, and by the managing director, production director, and personnel director in a third house; in two houses it was carried by the deputy managing director; in one by the manpower director; in one by a formally designated industrial relations director; in one by the production director and the general manager jointly; in two by the general manager; and in one by the production manager.[22] In general, one might have expected the differences in the posts allocated formal responsibility for industrial relations to reflect differences in the importance attached to industrial relations, with the greatest importance being attached to industrial relations in those companies in which responsibility for industrial relations was attached to the most senior posts. However, the differences in nomenclature were of limited significance: there was no disagreement among Fleet Street managers, senior as well as junior, about the central importance of industrial relations. Indeed, there was general agreement that it played a disproportionate role in management thinking, and that excessive attention could lead to inefficient confusion of responsibilities; junior management complained that senior management was unwilling to delegate authority, undermining their own authority and increasing the self-confidence of chapel officials.

iii

In summary, Fleet Street management was highly conscious of industrial relations, but had not developed very effective methods of dealing with them, either at industry or at house level. As indicated, the NPA possessed few resources, either material or symbolic, and was not regarded as an effective means of conducting negotiations or of developing a long-term strategy for the industry. It had no authority independent of that granted to it by its members, and its members were willing to grant it only limited authority. Similarly, the wide divergence of interests perceived by newspaper companies meant that they rarely acted collectively, although in the long term their interests diverged less widely than they believed. At house level industrial relations were primarily the responsibility of production and editorial management, with specialized staff performing an advisory role, although the precise scope of individual responsibilities, and the nomenclature, varied from house to house. This scheme of organization had considerable advantages, ensuring that industrial relations were seen as a means to an end, not an end in itself. However, in any circumstances the arrangement is likely to foster a plethora of specific understandings and agreements, adapted to specific circumstances, and designed to deal with short-term difficulties. In the specific circumstances of Fleet Street, with a highly developed bargaining awareness among chapel officials, the arrangement increased the likelihood of competitive sectional bargaining, to generalize advantageous sectional agreements. The bargaining awareness was based partly on tradition and partly on the variability of the product, frequent changes in layout, pagination, and print run providing frequent occasions for bargaining. This inevitably meant that management was preoccupied with dealing with specific bargains and conceived industrial relations as a 'fire-fighting' role — a term frequently on the lips of Fleet Street managers. There was thus little opportunity for considering industrial relations issues at length, and in the context of a comprehensive long-term company strategy. The importance of local custom and practice was reinforced by the high level of internal recruitment in the industry and the limited attention paid to providing formal training, inside or outside the industry. The development of industrial relations 'professionalism' may lead to an exaggeration of the role of theoretical knowledge and techniques; in national newspapers that danger is considerably less than the alternative one of excessive preoccupation with the practical and the customary, resulting in an inadequate sense of perspective.

The problems involved in organizing industrial relations in national newspapers are not unique to that industry. Most importantly, employers' associations generally experience difficulty in establishing coherent industry-wide industrial relations policies. In the chemical industry, for example, where market and technological factors might have been expected to favour the development of a strong industry-wide employers' organization, the Chemical Industries' Association explicitly recognizes the status of 'non conforming' member, a status *de facto* occupied by MGN in the NPA: the largest employer in the chemical industry, ICI, followed an independent policy in industrial relations.[23] Similarly, collusive agreements to forgo taking advantage of competitors' industrial relations difficulties have proved fragile, both inside and outside national newspapers. The divergence between industry-level negotiated wage rates and average earnings has been widespread throughout British industry, especially in the engineering industry. However, management's organization and handling of industrial relations in Fleet Street showed in exaggerated form the tendencies existing in other industries.

iv

Fleet Street unions have acquired a central place in British management demonology. They have maintained a monopoly over the supply of labour and influence over labour utilization unique in British industry, and have established a uniquely strong collective bargaining position. Earnings in the industry are significantly higher than for manual workers in manufacturing industry generally (even if the special position of linotype operators paid on the London Scale of Prices is ignored), although management and unions naturally disagree on the extent to which the differential is justified by the 'unsocial hours' worked in Fleet Street. Print-union officials, especially at chapel level, have shown a high degree of bargaining awareness and an ability to take advantage of favourable situations and of management errors. The fragmentation of bargaining institutions in the industry has favoured competitive bargaining, both between and within unions. The structure of trade unionism in Fleet Street is well known, through the excellent detailed study by the ACAS *Industrial Relations in the National Newspaper Industry* and the briefer Open University text, *Press, Papers, and Print: A Case Study*, referred to earlier. Only the briefest outline is therefore included in this chapter, focusing upon those elements most directly relevant to the approach to new technology.

There are five major Fleet Street unions – NGA, NATSOPA, SOGAT, SLADE, and the NUJ – together with the Engineers, Electricians, and the small IOJ. UCATT, COHSE, T&GWU, and GMWU also have a small number of Fleet Street members. The NGA and SLADE have traditionally been regarded as 'craft' unions, although both unions, especially the NGA, have expanded the scope of their recruitment outside traditional craft areas, with technological change and the decline of the 'core' recruitment groups. NATSOPA and SOGAT have traditionally been regarded as 'unskilled' unions, although both include workers more appropriately classified as skilled: NATSOPA includes highly qualified computer and supervisory personnel, whilst SOGAT includes the Scottish Graphical Association, covering workers recruited by the NGA in England and Wales. Two unions recruit journalists, although the IOJ has only a small membership, is not affiliated to the TUC, and self-consciously follows 'professional association' principles. Both the Engineers and the Electricians employed in Fleet Street act largely independently of their unions: the Engineers report to the North London District and are therefore outside the conventional AUEW divisional structure, whilst the Electricians are organized into a special Fleet Street Press Branch. Despite their wide differences, the Fleet Street unions share common features, and face common problems. As among proprietors, the major feature is a high degree of sectionalism, Fleet Street members acting more in response to pressures within Fleet Street than to pressures from the industry at large or from their national union officials; within Fleet Street, members responded primarily to the influences of their particular work situations. But, unlike management, union members profit from the sectionalism, using the fragmented bargaining institutions to maximize their rewards.

As with employers, the role of industry-level formal institutions has been slight. Before 1974, industry-level negotiations with the employers were conducted on behalf of the print unions by the Printing and Kindred Trades Federation, presided over by R. (Lord) Briginshaw of NATSOPA. However, the PKTF was dissolved in 1974, amid general disillusion with it, and the co-ordination of bargaining was continued on only an *ad hoc* basis. The PKTF was broken up partly by competing union interests, especially the classic difficulty of reconciling the interests of skilled and unskilled workers in formulating claims, and partly by personal differences. Its place was taken by the Printing Industries Committee of the TUC, which was established in 1975, and was envisaged as performing for the printing industries the co-ordinating role played by the TUC's Steel Industry Committee for that industry. The new committee was more comprehensive in membership than its predecessor, including representatives of the AUEW(E) and the EETPU, who had not been included in the PKTF, although initially

the work of the PIC was made more difficult by the absence
of the NGA, which was suspended by the TUC in 1972 for
failing to deregister with the Certification Officer following
the 1971 Industrial Relations Act, in defiance of the 1972
TUC vote against registration, leading the NGA to subsequently withdraw its TUC affiliation.[24] Despite the difficulties
posed by the NGA's absence — which proved only short-lived,
the NGA re-entering the TUC in January 1976, and paying its
affiliation fees for the period of exclusion — the PIC promised
to be more effective than the PKTF had been in its later
days, and was to be a major factor in the *Programme for
Action* negotiations. The greater promise was partly due to
the death of John Bonfield in January 1976, and the retirement of Richard Briginshaw, which removed two major and
mutually suspicious figures from the scene and reduced
personal rivalries, partly to the role of the TUC Secretariat
(especially Kenneth Graham) in providing an effective
'neutral' means of servicing the Committee, partly to the
commitment of W. H. Keys, general secretary of SOGAT
and the first — and to date only — chairman of the PIC, and
partly to the external pressures which made co-operation
between print unions especially necessary in 1975. The PIC
was not an authoritative body and, apart from the limited
services of the TUC, had no resources other than those granted
to it by its members. But it did provide a congenial arena for
considering the overall problems of unions in the industry,
outside the pressures of preparing for the annual round of
industry-level wage negotiations.

The PIC provided the major arena for the representatives
of the print unions, in practice the general secretaries, to
consider the overall problems of the industry together. The
negotiations over the JSC were to bring the general secretaries
of the print unions more closely together, and fostered
informal contacts between them. Co-operation between the
general secretaries was further fostered by the amalgamation
discussions between all print unions, and by the need to co-
operate when employment was threatened by unofficial
action involving groups of members of any union, as in the
NUJ dispute at MGN in December 1977.[25] However, the
degree of initiative allowed to general secretaries varied from

union to union according to political circumstances; although the authority of the SOGAT general secretary was traditionally greater than that of other general secretaries, no print-union leader possessed the personal authority characteristic of general secretaries in what H. A. Turner called 'popular bossdoms', on the model of Ernest Bevin in the T&GWU.[26] Print-union leaders, as the following chapters on the NGA and NATSOPA show, were constrained by complex internal political pressures, making it impossible for them to develop a united strategy for the industry, even if they had personally wished to do so: the rejection of *Programme for Action* indicated the dangers general secretaries faced when advancing too far on their own initiative. Nevertheless, informal co-operation between print unions, especially at general secretary level, developed considerably from 1975 onwards.

The PKTF and the PIC reflected the recognition by print unions of the importance of united action at industry level; the tensions which beset both organizations showed the difficulties of achieving unity. In 1975, as now, a more promising means of achieving an effective industry-level policy was through amalgamations, with the ultimate objective of 'One Union for the Printing Industry'. The major trend in printing trades unionism since 1945 has been the reduction in the number of unions; between 1945 and 1975 the number of independent printing unions dropped from fourteen to four. All printing unions extant in 1975 had been involved in amalgamations since 1945.[27] The NGA developed from a series of mergers in the 1950s and 1960s: in 1955 the London Society of Compositors merged with the Printing Machine Managers' Trade Society, to form the London Typographical Society: in 1964 the LTS merged with the Typographical Association, based in Manchester, to form the NGA; the NGA was joined by the National Union of Press Telegraphists and the Association of Correctors of the Press in 1965, by the National Society of Electrotypers and Stereotypers in 1967, and by the Amalgamated Society of Lithographic Printers in 1968. The much smaller craft union SLADE was joined by the United Society of Engravers in 1973. The largest non-craft union, SOGAT, was involved in seven mergers between 1945 and 1975, including the abortive merger with NATSOPA: SOGAT, then the National Union of Printing, Book-binding and Paper-workers, was joined by the Original Society of Papermakers in 1948, by the Card Edge Guilders' Trade Society in 1961, by the Monotype Casters' and Type-founders' Society and by the Papermould and Dandy Roll Society in 1962, and by the Pattern Card Makers' Society (Manchester) in 1963. In 1966 the NUPBPW joined with NATSOPA to form the Society of Graphical and Allied Trades, the NUPBPW forming Division A, NATSOPA Division 1. However, the merger was not successful, and in 1970 the two unions split up, the former NUPBPW retaining the name SOGAT. The new union was strengthened, the traditional craft/non-craft line further confused, by the merger with the Scottish Graphical Association in 1975. NATSOPA, apart from the abortive merger with NUPBPW, has been involved in only one merger since the Second World War, with the Sign and Display Trade union in 1972. The NUJ was not involved in merger activity, apart from an experimental period of dual membership with the IOJ between 1968 and 1972, which proved a failure, until after 1975. Neither of the maintenance unions has been involved in merger activity affecting their Fleet Street members. Since 1975 the NGA, SLADE, SOGAT, NATSOPA, and the NUJ have all been involved in amalgamation talks, but no further amalgamations have yet taken place (see below pp. 112, 158–67).

Since 1945 the structure of trade unionism, at national level, has thus been radically simplified; in 1975 it appeared that further simplification was imminent. An industry-wide policy towards the major issues facing the industry, notably new technology, thus appeared easier to achieve than in the years immediately following the Second World War, when trade-union organization was more complex. However, the simplification in structure was more apparent than real. Although the number of unions involved was smaller, each union was subject to a wide range of internal pressures, which rendered policy-making difficult for individual unions; the difficulties facing the NGA and NATSOPA are examined in detail below, in chapters 3 and 4. All unions were subject, in different degrees, to tensions between the interests of workers in national newspapers on the one hand, and in provincial houses and general print on the other; to the overlapping, but not identical, tensions between the interests of London and provincial members; and to conflicting pressures from occupational groups whose interests were differently affected by new technology. The problems faced by the unions involved were all the greater because of the incomplete absorption of recent mergers, and the survival of pre-merger attitudes. Finally, the tradition of chapel autonomy further limited the ability of the unions involved to formulate and enforce a coherent national policy on new technology. In view of historical patterns and recent tensions, it is thus hardly surprising that policy-making was confused and not always carried through effectively. The following pages discuss such issues in general terms.

Fleet Street provided higher earnings, shorter hours, and greater job control than other sectors of the printing industry. Although averages can be misleading, in April 1975 the lowest-paid group of Fleet Street production workers, NATSOPA Ancillary Workers, earned an average of £56·80 per week, the highest-paid group, NGA Composing Room Members, £130·70; the unweighted average for all Fleet Street production workers was £88.30.[28] Average earnings in manufacturing industry in April 1975 were £54·50 (for detailed figures see Table 2.2). For those members of the printing industry who were able or willing to move to London, and for those already living in London, entry into Fleet Street was thus highly desired. This favourable situation was maintained by effective bargaining, in the context of union control over the supply of labour. All print unions controlled the supply of labour to Fleet Street by apprenticeship or union membership conditions, or both. NGA members working in Fleet Street were required to serve an apprenticeship and at least two years' time outside Fleet Street; since vacancies were filled by the branch sending applicants as notified, and employers had little discretion in accepting applicants sent by the branch, the usual criteria for employment was seniority of branch membership. SLADE operated a similar system, without the formal requirement of two years' service. Entry into the newspaper section of the London

Central Branch of SOGAT was based on length of membership of the branch: waiting time was approximately twenty
years. Similarly, the London Machine Branch of NATSOPA
required four years' work in printing, followed by registration, and recruitment by seniority. Because earnings and
employment conditions in provincial newspapers and magazines, and in general print, were inferior to those in national
newspapers, as shown below (pp. 67-9), there was the
problem of reconciling the interests of an élite group with
those of the majority of members. The interests of the
majority might have been better served by a loosening of
the supply of labour, or by the use of the bargaining power
of the élite group in the interests of the majority, not those
of the élite group alone. The difficulty was resolved by
allowing maximum autonomy to the élite group, either in
policy or in practice: the problems this involved in the NGA
and NATSOPA are examined in the following two chapters.

In all print unions the London branches, and in the case
of the NGA the London Region, had traditionally been the
most powerful, because of their size, wealth, and history.
The degree of concentration was greatest in NATSOPA,
least in SOGAT: in 1974, 26,540 out of 55,992, or 47.40 per
cent of members of NATSOPA worked in the London region,
compared with 26,456 out of 193,804, or 13.66 per cent
for SOGAT. Comparable figures for the NUJ were 5,883
out of 29,433 (19.99 per cent), for SLADE 5,000 out of
16,925 (29.54 per cent) and for the NGA 24,298 out of
107.670 (22.57 per cent).[29] The overall figures underestimate
the significance of the London membership. For example,
although SOGAT had the lowest concentration, its national
leadership has been drawn primarily from the London Central
Branch of the union (of which the present general secretary
was secretary, and present president of the union also a
member). The administration of the casual system is the
responsibility of the London Central Branch, not of Head
Office; even before the Head Office moved out of Hadleigh
(Essex) in September 1976, the calls office was situated in
the London Branch office. Entry into national newspapers
was also controlled by the London branches. Hence the
London branches were more directly important to the

SOGAT London member than Head Office was. Similarly, although only 19.99 per cent of NUJ members were employed in London (and a further 1,112 or 3.79 per cent on national newspapers in Manchester), the highest earnings and the greatest prestige among journalists were obtained by working in London.

National newspaper membership overlapped with, but was not identical to, the London membership. Some national newspaper employees worked outside London (notably in Manchester, and to a very small extent, in Plymouth): in 1975 the NGA had 1,710 members employed in national newspapers in Manchester, SLADE 333, NATSOPA 4,225, SOGAT 850 and the NUJ 807. Many London members worked outside national newspapers. The proportion of London members employed in national newspapers varied between 96.58 per cent for the London Central Branch of the NUJ and a mere 5.61 per cent of SOGAT Printing Machine Branch members. The overall proportions of London members employed in national newspapers were 20.25 per cent of NGA members, 7.41 per cent of SLADE members, 46.72 per cent of NATSOPA members, 28.05 per cent of SOGAT members, and probably over 90 per cent of NUJ members (since the number of members of the NUJ London Freelance Branch working for national newspapers is unknown, although probably very substantial, it is impossible to calculate the overall proportion of NUJ London members working for national newspapers). The extent to which national newspaper employees were organized separately from other sectors of the industry varied from union to union and from occupation to occupation within unions: NGA and NATSOPA structures are outlined in detail below. However, within the London region, regardless of their size and the precise organizational arrangements, the national newspaper membership constituted the major grouping, except in SLADE, which was relatively small and contained a large group of members in the advertising industry.[30]

The print unions covered a wide range of occupations, with different economic interests, likely to be affected by new technology in different ways. Occupational differences were institutionalized in the branch structures of the print unions. For example, the circulation representatives, the process provers, and the publishing-room assistants were organized into three separate branches in SOGAT, although the publishing-room assistants, organized in the London Central Branch, were by far the most numerous, and the most important. Similar heterogeneity was evident in the NGA and NATSOPA. Only the NUJ could be regarded as an occupationally homogeneous union, although the position of editorial management constituted a serious problem for the union (especially symbolically, in view of the principle of editorial freedom); and even the NUJ comprised three branches, Magazine, Press, and Books, with very different interests.

Reflecting the geographical and occupational spread of members in the industry, trade-union structure was highly complex. For convenience, the structure is summarized in a simplified diagram (Fig. 3).

Although the formal structures of the print unions differed in detail, they shared important common features. The formal structure of print-industry unions follows the conventional pattern, running from national level, through region and/or trade group, to the district, branch, and chapel. However, the tradition of shop-floor autonomy has a longer history in printing than in other industries, although the significance of the tradition differs from union to union. The basic unit of union organization in the industry is the chapel, which comprises all the members of a specific group in a specific house, with a minimum size, in practice, of four. The fundamental principle of print trade unionism is the unity of the chapel: the FOC or the MOC represented chapel members to the outside world, including management — the 'FOC is the Union' in a more substantial sense than the often quoted phrase 'the steward is the union.'

It is often the F.O.C. who recruits the labour and allocates it to the different tasks. It is the F.O.C. who draws up the overtime and holiday rotas. It is also the F.O.C. and Chapel committee who are responsible for discipline. In effect . . . it is the F.O.C. who is the man manager . . . this control has now become second nature.[31]

The degree of co-operation between chapels varies widely. For example, NATSOPA RIRMA chapels, mainly comprising ancillary workers in a wide variety of settings, frequently act together, and NGA composing-room chapels normally elect an Imperial FOC, although the scope of his authority is limited. The Macgregor Royal Commission, following the views of ACAS, recommended that unions should develop Federated House Chapels, or at least should improve co-ordination between chapels, but moves towards a 'rationalized' chapel structure have been limited (see below, pp. 333-5, for developments at MGN).[32] The operation of the casual system in both the machine room (NATSOPA) and the publishing room (SOGAT) constitutes a limitation upon chapel cohesion in those areas, but the limitation is relatively minor — when employed at a specific newspaper casuals, even casual casuals, act as members of the chapel.

The extent to which chapel autonomy and cohesion is a threat either to management and union authority, or to 'good industrial relations', depends upon the policies adopted by the chapels: virtually autonomous work groups may constitute no threat to other groups, depending upon the stability of the environment and the degree of competition for scarce resources. However, in newspaper production there is an unstable environment and competition for scarce resources. Instability in the environment comes from variations in paging and in edition changes, as well as from the machine breakdown and raw-material problems encountered in any industrial setting. Even where the number of pages is small, the number of edition changes could be great — possibly even more than where pagination is high, because journalists have more time available. Competition for scarce resources, whether of money or of power, is inherent in industrial organization and likely to be especially acute in industries with economic difficulties, particularly economic difficulties following periods of prosperity. Accordingly, the potential for tension between chapels and management is considerable. The extent to which chapel autonomy threatens union authority obviously depends on the degree of devolution of authority and the extent to which developments in particular chapels can be insulated from outside. As will be shown below, the introduction of new technology posed especially acute tensions. On the one hand, chapels were sometimes willing

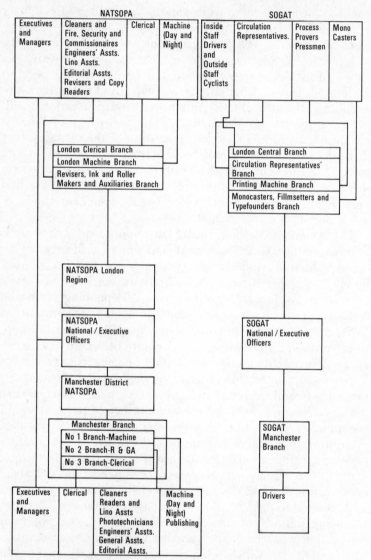

Note: There are also other unions organizing small numbers of members in the industry, including NUSMCH and DE (heating engineers), COHSE (nurses), GMWU (canteen staff), UCATT (bricklayers and painters) and TGWU (drivers).

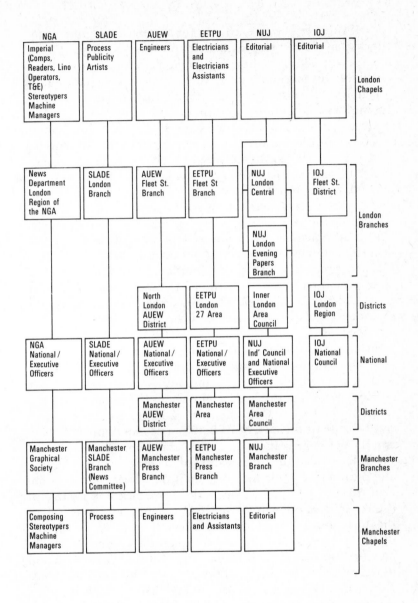

Fig. 3. The national newspaper industry — trade-union structure (simplified)
Source: ACAS, *Industrial Relations in the National Newspaper Industry*,
p. 290 (corrected).

to 'sell' future jobs in exchange for increased earnings, at the expense of future employment opportunities, in opposition to official policy; on the other hand, chapels were sometimes unwilling to accept changes which safeguarded basic union principles because of their inconvenience in particular circumstances, again in opposition to union policy.

Chapel autonomy was a long-standing feature of print-union tradition. But its importance increased rather than diminished in the early 1970s, as the proportion of members' earnings derived from chapel-level agreements increased. Before the Second World War industry-wide basic rates constituted the major part of members' earnings: by the late 1960s the gap between basic rates and average earnings was nearly 300 per cent, and widening. As Table 2.1 (p. 39) indicates, in 1975 average earnings for all print production workers, except readers, process workers, and outdoor publishing workers, were over three times the national minimum rates. Although part of the gap was due to house-wide agreements, by far the major part was due to chapel-level bargaining. The importance of chapel-level competitive bargaining is revealed in the short-term instability in differentials which accompanied long-term stability. Earnings were ratcheted upwards by competitive bargaining at chapel level, producing both short-term instability and long-term stability in differentials, and increasing earnings.

The effects of chapel autonomy were all the more disruptive because of the lack of fit between production technology and chapel organization. In British trade unionism in general the link between the organization of the process of production and patterns of union membership is only loose: the distribution of union membership reflects historical patterns of economic development and of recruitment policies, as well as the logic of the production process. For example, in the British motor-car industry the expansion of the T&GWU's membership owed much to the failure of the AEU to expand its recruitment outside traditional craft areas in the 1930s, although such expansion was official AEU policy, resulting in considerable difficulty in relating the interests of different sectors of the motor-car labour force to each other. Similarly in printing: Fig. 4 shows the location of occupations and union membership in the production process.

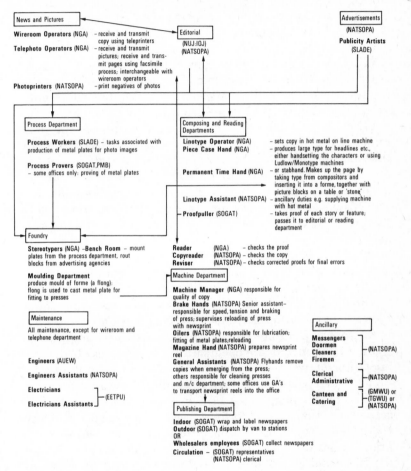

Fig. 4. The location of occupations and union membership in the production process. *Source:* ACAS, *Industrial Relations in the National Newspaper Industry*, p. 15.

The pattern of union membership is not closely aligned with the distribution of jobs required by the production process, members of different unions, with different conditions, different loyalties, and different rates of pay working alongside each other in the same departments. The boundaries between NGA, NATSOPA, and SOGAT members in the composing room, between NGA and NATSOPA members in machine and reading departments, as well as AUEW and NATSOPA members in engineering departments, were especially difficult to maintain. The checking of proofs is the responsibility of the reader, in the NGA, but the responsibility for checking the copy belongs to the copy-reader, in NATSOPA, and the checking of corrected proofs for final errors is the responsibility of the reviser, in NATSOPA. In the machine department the machine manager, NGA, is responsible for the quality of the copy, whilst the brake-hand senior assistant, NATSOPA, is responsible under the supervision of the minder for the speed, tension, and braking of the press, and for supervising the reloading of newsprint onto the press, and the oiler, NATSOPA, is responsible for lubrication, fitting metal plates, and the reloading of the newsprint. The high degree of interdependence in the production process, combined with the fragmentation of the union structure, and the focus of loyalties upon the union rather than the firm, inevitably results in tension.

In short, printing unions, like newspaper proprietors, traditionally acted independently. There was little co-operation between unions at national or at local level. The PKTF had collapsed, and in 1975 the PIC was still in the process of emerging as an effective means of co-ordinating action at national level. At local level there was no machinery for inter-union co-ordination. The formal structures of the print unions differed widely, as the detailed examinations of the NGA and NATSOPA show. However, all the print unions possessed highly complex structures, designed to ensure appropriate representation for sectoral, geographical, and occupational interests. In all unions there were differences in interest between members in national newspapers, and the rest, between the London and provincial membership, and between groups likely to lose by, or profit from, new technology. As the historical centre of the general printing industry as well as of national newspapers, London provided the major focus for political activity within all print unions, although the proportion of members working in London varied widely from union to union. Despite differences in historical development and in current coverage, all print unions permitted, in practice, a high degree of devolution of authority, especially to the London membership. Devolution had proved an effective means of maximizing earnings on Fleet Street, where all groups earned above the average for manual workers in manufacturing industry. However, in the 1970s the economic environment of the industry began to deteriorate, and employment contracted, especially in London. In 1975 it was expected that the rate of contraction would increase. Moreover, in some houses the effects of the industry's short-run difficulties were showing themselves in lower earnings. In this context the widespread introduction of new technology would inevitably pose major problems for the unions involved.

Trade union effectiveness depends upon the strategy being followed, and its appropriateness to the environment within which the union is operating. Since the Second World War the print unions had been primarily concerned with maximizing earnings, especially within national newspapers, rather than with maximizing employment, since employment was not seriously threatened until the 1970s. The unions had achieved major successes, especially in Fleet Street, as Table 2.2 shows.[33] During the period 1961–75 the average earnings for all occupational groups in Fleet Street exceeded the average weekly earnings in manufacturing industry; in 1961 the excess varied between 5.06 per cent for NATSOPA RIRMA members and 157.83 per cent for NGA piece-case hands. In 1972, when figures for RIRMA are not available, the range was between 69.17 per cent for SOGAT outdoor publishing staff and 168.27 per cent for NGA linotype operators. Earnings in the paper, printing, and publishing industry as a whole kept pace with increases in manufacturing industry at large, without reaching Fleet Street levels.[34] Even where national officials were opposed to selling jobs for higher earnings, because of the danger to

Table 2.2

Comparison between Earnings of Fleet Street occupations and average manual earnings in manufacturing industry

	1961 (April)		1967		1972		1975 (April)	
Average weekly earnings in manufacturing industry (£s)	15.7625		21.13		33.6		54 5	
	A	B	A	B	A	B	A	B
Lino operators	36.60	132.20	51.24	142.50	90.41	168.27	153.96	182.53
Time hands	26.69	69.33	38.63	82.82	67.14	99.82	103.68	90.24
Piece case	40.64	157.83	53.00	150.83	89.36	165.95	137.54	152.37
Readers	25.35	60.76	37.38	76.90	63.96	90.36	96.61	77.27
Stereotypers	38.39	143.55	49.14	132.56	74.01	120.27	102.94	88.88
Machine Managers	35.00	122.05	46.93	122.10	78.59	133.90	97.96	79.74
Machine Assistants	28.84	82.97	38.42	81.83	61.78	83.87	77.73	42.62
Publishing (indoor)	24.34	54.42	35.61	67.11	58.45	73.96	75.87	39.21
Publishing (outdoor)	25.27	60.32	37.45	77.27	56.84	69.17	75.54	38.61
Engineers	30.45	93.18	50.55	139.23	79.25	135.86	103.05	89.08
Electricians	26.19	66.15	42.94	103.22	76.09	126.46	108.51	99.11
RIRMA	16.56	5.06	40.27	90.58	n.a.		56.86	4.33

A : Average weekly earnings of selected Fleet Street production workers.
B : Gap between average weekly earnings in manufacturing industry and in Fleet Street, as percentage of average weekly earnings.
Calculated from ACAS, pp. 248, 257.

overall-employment levels, chapels in Fleet Street were reluctant to forgo the increased earnings offered by management in exchange for lower manning levels.

However, in the 1970s the economic situation in the industry began to change. This was partly reflected in changes in relative earnings levels; for all groups except linotype operators the gap between average weekly earnings and average weekly earnings in manufacturing industry was narrower in 1975 than it had been in 1972; relative earnings in the process, machine room, and publishing areas had all dropped sharply. Changes in employment trends, caused partly by declining demand, with the loss of contracts overseas, and partly by productivity increases, were ever more serious. The expansion of jobs in the industry which had occurred in the 1960s was succeeded by slow contraction. In the printing industry as a whole the number of workers employed fell from 155,800 in 1970 to 143,900 in March 1975, a drop of 7.64 per cent. There was a particularly sharp decline in employment in the industry in London: between 1970 and 1975 all the London branches of the production unions lost members, with the possible exception of NATSOPA clerical branch, for whom figures for 1970 are not available.[35] Over the same period employment in national newspapers, including Manchester and MGN employees in Scotland, the Midlands, and the West of England, dropped from 41,590 in 1970 to 37,367 in March 1975, a drop of 10.15 per cent.[36] The most marked decline was in SLADE, which was suffering particularly severely from the migration of general print, as well as from technological change, and in SOGAT Printing Machine Branch. The Printing Machine Branch was losing jobs with the development of photosetting, reducing openings in the process area. Both groups had relatively few members in national newspapers. The only area of expansion was among the journalists, but even the expansion in the Freelance Branch of the NUJ, by far the largest expansion, could be seen as a defensive reaction to increasing economic difficulties. Even freelance journalists were perceiving the need for defensive collective organization. In 1975 the PPITB predicted that national newspapers would lose 14,355 jobs, or 35.1 per cent of its 1975 labour

Table 2.3

Membership of branches with members working in national newspapers

	1970	1975	Change (%)
NGA London Region	26431	23633	−10.59
NATSOPA London Machine	8598	8161	−5.08
RIRMA	6977	6678	−4.29
Clerical	N/A	10450	N/A
SLADE London	5983	4907	−17.98
SOGAT London Central	23474	21160	−9.86
Printing Machine	4374	3420	−21.81
NUJ London Evening	353	399	−13.03
Central London	3834	3509	−8.48
Freelance	1079	1701	+57.65
IOJ London District	763	948	+24.25
AUEW Fleet Street	N/A	1018	N/A
EETPU Fleet Street	N/A	967	N/A

Source: Adapted from ACAS, Industrial Relations in the National Newspaper Industry, p. 284.

force, between 1975 and 1981; it was estimated that in 1981 the industry would employ approximately 26,000 workers. The major losses were expected to be in the origination area, with a decline in the number of compositors (NGA) by 50 per cent.[37] Part of the loss was to be achieved by natural wastage, the remainder through early retirement or voluntary redundancy. In short, a period of rapid contraction was anticipated in an industry already experiencing gradual overall contraction.

The worsening economic situation in Fleet Street in 1975 led managements to make a serious attempt to reduce production costs. Hence, there was a reduction in earnings amongst groups paid on piece rates with declining pagination — instead of increasing the rates to maintain earnings during a drop in pagination.

Table 2.4

Average weekly earnings: selected production
workers: House A April 1975–October 1975

	April 1975 (£s)	October 1975 (£s)	Change (%)
Linotype operators	209	183	− 12.44
Time hands	125	125	No change
Piece case	154	149	−3.25
Readers	125	125	No change
Revisers/copy-readers	97	97	No change
Process workers	105	108	+2.86
Stereotypers	168	164	−2.38
Publishing (indoor)	87	81	−6.90
Publishing (outdoor)	96	77	−17.71
Electricians	111	111	No change
Engineers	111	111	No change

Source: Confidential information.

For all newspapers, average earnings of all production workers rose by a mere £1.15 over the six months period.[38] A more significant change was the announcement of major plans to reduce labour costs, either simply by shedding labour to maintain financial viability (as at the *Observer* or the *Guardian*) or by introducing new technology, in the case of *Financial Times* with an apparently firm deadline. Fleet Street unions therefore had to adapt their strategy to face the new environment. In the early 1970s the strategy had been to maximize earnings, without loss of jobs if possible, but with the loss of jobs if necessary. Chapel independence and fragmented bargaining had helped Fleet Street members to achieve earnings levels which compared very favourably, even at the bottom of the scale, with the earnings of manual workers in manufacturing industry generally. In the new situation of 1975, in which external pressures exerted unusual influence upon employers to resist demands for higher earnings and to seek reductions in manning levels, attention shifted to preserving jobs. The fragmentation which facilitated maximizing earnings would be damaging in the new situation, enabling employers to play chapels off against each other, to the overall disadvantage of the unions. Accordingly, the new environment required a new approach, and to be effective the new approach required increased unity, both at national level and between chapels. The problems posed for the NGA and NATSOPA, the two unions most profoundly effected by management proposals for new technology, are examined in detail in the following two chapters.

v

According to J. T. Dunlop, in his classic *Industrial Relations Systems*, industrial relations systems comprise 'certain actors, certain contexts, an ideology which binds the industrial relations system together, and a body of rules created to govern the actors at the work-place and the work-community.'[39] The major actors are management, workers, and government. The decisive contexts are market, technology, and 'the locus and distribution of power in the larger society'.[40] The major concern of industrial relations is with the rules governing employment relations, and with the procedures for the establishment of the rules. Some industrial relations rules in Fleet Street were determined unilaterally by management, some unilaterally by trade unions, and some bilaterally. Management was solely responsible for decisions on long-term investment in the industry and, most importantly for day-to-day operations, for pagination. The unions were directly responsible for the supply of labour, the appropriate branches sending individuals to management on receipt of notification of vacancies. But collective bargaining was the major method of rule-determination, although its operations were heavily conditioned by decisions made unilaterally: wages, conditions, and, most importantly for the present study, manning levels were determined bilaterally. The technological, market, and political factors mentioned by Dunlop were central. As shown in the previous chapter, the technology of the production process changed little between 1890 and 1960, but began to change rapidly in the 1970s. However, its effect was to depend upon the speed of implementation, the subject for extensive discussion below. The industry's product market was dwindling slowly, but some houses were obtaining better financial results than others, and one house was expanding rapidly. The industry experienced cycles of boom and slump within the overall contraction, resulting in instability: 1975 was a year of unprecedented depression. The labour market was as important for industrial relations as the product market. Although the demand for labour was contracting in the 1970s, the trade unions maintained control over its supply; no 'reserve army' developed. The distribution of power in the larger society had only limited influence on industrial relations in the industry, although the industry was a major focus of political interest. The Government's major concern was with the maintenance of employment levels, but was constrained from direct involvement by the tradition of the 'independence' of the press, suspicion of Fleet Street proprietors, and urgent general economic problems.

However, industrial relations in Fleet Street were not determined solely by technological, market, and political constraints. The major feature of the industrial relations system in Fleet Street was its fragmentation. A high degree of local autonomy fitted well with the tradition and attitudes of both management and unions, rather than deriving from the structure of the industry or from its environment. Technology, market and government conditioned, but did not determine, industrial relations in Fleet Street.

The present chapter has been concerned with the overall features of industrial relations in Fleet Street. However, the complex interrelations between the structure of the institutions in the industry and the outcome of the negotiations over new technology can only be seen by a detailed examination of events within particular unions and particular houses. The new technology had the profoundest effects for the NGA, whose members were directly threatened by the development of computerized photocomposition. The attitude adopted by the NGA was therefore of decisive importance for the introduction of new technology. In the next chapter I therefore turn directly to the NGA and its approach to new technology.

Chapter 3

The National Graphical Association
and Technological Change

The changes which occurred in printing technology in the 1970s were diverse, and affected all sectors of the industry. Even within national newspapers there were great differences in the changes proposed for different houses, especially between quality and popular newspapers. Each proposal had different implications for the unions concerned. But the union generally most affected was the NGA — its members had the most to fear. This was partly the general truism that groups with more have more to lose. But, more specifically, the greatest savings in unit costs could be made in areas under NGA jurisdiction: the introduction of computerized photocomposition in the origination area promised greater savings than any potential changes in the machine room or in the publishing area. Indeed, technological change provided opportunities for members of other unions to progress at the expense of NGA members: greater use of photocomposition increased the work of SLADE members; remote access terminals increased the demand for NATSOPA clerical workers and for NUJ journalists; wider use of electronics in general meant more work for EETPU members; only SOGAT had little to gain from NGA discomfiture, and SOGAT members, traditionally regarded as 'labourers' by the NGA élite, felt little obligation to the NGA. The reactions of the NGA to management proposals for new technology were thus crucial to the success of those proposals. The aim of this chapter is to explain those reactions by placing them within the context of the NGA's overall organizational and strategic problems.

NGA members were highly conscious of their skills, and their craft status. This consciousness had both technical and political aspects. Its technical aspect was evident in the extensive and sophisticated interest taken in printing technology, shown in the union journal *Print*, in special union publications such as the magazine *New Technology*, and in formal and informal discussions at union gatherings. Its political aspect lay in the recognition that skill provided the justification for apprenticeship rules, the traditionally legitimated means of controlling entry into NGA occupations, and thus of limiting unemployment and maintaining differentials over other groups. The superiority of the skilled NGA craftsman over the unskilled members of other unions was a recurrent, although not a dominant, theme in the correspondence columns of *Print*. Hence in April 1967 one correspondent aggressively wrote: 'I think it is high time we got up and started to fight, and the fight is no longer between the men and the employers, but between the craftsmen and the labourers (that is the correct term, whatever they would like to be called).' A decade later a London member wrote in similar terms, opposing the proposed amalgamation with NATSOPA:

If the N.G.A. does need an ally, then why not another CRAFT union only: SLADE? . . . there is many a member who will say 'I don't want to be a Nat' whatever the Bienniel Conference might say.

We craftsmen have the skill, knowledge, technical ability, and determination to be the markers of our own best interests and to be a separate craft trade union — let's keep it that way!

We regularly see the effect of the amalgamation of craft and non-craft unions; the skilled workers become the minority, and naturally can never be in a position to be an effective and decisive body within those unions.

The Leyland toolmakers and British Airways engineers are examples — we would be in their position.

N.G.A. members, don't cringe in front of this member hungry NATSOPA. It will eat us just like an apple — spitting out the craftsmen like pips, and digesting our coffers and jobs as the flesh.[1]

Such craft defensiveness derived largely from declining employment opportunities and narrowing differentials, especially in general print: jobs and earnings initially held up comparatively well in Fleet Street. Between 1971 and 1974 the number of craft employees in Newspaper Society houses dropped by 1.0 per cent overall: but within this small overall change there was a large drop in 'traditional' sectors (12.0 per cent in hot-metal hand compositors, 10 per cent in process workers (litho artists etc.), and a massive increase in film and paper make-up compositors (from 408 to 1,054, or 160 per cent).[2] In the much larger general printing and publishing sector employment dropped from 220,400 in 1971 to 196,100 in 1976.[3] Detailed figures on the loss of jobs available to NGA members are not available from the same source, but within the relatively small, if significant, decline was a massive swing away from conventional letter-press printing. Earnings in printing and publishing declined relative to earnings in manufacturing industry generally. Average hourly earnings in provincial newspapers rose from 86.00p per hour in October 1971 to 160.00p per hour in October 1975, an increase of 86 per cent, and average hourly earnings in 'other printing etc.' rose from 78.01p to 144.81p per hour, a similar percentage increase. However, average hourly earnings in manufacturing industry as a whole rose from 71.95p per hour to 139.91p per hour, an increase of 95 per cent.[4] Trends in the basic day rate for compositors in Newspaper Society and BPIF houses closely matched this overall slight decline: between April 1971 and June 1975, the most comparable months for which figures are available, the basic day rate for NGA hand compositors on morning newspapers rose from £24·36 to £45·80, a rise of 88 per cent.[5]

In short, in the late 1970s the NGA faced a severe threat to its existence, with the undermining of the traditional skill and thus the basis of power of its major occupational group, compositors. New technology was accurately seen as a threat which would destroy the union, if not controlled. The union saw the collapse of similar unions abroad, especially the once powerful International Typographical Union in the United States: it regarded itself as the only print union succeeding in maintaining its traditional privileged position. The response to contracting employment opportunities included restrictions upon the number of apprentices, recruitment of members in non-traditional sectors and occupations, bilateral agreements on demarcation issues with other unions, and attempts at amalgamation to form 'one union for the printing industry'. The effectiveness of NGA strategy depended largely upon the action of outside bodies — employers and, especially, members of other unions: an overall assessment will be attempted below. But they also depended upon the effectiveness of the Association as an organization, its capacity to formulate consistent policies and to implement policies agreed upon. The union's ability to respond successfully to the threats posed by the new technology was reduced by its lack of organizational integration. The union's overall strategy towards technological change was one of conditional acceptance. But the ability to operate such a strategy depended upon preserving a flexible response to management initiatives. Controlled flexibility was difficult to achieve with the complex structure of the Association, especially the traditional authority of the chapel, and the special position of the London Region within the union.

To understand the NGA's strategy for dealing with technological change it is necessary to understand the structure and functioning of the union as a political organization. The following section therefore describes the union's constitution and structure, before turning to its policy towards new technology in section iii.

ii

The basic unit of government in all print unions is the chapel, which existed long before any print union; chapels formed themselves into local associations early in the nineteenth century, and local associations later evolved into national trade unions. According to NGA rules 'the democratic control of the Association by the membership is based on the chapel, through which complaints or aspirations of members may be conveyed to branch and regional meetings, and to the National Council.'[6] The rules do not define the scope and functions of the chapel: they merely provide for the establishment of a chapel in every office recognized by the union, and for the drawing up of chapel rules in every office in which four or more members are employed. However, the NGA *F.O.C.'s Handbook* contains a set of model chapel rules, which probably represent standard practice in large, well-organized chapels. The suggested rules provide for the election by the chapel of a chairman, father, deputy father, clerk, two auditors, and an unspecified number of committee members. By far the major role is played by the FOC. He interviews all NGA members engaged by management to establish that they have been cleared by the branch to begin work, heads all deputations to management, authorizes all circulars, petitions, and pass rounds, and generally ensures that chapel, branch, and national rules are followed within the office. Moreover, no member of the chapel is allowed to approach management without the consent of the FOC except on a purely personal matter — and 'personal' is defined narrowly to exclude all wages and conditions items. 'It shall be deemed an offence for any member to approach or make any suggestions to the management, other than of a personal nature, without the prior consent of the F.O.C.'[7]

For many NGA members 'the chapel is the union.' The chapel plays the primary role in fulfilling traditional trade union functions — the representation of members individually and collectively in conflicts with management, the formulation of in-house claims, the provision of sickness, death, and other welfare benefits and the effective implementation of national policy at local level. But, in addition, it performs many functions performed elsewhere by management: it regulates the work place through the control and administration of recruitment, work rotas, and discipline. Employees are hired through the union. The administration of work rotas extends beyond the drawing up of overtime rotas, often found in other industries, to include the allocation of work-tasks. The chapels are also responsible for the negotiation of house-level additions to national rates, which form a declining proportion of members' earnings in printing, as in engineering; this has further reinforced the historical importance of the chapel. As the National Council commented in their paper on collective bargaining presented to the Biennial Delegate Meeting in 1978: '. . . compared with before the war, when minimum went often near to maximum rates and average did not markedly diverge from normal working hours, the quantitative significance of independent workplace bargaining is now of an entirely different order.'[8] In both constitutional theory and practice 'the right to make final decisions on all matters concerning the work lies with the Chapel and the Chapel alone.'[9]

The FOC is the lynch-pin of chapel organization. He is

formally designated in the union's constitution, and granted
considerable authority by rule: the problem of integrating
shop-level representatives into the union machinery found
in many other unions does not formally exist in the NGA.
However, his authority derives more from his relationship
to the group than from his constitutional position. He is,
of course, elected only by members of the chapel, at the
Annual General Meeting, and is subject to constant informal
influence by them in the shop. This is especially powerful
because the average size of chapels, except in national newspapers, is small. The need to be responsible to chapel opinion
is made explicit in the FOC's *Handbook*; 'F.O.C.'s are representative of the chapel as a whole, and *adequate* [emphasis
in original] consultation with, and communications to,
chapel members will help create trust between everyone
(including managements).'[10] Hence FOCs are advised against
conducting business with management alone, and to keep
members continuously informed. Sykes emphasized the role
of the FOC as no more than *primus inter pares*:

> The Chapel as an *association* is of primary importance, the individual
> officers of secondary importance . . . [The FOC] makes no decisions
> himself and only participates — as a Chapel member — in the making
> of collective decisions. The Chapel is genuinely an association of equals,
> decisions are made by the assembled group, not by officials acting
> alone.[11]

Some chapels rotate the office of FOC among all members
of the chapel, thus sustaining involvement and preventing the
division of the group into leaders and led. However, this
exclusive emphasis upon the primitive democracy of the
chapel is misleading. FOCs derive their authority from the
group, decisions are a group responsibility, the group operates
according to principles of unity and equality, and group
sentiment is a very powerful force. But the FOC is more than
simply a passive channel for group feeling. This is partly
a matter of time and resources. According to the ACAS
survey, in national newspapers 9 out of 19 Imperial composing
FOCs were engaged nearly full time on chapel business, 7
more spent over half-time on chapel business, and only 3
spent less than half-time; 8 out of 15 machine manager
FOCs were nearly full-time, 2 were over half-time, and only

5 spent less than half-time. The likelihood of chapel officials being full-time was greater in dual- (or multi-) title houses than in single-title houses. On facilities, 15 out of 19 Imperial composing FOCs had office facilities available, as did 9 out of 10 machine-manager FOCs in dual-title houses (although only 1 out of 5 machine-manager FOCs did so in single-title houses, reflecting far simpler scheduling and production problems).[12] Facilities available to FOCs in provincial houses were fewer — only 1 out of 25 composing chapels, and 2 out of 17 machine managers' chapels had full-time FOCs — and facilities in general print were probably even less generous.[13] In addition to time and facilities, FOCs were relatively experienced in union affairs. It was customary to serve an apprenticeship in a lesser office, and once in office FOCs were likely to stay for several years: ACAS reported that the average length of time in office of Imperial composing FOCs in national newspapers was 6.7 years, the longest period in office 16 years.[14] The FOC played the major role in house-level negotiations, and acted as the link between the chapel and the union. As the National Council commented, the growth of plant-level bargaining had completely changed the role of FOCs:

Where they had a part to play in our traditional type of collective bargainings [sic] it was largely one of watch-dog, whose function was to see that union rules, collective agreements and customary practices were observed.

Today they are negotiators in their own right, and a substantial part of the workers' pay packets depends on their collective efforts and leadership.

Moreover, in such matters as overtime, it is they who uphold the principle of 'fair shares' and are involved in the detailed administration of its allocation. Their greater authority over union members is derived from their representing their members' interests on important issues which full-time officials have little or no say in settling.[15]

They also have wider contacts within the union than other chapel members; they represent the chapel at regular branch meetings, attend special training courses, including residential schools, and are far more likely to stand for union office. The force of group sentiment may be considerably stronger in the chapel than in other forms of work-shop level organization, for both historical and structural reasons. But even in a craft with a high level of occupational community and involvement in union activities, at least at chapel level, the FOC is likely to exercise more than a proportionate influence on chapel attitudes and actions.

Nominally, NGA chapels are fully integrated into the branch system. Branches comprise a number of chapels within a given territorial area, chapels are directly represented at branch meetings, chapel rules have to be approved by branches, and house-level agreements have to be approved by the branch. Branches are clearly charged with responsibility for ensuring that the policies of the National Council are carried out within a particular area. This is especially important during periods of technological change, when managements wish to alter work practices, or to install new equipment, for chapels are required to report to their branch secretary when any new item of equipment is installed and before any change is made in existing work practices.

Before concluding a new agreement with management (e.g. working conditions, overtime rates), or agreeing to any alterations in an existing agreement, chapels should seek the advice and ultimately the endorsement of the local Branch Committee . . . The Branch has the responsibility to ensure that there is no contravention of Branch or Association rules (or policy), National Agreements or customs of the trade. Finally, the agreement should be forwarded to Head Office for approval.[16]

Despite this provision, complaints were made by Head Office that chapels were agreeing to the installation of new equipment, or to new working practices, without informing either the branch or Head Office (especially galling to Head Office when chapels subsequently grumbled that Head Office was failing to provide protection against changes brought about by new technology). NGA president Les Dixon wrote in April 1977:

In many instances, and through apathy, our members have not been as vigilant as they should be and have allowed members of other unions to claim jobs that originally and traditionally were ours. Or they have allowed employers to install new equipment without notifying branch, region, and Head Office, thus allowing the vital initiative to be lost, regardless of . . . circulars . . . advising them of the importance of keeping us informed.[17]

The branch was charged with responsibility for ensuring that national policy was followed in its area. But the resources available for such oversight were limited, and effectiveness dependent upon the extent to which chapel officials placed confidence in the branch. Although the NGA has the reputation of being a wealthy union, and its subscriptions remain relatively high, the union's finances deteriorated in the 1970s.[18] Expenditure on branch-level administration was thus inevitably limited. The number of branches had declined since 1970, as a result of a comprehensive policy of reorganization and consolidation: between 1970 and 1975 the number of branches dropped from 188 to 131. Given the union's static membership this inevitably resulted in an increase in the average size of branch membership. Increased size, and increased technological change — alongside other trends common to the whole trade-union movement — increased the work load upon branch officials. To meet the increased work load the number of full-time branch officials increased, financed by a new administration grant from central funds, to supplement the money raised by branch subscriptions. There remained a major problem in the provincial press and in general print of ensuring that resources were available for effective branch oversight. However, the problem of lack of organizational resources at branch level has not been a serious one in national newspapers, where the relevant branch, the London Region, had nine full-time officers, with appropriate supporting administrative staff.

Branches of the Association are organized into seven regions — London, Northern, South-Eastern, Midland and North Wales, South-Western and South Wales, Irish, and Scottish.[19] The region is responsible for ensuring that National Council's policies are followed in its area, and 'such other functions as may be required of them by the National Council'. In addition to lay officials, the rules provide for the election by the region of a full-time regional secretary, paid for out of central funds: regional secretaries are not subject to re-election, and can be dismissed only by the National Council. Each region is responsible for holding an Annual Conference. The regions have a limited autonomy. For example, they are able, on the basis of a vote of regional members only, to levy a regional subscription on branches and to spend the money as the region thinks fit (subject of course to any general Associa-

tion rules on legitimate expenditure). But they are administrative rather than political groupings, and do not carry any great
authority on general policy matters. The regions elect nineteen
out of thirty-one elected members of the National Council,
but, with the very significant exception of London, this division of the electorate has administrative rather than constitutional or political significance. Even within the restricted
administrative sphere the scope of the regions is limited: since
the regional office is centrally financed, decisions about its
size are made centrally. The Annual Regional Conferences are
important meeting places for local members: but their major
importance is to provide an arena for national officials to present their views of major current issues, and to obtain some
feed-back from active rank-and-file members.

The London Region was an exception to this assessment
of the limited role of the region. In 1975 this comprised
approximately 23,000 members (just under a quarter of the
union's membership), of whom nearly 18,000 were master
craftsmen: 7,800 compositors and readers, 3,550 lithographic workers, 2,730 machine managers, 1,310 monotype,
linotype, and intertype operatives, 1,200 electrotypers and
stereotypers, and 1,100 telegraphic and electronic and
miscellaneous.[20] Only 20 per cent of London members were
employed in national newspapers, but they exercised a political
influence beyond their number in the region, because of the
comparatively large size of the chapels involved, the salience of
Fleet Street as an occupational ambition for all print workers,
and the gradual decline of employment in the industry outside national newspapers.

The NGA's standard chapel–region–branch–National Committee structure did not apply in London (defined as the
area within a 15-mile radius of the General Post Office,
Charing Cross): the London Region was a branch as well as
a region. Since the London Region and its relationship with
its constituent chapels on the one hand, and the National
Council and Head Office on the other, is central to understanding the impact of new technology in national newspapers,
it is worth examining the London Region in detail. The
London Region was the direct descendant of the London
Society of Compositors, and retained its own complex system

of representation and set of rules. Individual chapels elected representatives to (i) London advisories, 20 in each local-government area; (ii) 7 trade committees (non-Regional Council members), covering respectively composing, machine, news, readers, telecommunications and electronics, electro and stereotypers, and lithographic, (iii) Regional Council: 20 members, 5 from composing, 3 from machine, 4 from news (2 compositors, 2 machine managers), 2 readers, 2 telecommunications and electronics, 2 electrotyper and stereotyper, 2 lithographic; (iv) delegates to the Annual Regional Conference.[21] In addition, members in national newspapers elected delegates to twice-yearly News Department Delegate Meetings. The primary focus of interest for national newspaper members was the News Trade Committee, which provided the major forum for discussion of new technology on Fleet Street. But the Regional Council itself was very active and heavily involved, meeting at least fortnightly and being directly responsible for the regional officers. The relationship between regional officers and the union was different in London from elsewhere: the clause relating to the election of regional secretaries specifically excluded London; the London regional office was not provided for under rule. Instead, all London full-time officers (chairman, vice-chairman, secretary, deputy secretary, assistant secretary/organizer, financial secretary, assistant secretaries and trustees) were subject to ballot of the London membership every three years, at the same time, except for former officials of the NSES, NUPT, and ACP, whose personal positions were protected when their unions merged with the NGA.

The widely different interests and views amongst London chapels, and the ample opportunity provided for influencing regional policy, meant that creating a consistent response to the new technology proposals within the region was difficult. Hence the deputy secretary of the region, Ernie Welham, commented in April 1977: 'Because of different attitudes at chapel level it was becoming very difficult to formulate a policy that would satisfy a majority of members in the London News Department.'[22] These difficulties revealed themselves at successive annual conferences of the London Region, but most clearly at the November 1976 conference.

According to the report in *Print*, 'alarm, and not a little despondency, characterized a debate on the section of the report [by Regional Council] dealing with new techniques in national newspapers.' In moving the reference back of the section of the report dealing with new technology one speaker expressed his lack of confidence in a 'secret society of general secretaries': he was supported by another speaker who referred to the report as a 'load of old waffle'. After an extensive debate, in which considerable suspicion both of London and, especially, of national leadership was expressed, the report was referred back. The London Region deputy secretary's plaint that 'too many members still believed the era of feather-bedding was not past' was rejected.[23] Similarly, in November 1978 there was extensive debate over a resolution from the *Sunday Times* machine managers (who had sponsored the 1976 motion for reference back) that the National Council should pursue a policy of 'parity' for all members involved in new technology, and involve chapel representatives at all meetings. On this occasion the Regional Council successfully opposed the motion.[24]

The wide diversity in chapel interests made policy formulation difficult within the London Region. But the relationship between the London Region and the national office was even more difficult to manage, even after the creation of a more integrated structure in the re-organization of the union which came into effect in 1973. The NGA president complained: 'Unfortunately, in the NGA we still have members who regard themselves as individuals belonging only to a particular section arising out of our own amalgamation.'[25] This complaint referred largely to the London membership. The position of London was granted special recognition. On the National Council itself the London Region elected only 4 representatives, as did the Northern and the North Eastern Regions. However, the region's position was stronger on the Trade Group Boards, important both in themselves and as the electorate for 12 (of the 31) members of the National Council. Hence the Letterpress Trade Group Board by rule consisted of 5 London representatives (2 compositors, 1 machine manager, 1 reader, 1 electrotyper/stereotyper), and 15 provincial representatives; the Lithographic Trade

Group Board consisted of 4 London, 2 national, and 14 provincial representatives; whilst the Newspaper Trade Group Board comprised 5 London NPA (2 compositors, 1 machine manager, 1 E&S, and 1 T&E), 5 Manchester NPA, 1 London/ Manchester reader, 1 national T&E, 8 provincial Daily and Weekly, and 1 provincial T&E representative. The Trade Group Boards were not, in themselves, authoritative bodies: their decisions took the form of recommendations to the National Council. The extent to which Council payed attention to the views of the Trade Group Boards therefore varied. In normal circumstances Council accepted the views of the Trade Group Board; however, where Council had a well-defined view, it was likely to accept recommendations only when they accorded with existing views. It was alleged by opponents of the National Council policy that the News Trade Group Board's views were neglected in the discussions on the new technology.

The tension between the provincial members of the NGA and its London, especially Fleet Street, membership was reflected in the relative attention given to 'flat rate' increases, especially in the minimum rate, by the two groups. As one provincial member pointed out, 'the majority of our members live and work in the provinces and take home the flat rate which, compared with our brothers in the newspaper world, seems ridiculous'; some provincial members wished to focus attention on closing the gap between Fleet Street and provincal members.[26] There was also occasional resentment against what many provincial members regarded as the disproportionate attention paid by national officials to Fleet Street, symbolized in the resources devoted to the negotiation of the agreement on new technology with Mirror Group News-papers (see below). However, it would be misleading to see the National Council as neglecting the interests of relatively poorly paid provincial members. As the Association General Secretary stressed, the principles on key-stroking established in Fleet Street were central to the interests of members elsewhere.[27] Moreover, the National Council launched a special campaign to improve the position of the low paid in 1977, attempting to obtain above average increases, but this was short-lived, being suspended after government pressure because it breached the twelve-months rule of the Government's then pay policy. Finally, the bargaining tactics in provincial newspapers sometimes took advantage of the links between the provincial press and Fleet Street, for example the use of *Financial Times* comparisons and pressure in the Westminster Press (although it is noticeable that the dispute at the Westminster Press's *Northern Echo* in Darlington was not carried over to the *Financial Times*).

Despite the amalgamation and subsequent re-organization, the basic political division within the NGA remained between the London Region and the rest, between the old London Typographical Society and the Typographical Association. Just as provincial members sometimes felt that the union was paying disproportionate attention to London, so London members felt that the union was dominated by the old Typographical Association. The latter is more plausible that the former. The general secretary, Joe Wade, who succeeded John Bonfield in January 1976, was originally a 'TA' man from Blackburn, and ran second to George Jerrom, the London candidate, in the London Region; the president, Les Dixon, was also a TA man, although from Watford, just outside the London Region; the assistant general secretary, elected in 1976 at the age of thirty-two, was not significantly involved in union affairs before the merger; before winning national office he was full-time secretary of the Chiltern and Thames Valley branch, the nearest approach to a London candidate in the election. (The 'London' candidate, G. Jerrom, was not allowed to stand for the election, although he was nominated by three branches, because he failed the qualifying examination. The reasons for his failure are obscure, but he continued to be active in London regional affairs and was subsequently successful in winning election at national level.) The national officer for the News Trade Group, until his retirement from union office in 1976, was a former NUPT man from Lancashire. In the elections for national-level office held in 1977 and 1978 London Region candidates came third.[28] This political weakness at national level is likely to continue, as the proportion of union members in the London Region falls: it is no longer the largest region, being smaller than the Northern Region.

Some members of the London Region felt that national officers were too ready to reach agreement with management without consulting local representatives. Hence the national news officer was criticized for making a national agreement on photopolymer plates without observing 'the basic rules and requirements of consultation'.[29] The same feeling was expressed with regard to the national officers' attitude towards *Programme for Action*. One solution to this problem was thought to be the expansion of the role of the London branch: 'The London branch shall have full control (the National News Officer should be in London), and they should be supported by the National Council, which they are not at present'.[30] The London candidate for election as national officer in 1977 argued that greater scope should be given to regional, rather than national negotiations: he was defeated.[31] At the 1978 Biennial Delegate Meeting the London Region put forward a resolution that regional conferences should be called, a regional ballot held, and an eight-weeks deadline set before submitting a wage claim: the motion was rejected.[32] Attempts by the London Region to expand the scope of regional responsibilities thus failed.

The governing body of the union was the National Council, which met in Bedford once every six weeks: the National Council, in turn, elected an Executive Committee, which was required by rule to meet at least once between National Council meetings.[33] The Council consisted of thirty-one voting members (nineteen elected on a regional basis, and twelve by the Trade Group Boards) plus the seven regional secretaries who attended *ex officio* but did not vote. The members of Council were elected every two years, with no restriction upon eligibility for re-election. Candidates could be lay members or full-time branch officials: an obvious route to success for a branch official hoping for higher office was to gain national exposure and contacts through election to the National Council. The Council was responsible for its management of union affairs 'to the general body of members only'; Council members could be removed from office only by a Speical Delegate Meeting called specifically for that purpose.[34] Although the Council submitted a report to the BDM, it was not responsible to the BDM: indeed, 'in the event of any decision passed at a delegate meeting being found by the National Council to be inimical to the best interests of the Association, or incapable of administration, the National Council shall have power to deal with it, and any such decision shall be submitted to a vote of the members for endorsement.'[35] In addition, if Council was unable to implement a decision within twelve months of a biennial delegate meeting, it was required to issue a full statement to the membership. However, this apparent general sovereignty of the National Council was significantly limited by rule: before considering any proposal from an employer or group of employers, Council was required to 'ascertain' the opinion of the region or branch concerned; and before accepting or signing any agreement with employers 'involving a general alteration in wages, fringe benefits, or working conditions' the Council was required to submit the proposal to a ballot of the members affected.[36]

The overall policy of the NGA was made at the Biennial Delegate Meeting, the highest authority in the union, which met in June, normally for five days. Each branch sent one member for every 300 members, or part of 300 members. (The BDM was thus more flexible in its representation than either the National Council or the Trade Group Boards: this potential source of constitutional difficulty has not yet become significant.) The meeting considered the report of the National Council, which normally ran to about eighty pages, motions forwarded from branches, and such emergency resolutions as the meeting Standing Orders Committee recommended. As in other unions, the NGA Conference had difficulty in coping with the amount of business, especially in view of the time devoted to the report of the National Council: in 1978 delegates complained about the number of resolutions remitted because of lack of time, and the excessive amount of time devoted to fraternal greetings and votes of thanks.[37] Changes in the procedure of conference in the 1970s worked in different directions. Until the 1976 meeting approximately one-third of the time available to conference had, by rule, to be allocated to rules revision; this rule was changed in 1976 so that the provision applied only to alternate meetings. A second innovation worked in the opposite direction. The National Council presented three discussion papers to the 1978 meeting — on new technology, on work bypassing composing rooms, and on collective bargaining — which reduced the time available for discussion. Members of the National Council and national officers were required to attend the BDM, and could speak, providing that they 'are stating the definite views of the National Council', but could not vote (except the London and Scottish regional secretaries if they happened to have been elected as delegates by their regions).[38] In practice members of the National Council played a very prominent role in proceedings; the general president presided, the general secretary made a major speech, and national officers frequently presented the portion of the National Council report dealing with subjects for which they had major responsibility. The BDM was not a passive body: National Council recommendations were not invariably accepted. Hence in 1976 a vote of censure upon the National Council's handling of the 1975 NS/BPIF wage dispute was carried overwhelmingly; the general secretary's plea for the remission of a motion calling upon the National Council to insist on reduced working hours in all future agreements concerned with new technology was unsuccessful; and the National Council's policy of support for a pay policy, with provision for some move towards the restoration of differentials for skill and responsibility, was rejected (although by only 3 votes, 177 to 174).[39] Similarly, the 1978 BDM accepted a resolution instructing the National Council to negotiate a new manning agreement for machine rooms, and specifying the levels to be achieved, despite the Council's preference for being allowed discretion, referred back the section of the National Council's report on compositors' extras because of lack of progress, and insisted upon a ballot on the filling of the position of financial secretary, which had been filled by appointment by the National Council on the death of the previous incumbent.[40] The BDM determined NGA policy, which may run counter to that preferred by the National Council: the ban on work from unrecognized sources was an especially important policy decision made by the BDM, against the advice of the National Council. However, the relative infrequency of Biennial Delegate Meetings, the amount of time devoted to the National Council's report and speeches, and the discretion allowed to the Council by rule, limited the effectiveness of the BDM as a means of determining the application of NGA policy.

As has been shown, the NGA's structure was complex: it was a traditional 'closed' craft union in the process of developing into an embryonic industrial union. There were elements of traditional craft democracy, especially in the central role attributed to the chapel in the union constitution, and in the operation of the chapel. But there were elements of a very different tradition in the central role of the National Council, and of the general secretary in particular. The National Council played the major role in the joint negotiations with the NS/ BPIF in provincial newspapers and in general printing, and although central encouragement was given to local bargaining in the campaign to assist the low paid, it was local bargaining carefully monitored by the National Council. Moreover, there were groups within the union for whom chapel traditions had little meaning — for example, the Telecommunications and Electronics section, as well as the Executives, Technicians, and Overseers section; the merger with NUWDAT further weakened the traditional 'core' of the NGA (see below, pp. 112-3). The influence of the general secretary, as the major link between the National Council and the full-time officers, and the personification of the union to the outside world, inevitably grew, although the present general secretary has not established the strong personal position of his predecessor, John Bonfield. The general secretary was the 'chief officer' of the Association, 'responsible for giving effect to the policy of the National Council', and directly responsible for administration at Head Office, including publication of the union journal; the duties of the general president were to provide advice and assistance to the general secretary, as well as presiding over meetings and exercising 'general supervision'. The general secretary was the only Head Office official entitled to speak on all matters at meetings of the National Council: other officials might be called upon to speak about matters which were their direct responsibility.

Even in the NGA, Head Office grew in importance in the 1970s. This was shown at the most general level in the growth of expenditure on administration (although this of course covered branch as well as central administration): between 1973 and 1977 expenditure grew from £620,000 to £1.4 m.[41] This growth was due both to expansion of existing tasks and to the development of new resources – the growth of the education department, the creation of a research department, increased involvement in health and safety work. There was also an increase in the assistance provided by Head Office to branches, both over routine matters and in disputes. Expert assistance was available from Head Office to help with negotiations over new technology; 'a disputes Van' was bought, complete with electronic equipment, to assist in industrial disputes. The importance of professional assistance from the centre is likely to increase further during the continuing process of negotiating over the introduction of new technology. The publication of discussion papers, at the initiative of the National Council, was part of a similar trend. However, it is easy to exaggerate the importance of national institutions in general, both representative and bureaucratic, and the general secretary in particular. The NGA was not a centralized oligarchy, much less a 'popular bossdom': national institutions and officials determined general policy, but even general policy was subject to the BDM, and the translation of general policy into specific agreements required the consent of the members directly concerned.

The NGA was thus at a transitional stage. At the base of the organization remained the chapel, with its deeply in-grained tradition of craft pride, as a very powerful bargaining force with employers and a powerful political force within the union. However, technological change was undermining the chapels' bargaining power, NGA chapels no longer being always able to stop production. The importance of extensive-ness in collective bargaining inevitably increased the im-portance of branch, regional, and national institutions. Craft consciousness of skill survived, but the ability to exact a premium price for that skill through above-rate house-level increases diminished: a very high proportion of provincial

NGA members earned little more than the basic rate. Hence
the bitterness of many NGA provincial members against
economic trends in general, further fuelled by resentment
against the widely publicized Fleet Street earnings. This was
movingly expressed in an article in *Print* by the wife of
a Cotswold compositor, who described graphically the
decline in her family's standard of life, and evoked considerable sympathy from the provincial membership.[42] Since the
majority of NGA members were not employed in London,
and in London the Fleet Street members were only a minority,
the national institutions of the union were primarily responsive to the interests of provincial members; any other policy
would be democratically acceptable only in circumstances
in which Fleet Street issues involved principles which, if
conceded, would further weaken the position of provincial
members – as direct journalist in-put did. NGA national
institutions were thus less willing to regard Fleet Street
interests as as central to the interests of the NGA as the
Fleet Street chapels themselves were, or the London Region
was. This is not to suggest that NGA national leadership
neglected Fleet Street, for national leadership recognized
that Fleet Street was a desired occupational goal for many
members and of far more importance to the union than its
numerical importance implied: hence the considerable
attention to the *Mirror* negotiations. But the NGA national
institutions could survive a severe reduction in membership
in Fleet Street, whilst the London Region, already losing
jobs in periodical publishing and general print, could not.
The potential divergence between the London Region and
the remaining members of the NGA was thus not simply
a historical relic from pre-amalgamation days: it reflected
current economic and political interests.

The eventual outcome of attempts to introduce technological change in national newspapers depended heavily
upon the action of the NGA as the largest craft union. At
the very least, the NGA had sufficient strength to cause
considerable damage to newspapers attempting to introduce
major technological changes without their co-operation.
However, the NGA was not solely concerned with events in
Fleet Street, and reacted to them in the context of wider

changes in the printing industry: the union leadership had a wider constituency to consider. Within the provincial press and general print managements had been introducing photocomposition, web-offset, and a number of other technological changes for several years: the NGA had thus had to respond to innovations where its bargaining power was weaker than on Fleet Street. Its experience in dealing with the problems of this wider constituency inevitably influenced its approach to technological change on Fleet Street.

iii

NGA leaders recognized that the major problem facing the union in the 1970s was technological change; as Joe Wade continually stressed, this was far more important than current wages or employment levels.[43] Three alternative strategies existed for the Association: outright, total opposition to new technology; enthusiastic acceptance of new technology as the only means of reducing the amount of printing work going abroad; and conditional acceptance. In deciding between strategies the Association necessarily took account of employers' policies, and the policies of other unions in the industry: the Association paid little attention to the views of the Government, the Royal Commission on the Press, or other outside bodies. The employers were of course the initiators of change, believing that new technology would significantly reduce labour costs, and thus unit production costs: the fact that the NGA was responding to managerial initiatives conditioned its strategic thinking. Other unions in the industry partly shared NGA fears of employer initiatives and partly saw them as an opportunity to profit at the expense of NGA members. The NGA could not assume that other print unions would share their attitude towards employers' initiatives — hence the special enthusiasm of the NGA for amalgamation between the print unions. The NGA's overall strategy was necessarily defensive.

There was little support within the Association for total opposition to new technology, except occasionally for tactical purposes: the 'Luddite' element in the NGA was relatively small. Many members rightly suspected that the new technology would not be as efficient as many employers believed it would, that the technology was more difficult to get right, and that the quality of the work produced would decline. As one member wrote following a visit to the 1978 Newstec Exhibition:

[new systems] are costly to buy and maintain, temperamental and often it is necessary to install a second system as back-up . . . Supplanting well-proved straight-forward systems with complex ones for fashion's sake seems to me to not always apply. Deplorable hyphenation. Story mix-ups . . . a general sense of inaccuracy seen in the best newspapers.[44]

But it was generally accepted that total opposition would be pointless. Nor were there many enthusiasts for the new technology, although some members recognized that the new systems would be quieter and cleaner, and some younger members found electronics exciting. The NGA's strategy was based on the premise that the the new technology had to be accepted, but that its introduction ought to be gradual, negotiated, and, of course, not at the expense of NGA members' interests. Above all, there was to be no compromise on the basic issue of retaining NGA control over key-stroking. The warmth of the acceptance, the speed of introduction tolerated, and the exact price of that acceptance differed in different parts of the union: the national leadership, and members in the provincial press and general print, were less hostile than the leaders of the London Region, and the Fleet Street membership.

John Bonfield summarized the NGA national leadership's view of the new technology in an article in *Print* published in January 1976 (shortly after his death):

We go along with the introduction of the new technologies if only because the alternative is worse. But we demand that the threat to our members' employment that this necessarily entails is dealt with in just and humane social terms — which, first of all, means that there will be no compulsory redundancy . . . and that those who may wish to leave the industry at this time, for any reason, have reasonable guarantees for their future living standards.[45]

The alternative to failure to agree to the new technology was the further loss of business overseas and the expansion of work in 'unrecognized' shops, whether in-house for large organizations or in unorganized 'bucket-shops' for other customers. The compensation for loss of job property rights and the financial security to insure against a future decline in living standards could be provided by the employers, or if necessary the Government, as in the Dock Labour Scheme. 'While modification of old demarcation lines may well be made necessary in some respects because of the nature of some of the technologies, there is going to be no take-over of the composing function by any other union.' The same month Bonfield died in office, shortly before his retirement, and his colleague Roy Hutchins retired. But his policy was continued by Joe Wade, although with more militantly sounding rhetoric, at least in his early months in office (see quotation below, p. 234). He recognized that the union had no alternative to accepting the new technology, and that this would involve a reduction in the print labour force, and thus lost membership, but that the reduction was to be gradual, the financial terms generous, and the existing demarcation lines were to be preserved. The new technology was to lead to a reduction in working hours, not simply to the disappearance of jobs.

The National Council's policy was presented in a discussion paper to the 1978 BDM in Douglas, and accepted by the Conference.[46] The major elements in the policy were maintenance of NGA jurisdiction over typographic input; no compulsory redundancy, and the enhancement of payments for voluntary redundancy; reduction of the working week; extension of annual holidays; and improved pension and sick-pay arrangements. It was also recognized that present systems of hourly payments and the London Scale of Prices would have to be changed fundamentally. Existing wages systems would be inappropriate for new integrated systems because output would be dependent upon the speed and output of the technology, not the efforts of the individual operative, and it would be impossible to link effort to output in systems when input could be coming from three or four different sources: 'the bonus position for various sections would be dependent upon a number of outside non-controllable factors.' But the major strand in the union's policy remained retention of control over input: *the NGA has consistently maintained the input of typographical material is a composing function and consideration to changes in demarcation lines could only possibly be considered in the context of an amalgamation of unions in the newspaper industry'* (emphasis in original). Progress towards amalgamation was, at best, uneven.

The framework for the union's policy towards new technology was laid down nationally, by the full-time officials and by the National Council. But it was recognized that uniformity of application would be neither possible nor desirable: management proposals varied, and therefore the NGA's response would have to vary, within an established framework. This view was considerably strengthened at Head Office with the election of Tony Dubbins as assistant general secretary in 1976. Dubbins defeated two candidates already working at Bedford, John Jones and Ron Harris, by a substantial margin: 25,393 votes compared with 18,437 and 15,014 respectively. He was much younger than his rival candidates, and relatively experienced in new technology: he was the first major national official who had not had experience of conventional letter-press methods of printing. He had been full-time branch secretary of the Chilterns and Thames Valley branch, and responsible for negotiating a number of plant-level agreements on new technology.[47] He favoured the negotiation of further similar deals, whether in Fleet Street or elsewhere.

The outlines of the National Council's policy of conditional acceptance of new technology were not seriously challenged within the union. However, some groups within the union were more eager to stress the conditions than the acceptance. George Jerrom, the *Daily Mail* reader who stood unsuccessfully against Wade for the position of general secretary, argued that American manning levels were 'totally unacceptable' in Britain, as they would 'carve up' the NGA. The union should follow a 'clear policy of maximum job protection'.[48] Despite obtaining a majority among London members, Jerrom was very heavily defeated in the election for general secretaryship — predictably, as Wade had been a national officer for twenty years, and assistant general secretary, and was thus heir apparent. However, Jerrom's emphasis upon the need for maximum job protection was echoed by the 1976

Biennial Delegates' Meeting. The London Region proposed a resolution instructing the National Council to insist on reduced working hours in all negotiations over the introduction of new technology, and to institute a campagin for the 35-hour week in the next round of wage negotiations. Wade requested remission of the motion, not because he disagreed with the policy — National Council had already put forward the claim for a 35-hour week — but because the time was inappropriate. The BDM rejected Wade's argument, and carried the London motion overwhelmingly.[49]

The NGA's policy on new technology was formulated in the light of the needs of the membership as a whole, not simply the Fleet Street membership. Whereas a policy of outright opposition might have been sustainable for Fleet Street alone, it was not sustainable for the provincial press or general print. In all three areas the Association stood firm on the basic principle of NGA monopoly over origination, but was willing to negotiate on other matters, including manning levels. On this basis successful agreements were reached with employers in the provincial press, in general print, as well as in Fleet Street itself.

As in national newspapers, provincial newspaper managements wished to introduce new technology as a means of reducing unit costs.[50] As the ACAS inquiries showed, there was extensive use of photocomposition, VDUs, and web-offset machines, especially in larger houses. In 1977, many more houses had definite plans to introduce new technology within the next two years. In most cases the new technology was introduced without serious industrial relations problems: agreements provided protection against compulsory redundancy, retraining, guarantees against loss of earnings, and revamping of payments systems to provide for increased earnings. The absence of major industrial relations problems was because, in general, the industry was more profitable, and less competitive. Technological change coincided with increased work-loads, either because of the launch of new papers, an increase in the size of existing papers, or a move into jobbing printing work. (Although the optimism reported by ACAS in 1977 underestimated the potential threat of 'free' newspapers upon the revenue of established papers —

except of course where the free newspapers were off-shoots of traditional houses — and the long-term worries of the NGA about the loss of jobs.) The process was eased by the long-standing existence of a management–union Joint Standing Committee, containing six representatives of the Newspaper Society and six NGA representatives, set up in 1967.[51] The JSC, whose terms of reference were to 'promote maximum productivity, the efficient use of manpower, and the security of employment', met at six-monthly intervals, and provided an opportunity for continuing discussions of the problems posed by new technology, free from the tensions caused by attempts to resolve industrial relations crises. Finally, and most importantly, the proposals implemented in the provincial press were relatively modest; only one house attempted to introduce a completely integrated computerized system covering the editorial, administration, production, and marketing functions — the non-union *Nottingham Evening Post*. The increased flexibility in the use of labour required involved only members of one union: there was no inter-union redeployment. NGA chapels allowed redeployment between departments, for example between the composing room and the plate making department.

In its evidence to the Royal Commission in March 1976 the NGA stated that it did not feel that new technology created a major problem in the provincial press because the sector was expanding: in an expanding sector increased productivity did not mean lost jobs (although there was some concern about future opportunities forgone).[52] The union pointed with satisfaction to the experiments in Optical Character Recognition (OCR) which were being set up in Norwich, Carlisle, Sunderland, and Reading under joint Newspaper Society/NGA supervision, with the hope of reaching a national agreement. The agreement provided for a six-months trial period, during which NGA members would not press for additional money for operating the equipment in return for guaranteed protection of earnings levels for members selected for training. The effect of the new system upon NGA members was to be assessed at the end of six months. As events turned out, for different reasons three projected experiments did not go ahead; the only one that

Table 3.1

Technical processes used by provincial newspaper houses

Technology	percentage of houses† by numbers employed					percentage of total sample
	less than 100 employees	101–250	251–500	501–1,000	more than 1,000 employees	
Origination Department						
Hot metal linotype	73	73	69	74	80	74
Computer						
Typesetting	22	35	41	63	20	36
Photocomposition	23	60	51	58	40	43
OCR	0	6	10	10	0	4
VDU	7	29	26	32	20	19
Machine Room						
Letterpress	70	70	68	74	100	70
Web-offset	20	35	32	42	20	28
Photogravure	0	1	0	0	0	1

Number of houses introducing new technical processes in the next two years

Equipment	percentage of houses by numbers employed					percentage of total sample
	less than 100 employees	101–250	251–500	500–1,000	more than 1,000 employees	
Computer-Typesetting	2	8	28	21	0	10
Photocomposition	8	17	38	42	20	22
OCR	2	4	13	0	20	7
VDU	8	4	41	37	40	16
Web-offset	1	2	8	0	0	3

Source: ACAS, *Industrial Relations in the Provincial Newspaper and Periodical Industries*, pp. 10, 11.

did, on a joint basis, was in Carlisle; it showed that OCR had no harmful effects on NGA members. The joint experiment was, however, very limited, and OCR was to play no role in Fleet Street. Elsewhere, individual newspapers went ahead with introducing new technology, in some instances (Portsmouth and Peterborough) involving the use of non-NGA members for key-boarding. The attempts to break the NGA monopoly of key-boarding inevitably resulted in strike action. The dispute at Sharmans in Peterborough in 1976 lasted for seven weeks, and eventually resulted in victory for the NGA.[53] At Portsmouth the NGA negotiated an agreement for the retention of NGA control for two years, despite management's desire for direct input, a success the union partly attributed to the support of local NATSOPA chapels.[54]

Provincial newspaper proprietors favoured local level negotiations to secure agreement on technological change: they believed, correctly, that local negotiations would be more rapid and more flexible than national-level negotiations. They were also likely to be more successful, in that individual chapels were more likely to agree to manning reductions through natural wastage as a means of boosting their own earnings, even at the loss of jobs for future workers, than higher-level bodies, concerned with the overall level of NGA membership. The NGA was concerned to see that individual chapels did not mortgage the union's future, and insisted that chapels obtain branch approval before signing new technology agreements. A number of chapels, after obtaining branch agreement, did sign agreements allowing increased flexibility in the use of labour, the running of high-capacity machinery, the loss of future jobs, and the effective de-skilling of the composing function. Partly to control and channel this process the National Council called a conference of FOCs and branch secretaries in provincial newspapers in March 1977 to consider the establishment of guidelines on the introduction of new technology, put forward by the News Trade Group Board and the National Council. The conference endorsed the guidelines which comprised no compulsory redundancy, employers' recognition of obligations on sick pay, and above all the maintenance of existing demarcation lines.[55]

The threat to compositors' jobs was even greater in general print than in provincial newspapers. Both managements and unions were concerned about the growth of in-plant printing in the 1970s, and successfully organized resistance to a government proposal that printers in local government offices should be able to tender for outside contracts. Recognizing this common interest, a joint committee of the BPIF, the NS, and the NGA was set up to survey the overall pattern of origination, and the impact of the diversity upon work in composing rooms.[56] However, progress was slow, and the NGA 1976 BDM resolved to reimpose a ban on all work from unrecognized sources, despite a request from the National Council for the motion to be remitted: the mover of the motion commented 'We feel we are not getting to grips with the situation. The only way to insert a little urgency would be to reimpose the instruction that work from unrecognized sources should not be handled.'[57] The National Council was not enthusiastic about the ban, recognizing that it might result in less work for NGA members in machine rooms, as well as for members of other print unions, but were bound by the BDM decisions. Since the ban was directed directly against customers, and only indirectly at print employers, it had little effect upon print management, and the BPIF reported in January 1977 that the industry had 'generally remained quiet.'[58] The main direct result of the ban was conflict between NGA and SLADE, whose members in the agency and studio field were an 'unrecognized source'. SLADE and the NGA were in direct competition for members in that area, since the NGA's methods of changing an unrecognized into a recognized source was by recruiting members, where appropriate, in the studio and agency field. After intervention by Bill Keys, as secretary of the TUC Printing Industries Committee, an agreement was reached between the NGA and SLADE in December 1976 whereby NGA members would do all type-work in the field, SLADE members visuals, and there would be a 50/50 division where there was an overlap. All work coming from such sources would have a joint NGA/SLADE label authenticating the work.[59] Following the conclusion of the agreement SLADE agreed to join the discussions on amalgamation already taking place between NGA and NATSOPA. Detailed arrangements were made for preparing a fair list of shops, arrangements were made for filling in the joint label and steps taken to trace work which came from unrecognized sources. However, in the nature of the case it is impossible to establish how effective the ban was: there is no way of knowing of work which went elsewhere, no way of policing the extent to which members colluded with management to do work lacking the label, and considerable difficulties in tracing work from unrecognized sources back to its source, to ensure future compliance or to organize workers into SLADE or the NGA, as appropriate. It is doubtful whether the ban made a major contribution to saving compositors' jobs, although it may have driven work from 'unrecognized sources' underground.

The NGA's ban on work from unrecognized sources indicated the extent to which the NGA was prepared to go to maintain control of origination. But the special significance of the dispute is the extent to which it showed the NGA's dependence upon other unions for success. The joint-origination label designed in co-operation with SLADE was only one of several inter-union agreements to which the NGA was a party. In addition, there were reciprocity agreements between NGA and NUWDAT over members employed on letter-press and photogravure machines (before the merger of the two unions in 1979), with SOGAT (MMB) over members employed on platens and vertical Miekle machines, and agreements with NATSOPA over readers and machine managers in daily-newspaper offices. The development of small, highly flexible and easily operated presses in the 1970s vastly expanded the opportunities for low-cost printing: large organizations found it cheaper, as well as more convenient, to produce material in-house than to put it out, reserving putting out for especially large runs or where quality was especially important. The growth of in-house printing in local government was especially extensive. In an attempt to secure the return of the work to the industry, or, failing that, to obtain the transfer of workers engaged on origination work to the NGA, or, as a last resort, dual membership, the NGA undertook extensive discussions with NALGO, APEX, TASS, ASTMS, USDAW, TSSA, GLCSA, NUPE, CPSA, IPCS, and even the NUS, as well as other recognized printing unions. The discussions had mixed results: those with APEX were as successful as the NGA National Council felt it could 'realistically expect': NGA members were to be offered any vacancies which occurred in printing establishments organized by APEX, the NGA members having dual membership. APEX agreed not to organize any further print origination or printing establishments, to involve the local NGA branch secretary in any negotiations with management, and to establish a joint national committee to resolve any problems impossible to resolve at local level. Discussions with other unions were less successful, and stalemate was reached. Although the negotiations with ASTMS were notably unsuccessful, most controversy was aroused by the negotiations with NALGO. NALGO organized approximately 1,400 members in local-government printing, whose work was held up by NGA members as lacking the appropriate label. NALGO refused to agree to the transfer of their members to the NGA, and pursued a claim under the Bridlington formula against the NGA at the TUC. The NGA National Council recognized that the claim would be successful, as NALGO was the appropriate union for local-government workers, and suspended the ban on work from NALGO members, although on inconvenient terms: NALGO officers were to obtain permission from NGA Head Office for any individual piece of origination which they wished to have processed through NGA offices. No satisfactory solution to the problem has yet been reached.[60]

The NGA was dependent upon other unions for effective control over work from unrecognized sources. The union found itself in special difficulty in dealing with the problem because of the TUC Disputes Committee's interpretation of the Bridlington principles. The TUC Disputes Committee did not lay down general criteria for resolving inter-union conflicts; judgements were based upon organizational dominance and bargaining rights for the relevant bargaining unit.[61] '[The TUC] has made absolutely clear to us . . . that no union has any sole right to organise staff in a particular industry, or trade category or to claim sole rights to particular areas of work.'[62] The NGA felt that this mode of procedure worked to the disadvantage of craft unions and to the advantage of general and industrial unions: once unions like ASTMS or the GMWU had negotiated sole bargaining rights with an employer, the NGA was prevented from recruiting workers engaged on in-house printing by the Bridlington agreement. Accordingly, the NGA called for a TUC inquiry into the operation of the Bridlington principles at the 1978 TUC. Although the motion was successful, the subsequent review by the TUC recommended no change in the Bridlington principles or in the mode of operating the procedure. The General Council recognized the difficulties caused by the impact of new technology in printing, but commented: 'it is this process of change which makes it very difficult for the TUC to contemplate prescribing the rights of members of particular unions to particular work.' Accordingly, the General Council asked the TUC PIC to 'give further consideration to the practical problems involved in defining prescriptive rights', and promised to reconsider its views in the light of any further comments. The General Council did not wish to become involved in inevitably complex and contentious attempts to reform 'Bridlington'.[63] The NGA's concern over the effect of the Bridlington principles in restricting their ability to 'follow the process' wherever it was carried out was well founded: the Association had been prevented from maintaining its monopoly over origination by other unions. However, the NGA's focus upon the deficiencies of the Bridlington principles, and upon the need for their reform by the TUC, was misplaced. The principles were little more than a set of working rules to limit inter-union disputes or to resolve them once they had broken out by, in effect, General Council mediation: it was unrealistic to expect the TUC to use them as the basis for favouring a particular type of structure for the trade-union movement as a whole (by 'process') — their role was more modest. Moreover, Disputes Committees were not simply a means of legitimating the position of large, heterogeneous unions: research by Kalis indicated that the T&GWU was successful in seventeen cases in which it was involved before the committee and unsuccessful in eighteen.[64] The NGA's problems stemmed from technological change, not from TUC policy, as the General Council recognized. The NGA's policy of concluding bilateral agreements with the unions involved, and of attempting to build a single union for printing, offered more prospect of success than criticism of the operation of the Bridlington principles.

In both provincial press and general print the NGA's policy of cautious acceptance of new technology was successful in controlling the pace of innovation, without totally stopping it or causing major industrial conflicts. As the ACAS survey indicated, a number of newspapers introduced photocomposition, web-offset printing, and other changes, within existing demarcation lines. This relatively sanguine view was shared by the NGA, especially by its leadership, and by the employers' organizations. In general print the repercussions of the ban on work from unrecognized sources was partially responsible for a worsening of relations between the NGA and the BPIF, together with a deterioration in 'normal' wage negotiations. Moreover, the union's attempt to 'follow the process' into areas outside the NGA's traditional jurisdiction brought conflict with other TUC unions. The union was on the defensive in provincial newspapers and in general print, both against employers and against other unions. This increased the importance of maintaining basic principles on Fleet Street. Both the NGA National Council and the London Region argued that new technology could be introduced on Fleet Street only within existing demarcation lines. However, there were differences in the degree of willingness to contemplate changes in manning levels, which depended partly upon the credibility of management threats to close down: the NGA national leadership attached more credence to management threats than the London Region did. The NGA national leadership was more aware than London of developments in the provincial press and general print, and responsive to the problems they posed; the national leadership could face changes which increased work outside London with equanimity, for example in Manchester NPA chapels, whilst the London Region could not. The national leadership was therefore prepared to adopt a more flexible attitude towards new technology in national newspapers than the London Region was, partly because of a greater fear of management threats, and partly through having less to fear.

The NGA policy towards new technology was the same in national newspapers as in provincial newspapers or general print: a willingness to accept new machinery conditional upon acceptance of the NGA monopoly over key-boarding. On this there was no disagreement between Bedford and London. But the difference in perspective between the national officials and members employed in national newspapers was revealed spectacularly over the rejection of *Programme for Action* in March 1977, discussed in detail in chapter 5. When the Joint Standing Committee was discussed in the autumn of 1975 the NGA was not involved; Joe Wade joined the discussion in January 1976. The Joint Standing Committee's proposals were published in December 1976, signed by Wade along with the other General Secretaries involved, and by representatives of the EETPU and the AUEW. The National Council decided to organize special consultative meetings in London and Manchester, before organizing a ballot of the relevant membership. Wade was very much in favour of the proposals:

It is my hope that the decision will be in favour for, in my view, a rejection of these proposals can lead only to the death of two or three national newspapers. The appalling consequences which would flow from this in terms of unemployment would not only generate a great deal of human misery, but would inevitably create such a drain on our financial resources that it would have a very serious effect on our bargaining power.[65]

The two special meetings in London and Manchester rejected the proposals. Their rejection was confirmed by a ballot of members, who voted by a majority of 2,899 against the proposals: the overall voting was 3,778 against, 889 for. The majority against the proposals in London was more substantial than elsewhere: 2,855 (82.11 per cent) against, compared with 622 for; elsewhere (primarily Manchester members) the voting was 923 (77.56 per cent) against, 267 for. Wade was very disappointed at the result of the ballot, but expressed the view that the vote was against the specific proposals of the Joint Standing Committee, not against new technology as such:

no one should construe this to mean that [our members] are opposed to the introduction of new technology. They are as aware as anyone else that this is necessary if the national newspapers are to survive. So it is clear to me that it is not the technology they are opposing or, indeed, a rationalisation of the manpower situation, but the methods proposed by the Joint Standing Committee.[66]

Whatever Wade's interpretation, his views were not shared by his newspaper membership. The approach represented by the JSC was comprehensively rejected, and the NGA, like other organizations, made no further attempt to establish a joint approach to the introduction of new technology in national newspapers.

Following the collapse of the JSC initiative, the NGA responded to management initiatives by attempting to negotiate the introduction of new technology within existing demarcation lines on a house-to-house basis: negotiations at TNL and MGN are discussed below, in chapters 7 and 8. The major agreement negotiated was at MGN in August 1977, when agreement was reached on increased earnings in exchange for lower manning levels, within existing demarcation lines (see below, pp. 325–6). The agreement involved the amalgamation of five chapels in Fetter Lane, the buying out of the London Scale of Prices, a reduction in manning in London, and the complete abolition of the Manchester composing room from 1982, when facsimile transmission from London for printing in Manchester would be introduced, and a complete change in shift patterns. Workers employed in Manchester on hot-metal composing would have employment guaranteed until retirement, death, or voluntary redundancy, even after the department was closed in 1982. The NGA president, Les Dixon, claimed that the agreement represented a 'breakthrough': 'We have secured an agreement which ensures that the new technology which affects the Association is in our control. We will have an agreement which protects the terms and conditions of employment and guarantees that there will be no compulsory redundancy.'[67] Despite the substantial loss of jobs at Thomson Withy Grove, who printed the *Daily Mirror* under contract in Manchester, the agreement was accepted by the membership. The decision of MGN management to buy out jobs within existing union demarcation lines confirmed the NGA's policy of insisting upon control of origination, and made it less likely that other managements would attempt to undermine that monopoly: events at TNL indicated the problems encountered in attempts to modify demarcation lines.

The NGA was thus more successful in general in national newspapers than in other sectors of the industry. But even in national newspapers the Association was not unassailable. As the general secretary argued when ordering casual machine minders to return to work during unofficial strikes at the *Observer* and *Reveille* in June 1978, 'The National Council do not believe these [closure] threats are bluff. We are in a new ball game as far as newspaper production in concerned. Proprietors of national newspapers now have much wider financial interests. If they could not get uninterrupted production, they will place their investment elsewhere.'[68] The extent to which large conglomerate multi-national companies will adopt a different attitude from traditional proprietors remains to be seen: at present the new proprietors appear to regard national newspapers as a prestige symbol, whose losses can be tolerated provided they do not become too great, or the evident industrial relations problems too obvious to ignore. But the NGA leadership believed that the traditional presumption that disputes procedures could be ignored because, in the last resort, the paper must appear, no longer obtained: the view was not universally held within the union.

iv

In this chapter the constitution and structure of the NGA, and the overall development of its policy towards new technology have been examined: the detailed application of that policy in three Fleet Street houses is examined in chapters 6, 7, and 8 below. The NGA was more threatened by new technology than other printing unions were, as the major technological changes were in the origination area: computerized photo-composition, and the potential for remote-access composing thus made available, was a major threat to compositors, the core membership group of the NGA. As assistant general secretary Dubbins pointed out to the 1978 Bienniel Delegate Meeting, 'it is possible, within a relatively short period of training to be able to learn the new techniques of IBM composition, paste-up, small litho-printing, and to produce origination and printing acceptable to many customers without having gone through a craft apprenticeship.'[69] The product might not be the best, but it would be acceptable. Dubbins recognized that craft exclusiveness was not a realistic basis for maintaining members' living standards: where high earnings depended solely upon the retention of control over a process which in itself was relatively simple, the attraction to both managements and members of other unions of breaking that monopoly control were considerable. The NGA's policy towards new technology was therefore one of conditional acceptance: recognition that complete opposition would be impossible, combined with insistence that the NGA should retain a monopoly over key-boarding. Pursuit of this strategy proved difficult, but not impossible. The Association developed a broad framework of policy for all sectors — no compulsory redundancy, improved pensions, holidays, and sick-pay, reductions in the working week, and continued control over key-boarding — but permitted local variations within that framework. The union was unable to prevent a loss of jobs, but it retained more control over the pace at which jobs were lost than comparable unions elsewhere, notably the ITU in the United States.

Technological change brought the NGA into conflict with both employers and other unions. Over all, the union was successful in preventing employers from making major technological changes at the expense of NGA members, where necessary at the cost of considerable conflict, as at Sharmans in Peterborough or TNL. But whereas the union succeeded in preventing major changes in areas where it already organized members, it had less success in preventing the seepage of work away from traditional printing establishments. Its attempts to prevent that seepage, notably by the ban on work from unrecognized sources, brough the Association into conflict with SLADE, NALGO, ASTMS, APEX, as well as with the NUJ. This involved a further tension between the NGA and the TUC, which had not forgotten the NGA's independent attitude towards the Industrial Relations Act of 1971. The outcome of the conflict with SLADE was a formal agreement on work from unrecognized sources, and the entry of SLADE into detailed discussions about the possibility of merger with the Association. But the outcome of tension with other unions was less satisfactory, and discussions with NALGO, ASTMS, and the NUJ made slow progress.

The difficulty in reaching bilateral agreements with other unions gave further impetus to the NGA's interest in amalgamation with other unions to form an industrial union for the printing industry. Despite hesitations amongst some members, the NGA national leadership was firmly amalgamationist. According to Joe Wade,

In my view amalgamation is the only way in which we can stop inter-necine warfare breaking out among the unions from time to time; the only way we can have effective control over manpower in the industry; the only way we can adequately protect our members' interests in the face of new technology; the only way we can raise our members' living standards to realistic levels; and the only way we can obtain real participation by the unions and their members in the industry.[70]

The union's objective was one union for the printing industry, not the creation of a craft 'bloc' within the industry: hence the discussions with NATSOPA preceded those with SLADE, and the discussions with SLADE were part of a three-sided arrangement including NUWDAT. The NGA national leadership, if not all NGA members, recognized that a merger with another craft union might exacerbate already extensive tensions between craft and non-craft workers within the industry, and would at best only provide a short-lived defensive alliance against technological change. For SLADE was suffering, in a more acute form, from similar problems to those of the NGA. Since NATSOPA was the main non-craft union recruiting members in areas adjacent to the NGA's jurisdiction, amalgamation with NATSOPA offered the most promising avenue. As shown below (pp. 161–2) for reasons unrelated to new technology the proposed amalgamation with NATSOPA did not take place. Nor did the proposed merger between the NGA, SLADE, and NUWDAT, as SLADE members rejected the terms by an overwhelming majority.

However, the small NUWDAT merged with the NGA in October 1979, and the same year the NGA began extensive discussions with the NUJ, with the long-term objective of possible amalgamation.

The NGA successfully resisted incursions into its monopoly of key-boarding in the traditional printing area. But its success was expensive to achieve, and probably short-lived. Attempts at a more permanent solution through the negotiation of bilateral demarcation agreements with other unions whose members might benefit from the end of the NGA monopoly or through amalgamation have so far had only limited success. Agreement was reached with SLADE over recruitment in the agency field: but the agreement poses such obvious operational difficulties that it is likely to be short-lived. More importantly, agreement was reached with the NUJ in 1975 whereby the NUJ recognized for national newspapers that setting, proof-reading, and the assembly of type, however performed, were under the jurisdiction of the NGA. The NUJ also recognized the NGA's responsibility for the transmission of documents or pages by facsimile reproduction, the conversion of copy in the form of magnetic or punch-tape or direct impulse for on-line input into data processing or type-setting equipment, Optical Character Recognition, and 'any operation which involves the transmission of photographic prints and the reception and distribution of the same'. However, relations with the NUJ deteriorated in 1976, when the NUJ refused to agree to the transfer of NUJ members engaged on origination work in publishing houses to the NGA, and one NGA official commented that amalgamation discussions could only include the NUJ after 'modification' of NUJ attitudes: the NUJ policy on new technology developed in 1977 and 1978 indicated that modification was possible (see below, pp. 341–3).[71] Nevertheless, in general, the very considerable effort expended on amalgamation discussions has proved fruitless, and in 1979 the NGA was further away from amalgamation than it was in 1976.

The NGA national officials saw the solution to the problems posed by new technology in bilateral agreements, or preferably in amalgamation. But this is a very long-term solution. As the first section of this chapter indicated, the merger between

the LTS and the TA in 1964 did not result in a perfectly integrated union — the LTS retained considerable autonomy as
the London Region. The attempt to integrate the union more
closely in the 1972 revision of the organization, with the
formation of Trade Group Boards, met with considerable
success. But the feeling amongst provincial members that
London members are unfairly advantaged and the feeling
amongst London members that their 'country cousins' are
a source of weakness persist. Substantial policy differences
remain between the national leadership and the London
membership. Moreover, although integration may be achieved
at national and regional level, the focus of union power and
involvement is at chapel level. This is partly a matter of rule:
all agreements are subject to a ballot of the chapels affected.
But it is more a matter of power: the focus of bargaining power
within the NGA lies with a small number of powerful chapels
in national newspapers. The limited success of attempts to
co-ordinate tactics even at individual house level through the
election of Imperial Composing FOCs, and the unpopularity
of proposals for a system of Federated House Chapels, at
least with the London national newspaper chapels, indicate
that chapel separatism even within the same house remains
a considerable force. Chapel autonomy has survived considerable organizational upheaval, and would survive further
change; the success of any policy on new technology therefore depends upon securing chapel agreement.

The NGA, as the union most affected by the new technology, has been examined here in detail, to indicate the
organizational and political context within which responses
to new technology were worked out. New technology posed
different threats and different challenges to other printing
unions: for SLADE members the new technology posed
similar dangers as for NGA members; for NATSOPA members
it provided an opportunity to expand their influence at the
expense of the NGA; for SOGAT members changes at the
quality newspapers had few consequences; for NUJ members
it offered increased power, and changed working practices.
As a contrast with the approach adopted by the NGA, the
following chapter examines the structure, functioning, and
policy of NATSOPA.

Chapter 4

The National Society of Operative Printers, Graphical, and Media Personnel[1] and Technological Change

In 1975 the NGA viewed new technology with concern, and even alarm; NATSOPA viewed it with hope, and even anticipation. The major reason for the contrasting attitudes is clear. NGA members had traditionally formed a craft élite in the industry, whilst NATSOPA members had been restricted traditionally to 'semi-skilled' jobs, confined by demarcation barriers erected by the NGA and accepted by management. Even in the area in which the earnings of NATSOPA members most nearly reached those of NGA members, the machine room, NGA members retained at least a 10 per cent differential.[2] Restricted promotion opportunities were especially frustrating to Fleet Street machine-room workers, since promotion was frequent in provincial houses, where many NGA machine managers were former NATSOPA members: the most contentious industrial relations frontier in Fleet Street was in the machine room, between NGA machine managers and NATSOPA machine assistants. The NATSOPA general secretary, Owen O'Brien, saw new technology as ending the barriers of craft exclusiveness, to the advantage of his own members: 'speaking realistically, the lines of demarcation will not be blurred, they will be *obliterated* [emphasis in original]. The sooner practical people in all the unions come to terms with reality the better for all concerned . . . instead of trying to maintain an out-moded guild mentality that should be interred in peace.'[3] For O'Brien, new technology offered an opportunity to fulfil a historic mission for his union: it had been founded in 1889 as the Printers' Labourers' Union, and renamed the National Society of Operative Printers *and* Assistants in 1911, but the 'and' had historically represented aspiration rather than achievement. New technology appeared to provide the means whereby the aspiration of 1911 could become reality in the late 1970s. However, the general secretary's enthusiasm for new technology was not universally shared within the union: NATSOPA members, like the members of the NGA, rejected *Programme for Action* when it was presented to them for approval.

Like the preceding one, this chapter contains an account of the organization and structure of the union, before a detailed examination of the union's policy towards new technology. NATSOPA's organization and structure is more centralized, and simpler, than that of the NGA: the powers of the Executive Council are greater, both in rule and in practice, and those of the chapel less. It might therefore have been expected that the general secretary's welcome for new technology would have formed the basis for union policy, and new technology seen as at worst an inevitable disruption. However, no print union leader has ever been able to exercise the authority of a Bevin or Deakin, even in NATSOPA: even charismatic and firmly established leaders like George Isaacs and Richard Briginshaw were incapable of ensuring complete obedience, and on occasion had to use unorthodox means to maintain authority. The production process in national newspapers facilitates strong workshop union organization and does not permit domination by central union hierarchies, whether autocratic or bureaucratic: the most workable system of government is one of fragmented oligarchy. It is perhaps surprising that NATSOPA members should have disregarded the advice of their general secretary and Executive Council, and rejected *Programme for Action*, in view of the efforts of the leadership to secure acceptance; but it is hardly inexplicable. The rejection was due partly to suspicion of the promised benefits of new technology, partly to dissatisfaction with the terms of the agreement, especially the acceptance of voluntary redundancy, and partly to long-standing opposition to the national leadership amongst politically strategic groups within the union. The following chapter documents and explains this complex situation.

i

In 1974 NATSOPA had a membership of 55,992, including just over 4,000 members who had joined on the merger of the Sign and Display Trade Union in 1972; this represented a small increase over the membership of 1964 (46,351), although of course the intervening decade had seen the massive expansion and contraction associated with the abortive merger with NUPBPW between 1966 and 1969.[4] The membership was heavily concentrated in London, with a small concentration, employed almost entirely on national newspapers, in Manchester: in 1974 47.40 per cent of members (or 26,540) belonged to the three London branches, which understates the concentration of members in London since the Sign and Display Trade Section and the Technical, Administrative, and Executive Section, which were not geographically based, also included a large number of London members; a further 8.6 per cent of members belonged to the Manchester District.[5] The remaining membership was widely scattered, mainly in provincial newspaper houses; the only occupational differences between provincial and national newspaper membership were that there were no NATSOPA members in machine rooms in Scotland, and NATSOPA rather than SOGAT manned publishing rooms in provincial newspaper houses. There were comparatively few NATSOPA members in general print, especially outside London.

As in other print unions, the basic unit of organization was the chapel: in every establishment in which they were regularly employed NATSOPA members were to form themselves into chapels. The reference to 'regular' was important: because of the importance of casuals, not all NATSOPA members belonged to a chapel; casuals were members of the appropriate branch, not chapel. The chapel elected an FOC, to be responsible for collecting dues, chairing meetings, and acting as a link between the chapel and the branch.[6] The importance of the chapel, both to the member and to the union's organization, varied: as in other unions, chapels in national newspapers were both more important to the member, and more powerful in the union, than chapels in other sectors. Hence, except for RIRMA chapels, NATSOPA chapels in Fleet Street were as likely to have full time FOCs as the chapels of other unions: in dual- or multi-title houses, 16 out of 17 NATSOPA machine chapels, and 7 out of 8 NATSOPA clerical chapels had at least one official spending nearly all his/her time on chapel business, although only 8 out of 55 RIRMA chapels did so: in single-title houses the comparable figures were 3 out of 6, 1 out of 4, and 0 out of 18 for full-time chapel officials.[7] NATSOPA machine and clerical Fleet Street chapels were also relatively large: in dual or multi-title houses the average size of machine chapel was 303, and clerical 480, in single-title houses 57 and 114 respectively. These were by far the largest chapels in multi- or dual-title houses, and exceeded only by the Imperial Composing, NGA, and the NUJ in single-title houses. Table 4.1 summarizes the comparison between NATSOPA and other major print chapels. The table also illustrates incidentally the extreme sensitivity of industrial relations in the machine room: nearly all machine chapels in multi- or dual-title houses had officials spending nearly all their time on chapel business, although the average size of NGA machine managers' chapels was only 46 men.

Fleet Street chapels, especially machine chapels, were extremely powerful, both within the house, and within the union, partly because of their bargaining role at house level, and partly because of their size. However, the chapel did not play the central role in NATSOPA organization or NATSOPA spirit that it played in the NGA. This was forcefully expressed in the Model Chapel Rules endorsed by the Governing Council (in 1940):

As Chapels owe their existence to the fact that they are created under the rules of the Society, and all members of the Chapel must be members of the society, no Chapel can be affiliated to, associated with, or subscribe to any movement of any kind that is not recognized by the Society (§ 12)

In no circumstances can Chapel Rules over-ride or take precedence over the Society's Rules (§ 17).[8]

All chapel rules were subject to the approval of the Branch Committee, and no rules could be approved which were inconsistent with Model Rules laid down.[9] The FOC was not accorded the central role in local affairs he was accorded in the NGA: for example, there was no provision that he should

Table 4.1

Distribution of chapel facilities in Fleet Street.

Union/chapel	Number of chapels in sample (a)	Number of chapels with at least one official spending nearly all time on chapel business (b)	Number of chapels + office facilities (c)	Average number of employees per chapel (d)
Dual- (multi-) title houses				
NATSOPA Clerical	8	7	8	480
NATSOPA Machine	17	16	15	303
NATSOPA RIRMA	55	8	19	43
NGA Imperial Composing	14	8	12	154
NGA Machine Managers	10	7	9	46
SOGAT Publishing	21	15	14	239
NUJ	15	—	4	156
Single-title houses				
NATSOPA Clerical	4	1	1	114
NATSOPA Machine	6	3	3	57
NATSOPA RIRMA	18	—	7	14
NGA Imperial Composing	5	1	3	83
NGA Machine Managers	5	1	1	13
SOGAT Publishing	8	1	4	42
NUJ	5	—	—	89

Source: ACAS, Industrial Relations in the National Newspaper Industry, pp. 274-5.

be present at all discussions between NATSOPA members and management. The FOC was to be present at all chapel meetings, and to be consulted on all matters in dispute; but he was to communicate all matters to the branch secretary within seven days of the chapel meeting. Accidents were to be reported to the branch secretary by the FOC within twenty-four hours: failure to do so was punishable by the Branch Committee. Failure to obey the chapel rules was dealt with under the authority of the branch, not of the chapel: 'Members of the Chapel refusing to obey the approved Chapel Rules shall be reported to the Branch Committee, who in their discretion may impose a fine not exceeding the sum of £10, expel, or otherwise deal with such members.'[10] Similar provision obtained for failure to attend chapel meetings. In short, the chapel was more the work-place arm of the branch, and the FOC a link between higher union bodies and the work-place, than in the NGA.

The relationship between the chapel and the branch was more two-sided in NATSOPA than in the NGA. Chapel autonomy was central to the historical development and ethos of the NGA: chapels had preceded national organization by centuries, and the union's constitution formally recognized the central place of the chapel. NATSOPA's structure represented a very different historical development, from the centre outwards, a very different strategy, open rather than closed, and a very different ethos. However, NATSOPA Fleet Street chapels were heavily influenced by the organization and practices of other Fleet Street chapels, where their labour organization and bargaining power permitted them to be so, notably in the machine room. The central role of machine assistants, especially brake hands, in the production process, and the effective control of the supply of labour by the calls office administered by the London Machine Branch, permitted Fleet Street NATSOPA machine chapels to assert their independence both against management and against the national union leadership. There was thus a contrast between the formal position of NATSOPA chapels and the substantive position, especially for Fleet Street machine chapels. The industrial stability and the political sensitivity which would have permitted this position to be stablized were notably absent, maintaining a central organizational weakness within the union.

The branch was more important in NATSOPA than in the NGA. As in other unions, all members of the union belonged to a branch, branches consisting of 'any number of members considered by the E. C. [Executive Council] sufficient to form a Branch, resident or working in one town or area.'[11] Since the size of branches varied widely, an average figure for branch size would be misleading, even if it were available: by far the largest branches were in London and Manchester.[12] The London membership was divided into three branches: Machine branch; Revisers, Ink and Roller Makers and Auxiliaries (RIRMA); Clerical, Administrative, and Executive Personnel, the latter being the largest.

Table 4.2

Membership of London branches of NATSOPA

	1966	1970	1974	1975
London Machine	9184	8598	8373	8161
London RIRMA	N/A	6997	7034	6678
London Clerical	N/A	N/A	11133	10450

Source: Adapted from ACAS, Industrial Relations in the National Newspaper Industry, p. 284.

Branch administration was in the hands of a Branch Committee, assisted by a branch secretary who might or might not be full-time. Chapels elected delegates to branch meetings on the basis of 1 delegate for every 5 members. The branch, at its meeting, elected its chairman, committee men, secretary, and, when required, scrutineers, except in towns where District Offices were located (including Manchester), in which case the secretary was appointed by the Executive: the size of the committee, and the scale of allowances for attendance, was decided from time to time by the Executive.[13] Ballots of the whole membership for the election of branch officials were held only by the specific direction of the Executive, except in London, where committeemen were elected biennially by ballot vote of the branch membership.

In London, branch officers were assisted by a substantial administrative staff (twenty-nine), required to deal with the operation of the 'call' system; there were few auxiliary administrative staff outside London. In view of their importance, the secretaries of the three London branches were elected on the same basis as the general secretary, namely triennially by secret ballot. Symbolically, ballot papers for union elections were distributed to the branch secretary; it was the responsibility of the individual member (or his FOC acting on his behalf) to claim the ballot paper, and the responsibility of the branch secretary to return unissued ballot papers to the official responsible for scrutinizing ballot papers.[14]

Although branches, especially the London Machine Branch, were more important in NATSOPA than in the NGA, branches were subject to strict Executive regulation. Hence, branches could be formed and dissolved by the Executive; the Executive could direct any district or branch to hold a ballot, either for the election of officials or for the approval of policies. Although the branch could adopt schemes for supplementary contributions and benefits, following branch ballots, subject to the approval of the Executive, Executive oversight of branch funds was exceptionally strict:

The Branch and district bank balances to be kept in hand by any Branch or district offices shall not exceed such sum as the E.C. shall determine. The Bankers have standing instructions to transfer to the General Fund any surplus over the amount prescribed by the E.C. standing to the credit of Branch or district accounts on the last Saturday of each month.[15]

Similarly, the Executive's bankers were to transfer money from the General Fund to branch or district funds when the level of the latter fell below the Executive's figure. This strict central control of branch finances gave added force to the criticisms of the mishandling of the union's finances, discussed below, pp. 129–30. Under rule, the Executive was thus able to exercise full control over branch activities; the extent to which it would wish to do so, of course, depended upon the issues and the branches involved — the Executive would naturally hesitate before using the full authority provided by rule over the London machine branch.

Outside London, NATSOPA's district and regional organization was slender. There were no district or regional committees. Instead, district meetings of branch delegates were called biennially, the reports of the conferences being published and resolutions being forwarded 'for the attention of the Executive Council'.[16] In London, the three branches elected a London Branches Central Committee, consisting of eleven members — five from the machine branch, three from RIRMA, and three from clerical; the chairman and secretary were the chairman and secretary of the London Machine Branch. Elsewhere, the districts were merely groupings of branches devised for administrative convenience and, more importantly, for electoral purposes. Within each district, a district secretary, appointed by the Executive, was responsible for the 'supervision' of branches, providing advice and direction: the district secretary was thus the Executive's local agent, responsible to the general secretary (rather than to the branches within the district or to the district membership by ballot).[17]

The government of NATSOPA centred upon the Executive, which, subject to the Governing Council, 'shall administer all the affairs and business of the Society'; since the Governing Council only met biennially, and the Executive was in any case only obliged to 'have due regard to any directions given to it by the G.C.', the Executive was not subject to close control.[18] It controlled the work of the general secretary and the national assistant secretaries, although of course they were elected by the whole membership, and appointed all district officials. It had authority 'to construe the rules and to determine on all matters wherein the rules are silent', its decision remaining binding until explicitly reversed by the Governing Council or ballot of the membership. Even if the Executive's interpretation were to be reversed, acts done under it were to remain valid. The Executive had authority to fine members up to £20, or 'to expel in its absolute discretion any member who, in its opinion, is acting contrary to rules or in a manner detrimental to the Society's welfare'; it also had the authority to relieve any full-time paid official of his duties (on payment of four weeks' salary), and to remove or suspend from office any office holder, including an elected member of the Executive, for acting 'in a manner contrary to the interests and welfare of the Society', subject to appeal to the Governing Council. Indeed, the only officials who could not be suspended by a majority of the Executive were elected members of the Governing Council.

The Executive Council consisted of 20 members, elected for two years, but eligible for re-election: candidature was restricted to lay members. The 20 seats were distributed: 4 London Machine Branch; 2 London RIRMA (R&GA section); 1 Ink and Roller Division; 2 Manchester branch; 4 General Clerical, Administrative and Executive Personnel membership; 2 South Eastern District; 1 North Western, excluding Manchester; 1 Sign, Display and Trades Section (subsequently merged with the RIRMA branch); 1 from each remaining district, including Scotland. The general secretary attended meetings of the Executive, but had no vote: he was also responsible for preparing the Executive agenda. The quorum of members was seven, but the London members of the council were empowered to act as an Emergency Committee of the Council, either 'as necessity arises' or 'when called by the general secretary'.[19] The Executive was thus a relatively small body, mainly oriented towards London. It was also oriented towards the machine-room membership, especially among the representatives drawn from NPA houses. There was notably limited representation of TAE&A members (of whom there were 2,390 by the end of May 1978), leading the News Group TAE&A chapel to protest at their exclusion from the Executive early in 1977: the position was remedied by the 1978 Governing Council, which agreed to the allocation of an Executive Council seat to the TAE&A Section.[20] The same Governing Council also agreed to increase the representation of clerical workers, although the general secretary successfully asked for time to consider the 'mechanics' involved, since some sections of the Association were possibly over-represented.[21] As a lay body, with considerable authority, the Executive Council was in a position to act independently of full-time Head Office officials, and formally subject to membership control through frequent re-election. Historically, they have been subject to influence by the full-time officers, notably a

succession of important and long-lived general secretaries —
there have only been four general secretaries since 1909,
of whom one held office for only three years, and one
assumed office in 1975 — and re-election is frequent.

The Executive Council was subject to the Governing
Council: 'the Governing Council shall have supreme control
and management of all the affairs and officers of the
Society, and its decisions shall be final and binding upon all
members.'[22] The Governing Council had authority to 'give
any directions to the E.C. it considers necessary for the
management of the affairs and officers of the Society.'
Members were elected by districts, on the basis of 1 member
for each 500 members, with a minimum of 2 delegates per
district, giving a Council of approximately 100 members:
35 elected delegates constituted a quorum. The Council
met biennially, but the Executive could call a special meeting
if it considered circumstances warranted, or the Governing
Council could itself decide to call a special meeting, as it did
in 1978 to consider a special report upon the union's finances
(see below, p. 129). No member of the Executive Council
could be an elected delegate to the Governing Council,
although the president of the union presided over the meetings
of Council. In 1978 members of the Executive Council and
district and branch secretaries for the first time spoke on
policy issues at the Governing Council. If a member of the
Governing Council proved unable to attend a meeting, his
place was filled by the co-optation of the next eligible candidate from the district affected, or a ballot was held where no
eligible candidate was available; there was no provision for
Executive initiative. The Governing Council elected an
Appeals Committee of members to decide upon appeals
against decisions of the Executive, where Rule allowed
appeals; the Committee was to meet at least annually, and
otherwise at the initiative of the Executive. The union's
constitution attempted to maintain a separation of powers,
severely limiting the role of Executive members on the
Governing Council. There was no guaranteed representation
on the Governing Council, in contrast to the Executive; as
the RIRMA and, especially, the clerical branches increased in
size, their representation on the Governing Council increased,

and the influence of the machine branches waned. There was thus the potential for misalignment between an Executive disproportionately influenced by the London branches (especially by the machine branch) and the Governing Council.

Although the Governing Council possessed 'supreme control' of the union's affairs under rule, its ability to exercise this control was limited, owing to its infrequent meetings. Moreover, the meetings of the Governing Council were largely taken up by discussion of the Executive's report, delegates raising questions on the report, and members of the Executive or full-time officers replying, as the report was taken, paragraph by paragraph. The Governing Council was not a rubber-stamp, as is indicated by the Executive's failure in 1978 to prevent the appointment of special auditors to investigate the Association's accounts and to report back to a special meeting of the Governing Council; but it could not exericise direct control over union policy, especially during periods of rapid change in the industry.[23] The major responsibility for the development of union policy towards other unions and towards new technology, as well as in routine collective bargaining, therefore lay with the Executive, and especially the full-time officers at the Head Office in Borough Road, South London. Where consultation with the membership was required rapidly over important issues of principle the Executive organized a ballot of membership, as it was permitted to do by Rule, rather than calling a special meeting of the Governing Council, as over union policy towards the continuation of pay policy in August 1977; the ballot endorsed the Executive's policy of refusing to support the continuation of the Social Contract, ending the policy of support for the Social Contract endorsed at the 1976 Governing Council.[24]

Under rule, the general secretary 'shall be responsible for the carrying on of the business and work of the Society, and control the staff at the Head Office.'[25] He was required to attend all meetings of the Governing Council and the Executive Council, and could attend any Branch Committee meetings he wished, with the right to speak but not to vote (a significant right during the union's troubled history in

Fleet Street in 1977-9). At Governing Council he normally moved a resolution introducing the discussion of the Executive's report and could take part in discussions as spokesman for the Executive, although he could not vote. He acted as the main route of access to the Executive Council, since all correspondence was conducted by the general secretary on behalf of the union; draft replies to correspondence were normally prepared at Head Office, subject of course to approval by the Executive; and the Executive deferred to Head Office judgement on exceptional as well as routine matters. Hence the union's policy during the NUJ closed-shop dispute at Darlington in 1977, which resulted in a strike by NATSOPA members for twelve weeks, was largely left to the general secretary: similarly, the general secretary was directly responsible for initial discussions with other unions over possible mergers, reporting back to the Executive as appropriate.[26] However, the position of the general secretary was not inviolable. He could be removed from office by resolution of the Executive 'if he be, in the opinion of the E.C., incompetent, and remove him from his office and expel him from the Society if he be, in the opinion of the E.C., a financial defaulter in regard to the moneys or securities of the Society, or guilty of wilful neglect of duty, or any act knowingly committed against the interests of the Society.'[27] In view of the circumstances in which Edwin Smith 'retired' in 1909, with the Society's accounts in confusion, and the criticisms made of Briginshaw's conduct of the union's finances in the 1970s, culminating in the issuing of writs in 1979, the clause on financial irregularities was not totally irrelevant.[28] Equally relevant was the provision for triennial election of all full-time officials, including the general secretary. Both George Isaacs and Richard Briginshaw established such dominance in the union that re-election became a formality: there was no opposition to either incumbent on the seventeen occasions in which they stood for re-election between 1918 and 1974.[29] But the re-election of the present general secretary was challenged in 1978.

Two general secretaries have dominated the history of NATSOPA, George Issacs and Richard (now Lord) Briginshaw; Isaacs was general secretary from 1909 until 1948, and

Briginshaw from 1951 to 1975. Both men established very powerful positions in the labour movement, surprisingly so for leaders of a small, not especially wealthy, union. Isaacs was a member of the TUC General Council from 1932 until 1945, a Member of Parliament 1923–4, 1929–31, 1939–59, and Minister of Labour in the 1945 Labour Government; Briginshaw was a member of the General Council from 1965 to 1975, and served on the important Economic and Finance and General Purposes committees. Although possessing more influence in the labour movement than many leaders of unions of a similar size, the present general secretary, Owen O'Brien, has not established the presence, within or outside the union, of his predecessors — and is unlikely ever to do so, not least because he did not achieve office as general secretary until the age of fifty-five. He is not a member of the TUC General Council, nor is he the chairman of the TUC Printing Industries Committee, although Briginshaw had been the chairman of its nearest predecessor, the Printing and Kindred Trades Federation: it is impossible to say whether this contributed to a weakening of O'Brien's position within the union. Like all his predecessors, O'Brien served his union apprenticeship in the London Machine Branch (LMB). He was born in Stepney in 1920, and entered 'the print' in 1934. His first full-time union post was as Assistant Secretary of the LMB, to which he was elected in 1951; in 1952 he was elected secretary of LMB, and by virtue of that office also became secretary of the London Joint Branches. In 1963 he was elected national assistant secretary, on J. T. Allen's retirement, and in 1975 he succeeded Briginshaw as general secretary. His period in office has been marked by bitter conflict within the union, over ideologies, personalities, and policies. O'Brien has been identified as 'right-wing', a staunch supporter of the Labour Party, and in industrial relations of the need to negotiate flexibility with employers: his personal relations with some employers have been more cordial than some NATSOPA members thought appropriate. He has been singled out for criticism by the Socialist Workers' Party, the *Socialist Worker* publishing detailed criticisms of his administration, based upon leaked confidential information, during his campaign for re-election in the spring of 1978.[30] The

intricate ideological and personal rivalries involved are beyond
the scope of this study, although they have contributed
significantly to the confusion of NATSOPA policy in Fleet
Street: tension between the general secretary and R. A.
Brady, FOC at the Thomson's (*Sunday Times*) Night Machine
Chapel, chairman of the LMB, and a machine branch Executive
member has been especially marked. Nevertheless, a brief
account of the major issues involved is necessary, since they
played a major role in internal discussion within the union
from 1977 onwards, severely restricting the time and energy
available for the development of union policy, and weakening
the authority of Head Office.

The general secretary was accused of having been involved
in alleged financial irregularities over the sale of Association
property in Blackfriars Road and Maymott Street, London,
in 1972, the movement of Association funds into Swiss bank
accounts, and the creation and liquidation of private companies financed from Association funds, accusations which
the general secretary appropriately termed 'libellous'.[31]
There is no evidence that the general secretary was associated
with irregular financial practices, and the Governing Council
in June 1978 accepted his account of his own actions.
Nevertheless, there was sufficiently strong feeling within the
union for the 1978 Governing Council to reject the Executive's
Financial Report, to call for a second audit of the union's
accounts by new auditors and to provide for the calling of
a special Governing Council to consider the auditor's report
when available. The new auditor's report revealed details of
financial irregularities and the Association subsequently sued
Lord Briginshaw and others for misappropriation of funds;
at the time of writing the case is still pending.[32] The effect
of the controversy was inevitably to weaken the authority
of the general secretary, as the official responsible for Head
Office administration: notwithstanding his own presumed
probity, many members believed that he had failed to launch
a major investigation on his own or the Executive's initiative,
although the union President denied this.[33] The general
secretary's political weakness was revealed in 1978 when,
contrary to tradition, there was a real contest when O'Brien
stood for re-election: B. A. Fitzpatrick, the left-wing FOC of

the *Sunday Times* Clerical Chapel, obtained 10,133 votes, losing by 7,104 votes after a bitter campaign.[34] There was a further electoral challenge to the general secretary when his brother, a national assistant secretary, stood for re-election in September 1978: E. O'Brien was successful on the first ballot by 1,123 votes, receiving 10,918 against 5,643 for Fitzpatrick and 4,152 for R. A. Brady.[35]

Since 1975 the affairs of NATSOPA have attracted wide attention, the *Observer*, with some exaggeration, suggesting that 'the activities of Lord Briginshaw and his colleages are likely to become the biggest talking point in the trade union movement for two decades.'[36] (It is hardly accidental that the *Observer* Night Machine Chapel was a vociferous critic of the O'Briens.) The criticism has been largely personal and ideological, although the wide discretion legitimately allowed to Briginshaw under ballot certainly did not facilitate rigorous financial control, and one accountant (not directly employed by the union) has been found guilty of forging a document (with intent to defraud the Inland Revenue) whilst engaged upon NATSOPA affairs.[37] According to the union President, H. T. Ball,

officers have been maliciously attacked, mud has been slung; they have suffered smears on their characters and questions as to their integrity . . . our officers are unable to respond to these faceless attackers who hide behind the skirts of journalistic privilege. . . . A small, but active, minority within our Union . . . seems to disagree with the majority view of how we should operate and because they cannot win by demo-cratic means they resort to underhand tactics . . . Recent articles in the National Press and Periodicals . . . have been a deliberate attempt . . . to force our members' thinking processes along certain lines . . .[38]

Discussions at the 1978 Governing Council were coloured by attitudes towards the general secretary's handling of the Association's finances.

My impression of this year's Governing Council was one of dismay and disgust for the way the General Secretary was treated by the people who had only one aim and that was the downfall of Owen O'Brien. (London RIRMA delegate)

In the past I have admired London Machine delegates for their ability to express themselves in a constructive manner; but, regrettably, all I could admire this time was their courage — their courage to take on the

President and the platform. This militancy created an atmosphere of them and us — them being the London Machine delegates and us being the other delegates. (Northern District delegate)[39]

Although much of the bitterness in the conflicts had ideological and personal roots, and the issues involved were transitory, they paralleled conflicts on union structure and expressed themselves in structural terms. At a structural level, the issues involved were those of branch autonomy, especially the autonomy of the London branches, and to a lesser degree chapel autonomy. Hence the London Machine Branch resolved that, whilst it supported the principle of amalgamation with SOGAT, amalgamation should involve the maintenance of existing branches ('no branch may be merged with another, or broken up, without a ballot vote of that branch'), and branches in the new union should have as much autonomy as branches in SOGAT: the LMB had in view the independence of the London Central Branch of SOGAT.[40] Hence also the insistence of NATSOPA members at a mass meeting at Times Newspapers in November 1978 that 'no Agreements to be negotiated without the participation of all individual Chapel officials and the agreement by those Chapels, which must be kept in existence.'[41] Feelings against reorganization from above were especially strong at The Times since the chapel structure was reorganized in 1978, with the formation of Thomson's Day Chapel, despite the opposition of the Thomson's Night Machine Chapel, from whom the new chapel was formed. As shown above, the Executive Council was responsible for organization, and for ensuring that agreements negotiated were consistent with union policy: normally, the Executive concurred with branch decisions, sometimes even without the full details of the agreement being tabled. However, the Executive did not always concur: for example, when the London Machine Branch Committee rejected an agreement negotiated by the *Sunday People* Machine Chapel, since it involved reduced staffing, the Executive upheld the chapel's appeal against the decision.[42] The most important, and complex controversy over the respective roles of the Executive, branch, and chapel arose during the disputes at Times Newspapers in 1977–9, and is discussed below, pp. 142–53.

NATSOPA was established in September 1889, as the Printers' Labourers' Union. Its core group has always consisted of machine-room assistants, especially in the newspaper industry, although the expansion of recruitment amongst clerical, technical, and executive staff, is gradually reducing the numerical importance of machine branches within the union. The closure, or movement outside London, of large general printers, and the increasing importance of small and medium-sized printers, with versatile machinery and small staffs, is further reducing the importance of machine assistants to the union. Although the union possesses the same chapel structure and nomenclature as the NGA, the chapel is not the focus of traditional loyalties: the branch, Executive Committee, and Head Office play a more prominent role in both the constitution and the politics of the society. Hence the branch is responsible for many aspects of chapel discipline, whilst the Executive has the ultimate responsibility for construing the Society's rules, or, where the rules are silent, making a ruling, subject to the biennial Governing Council. In practice, the Executive Committee allows considerable discretion to the general secretary, and where it exercises its authority pays considerable attention to the views of the general secretary. In London, the importance of the branch for the individual member's working life is reinforced by branch office administration of the casual system; casuals are members of the branch, but not of the chapel. The relative importance of the branch is reinforced by the high level of turnover amongst clerical workers in the industry, many of whom do not remain employed in any one house sufficiently long to develop group loyalty. For members of the TAE&A section there is the further pull away from chapel solidarity exercised by loyalty to management, and individual career ambition: although union membership and the acceptance of constitutional trade-union practices may be consistent with managerial and supervisory positions, the intense solidarity of traditional print chapels is not.

The structure of NATSOPA is thus formally, and to some extent in practice, highly centralized. However, the centralization is incomplete. The central core of the union has traditionally been the London Machine Branch, whose 8,000

members employed mainly in the high-paying national newspaper industry have traditionally supplied the top national
leadership of the union, but who have retained considerable
independence, including significant financial resources. This
position within the union is being undermined as the branch
declines in membership and the clerical membership expands.
1977 saw the election of the first president of the Union
drawn from outside the London Machine Branch, when Bert
Ball (FOC *Mirror* RIRMA) defeated R. A. Brady (London
Machine) by 5,587 votes to 4,987, the selection of the first
RIRMA trustee, and the election of the first RIRMA national
assistant secretary.[43] In the ballot for national assistant
secretary there was no candidate from the London Machine
Branch on the second ballot, although all previous national
assistant secretaries had been from the LMB; the LMB vote
was split on the first ballot, and the run-off was between
the successful RIRMA candidate, J. A. Moakes, and the
secretary of the Manchester branch. The tension between the
LMB and the Executive was increased by ideological and
personal differences, but not caused solely by them: the
tension arose from the diminishing importance of a formerly
dominant group. With the growing importance of RIRMA
and clerical branch members on the Governing Council and
the Executive, the insistence upon branch autonomy by the
LMB is likely to increase. Since members of the branch play
a crucial role in the production of national newspapers this
tension is likely to have a continuing effect upon the implementation of technical change in Fleet Street, as experience
at TNL between 1977 and 1979 confirmed.

ii

Of the general secretaries who signed *Programme for Action*,
Owen O'Brien made the most conspicous efforts to persuade
his members to support it. He spoke on its behalf at mass
meetings of the members involved in both London and Manchester; he regarded the London meeting as 'negative', failing
to consider the proposals on their merits, whilst the Manchester
meeting was more constructive. *Programme for Action* must
'not be sloganized out of existence'; it did not undermine

traditional trade-union rights.[44] The Executive also endorsed the proposals, after extensive discussion: 'The Executive Committee being cognizant of the general difficulties in the industry, recommend the adoption of the proposals contained in the documentation.'[45] Despite the general secretary's campaign and the Executive's decision, the NATSOPA members involved rejected the programme narrowly by 4,598 votes to 4,296, the majority against in London outweighing the majority in favour in Manchester. The general secretary regarded the result as unsatisfactory, but of course accepted it. Since technological change would continue, and the union could not act as 'King Canutes', it would be necessary to negotiate changes on a 'house by house' basis.[46] As for the Joint Standing Committee itself, the Executive in April decided to continue to support it as an arena for discussing training and as a channel for the prospective funds from the European Social Fund.[47]

This brief account of the progress of *Programme for Action* within NATSOPA touches upon all the elements in the union's approach to technological change: the general secretary's commitment; the Executive Committee's more hesitant support; the hostility of the active London membership and the acceptance by the Manchester membership; the resultant almost even division of opinion amongst the newspaper membership; and the eventual adoption of a 'house by house' approach to new technology.

The general secretary believed that newspapers were under increasing threat from television and radio, both as sources of news and as advertising media. These threats were undesirable both because of the political importance of the press to effective democracy, and the economic livelihood of union members. Implementation of new technology was the only means of ensuring the long-term viability of the industry and thus the economic position of NATSOPA members: refusal to accept new technology could lead to a repetition of American experience, where complete opposition led to the growth of non-unionized shops. New technology would involve the loss of jobs: 'there is no doubt that the labour force would be reduced.' But 'our agreement with the publishers [on the JSC] is that there will be no compulsory redundancy brought about by new technology', and 'adequate compensation for voluntary redundancy would be negotiated.'[48] The introduction of new technology would also provide an opportunity to solve two major problems facing the union: the casual-labour system; and the barrier against the promotion of machine assistants to machine managers in Fleet Street houses (except the *News of the World*). O'Brien had a long-standing ambition to 'decasualize' casual casual members, by the introduction of a scheme modelled on the Dock Labour Schemes, whereby registered workers would receive a guaranteed minimum fall-back wage. He believed that such a scheme would be easier to establish for newspapers than for the docks, because of the smaller numbers involved (although the discussions on the JSC showed the difficulty in agreeing on such a scheme in principle, in addition to the financial difficulties).[49] The introduction of new technology and the flexibility in the use of labour it involved opened up promotion possibilities previously closed to NATSOPA members: 'members of this Society with the skills and aptitude to operate the new processes should be given opportunities to do so. We believe that the old guild concept of production in the industry should now be filed away in the archives of history.'[50] In short, '[new technology] cannot be sloganised away, and we intend to grasp and control it primarily in the interests of the members we serve . . . This means more than marching the troops up the hill and down again.'[51] For these reasons O'Brien believed that NATSOPA should be in the vanguard of supporters of technological change.

The general secretary's conception of a technologically advanced industry, with the career open to the talents, was not simply a campaign product. He was especially active in encouraging training for new technology, both within NATSOPA, and in the industry generally. He was a strong supporter of NATSOPA courses on new technology, which were put on at the union's holiday home and conference centre at Rottingdean, the London College of Printing, and elsewhere; speakers included members of other unions, notably the NGA, journalists interested in new technology, such as Rex Winsbury, and management representatives (including the joint general manager of the FT, Justin Dukes), as well as NATSOPA officials.[52] He was the only union general secretary to take a serious interest in the work of the Printing and Publishing Industry Training Board (PPITB), serving as chairman from 1977 until the present. He was also a member of the court of Cranfield Institute of Technology, a non-UGC management education centre whose director, Philip Sadler, had worked in printing, and published one of the few books on the organization of the industry.[53] He was willing to give a public blessing to technological innovations which he supported, such as the introduction of a di-litho press at Sefton Newspapers, Southport, or, more controversially, the FT's introduction of facsimile transmission to Frankfurt in 1979: after visiting the Frankfurt operation he commented that the system appeared to be working 'effectively and without trauma'.[54]

The general secretary's views were echoed by other members of Head Office staff, notably the national assistant secretaries E. O'Brien, Owen's brother, and, until his retirement through illness in July 1977, A. Davis. As the national officer directly responsible for the Technical, Administrative, Executive, and Advertising Section, the product of internal reorganization in 1977, E. O'Brien was naturally sensitive to the opinions of that group, whose members were likely to gain as a result of technological change. A. Davis was the chairman of the Society's Working Party on New Technology 1975–7. The Society's Executive generally agreed with the Head Office view. Hence *Programme for Action* was accepted. The FT's development plan was accepted: 'this Union, at Executive level, has no reservation in principle in cooperating with *The Financial Times* for bringing in new technology.'[55] Similarly, the Executive Council in January 1978 endorsed the agreement of the MGN Combined Reading and Composing Room Chapels (part of the RIRMA branch) to begin training for photocomposition at the *Reveille*, months before the NGA reached agreement at MGN.[56] During the Times dispute the Executive Council was willing to accept the 'Booth' formula of 8 March, involving the acceptance of new technology in principle, subject to the maintenance of the principle of voluntary redundancy, the union agreed to 'the application of new technology in accordance with a timetable to be agreed and with arrangements for future joint reviews', and to 'a timetable for implementation of staffing levels agreed [to be] negotiated during the period between the signing of this agreement and resumption of publication.'[57] In the provincial press, the Executive's policy was to endorse new technology agreements negotiated by chapels, even where the loss of jobs was involved, on a local basis.

However, the Executive Council was less committed to new technology than the general secretary, inevitably in view of its heterogeneous composition. The Executive contained at least two long-standing critics of the O'Briens, including Brady from the London Machine Branch and Fitzpatrick from the Clerical, Advertising and Executive Branch. The controversy over the union's finances, and even more the events at The Times, weakened the influence of the O'Briens, with the evident failure of their cautious approach to events at The Times and the prominent successful roles played by O'Brien's critics Brady and Fitzpatrick during the dispute. Hence the resolution submitted by the Executive on the Society's behalf to the 1979 TUC emphasized strongly the need for joint control of new technology and the distribution of the rewards to the workers through reduced hours, increased holidays, and other benefits: '[the TUC] views with grave concern the attempts ... to introduce New Technology by management dictate . . . New Technology [is] to be introduced only where joint agreement exists between Unions and Employers and under democratic supervision at plant and industry levels.' The resolution was merged into a composite resolution on new technology, linked to the TUC report *Employment and Technology*, and accepted.[58] Although never Luddite, since it continued to endorse agreements on new technology, the Executive was less well disposed towards new technology at the end of 1979 than it had been four years earlier: worried by their role in the *Times* dispute, the August 1979 meeting of the Executive established a special subcommittee to investigate the work of the TAE&E section at TNL, and instructed the chapel not to carry out work which belonged to other branches.[59]

It is impossible to gauge NATSOPA rank-and-file members' attitudes towards new technology or the trend in those attitudes: there was no concerted campaign on the issues, and no survey evidence is available on membership opinion. As mentioned above, the membership rejected *Programme for Action,* although by a much narrower margin than in the NGA: but whether this represented opposition to new technology in general, or simply to the specific package represented by *Programme for Action*, it is impossible to say. That the membership was willing to endorse some of the manpower consequences of new technology was shown by their support, by the large majority of 10,609 votes to 2,822, for a new rule on Industry Severance Grants. Workers accepting voluntary redundancy or early retirement were to obtain their branch's written permission; if permission was granted they were to give a written undertaking to leave the industry or face expulsion from the union.[60] Workers who accept voluntary redundancy 'should no longer be a liability to the industry, the union, and in particular to [their] fellow workers.'[61] The rule was not a dead letter, since the union expelled four members of the *Mirror* Day Staff Chapel for refusing to give the undertaking required, and resisted their appeal through to the TUC's Independent Review Committee (which decided that it had no jurisdiction).[62] More significantly, throughout the period chapels adopted a pragmatic approach to new technology. Agreements on new technology were especially frequent in the clerical area. However, although agreements continued to be made throughout the period, the difficulties involved appeared to increase in 1978 and 1979. As indicated earlier, the policy of the London Machine Branch Committee in 1979 was to refuse to approve agreements which involved reduced staffing. Complete pragmatism is impossible: by 1979 the pragmatism was being applied more selectively.

The tone of discussion at union conferences, and in the correspondence columns of the union journal, also grew more hostile towards new technology. The conclusions reported following technology appreciation conferences in 1979 were less positive than those reported three years earlier. As one writer summarized the experience of a weekend seminar on new technology, organized by CA&EP chapels in

1979: 'the basic feeling was that we should not negotiate our technology agreements on the basis of more money for a smaller number of staff, but should negotiate on the basis of no job loss, along with better social conditions, such as hours, holidays, etc., and with in-depth training.' The secretary of the London CA&EP branch summarized the position succinctly: 'the basis of any agreement must be the *status quo*'.[63] Although members' letters in the union journal may reflect editorial selectivity as much as membership opinion, increased disquiet about new technology was evident in the journal correspondence columns in 1979 (and changes in editorial practice are themselves likely to be a response to perceived changes in members' opinions). The issues of March and April 1979 contained a number of letters from London clerical members expressing diquiet with trends in union policy, including policy on new technology. According to one member, NATSOPA should oppose reduction in manning through natural wastage because it reduced employment opportunities for school-leavers, increased the workload for those remaining, and limited career expectations by disrupting internal transfers (management only permitting transfers if the job vacated was lost).[64] According to another, VDUs should be permitted in newspaper offices only on condition that no jobs were lost, that the working week was shortened and regular overtime ended, with compensation for earnings forgone.[65] The following month a London clerical member of the Governing Council wrote expressing his opposition to new technology on the grounds that it increased unemployment and increased employers' profits. Equal division of the direct savings made on wage costs was inadequate because it under-stated the advantages to employers of reduced labour; the indirect costs of employing labour were often larger than the direct costs, and ought to be taken into account in calculating savings.[66] Although the opposition to new technology was most vociferous in London, there was also some disquiet among provincial members: growing concentration of ownership and the development of VDUs made it possible for production facilities for weekly newspapers to be concentrated, with consequential loss of jobs especially among composing and machine room members.[67]

Rank-and-file members of NATSOPA were not entrenched opponents of new technology: there was no general fear that the economic value of their skills and experience would be undermined, nor that there would be a catastrophic loss of jobs. Nor was there opposition to the possible 'de-skilling' of work (although there was some concen about the effect of word processors upon clerical work). However, there was sufficient concern over the employment consequences of technological change to reduce the appeal of the general secretary's enthusiasm. This made it possible for groups opposed to the general secretary on other grounds to obtain additional support, especially where official policy appeared to fail.

New technology did not threaten the existence of NATSOPA, as it appeared to threaten the NGA. However, although technological change itself might be an opportunity as much as a threat, it was recognized that Fleet Street managements would use the occasion provided by the installation of major new equipment to make substantial savings in labour costs, even in areas unaffected by new technology; indeed, given the traditional Fleet Street practice of seeking compensating payments when the existing differentials are upset by management buying agreement on new technology from groups directly affected, managements would be guilty of incompentence if they failed to do so. Substantial reductions in NATSOPA manning levels were wanted at both the Financial Times and The Times, although the new technology primarily involved NGA members. The complex interaction between new technology, management attempts to reduce production costs, and NATSOPA's intricate internal political systems, was especially evident at TNL, where NATSOPA members were centrally involved in events surrounding the suspension of the newspaper in 1978. The overall story of technological change at TNL is discussed below, chapter 7; in this chapter the concern is with TNL only in so far as it sheds light on NATSOPA and its approach to new technology.

Although highly visible, the national newspaper industry is comparatively small and geographically concentrated: the union members actively involved in union affairs outside the chapel are relatively small in number and are well known to each other. Personal relations are thus perhaps more important than in larger industries or organizations, in which personal differences can be minimized by career mobility. In print-union politics this is impossible; the numbers involved are small and job mobility is very limited: personal relationships are therefore disproportionately important, and personal rivalries particularly intense. In NATSOPA, this was reinforced by O'Brien's identification with the right wing of the Labour Party, and his hostility towards Trotskyite infiltration of the party. The union was thus a prominent target for left-wing activists; in view of the high level of demand for clerical workers in London, and the high turnover in the NATSOPA clerical section, it was also a relatively easy union to join, unlike the NGA. One element in NATSOPA's reactions to events at The Times was long-standing personal rivalry between the O'Briens and R. A. Brady, the FOC of Thomson's (*Sunday Times*) Night Machine Chapel. Brady had succeeded Owen O'Brien as secretary of the London Machine Branch in 1964, defeating E. O'Brien on a second ballot. He resigned from office in 1968, and in the ensuing election B. Rudd defeated E. O'Brien. However, following his successful election, Rudd indicated that he would be unable to assume office because of domestic circumstances, and the Executive Council thereupon declared E. O'Brien as branch secretary. Following his resignation, Brady was a frequent candidate for national union office, usually in opposition to candidates associated with the O'Briens.[68] In 1977, for example, he stood for election as president, coming second to H. T. Ball (4,987 votes against 5,587); in 1977 he attempted to stand for election as a national assistant secretary, but was disqualified because his seconder was three weeks in arrears in paying his dues; in 1978 he stood against E. O'Brien for national assistant secretary, coming third, behind O'Brien and B. A. Fitzpatrick.[69] As a member of the Executive Council he was frequently involved in arguments over the leakage of confidential documents to anti-O'Brien groups, and over the importance of collective responsibility. A second active FOC at TNL was also a prominent critic of the O'Briens, B. A.

Fitzpatrick, although he did not always agree with R. A. Brady: both men stood against Ball for president in 1977 and against E. O'Brien for election as national assistant secretary in 1978.[70] It was thus likely, on ideological and personal grounds, that any dispute at New Printing House Square would involve tension between NATSOPA Head Office and the FOCs mainly involved.

The first important dipute at TNL in the period involving NATSOPA occurred in March 1977. Although the dispute did not involve new technology, it was important for its effect upon relations between NATSOPA Head Office and the union's membership at TNL: the 1977 dispute was not forgotten when the larger 1978-9 dispute began. The roots of the 1977 dispute lay in unresolved problems stemming from *The Times*'s move to New Printing House Square in 1974: the division of responsibilities and the relative payments between NATSOPA members employed on *The Times* and the other Thomson publications had never been satisfactorily resolved. According to management, the dispute arose over a claim by Thomson's NATSOPA Machine Chapel for £1·50 per night for cleaning duties; according to the chapel it arose because management had failed to ensure the presses were cleaned adequately.[71] Management refused payment, basing its refusal partly on the grounds that the payment would have been contrary to pay policy, which NATSOPA had accepted. The dispute began with the loss of copies on 24 February, but worsened on 2 March when management threatened that workers refusing to work normally would be treated as having terminated their engagements; the grievance should be taken through the proper grievance procedure. The undertakings were not given and the paper was suspended on Friday 4 March. Following discussions between management and national and branch officers over the weekend of 5-6 March, a formula was agreed: cleaning duties were to be removed from the night staff and more men were to be recruited to the day staff to perform the increased work; the night staff would be responsible solely for production and for normal 'wipe-up'; a separate Day Staff Chapel would eventually be formed.[72] The agreement was rejected by chapel members on 6 March.

The following day the Executive Council ordered the men to return to work. The members still refused to return, and the chapel FOC, deputy FOC, and committee were called before the Executive on the Tuesday. The Executive expelled four of the members involved, the fifth giving the assurances requested by the Executive Council. When The Times members still refused to return to work on the basis of the formula negotiated, the Executive sent telegrams of expulsion to the 120 members, and began to discuss the possibility of supplying alternative labour. However, following intervention by the TUC, the men agreed to return to work on 10 March and to put the grievance into procedure; NATSOPA withdrew its expulsions.

Although the dispute began as a dispute with management over cleaning duties, it developed into a challenge to the NATSOPA Executive's authority. Owen O'Brien was quoted as saying, 'We will have a confrontation with people who intend, if they get their way, to undermine the authority of this union. We will meet that challenge to the union and its executive.'[73] The *FT*, with some exaggeration, described the Times management as 'almost spectators as Mr. O'Brien struggled to control his rebellious members.'[74] The Executive was supported by the London Machine Branch, a mass meeting of Fleet Street FOCs and MOCs, and provincial branches. The Executive thus successfully mobilized support for its strong stand against disobedience to its authority. Although the members involved were reinstated, seven chapel officials involved were charged with disregarding legitimate union authority under Rule 20 § 1 (a): 'any member shall cease to belong to the Society . . . (a) if he has not obeyed any order (by these rules authorized to be given) of the G.C., E.C., or B.C.'[75] The Executive banned the seven involved from holding union office and fined them £25 each. The Executive's decision was upheld by the Governing Council's Appeal Committee in November, but the fine was reduced to £5 each.[76] The Executive also pressed ahead with the proposed chapel reorganization, despite strong and continuing opposition from the Thomson's Night Machine Chapel: the Executive even voted to suspend the rule whereby proposals for chapel reorganization were required to lie on the table for three months. Despite this constitutional irregularity, the Appeal Committee rejected the Thomson's Night Machine Chapel appeal against the Executive. (As permitted by rule, the chapel asked the Executive for re-imbursement of expenses incurred in conducting the appeal, but the request was refused, on the grounds that proper dockets were not produced).[77] A further consequence of the March dispute was the temporary resignation of the Secretary of the London Machine Branch, John Mitchell. Despite a procedural wrangle over the propriety of taking the motion, a Delegate Meeting of the LMB passed a motion criticizing the committee: the critical motion was supported by a member of the LMB Committee, despite collective responsi-bility. Thereupon Mitchell and Brady (as chairman of the LMB Committee) both resigned. Brady quickly withdrew his resignation, denying that his action in resigning had been due to the critical resolution, but not providing any alterna-tive explanation; Mitchell pressed ahead with his resignation, but subsequently withdrew it when supporters of the critical motion made it publicly clear that they had been criticizing the national Executive Council, not the London Machine Branch Committee.[78]

The March 1977 machine room cleaning dispute at The Times did not directly involve new technology, although it stemmed directly from reorganization on the move of *The Times* to join the *Sunday Times* in Printing House Square. However, it did indicate the sensitivity of issues of changes in working practices, even where members of the same union branch were involved: all the workers involved were members of the NATSOPA London Machine Branch. The issue involved was that of the association between the organization of work and chapel structure: the changes proposed by the Executive would involve a permanent reduction in the work of the Thomson's Night Machine Chapel: the transfer of cleaning duties to day staff was seen as a preliminary to the creation of a seven-day Thomson's Day Chapel, in place of the then existing five-day Times Day Chapel.[79] The chapel did not favour external involvement, whether by Branch or by Executive. Moreover, industrial relations at the paper were especially sensitive because of what was seen as the

constraining effects of government pay policy and the uncertainties following the rejection of *Programme for Action*.
The political alignments which emerged over the strike
recurred over subsequent issues: the Executive was supported
by the Branch Committee, the branch secretary, and such
provincial branches as publicly expressed an opinion. But
the Branch Committee included members actively opposing
the Executive, and the Branch Delegate Meeting supported the
chapel: although the Branch Delegate Meeting had no constitutional authority, it was an important expression of influential Fleet Street opinion. Amongst Fleet Street chapels, the
IPC (King's Reach) and the MGN Clerical Chapels publicly
supported the Executive; the *Observer* and the *FT* Night
Machine Chapels wrote to the Executive Council supporting
the dissidents.

With the expenditure of considerable energy and political
capital, the Executive succeeded in enforcing its authority
over TNL NATSOPA members, at least to the extent of
obtaining substantial endorsement from the Governing
Council Appeal Committee — not a formality. The chapel
officials involved were excluded from office. But the struggle
weakened further the general secretary's position, already
under stress from continuing criticism of the conduct of the
union's financial affairs. It was against this background that
the Times management in April 1978 threatened NATSOPA,
along with the other print unions, with the suspension of
publication if new agreements covering guaranteed continuity
of production, new disputes procedures, and new technology
were not successfully negotiated within six months.

The story of the implementation of new technology at
Times Newspapers, and of management's attempt to assert its
authority in 1978-9, is discussed below, pp. 254-301. However, in view of the special problems facing NATSOPA leaders
in their relations with their members at TNL, it is necessary
to consider the events of 1978-9 in so far as they involved
NATSOPA members here. NATSOPA members were not, in
the long run, likely to be so affected by the proposed new
technology as NGA members. The major impact of the introduction of electronic equipment, including Visual Display
Terminals and computers, would be upon NATSOPA clerical

members: the use of VDTs by tele-ad receptionists for financial checking and other operations would involve an expansion of their role, even if NGA opposition prevented management from ever using NATSOPA members to input material. However, many of the changes envisaged in the clerical area were simply the continuation of standard procedures for office automation. No major change was envisaged in the machine room; the existing rotary presses were to be retained. However, NATSOPA members were involved in many of the unofficial disputes which prevented continuity of production, and in the restrictive practices which management saw as unnecessarily increasing labour costs: Thomson's (*Sunday Times*) Night Machine Chapel imposed more restrictions on operations than any other single chapel (although of course their number did not necessarily indicate their importance). The reduced manning levels which management hoped to negotiate were to include NATSOPA members, especially in the machine room: indeed, the Thomson's (*Sunday Times*) Night Machine Chapel was to decline proportionately more than any other single chapel, from 540 to 318.[80] The Times management's proposals for the reorganization of production thus directly affected the interests of NATSOPA members: an inherently difficult situation was made even more difficult by the strained relations existing between NATSOPA chapels at TNL and the Executive Council.

Times management's letter to the general secretaries on 26 April, threatening the suspension of publication if agreements were not concluded by 30 November 1978, was considered by the NATSOPA Executive at its regular May meeting. Although the Executive objected to negotiating under threats, it agreed to negotiate and suggested a meeting with Times management: 'we would suggest the meeting takes place at national level, with Branch officials of each Branch being in attendance, and thereafter the matter will be dealt with by Branches and Chapels, co-ordinating their activities through a National Officer.'[81] The Executive stated that it shared management's concern at continuing interruptions to production. This concern was not simply a pious formality, since the meeting which considered Times management's letter also considered a resolution from *The Guardian* TAE&A Chapel expressing '[its] very grave disquiet concerning the present situation in Fleet Street . . . it is essential that trade unionists at all times should observe and abide by the existing and negotiated dispute procedures and that if they do not, then their membership of their union should be terminated.'[82] This feeling was shared among TAE&A members at TNL itself, where the chapel passed a resolution deploring the actions of a minority in putting jobs at risk, particularly since 'in the main the problems arising within Times Newspapers are caused by casual workers who own allegiance to no particular newspaper.'[83] Further disruption should lead to expulsion. The Executive Council was not required to act upon either resolution; but the resolutions indicated a trend in sentiment in an important small but growing section of the union (which of course included many middle managerial staff).

The Executive's policy over the TNL dispute was to deplore both management's threats and the continuing unofficial disputes, and to reaffirm willingness to negotiate. However, Times management were reluctant to negotiate with the unions involved separately, and the NGA refused to negotiate under duress: the Times management there-fore delayed replying to the NATSOPA Executive's letter proposing a meeting, to the general secretary's predictable irritation. In early August he wrote to The Times: 'we on our side are surprised that from the 15th May to date we have not received a reply to our communication beyond Mr. Nisbet-Smith's letter of the 17th May which indicated "We shall be in touch with you at the earliest possible oppor-tunity." ' Although recognizing that NATSOPA itself was not responsible for the delay in starting serious negotiations, Times management did not wish 'to fragment discussion at this primary stage'. The uncertainties in Times management's views were obvious in their letter to O'Brien at the end of August:

In view of NATSOPA's positive response, and similar replies from two other unions [NUJ, SOGAT] we will now need to determine the appropriate steps required by the situation, i.e. whether we should continue to meet with all Unions agreeable to such discussions, or

individually with each. As [these] matters concern widespread membership, the Company's view is that the first course would clearly be the
most effective.
We shall therefore continue to pursue this course, even if at a subsequent
collective meeting with General Secretaries it is agreed that matters
would best be progressed with individual Unions ... [It is of] particular
importance to the Company's general position that matters equally
affecting all its staff are discussed openly and collectively, at least so
far as common principles are concerned, before talks begin on specific
staff areas.[84]

By the following month, Times management recognized that
their hope of agreeing basic principles with at least the general
secretaries of all the print unions was a forlorn one, and
NATSOPA national officials and London branch secretaries
met Hussey and other members of Times management on
26 September. In view of the need to avoid leap-frogging
claims, the reluctance of Times management to meet print
union leaders separately is understandable. But the management conveyed the impression of stalling, and seeking confrontation, making the NATSOPA Executive's position
difficult to sustain when faced with conflicting internal
pressures. Some members desired the punishment of union
members at The Times who were continuing unofficial
action, and others wished to refuse to discuss anything with
Times management until the threat of suspension was lifted.
Times management tactics had the effect of weakening the
authority of the NATSOPA leadership, and in so doing
contributing to what the management itself diagnosed as
a major source of Fleet Street's problems, the weakness of
union officials.

During the period between the announcement of the
threat of suspension and the carrying out of the threat,
NATSOPA's policy, at Executive, branch, and most but not
all chapels, was one of willingness to negotiate, and protest
at the delays of Times management in bringing forward
detailed proposals. As Owen O'Brien wrote in his introduction
to the correspondence between NATSOPA and Times
management, published in November:

Although some of our Chapels [including Thomson's Night Machine
Chapel] had indicated that they were not prepared to meet during all
these months . . . the company have dealt with this matter in a non-

chalant way, i.e. by convening a meeting on the 26th September, which could easily have been held on the 26th May, and we are demanding that the duress under which our people have been placed should be withdrawn, and the customary form of collective bargaining . . . should be maintained. In such circumstances, I am sure reasonable people could reach reasonable conclusions.[85]

When he wrote, on 14 November, O'Brien had not received from management a copy of the section of management's proposed agreements envisaged as being common to all chapels, and due to be negotiated by full time officials. As late as 20 November, the general secretary believed that a new disputes procedure could be negotiated by the original deadline of 30 November, and that the remaining issues could be negotiated without duress; in the meantime, the *status quo* would remain, and the suspension be lifted. According to the general secretary, the problems at The Times were 'no greater than those which have been overcome in other newspaper offices'.[86]

The carrying out of the threat to suspend publication, and the failure of the first abortive Booth initiative, brought unity between the Executive and the chapels involved, and between the chapels themselves. The FOCs at TNL themselves commented on the surprising success of Times management: 'Marmaduke Hussey has probably succeeded in uniting all NATSOPA chapels on a scale never thought possible under normal circumstances.'[87] To maintain chapel unity, a NATSOPA *ad hoc* committee was formed by the *Times* chapels, chaired by Fitzpatrick; it was also supported by the *Times* Day Staff Chapel, the Thomson's (*Sunday Times*) Night Machine Chapel, the *Times* Clerical Chapel, the *Times* RIRMA Reading and Composing Chapel, the *Times* RIRMA Monocasters Chapel, the *Times* Night Machine Chapel, the *Times* Day and Night RIRMA Editorial Assistants Chapel, the *Sunday Times* RIRMA Reading and Composing Chapel, and the RIRMA Canteen Chapel — only the TAE&A members failed to provide representation. The objective was unconditional reinstatement, and negotiation on new technology agreements at leisure; there was no opposition to new technology as such — 'agreements must be reached for the future that allow the transition from old to new technology and provide the people affected with a real choice about their future and, most important of all, time to consider the alternatives'.[88] The NATSOPA *ad hoc* committee's statement echoed in almost precise terms the official NATSOPA view: '*Our position is quite clear* [original emphasis]. If the company want to resume publication, then they must reinstate all those dismissed, republish and we will then negotiate for as long as it takes without duress from any quarter.'[89]

Although there was agreement amongst NATSOPA chapels on unconditional reinstatement and negotiation without duress, there was disagreement on how to respond to management's refusal of reinstatement, and over how any negotiations should be handled. The Thomson's (*Sunday Times*) Night Machine Chapel was against discussions until the suspension was lifted.[90] But one of the RIRMA FOCs believed that the union had to negotiate to avoid the danger of a multi-national corporation simply withdrawing its investment; workers were more tied to the industry by their skill and experience than multi-national corporations by their investment: ' . . . the changes at T.N.L. are very difficult to accept but with some resolve and negotiating ability I feel that it will not be the calamity that some anticipate.'[91] The range of opinion within the union was apparent in the response to the 'Booth' formula of 8 March 1979, whereby employees were to be re-engaged until 17 April, to allow negotiation of a timetable for agreements on new manning levels and new technology; if any appropriate issues were unresolved on 7 April ACAS was to be called in to arbitrate. The Executive Council accepted the formula: it wanted the withdrawal of the New Agreements Project proposals, no arbitration, and no deadline. The Thomson's (*Sunday Times*) Night Machine Chapel accepted the proposals, but was not prepared to negotiate on the management's NAP, which was tantamount to rejection. The *Sunday Times* Clerical Chapel rejected the proposals because of the deadline, the arbitration by ACAS, the failure to reinstate four clerical employees allegedly summarily dismissed, and the acceptance of redundancy implied by the phrase 'subject to the preservation of the principle of voluntary redundancy'. The *Times* Day Staff Chapel, and *Times* clerical workers accepted the formula,

as did the RIRMA chapels.[92] The negotiations permitted
by the temporary re-engagement proved abortive, Times
management insisting upon acceptance of the principles
of the New Agreements Project before republication.
NATSOPA officials, as well as chapel officers, shared the
view that Times management were not seriously interested
in negotiation: 'Any seasoned negotiator would have recognized that no new interest to negotiate existed at all. [Times
management] had a scheme of things, a plan, a "green
field" project which must not be fundamentally altered, nor
phased, nor deflected from. In that atmosphere no negotiations as such were possible.'[93]

In view of the tangled history of relations between national
officials and the Times chapels, and the legacy of the March
1977 dispute, the issues of responsibility for the conduct of
negotiations and the ratification of agreements were central.
According to a report in the union journal, at a mass meeting
on 16 November of NATSOPA members employed at The
Times 'it became apparent that the vast majority of our
members wished negotiations to be dealt with by National
Officers and the E.C.'[94] Leaders of RIRMA and TAE&A
members publicly stressed that responsibility for negotiations should rest with national officials.[95] Not surprisingly,
Times machine chapels asserted the role of chapel officials,
a view which gained majority support from a mass meeting
of Times NATSOPA members after the beginning of the
suspension: 'no Agreements to be negotiated without the
participation of all individual chapel officials and the agreement by those chapels, which must be kept in existence.'[96]
The Executive Council's policy before the suspension was
that, after an initial meeting at national level, with branch
officers in attendance, negotiations would be conducted by
branch and chapel officials, under the co-ordination of a
national officer.[97] However, following the Executive meeting
which accepted the Booth formula of 8 March, the Executive
Council announced:

we proceed to negotiate a solution of The Times problem under the
sole direction of the General Secretary and the E.C. with such national
and branch officials as the General Secretary may deem necessary in
line with the constitution of the Society . . . the matter be left in the

General Secretary's hands to coordinate the details of the negotiations being set up.

At that stage, there was no mention of the involvement of chapel officers. Mindful of past experience, the union President 'reminded the E.C. that these decisions were binding on all members of the Council.'[98] However, it became clear that any attempt to restrict negotiations would be impracticable if it was seriously hoped to obtain chapel agreement. Accordingly, during the detailed negotiations under the Booth formula O'Brien indicated that 'national officials should not involve themselves in the negotiations, and . . . in view of the conflicting statements being made at senior and line management level a meeting should be arranged between the General Secretary and national officials and senior management, at which Chapel representatives should be in attendance.'[99] Having established general principles at national level, it was appropriate to hand over detailed negotiations to the chapels; but the general principles proved empty and the chapel negotiations made no progress.

The standard procedure for ratification of agreements concluded by officials was the circulation of copies of the agreement to members affected, and discussion at chapel meetings; if approved by the chapel meeting, agreements were forwarded to the branch committee and the Executive Council for endorsement. Anticipating difficulties in securing acceptance by chapel meetings for agreements negotiated, some RIRMA members at The Times proposed that agreements should be submitted to members for approval by secret ballot.[100] However, the proposal was not favoured by other chapels at The Times, nor by the London Machine Branch Committee: 'we cannot accept the principle of Ballot paper votes across the Board to all NATSOPA members at T.N.L..' The branch committee favoured existing practice. Although the Executive Council possessed authority under rule to arrange secret ballots where it thought appropriate, it merely 'noted' the proposal, and took no action, perhaps because it thought existing arrangements were satisfactory, or perhaps because any attempt to extend the use of secret ballots, in current circumstances, would provoke conflict in the union.

The final moves towards a settlement of the Times dispute could have been predicted from earlier events involving NATSOPA members at The Times. The Executive accepted the terms of the agreement negotiated on 27 July; but this was not accepted by all NATSOPA members at The Times. Members of the CA&EP and TAE&A chapels accepted the principles, and indeed went so far as to attend computer appreciation courses on the new technology, without consulting the Executive.[101] However, the machine room chapels did not: the *Sunday Times* Machine Room Chapel were reported as being unhappy with the new disputes procedure, and wanted an increase in the one-off payment to members on resumption of work from £100 to £500.[102] Throughout August and September NATSOPA members negotiated 'working agreements' with Times management, all chapels reaching agreement by 21 October. Although the major issue of principle inhibiting the successful conclusion of the negotiations for resumption involved NGA and not NATSOPA members, considerable delay occurred before the detailed agreements were concluded between all NATSOPA chapels and Times management, despite NATSOPA Executive's early acceptance of the basic principles of the resumption formula. To expedite settlement, in September the Executive explicitly decided to short-circuit the procedure for approving agreements: if chapels and the branch approve an agreement 'they can anticipate the authority of the E.C. to return to work.'[103] The NATSOPA chapels retained the initiative after the resumption of work, concluding only framework agreements to permit resumption; at the time of writing, December 1979, no final agreements have been negotiated between NATSOPA chapels and TNL management.

Events at TNL indicated the difficulties the union's administration faced in ensuring smooth industrial relations in normal circumstances. Personal, political, and policy differences in the union made the pursuit of a consistent policy by the union leadership difficult; consistency was easier to achieve for the anti-O'Brien forces, since it involved simply consistent opposition. As indicated, chapel officials at TNL had long been opponents of the general secretary. It was therefore likely that The Times's attempts to introduce new technology would face difficulties from NATSOPA chapels, even if the proposals posed no threat to NATSOPA members, and even if new technology was supported in principle by the general secretary. Although the general secretary supported *Programme for Action*, a mass meeting of *Times* NATSOPA members declared, 'We deplore Times Newspapers in seeking to reinstate *Programme for Action* after it being rejected by the members of NATSOPA, which the E.C. must support.'[104] The likelihood of new technology being acceptable to NATSOPA members was substantially reduced when Times management linked new technology with guaranteed continuity of production and new disputes procedures in April 1978, and threatened suspension if the proposals were not accepted. The Times management's delay in meeting NATSOPA leaders and their refusal to lift the suspension even when offered the rapid negotiation of new disputes procedures, made it difficult for NATSOPA leaders to reconcile the maintenance of a policy of reasonable willingness to negotiate with control over their Fleet Street members. The effect of the Times management's conduct during the dispute was to weaken further the NATSOPA Executive, and in so doing reduce the chances of new technology being acceptable to NATSOPA members. The apparent success of Fitzpatrick and Brady in negotiating favourable terms for the return to work, without any long-term commitment, inevitably increased their support at chapel level. TNL clerical members were not traditionally opposed to the O'Briens, as machine-branch members were; but the effect of the suspension was to increase anti-O'Brien feeling amongst TNL clerical members. In 1977 the NATSOPA Executive had expelled seven members at TNL for refusing to obey Executive instructions to return to work, and, although reinstating them, resisted pressure to remove the punishment; in 1979, when some NATSOPA chapels refused to agree to the terms for the return to work at TNL, the Executive in effect surrendered authority for concluding negotiations to the chapels.

NATSOPA members were less threatened by new technology than NGA members were: there was no NATSOPA principle equivalent to the NGA principle of unilateral control of key-stroking. However, NATSOPA members were affected by the same economic trends as NGA members: the growth of small printing houses, sometimes non-unionized, the movement of general print away from London, the growth of in-house printing, the concentration of ownership, and the potential for regionalization of production facilities; above all, by the desire of Fleet Street managements to reduce labour costs. In the clerical area this could be achieved by the same techniques of office automation that were being used in other sectors of industry, including computerized accounting and information systems, word processors, and other electronically based innovations. In the machine room this could be achieved simply by more efficient use of man-power, without major technological changes. However, technological change also offered opportunities for NATSOPA members, especially in the clerical area. In newspapers, as elsewhere, the increased use of electronic office equipment would result in more responsible clerical work, although possibly for fewer employees: in view of the high turnover of clerical employees in national newspapers and the high level of demand for clerical workers in London, this reduction would not be a serious blow to overall employment levels.[105] Moreover, any decrease in the number of clerical staff required on production-related tasks could be absorbed through increased employment in marketing. The reductions in manning levels in the machine room had no obvious solution. However, the long-term solution to the problem of manning levels in the machine room lay in decasualization, since the majority of machine-room assistants were employed on a casual basis, and could be successfully resolved only on an industry-wide basis (see below, pp. 189–92).

Owen O'Brien, like Briginshaw before him, believed that technological change would benefit NATSOPA members: by breaking down traditional demarcation lines it would provide the opportunity to end finally the historic association of the union with unskilled labour. 'The craftsman has had his day. I believe today it is not so much a question of craft as skill. You have to acquire a skill which is different from the type of skill that the craftsman had to obtain.'[106]

Instead of requiring craftsmen with all-round capabilities attested by the successful completion of apprenticeship in adolescence, the new technology required workers with specific skills relevant to particular processes, or even to particular machinery. The rate of change in production methods was so rapid that it was a waste of time to spend years in extended apprenticeships, on the assumption that the time invested and experience gained would constitute a life-long investment; training should comprise shorter periods of time and be related to specific objectives.[107] NATSOPA members could acquire new skills through such training methods just as successfully as NGA members. Hence O'Brien's enthusiastic support for the work of the PPITB, engaged on developing training programmes on such principles. Moreover, NATSOPA recruited the technical and managerial staff likely to increase in number with new technology through its TAE&A section: in 1978 the Governing Council established an Executive seat for TAE&A members, and the union's recruiting efforts were increasingly concentrating in that area, indicated by the decision in August 1979 to provide for a national officer and organizer for the section.[108] Where new technology involved the loss of jobs, the general secretary believed that savings should be shared on a 50/50 basis, with the workers who accepted voluntary redundancy leaving the industry.

These views were far from universal within the union. Although some of the opposition was primarily factional, other opposition was based upon the long-term dangers of selling jobs, a sentiment on which factional opposition was able to capitalize. For example, a number of members of the MGN clerical chapel expressed their disillusion with the agreement negotiated at MGN which involved the loss of 100 clerical jobs: 'these jobs are not the property of any one member or chapel to sell.'[109] Neither natural wastage nor voluntary redundancy was acceptable. Redundancy payments were simply 'an attempt to reduce resistance to the creation of unemployment. We should have no truck with them.' The workers who remained were faced with harder work and a pay increase losing its attractiveness through inflation, but negotiated under an agreement due to last for four years. It was misleading to suggest that individual members and chapels were selling jobs, since agreements were subject to approval by the branch committee and Executive Council, and it was the Executive's policy to encourage new technology, at the appropriate price: however, the sentiment was an important one, which gained increased currency as events at The Times unfolded.

The policy which the general secretary had outlined to the Royal Commission in 1974 remained in 1979: a belief that the properly supervised joint introduction of new technology would provide the basis for a more prosperous Fleet Street. However, the general secretary suffered a number of set-backs during the period, on new technology as well as on other issues. On a large scale, *Programme for Action* was rejected, despite his strong support for it within the union. At house level, the eventual outcome of the confused events at TNL weakened the authority of the NATSOPA Executive, and the MGN agreement was beginning to reveal short-comings. At chapel level, specific agreements continued to be negotiated in line with Executive policy, but the London Machine Branch Committee was opposed to the principle of reduced staffing, and even the RIRMA Chapel at the FT complained about the conduct of the London RIRMA branch secretary during industrial action over the Eurobond issue.[110] In the overall employment situation of 1979, with rising unemployment, selling jobs was becoming difficult, even where chapels were not discouraged from doing so by the Executive Council.

iii

NATSOPA leaders, like NGA leaders, saw joint action as the most effective means of ensuring union control over the introduction of new technology. Joint action took several forms: between chapels at house level, between branches, and between unions at national level. The ultimate aspiration was the creation of a united printing industry union: as Briginshaw said to the Royal Commission in 1974, 'The prime need is one union for the industry. There are no insuperable obstacles to the achievement. There are no good reasons against. There are only excuses.'[111] But the progress towards unity was patchy. Joint action between chapels, and between branches, was largely limited to emergency action, as at The Times in 1978-9; joint action at national level, especially through the Printing Industries Committee of the TUC, was more permanent, and in a limited way more successful, whilst the moves towards the creation of a single print trade union began promisingly, only to fade. This section examines NATSOPA's involvement in joint action, and its relation to new technology.

United action, at any level, could be based upon complementary interests, or upon pressure, internal or external. NATSOPA shared a common interest with other print unions in promoting the expansion of the industry, and in protecting employment prospects; as shown in earlier chapters, the industry's overall economic situation exerted pressure towards unity. However, NATSOPA's interests were not always complementary to those of other print unions: in a declining industry the best means of protecting employment prospects was often at the expense of other unions in the industry, whilst attempts to move outside traditional areas of recruitment often constituted incursions into the jurisdiction of other unions. Hence technological changes working to the advantage of clerical workers could operate to the disadvantage of NGA members; and moves into the advertising world, following the merger with the Sign and Display Trade Union, encountered opposition from SLADE, recruiting in the same area through the SLADE Art Union. In practice, united action constituted a means of achieving traditional objectives, not an end in itself. Where united action provided the best means of resisting employers, NATSOPA actively promoted unity; where united action provided the best means of controlling potentially dangerous external developments, such as new technology, NATSOPA was willing to join with other unions more enthusiastically than the NGA. But there was no significant sacrifice of NATSOPA's interests, at national or chapel level, in the interests of unity. Like virtue, unity was desirable in principle, but could be inconvenient in practice. It was therefore practised only when external pressure made it necessary.

During the suspension of Times newspapers, members of

NATSOPA were prominent in the co-ordination of opposition to management. Unusually for a clerical FOC, B. A. Fitzpatrick was the chairman of the All Union Liaison Committee at TNL, the body responsible for co-ordinating policy between chapels; John Mitchell, the secretary of the London Machine Branch, was the secretary of the parallel branch committee, the London Printing Branches Liaison Committee, comprising London officers of all the print unions. A mass meeting of NATSOPA members, organized by the Joint NATSOPA *ad hoc* committee at the Friends House, Euston Rd., on 4 January, was addressed by the acting FOC of the *Sunday Times* NUJ Chapel, John Fryer, and by the FOC of the NGA machine managers.[112] According to the *Times Challenger*, the meeting was 'an important expression of the cooperation which has developed at Times Newspapers between trades union chapels.' The Times dispute produced unity between NATSOPA chapels and other chapels. However, the unity resulted in no permanent institutions: at the return of the newspapers in November 1979 there were no institutional innovations, although the contacts made and the sentiments generated were not forgotten.

However, chapel unity could prove dangerous to union Executives in the long run. Although there was no danger in temporary arrangements caused by intransigence on the part of the employer, and unity in general was desirable, the Executive wished to ensure that inter-chapel arrangements did not threaten existing institutional arrangements or traditional objectives. Hence the comment from one clerical member that: 'our F.O.C.'s handbook encourages [Federated House Chapels], but unfortunately conducting negotiations through Federated House Chapels jointly with other Societies in frowned on. This reduces the usefulness of our participation.'[113] In practice, unity between chapels of different unions was mainly confined to specific disputes, there being few Federated House Chapels, even in the provincial newspaper industry. The most practicable method of achieving unity between unions, as well as the one preferred by union national officers, was initially negotiation at national level.

Historically, the major means of achieving united action between the print unions was through the Printing and

Kindred Trades Federation (PKTF), founded in 1901 to co-ordinate discussion between all print unions on matters of common interest (see above, pp. 53-4). Although negotiations were conducted by the PKTF, the agreements were of course subject to approval by the unions involved individually, and held by individual unions with the employers. The PKTF fell into disrepute in the late 1960s, as the process of mergers created stronger print unions: it proved easier to work through a federal body comprised of a large number of relatively weak organizations than through one comprising a small number of large ones, especially where the unions involved were dominated by powerful general secretaries. NATSOPA leaders felt that the unions involved were not giving full commitment to the organization. Even before the dissolution of the PKTF NATSOPA leaders had supported the principle of an inter-union committee under the aegis of the TUC (like the Steel Industry Committee established in 1967): the dissolution of the PKTF made such an institution all the more necessary.[114] The responsibilities of the PIC were more limited than those of the PKTF had been; it was a forum for the exchange of information rather than for collective bargaining. However, NATSOPA leaders felt that the PIC was more effective than the PKTF had been: 'the unions are prepared to be more open in their discussions than they were before in the days of the Federation, when you had three cards down and a couple up your sleeve. It seems to me that there are more cards on the table now.' However, the failure of *Programme for Action* led to some disillusion with the PIC in NATSOPA, as elsewhere, E. O'Brien commenting in October 1977 that 'vital matters, including new technology, appear to have been sacrificed on the altar of parochial interest'.[115] NATSOPA felt particularly aggrieved that its interest in recruiting more clerical workers was being disregarded, for example where SLADE/ NGA 'fair shop' certificates were being issued even where clerical workers were not organized. Despite these reservations, NATSOPA remained fully committed to the PIC, which has continued as a useful arena for the discussion of matters of common interest, including technology and training.

Although the PIC was an important arena for multilateral

discussions, NATSOPA's major efforts at united action were directed towards amalgamation, initially with the NGA, and subsequently with SOGAT. The union had previously merged with the NUPBW in 1967 when NATSOPA formed Division I of SOGAT: however, the merger had not worked, the two unions continuing as independent bodies, and failing to agree upon a new rule book; it was dissolved in 1970. However, NATSOPA continued to believe that the long-term future of trade unionism in the industry depended upon the eventual creation of a single print trade union. The Governing Council at Bournemouth in June 1976 passed a formal resolution on the need for one union in the industry, and welcomed the NGA general secretary, Joe Wade. Informal talks began between the two general secretaries the same month.[116] It was thought that NATSOPA and the NGA were natural partners: members of the two unions worked closely together in the composing and machine rooms, and in provincial houses large numbers of NGA members were former members of NATSOPA, promoted from machine assistants. Since the merger was intended as the first step towards a single print union, and not to form a bloc alliance, the general secretary of SOGAT was kept informed.

Discussions with the NGA continued until the spring of 1978, before being broken off by mutual agreement. The scope of the talks was expanded early in 1977, when SLADE and NUWDAT joined the discussions, resulting in increased complexity and delay (see above, pp. 000–0). In addition to constitutional and organizational difficulties, a major difficulty was posed by new technology: for example, a meeting scheduled between NATSOPA and NGA representatives to discuss 'outstanding questions', including new technology, was cancelled by the NGA.[117] There had been some success in reaching joint agreements between NATSOPA and NGA, most notably the 50/50 agreement on direct-lithographic processes, which operated effectively at the first di-litho press opened by Sefton Newspapers in Southport early in 1978.[118] But even outside Fleet Street conflict between NATSOPA and NGA arose over new technology, notably at Bradbury-Wilkinson's, a general print shop, where an agreement between management and the NGA, widening differentials between NGA and NATSOPA members in the machine room, resulted in a six-week strike.[119] In national newspapers there was resentment over the NGA's lack of consultation with NATSOPA over stoppages at MGN's *Reveille*, which were seen as typical of the NGA's cavalier attitude towards other unions. It was therefore hardly surprising that NATSOPA announced its withdrawal from the discussions when the proposals were ready to be put to ballot; according to O'Brien, although the discussions had begun optimistically, 'it [became] obvious that the task was almost insuperable' when SLADE and NUWDAT became involved. Despite their withdrawal, NATSOPA publicly hoped that the ballot on the merger between SLADE, NUWDAT, and the NGA would be successful.[120]

Even during the early stages of the amalgamation discussions with the NGA public opposition had been expressed within NATSOPA: the Sheffield branch forwarded a resolution to the Executive stating that 'amalgamation with the NGA [would be] totally repugnant.'[121] The Executive rejected the motion as being contrary to Executive policy. But the alignment of the NGA alongside SLADE over recruitment in the advertising industry, the neglect of NATSOPA's interests by the NGA and SLADE over the publication of the fair list and the conflict at Bradbury-Wilkinson's reinforced NATSOPA resentment against what was seen as traditional craft arrogance. This resentment developed into hostility in 1979 when NGA began recruitment amongst clerical workers, in effect poaching potential NATSOPA members.

In July 1979 NATSOPA joined with SOGAT in issuing a joint warning to employers against intervention by other unions in clerical and other non-manual sectors of the industry:

Our organizers are reporting from various parts of the country that not only are Unions from outside the industry recruiting in this field, but there are unions from within the industry who are entering what has traditionally been the sphere of influence of either SOGAT or NATSOPA . . . we cannot sit idly by and accept that our jurisdictional position is undermined; and we would like a reiteration from your association [the Newspaper Society] that the unions that are recognized as being appropriate in these areas are either NATSOPA or SOGAT as defined in the local area where we have excellent arrangements and there is no record of disputes occurring between us on this matter.[122]

The NGA recruited tele-ad girls at the *Surrey Advertiser* and *Aldershot News*, and reinforced its position by blacking copy from NATSOPA members. There was further NGA recruitment at the *Ormskirk Advertiser* and the *Huddersfield Examiner*. In December 1979 a two-week strike occurred at the *Warrington Guardian*, over management's recognition of individual membership of the NGA and the promise of recognition if NGA recruited 51 per cent of the relevant group.[123] To stop the encroachment NATSOPA took the NGA to the TUC Review Committee and informed the Newspaper Society that NATSOPA members would strike wherever employers granted recognition to clerical workers organized in other unions. The NGA's justification for the recruitment of clerical workers was the existence of a clerical section within NUWDAT, which provided a toe-hold in the clerical area which might be constitutionally justifiable in trade-union circles, although the union began recruitment before the merger with NUWDAT became operational on 1 October 1979. It also promised not to recruit where NATSOPA already had a sustantial membership in the clerical area. But NATSOPA interpreted the NGA's action as unjustifiable aggression, provoked by fears of the effect of technological change. As Owen O'Brien emphasized,

Because of their apparent fear that the new technology will cause a loss of membership in their traditional areas, the NGA is endeavouring to move into fields into which it previously would not have ventured [italics in original] .[124]

The reasons for the attempts to organise in this field can only be considered a rearguard action, not to promote clerical workers but to defend ageing and out-of-date so-called crafts (it is surprising what new technology can do).[125]

NATSOPA's resentment was all the greater because the NGA could only find an opening through NATSOPA's failure to achieve closed shop agreements in the clerical area (or any agreement at all in provincial weekly newspapers until 1979), a failure NATSOPA felt partly resulted from the NGA's long-standing unhelpful attitude to NATSOPA's attempts to achieve 100 per cent organization among clerical workers.

Throughout NATSOPA's discussions with the NGA SOGAT had been kept informed of progress. Following the breakdown of the discussions with the NGA in 1978 the informal discussions between NATSOPA and SOGAT were placed on a firmer basis, and the Amalgamation Panel of the Executive Council, which had been involved in discussions with the NGA, was appointed to carry on discussions with SOGAT.[126] The interests of the two unions were more similar than the interests of NATSOPA and NGA, as the earlier unsuccessful merger had indicated: the merger had failed for organizational reasons rather than for reasons of principle. Despite disagreements in specific plants on manning levels and the new technology, as at Bradbury-Wilkinson's (Saltash) in 1979, both unions had a similar interest in resisting NGA encroachment, although NATSOPA more than SOGAT; both resented the NGA's aristocratic craft attitude; and both general secretaries had been strongly committed to *Programme for Action*, especially as a means of solving the casual problem. Amalgamation between the two unions would facilitate recruitment amongst white-collar staff, especially in areas ancillary to printing, such as ink, paper, and the expanding office-supplies sector. In view of the failure of the earlier amalgamation, it was recognized that rules would have to be drawn up before the merger rather than afterwards. Accordingly, detailed Amalgamation Panel proposals were presented to the Executive early in March 1979, and 'taken' at a special meeting of the Executive Council on 23 April 1979: the Executive expected the proposals to be submitted to membership ballot.[127] It was hoped that the rules of the new union would be based on the same principles as NATSOPA's rules, especially relating to the re-election of officials, but it was 'not a break-point': the Governing Council in 1978 had in fact rejected a motion from the London Machine Branch which would have made amalgamation conditional upon the re-election of officers.

The NATSOPA Executive Council was enthusiastic about the merger, and in June suggested to SOGAT a joint meeting of Executives to overcome outstanding difficulties. However, some members of the union were less enthusiastic, and were eager to use the Executive's eagerness over amalgamation to prosecute other campaigns, especially the issue of the union's financial affairs. The London Machine Branch Delegate Meeting passed a comprehensive resolution which effectively stymied the Executive. The meeting favoured amalgamation in principle, but on condition that: full-time officers would not be allowed to sit on the Executive Council (although they were permitted to do so under SOGAT's rules); full-time officers were to be subject to re-election (although they were not required to do so under SOGAT's rules); the existing branch structure would be maintained; the new constitution granted as much autonomy to branches in the new union as permitted to existing SOGAT branches (which was considerably greater than the autonomy granted to NATSOPA branches); full information on the terms of the merger would be circulated before decision, to permit full Chapel and Delegate Meeting consideration; and there would be no undue haste, since 'the financial affairs of this union must be fully declared to the membership prior to such amalgamation.' Many of the conditions were sensible, although scarcely designed to facilitate the amalgamation discussions; amalgamation was even more desirable for NATSOPA than SOGAT, and SOGAT was by far the larger union. However, the reference to full disclosure of the union's financial affairs was an impossible condition for the Executive to meet, since the intense publicity which had already been given to the union's financial affairs might reasonably be regarded as full disclosure. The Executive 'NOTED' the motion (capitals in original): it did not, as it had done two years earlier to a motion from Sheffield against merger with the NGA, reject the motion as inconsistent with Executive Council policy, although it clearly was.[128] Correctly anticipating difficulties, and that NATSOPA would seek to reopen issues which it had assumed were closed, SOGAT refused NATSOPA's request for a joint meeting of Executives. Instead, O'Brien met the SOGAT general secretary. In the event, NATSOPA Executive decided that it could not 'finalise' the terms of the agreement with SOGAT until the next Governing Council, due in June 1980, and accordingly the discussions were suspended.[129] The issues which prevented proceeding with the discussions included the long-standing issues pin-pointed in the LMB Delegate Meeting's resolution: re-election of full-time officers, the eligibility of full-time officers for election to the Executive Council. The NATSOPA Executive rejected the principle that full-time officers should be eligible for election to the Executive Council and believed that it lacked a mandate to accept the principle of life tenure for full-time officers, although both principles had been accepted by the amalgamation panels.

Despite the complementarity of interests between NATSOPA and SOGAT the amalgamation proposals proved abortive: instead, SOGAT pressed ahead with its merger discussions with the NGA. The reason for the failure of the negotiations, on NATSOPA's side, was not the Executive's dissatisfaction with the terms agreed, but the incoherence of the union's internal political system, the impossibility of formulating a consistent policy at national level and effectively ensuring its acceptance throughout the union. Despite the formal authority of the Executive Council and national officials the union leadership did not feel sufficiently confident to risk putting the merger proposals to a ballot of the membership: it informed SOGAT that a decision would have to await the next meeting of the Governing Council, in June 1980. Part of the difficulty lay in the inherent fragmentation of the union, the division between machine, RIRMA, and clerical chapels: but the occupational heterogeneity was not different in kind from that of other print unions, and the external problems faced by the union were less difficult than those faced by the NGA. The failure of the amalgamation discussions with SOGAT was symptomatic of the disarray within NATSOPA at the end of the 1970s, with the national leadership preoccupied with internal conflicts scarcely related to the long-term problems of the industry. The new national assistant secretary, John Moakes, presented a gloomy catalogue of difficulties facing the union in November 1978:

the steady, remorseless contraction of printing in general — particularly in London; changes brought about by the new technology; employers' allegations of over-manning; years of frustration resulting from wage controls; internecine warfare within out own ranks; unofficial disputes across the whole spectrum which are virtually bleeding our industry to death; failure to honour agreements freely entered into; the new found toughness of some employers who are prepared to close down rather than concede; the danger of collective control being lost as a result of minority activists who appear to be more politically than industrially motivated. The list is endless.

Optimistically, he thought that united action with other print unions and the successful conclusion of the amalgamation discussions with SOGAT would be means of dealing with the problems faced by the Society.[130] A year later the union was involved in conflict over the organization of clerical workers with the NGA, and the merger discussions with SOGAT had been suspended: the union faced the prospect of isolation from other unions in the industry. Internal conflicts, including the conflict over the union's financial affairs, which attracted wide press publicity (usually un- favourable) and diverted official attention away from the industry's serious problems, had undermined the most promising medium-term solution to the union's problems.

iv

In 1975 NATSOPA appeared poised for expansion, either through recruitment or through merger. The union's spheres of jurisdiction included the major areas within printing not fully organized, clerical workers, and technical and super- visory staffs. The union devoted major recruiting energies into both sectors, especially the latter. Outside printing, the union hoped to recruit in advertising, building upon the basis provided by the Sign and Display Trade Union, which merged to become the Sign and Display Trade Section of NATSOPA in 1972. The emergence of new leadership at the top of the NGA and SOGAT, as well as NATSOPA, the success of the Printing Industries Committee, and the united front presented to the Royal Commission, augured well for substantial progress towards unity amongst print unions. The scope for expansion for NATSOPA on the fringes of the industry was counter-balanced by threats to employment prospects amongst the historically central machine-room membership, as employers, especially in Fleet Street, attemp- ted to reduce manning levels; but there was no fundamental threat to the machine room comparable to the threat to the composing room. The breakdown of demarcation lines by new technology was seen as helping NATSOPA, by increasing promotion opportunities for union members. The prospects for the late 1970s looked promising.

The promise was not realized. Recruitment in the clerical area remained difficult; the union complained of the lack of assistance given towards the achievement of 100 per cent clerical organization by other unions, and felt that it had not been given adequate recognition for its support of the NUJ in the Darlington *Northern Echo* dispute in 1977. By 1979 the union was engaged in conflict with the NGA over recruitment of clerical workers in provincial newspapers. The expansion of effort in the technical and supervisory area encountered difficulties: existing chapels objected to the organization of supervisory workers in a separate section, and the attempt to establish a full-time post of organizer for the TAE&A section failed at the first attempt, no appropriately qualified candidate putting his name forward for office. The attempt to expand recruitment in the advertising sector made little headway. The union's amalgamation discussions with NGA and SOGAT failed, neither set of proposals being submitted to membership ballot. By the end of 1979 the union faced the prospect of isolation from other print unions, with the NGA involved in detailed discussions with SOGAT, and the NUJ voting to join the discussions. New technology had not provided the breakthrough anticipated. In national newspapers, management at the FT had not pursued their 1975 development plan, despite the favourable reaction of NATSOPA national leadership, and both MGN and TNL managements had accepted the principle of the introduction of new technology on the basis of existing demarcation lines; in provincial newspapers NATSOPA members were less disadvantaged, but there was no major move to reduce demarcation barriers. Instead, new technology was being introduced on conventional lines, but with reduced manning levels — a process causing maximum disadvantage to NATSOPA members.

Some of the reasons for NATSOPA's difficulties in the late 1970s were external; the collapse of the joint union-management industry-level approach which produced *Pro-*

gramme for Action, and management tactics over new technology. But major reasons for NATSOPA's failure to realize the promise of 1975 were also internal: the continuing internal political conflict between the O'Briens and an important section of the union's membership. The major immediate issues in the conflict were the allegations of financial misconduct against Briginshaw and the present general secretary's association with his predecessor's alleged misconduct. However, the issues were more long-standing and wider. Some had their roots in personal political rivalries, others in ideological differences. But there was a fundamental tension between the union's formal structure, based on the 'open' models of the 'new' unionism of 1889, and the *de facto* power of the Fleet Street chapels: even in a stable environment the relation would have required skilful handling. At the simplest level, the continuing conflict left officers with insufficient time to carry out their duties — criticism was voiced of the failure to circulate details of the NS/BPIF offer in May 1979, provoking the general secretary to complain that 'the pressure that is being placed on the officers and staff . . . at the present time is straining our administrative resources to their limits.'[131] The Society's internal conflicts inevitably prevented the development of a consistent policy and undermined the credibility of the union in its relations with outside bodies, whether employers or other trade unions: hence the confusion over the negotiations which led to the republication of Times newspapers, and SOGAT's belief that NATSOPA had reneged upon its undertakings in the amalgamation discussions. The union's politics between 1975 and 1979 were dominated by sectional factionalism, which prevented the realization of the aspirations of 1975.

The preceding chapters have outlined the structure of industrial relations in Fleet Street and the major factors which influenced the development of policy towards new technology in two of the unions centrally involved, the NGA and NATSOPA. Reference has already been made to events at two of the major Fleet Street companies involved in new technology, TNL and MGN. The following chapters are concerned with events in Fleet Street between 1975 and 1979, examining in detail the industrial relations consequences of proposals for technological change. The initiative for the introduction of new technology came from several news-papers almost simultaneously. Since both managements and unions feared that a house-by-house process would result in confusion, both sides hoped that an industry-wide framework could be negotiated. The Royal Commission on the Press and the Labour Government also favoured an industry-wide joint approach. The attempt to develop an industry-wide approach is therefore examined in the following chapter. However, the approach failed; the Fleet Street members of the unions involved, except the NUJ, rejected the joint proposals produced. In default of a national agreement individual houses either suspended their proposals or pressed ahead, with widely different consequences. Chapter 6 affords an examination of events at a house which suspended its development plan, the Financial Times; chapter 7 deals with a house which was obliged to modify its proposals following a major industrial conflict, TNL; and chapter 8 with a house which successfully carried through its proposals, after exten-sive delay, but has not seen its hopes realized, MGN.

Chapter 5

The Joint Standing Committee for National Newspapers

In the 1950s and 1960s abortive attempts were made to establish national joint committees betweeen employers and unions in the national newspaper industry, most importantly with the Joint Board for the National Newspaper Industry, set up in 1964 following the recommendation of the 1961–2 Royal Commission on the Press.[1] However, these attempts foundered. The Joint Board commissioned a thorough research report on the industry from the Economist Intelligence Unit, and, following the report, established a Joint Management Committee to 'take the question of labour supply and demand out of the field of collective bargaining'.[2] But the attempt failed, 'the main stumbling block being the problem of deciding how savings from improvements in productivity should be shared among the members of the trade unions', or between trade unions and management.[3] The Joint Board disappeared without making any significant contribution to solving the industry's problems. The supporters of the Joint Standing Committee in 1975 were aware of the failure of previous similar attempts, and of the need to avoid a repetition of the events of 1964–7. They believed that the industry's economic difficulties were so severe and the technological changes impending so radical that history would not repeat itself. The aim of this chapter is to show why history did repeat itself. Part of the explanation lies in the particular circumstances of the industry and the history of the joint body, and part in the general difficulties of establishing joint bodies in an industrial relations system as impregnated with collective-bargaining assumptions as the British system.

i

In view of the industry's economic situation, it was hardly

surprising that in the summer of 1975 both union leaders and employers were seriously concerned about the economic situation in Fleet Street. In a broadcast at the end of August Joe Wade, then still assistant general secretary of the NGA, called for national-level talks between employers and unions on employment prospects in the industry, to which the director of the NPA, John Dixey, replied favourably at a meeting held during the TUC at Blackpool in September.[4] Also in September the NGA National Committee decided to write formally to the NPA asking for a meeting to discuss the situation created by declining revenue and employers' proposals for the introduction of new technology. Simultaneously, union leaders on the TUC Printing Industries Committee made it clear at one of their regular meetings with the Royal Commission on the Press that they wished to meet with employers to discuss the situation. The employers accepted through the NPA, and a joint meeting was arranged on 5 December.

The TUC Printing Industries Committee's views were published late in November.[5] The committee believed that there was an 'unprecedented crisis' in Fleet Street, with some newspapers in danger of closing, mainly due to rising newsprint prices and falling revenues. Although the committee denied that high labour costs were the major cause of the industry's difficulties, it recognized that manning levels were a contributory factor. Reduced manning could be achieved by natural wastage and voluntary redundancy, without compulsory redundancy. National-level discussions were necessary to establish guidelines within which negotiations could proceed at house level. The discussions would cover provision for improved pensions, early retirement, voluntary redundancy, retraining, alternative employment opportunities, and decasualization, as well as means of obtaining outside financial assistance, both from the Government and from the EEC. In exchange for jointly agreed arrangements on these matters, the PIC was willing to examine the effects of technological change on demarcation lines, and accepted that some blurring of existing demarcation lines might be necessary.

The major initiative for a joint approach to the industry's

problems came from W. H. Keys, as chairman of the PIC, and the union document provided the basic agenda for the joint meeting. The Fleet Street employers were happy to respond to the union initiative, seeing it as an indication of a realistic approach to the industry's problems. Indeed, they saw considerable advantage in stressing that the initiative came from the unions, partly because it obviously enhanced the chances of any agreement made being effective, and perhaps also out of an awareness that any future agreement involving government expenditure would receive a more sympathetic hearing from a Labour government if the initiative came from the unions rather than the distrusted newspaper employers.

The employers hoped that joint discussions would result in the formation of a joint national body to quantify the costs of pensions and severance payments, to establish national parameters for house-level negotiations, to monitor house-level agreements, and to obtain funds, both from within and from outside the industry, to alleviate the social consequences of change. At the same time, the employers hoped that the discussions would help in obtaining guaranteed continuous production under existing technology. Although there was an obvious difference in perspective between the employers and union leaders, there was also an obvious possible trade-off between the employers' interest in reduced manning levels, whether under existing or under new technology, and the union leaders' interest in enhanced social benefits. This trade-off was all the more likely to occur in a situation in which the industry was under close public scrutiny by the Royal Commission and public opinion expected a favourable response from the employers to the union proposals.

The meeting between the employers and union leaders to discuss the union proposals took place at the Waldorf Hotel on the morning of Friday, 5 December.[6] The employers' side comprised representatives of all the NPA houses, together with Mirror Group Newspapers, Thomson Withy Grove, and the NPA itself. The union side consisted of representatives of SOGAT, NATSOPA, EETPU, NUJ, and the TUC itself: neither SLADE nor AUEW nor the NGA were represented. SLADE followed its customary practice of ignoring developments in the industry — as it was to do throughout the existence of the Joint Standing Committee — and played no part at all. The AUEW were, at that stage, willing to enter into separate discussions with individual employers about new technology, but not to join in general national discussions. More surprising was the absence of the NGA. The NGA was not a member of the TUC at that stage, having been expelled for not de-registering as a trade union following the 1971 Industrial Relations Act, and was therefore not involved in the discussions of the Printing Industries Committee. The NGA failed to attend because, although it had initially sponsored the idea of a general discussion between employers and unions, it was unwilling to enter into discussions with employers without a satisfactory guarantee that there would be no compulsory redundancy: at that stage the employers were unwilling to give such a guarantee as a pre-condition for discussions. The Association also suspected that other unions were using the joint discussions as a means of weakening the NGA's position, and wished to obtain guarantees from other unions that existing demarcation lines would be retained under new technology 'as far as is practicable'.[7]

Despite the fears of some employers that the discussions would be undermined by divisions amongst themselves, which would allow union leaders sceptical of the initiative to opt out of the discussions, the meeting was successful and agreement was reached on a joint statement or 'declaration of intent'. The joint statement, issued the following Monday, 8 December, read:

At a joint meeting of all national newspaper publishers and Senior Union representatives it was agreed that there should be no compulsory redundancy in the areas covered by the introduction of new technology and methods.

In return for that undertaking the Unions stated that they would cooperate in management plans for the introduction of new technology and methods in individual offices.

It was also accepted that the above undertaking could not apply where a newspaper was in such a financial position as to jeopardise the future employment of its staff and in such other circumstances as to be mutually agreed between the parties.

Publishers agreed to examine with the Unions concerned the system of employment of casual staff in national newspapers, with a view to its progressive elimination, the employers accepting their social obligations to all those employed in the industry. A working party of the employers and unions has been set up for this purpose.

The meeting accepted that an appropriate method of improving efficiency and achieving long term viability of the industry was the introduction of voluntary redundancy in appropriate areas.

It was also agreed that early retirement and adequate pension schemes should be established with the same objective.

It was also accepted that in both these cases it was necessary to establish that if those concerned left the employ of the industry and ceased to be the responsibility of the Unions, the social obligations would need to be accepted.

With these points in mind it was agreed that working parties should be set up to make recommendations to the main group.

In view of this it was agreed that the unions would immediately examine the implications of continuing recruitment into the national newspaper industry.[8]

The prerequisite for continuing discussions was that employers guaranteed that there would be no compulsory redundancy. Even if union leaders were willing to contemplate compulsory redundancy (on conditions) there was no prospect of union leaders being able to carry their members with them. The employers were reluctant to provide firm guarantees, partly for the general reason that it would reduce their room for manoeuvre in the future, and partly because the financial difficulties of some houses, especially the *Observer*, were so acute that it might prove impossible to back up any guarantee. However, the employers recognized that failure to provide satisfactory guarantees would end the talks, incurring the special resentment of Keys and O'Brien, who had taken the lead in organizing the talks, result in unfavourable publicity, increase the difficulty of changing manning levels or introducing new technology, and in any case increase resistance to any attempt to implement compulsory redundancy schemes. Since success in sustaining union co-operation in changing manning levels or introducing new technology rested upon launching the talks, the employers provided firmer guarantees than they had initially intended. At the very least, if unions failed to 'deliver' upon their side the employers would be released from their obligations.

Moreover, the guarantee was not totally unconditional. Compulsory redundancy was accepted where a paper's financial position was so serious that failure to implement compulsory redundancy would jeopardize its future. And there was some ambivalence about the phrase 'in the areas covered by the introduction of new technology and methods'. It was wider than the initial employers' hope to limit any guarantees to 'the present exercise', but could be limited if manning levels were to be reduced in areas not affected by new technology, like the publishing room. (On the other hand such a move would have been so contrary to the 'spirit' of the agreement that the agreement would have lost its relevance anyway.)

The joint statement represented a declaration of intent: fundamental issues were unresolved, including the precise scope of any national-level agreement even on issues where employers and unions were in substantial agreement, namely pensions. For example, how far was the scheme to be tailored to the financial resources of the financially weaker houses? However, it was agreed to establish joint working parties on pensions, voluntary redundancy, and decasualization to work out detailed policies for submission to future joint meetings. A second, smaller-scale, joint meeting was held on 8 January 1976 at which the unions presented further proposals, building upon the joint statement a month earlier. The unions proposed joint supervision of new technology at national and house level, with union 'demarcation committees' at both levels, to consider demarcation issues. In addition, detailed proposals were made for voluntary-redundancy terms and pensions. The major principle regarding voluntary-redundancy terms was that employees should have the choice between enhanced redundancy payments (linked to age, but with younger workers receiving higher levels of earnings per year of service), and an income-preservation scheme similar to that proposed by the Financial Times (see below, pp. 229–30). The union objective on pensions was 67 per cent of final earnings, based partly upon existing house pension schemes, and partly upon a special supplementary scheme funded by the industry as a whole. Decasualization was to be achieved by allocating casuals either to a single employer or to a pool of labour supported by the industry, on the model of the Dock Labour Scheme. The employers agreed to cost the proposals, to begin groundwork with NATSOPA and SOGAT on decasualization, and to join with the unions in asking the Royal Commission on the Press to delay its Interim Report for a month to enable management and unions to submit joint evidence.

The second full meeting of the two sides took place on 16 January at the offices of the NPA. The employers recognized that they had to make a positive contribution to the discussions, and either to accept the union proposals or to offer constructive alternatives. This was all the more necessary because of the need to justify the request for delay to the Interim Report of the Royal Commission: failure to progress would be publicly damaging. On the other hand, the detailed costing of the redundancy payments and the improved pensions proved high: £35m–40m for Option A of the severance proposals and £145m for back-service pension payments, and an increase of £7.2m per year for future service. The employers felt that they could not finance such payments from industry sources, and were unable to make definite commitments without firm sources of finance from elsewhere. Accordingly, the employers wished to emphasize the general areas of agreement, especially joint supervision of the introduction of new technology, but to avoid premature specific financial commitments. The joint statement published following the meeting indicated that substantial progress had been made: general agreement was reached on the broad terms of redundancy compensation, on the need for improved pensions, and on the desirability of decasualization; working parties were to be set up on the three areas, charged with reporting back to the full joint meeting within a month; when the working parties had reached agreement 'the two sides will set up a Standing Joint Committee to supervise introduction of new technology and methods as well as the industry's utilization of its work force.' The employers succeeded in gaining union recognition of the principle that future savings in labour costs would not be shared amongst remaining workers, but used to finance severance payments and improved pensions. The two sides undertook to present joint evidence on these lines to the Royal Commission on the Press.

The Joint Industry Statement to the Royal Commission summarized the progress made in the three working parties and concluded that the savings made should be used to provide adequate redundancy payments, improved pensions, retraining facilities, and greater employment security for workers remaining.

Both parties equally recognise that the savings achieved as a result of this agreed programme must not be dissipated through lost production and attendant losses in revenue arising from unofficial stoppages of work. All unions involved in these discussions therefore reaffirm the need for union members to observe strictly the existing national and house disputes procedures so that continued production in the future can be assured. The employers on their part reaffirm that there will be continuing close consultation with unions and in particular that the introduction of new technology and methods will be dealt with in accordance with the terms of this joint statement.[9]

At an early stage in the discussions of the working parties it became clear that money would have to be obtained from outside the industry, even to finance a minimum programme. The joint presentation of evidence to the Royal Commission was part of a move to explore the possibility of financial assistance from the Government, although the employers had strong reservations about obtaining financial assistance from government sources because of a potential threat to the freedom of the press. In the event the Royal Commission did not propose generous financial assistance, although the Government was prepared to consider it (see below, pp. 337-8). A less controversial source of funds was the European Social Fund of the EEC. However, funds from the EEC could be obtained by a joint institution only, entrusted with responsibilities in the public interest. To satisfy the appropriate authorities that the joint discussions qualified as a joint social institution the two sides agreed, on 26 March, to the formation of a Joint Standing Committee before the working parties reported, subject to the approval of union Executives, the council of the NPA, and Mirror Group Newspapers. The Joint Standing Committee was to come into operation when the working parties had completed their discussions.

Its initial institutional existence was therefore shadowy — an essence without a form. An application for funds from the EEC for financial assistance with the cost of retraining was therefore submitted, through the appropriate British government channels, at the end of March.

The Joint Working Parties made slower progress than expected, and the further projected meeting of the full Joint Standing Committee was held over. Both the pensions and the voluntary-redundancy working parties made substantial progress, and by early May had prepared agreed reports: the Working Party on decasualization made slower progress. The following sections deal briefly with the issues covered by each Working Party in turn.

Union representatives claimed that pensions in the industry were seriously inadequate, and constituted a major reason why workers were unwilling to retire, even when they reached retirement age: in 1975 the industry employed an estimated 1,048 production workers aged 65 or more. The Royal Commission's research indicated that pensions arrangements were not significantly worse than in private industry generally, although there was of course scope for improvement.[10] The Government Actuary analysed twenty-two pension schemes, operated by nine Fleet Street houses. All houses had either separate schemes for different groups of employees — usually management/supervisory, journalists, and production workers — or more generous pension levels for more senior staff. Unlike much of private industry, all employees, including 'regular casuals', were eligible for membership, subject to relatively brief waiting periods — five houses made membership compulsory. The majority of schemes (fifteen) were 'fixed salary' schemes, although only 'about a half' of final salary schemes were based upon gross earnings: seven of the fifteen schemes provided pensions based upon one-sixtieth per year of service, the remainder on lower rates of benefit. Of the non-final salary schemes, three were 'average salary' schemes, three were fixed benefit schemes, and one was financed entirely by employees' voluntary contributions. ('Average salary' = pension based upon pensionable salary earned that year: 'fixed benefit' = pension accrual based on a flat rate independent of salary earned.) The Government

Actuary judged that the Fleet Street pensions schemes provided retirement benefits comparable with those general in private industry, but did not make comparable provision for widows' pensions: 'about three-quarters' would have needed improvement to meet the criteria for contracting out of the supplementary second tier of the National Insurance pensions scheme.

Both managment and unions agreed that improved pensions for Fleet Street production workers were socially desirable, and necessary to facilitate changes in manpower levels in the industry. At the very least, improved pensions were necessary to provide for employees over pensionable age still working in the industry. The unions' ideas were presented to the employers early in January 1976. Their objective was a retirement pension of 67 per cent of final earnings; workers leaving the industry were to receive either a frozen pension, an endowment life-assurance policy or an annuity, or early pensions if close to retirement age. A separately financed fund was to be established to finance supplementations to company benefits, as a means of ensuring similar benefits for different houses: employers with poor pensions schemes were to make greater contributions. The employers' response was cautious but encouraging, setting up a working group to examine the union proposals. Although employers wished to give impetus to the joint discussions, it was obvious that the union proposals would be extremely expensive and highly complex to administer. The employers' representatives undertook to obtain relevant information from employers and to invite experts to cost union proposals on the basis of available figures — although it was recognized that future costs would be based upon different figures, as a major aspect of the exercise was to reduce labour in the industry. Detailed discussions were held in the early months of 1976 under the aegis of a Pensions Working Party, consisting of representatives of all of the publishers and unions concerned: despite the wide differences of view, an agreed report to the Joint Committee of managing directors and general secretaries was ready by the beginning of May, although union representatives felt that they had substantially failed to achieve their original objectives.

The initial union proposals were not carefully defined — inevitably, as a first attempt in a highly complex area. There were five major areas of uncertainty which required exploration: costings; the link between company and 'industry' schemes; the relationship between the proposed scheme and state pensions; the extent to which pensions should be set against new technology savings; and administrative arrangements. Although the scheme was never finally worked out, much less implemented, because of the overall rejection of the Joint Standing Committee by union members, it is worth examining these five areas briefly, for they indicate the ramifying social consequences of the proposed new technology.

The trade unions did not make any detailed statements about the financial assumptions upon which they had based their proposals. How would the pension be linked to years of service? (The maximum then permitted by the Inland Revenue was two-thirds of final salary after ten years of service: more usual was two-thirds after forty years, pro rata.) Were earnings to be full earnings or basic rates? Was the final year to be simply the final year or the average of the best three over the final ten? Should provision for back service be on the same basis as future service? Should employees be expected to pay increased contributions? On the assumptions that pensions would be related to length of service, with a maximum of 40/60ths, that earnings would be full earnings in the final year of service, that back service would be included on the same basis as future service, that 50 per cent widows' benefit would be paid, and that staff included regular (but not 'casual') casuals, the employers calculated the cost of the unions' proposals at £72m for back service, and £7.5m as additional to existing future pensions commitments. The employers, especially houses in poor financial circumstances such as the *Guardian*, regarded this as impossibly extravagant, especially since they regarded severance payments and re-establishing financial viability as the first charges upon future savings in labour costs. They therefore hoped that some of the additional finance that might be available from the Government in the context of major changes in the industry might be used to fund pensions improvements. However, in the Government's view pensions in the industry were already above the level normal in private industry, and there was therefore no possibility of government finance. The employers therefore put forward a much reduced scheme, which would constitute a minimum target for individual houses. Pensions were to be based upon ½ per cent of final earnings for each year of service prior to 1977, and 1 per cent for each year of service after 1977; final salary was to be the average of the best three tax years of the last ten; and earnings were to be PAYE earnings, without any deductions. Workers retiring after forty years' service would receive about 60 per cent of final earnings, when the scheme reached maturity, derived from their occupational pensions and from the state pension. The employers estimated the extra cost of the new terms at £13.0m, with additional annual contributions of approximately £2.0m. Importantly, the extra costs of the pensions were to be conditional upon final agreement, at national and house level, on necessary manpower savings. The Joint Working Party's final report to the main Joint Standing Committee contained the employers' offer, to the scarcely surprised disappointment of the trade-union representatives.

Formulating proposals on the relation between occupational pensions schemes and state pensions schemes was complicated by the need to take into account the two-tier pensions structure established by the 'Castle' Social Security Pensions Act (1975), which was due to come into full effect in April 1978. Occupational pension scheme trustees had to decide whether to contract out of the second tier – participation in the first tier was compulsory. The situation was further complicated by the differences in pensions arrangements between houses, and therefore the differing attitudes towards contracting in. There was no divergence between unions and employers on this issue. For the unions, the source of the funding was irrelevant; for the employers, the decision to contract in or to contract out depended partly upon actuarial calculations and partly upon the complex problems posed by members of occupational pensions schemes who were not employed in national newspapers. In the event, the components of the minimum-pensions objective were not specified precisely: it was recognized that different houses might wish to adopt different attitudes towards the second tier in the state pensions scheme. It was explicitly agreed that the basic state pension, for which employers' contributions were compulsory, would be counted in the pensions calculations.

Possible differences in attitude towards state pensions schemes were only one aspect of differences between houses, which made the construction of a detailed national scheme impossible. There were differences between houses in the levels of pensions paid, the coverage of different schemes, the number of employees outside national newspapers included in the newspapers scheme, as well as the level of employee contributions. It was therefore agreed that the national level agreement should simply comprise the establishment of a minimum objective, which houses would attempt to achieve as they made progress in labour savings at house level. The JSC envisaged that the Joint Working Party would remain in being to monitor progress towards achieving the minimum objectives and to consider outstanding issues, including non-scheme members, continuing casuals, transferability, and the implications of the 1975 Social Security Pensions Act.

Throughout the discussions the employers maintained that improved pensions could be financed only out of the savings made by changes in manning levels and the introduction of new technology. The total benefits 'package' could not be improved by new money without being included in the increase in earnings which would affect the implementation of the conditional tax changes announced in the April 1976 Budget, and accepted by the TUC under the Social Contract. Union representatives argued that improved pensions were a separate issue from prospective savings, and should not be made to depend upon prospective savings from new agreements. The final agreement bridged the gap between the two positions by stating that individual companies would have to decide upon the timetable for achieving the minimum levels 'against the background of the progress made in the manning and new technology programmes affecting their particular enterprise'; the new levels could only be financed if 'part of the economic benefits expected from the revised manning arrangements and the use of new technology [were to be] available for pension purposes.'[11] The door was not closed on the possibility that some of the finance for improved pensions would be 'new money'; but such new money would be conditional upon some savings under new agreements.

The decision to restrict the national level to establishing minimum objectives was a disappointment to some union officials, who hoped that a national scheme would facilitate transferability of pension rights between employers. Indeed, at one stage it was suggested that pensions might be organized on an 'occupational' basis, directly involving the unions in pension-fund management. The employers were sceptical of the transferability of pension rights, partly because of the wide variations in pensions (at least some of which would remain even after the completion of the Pensions Working Group scheme, which was only a minimum scheme), and doubtful of the need because of the low level of movement between houses once workers had obtained jobs in Fleet Street. The question of transferability was deferred for further discussion. The employers' view that transferability was irrelevant was misleading, since the intention of the Joint Standing Committee was to encourage the restructuring of the labour force on Fleet Street. Although the major element in this process involved workers leaving the industry, the disturbance would probably also be accompanied by increased mobility between houses: past experience would no longer be an accurate guide. Moreover, the amount of movement between Fleet Street houses differed for different groups of workers: NATSOPA members, especially in supervisory and clerical areas, had a higher level of movement than other groups, and therefore a greater interest in transferability.

The Working Party on Pensions successfully reached agreement early in May 1976 on the terms of its report to the Joint Standing Committee. The Joint Standing Committee in due course agreed to the report, which was published in November 1976.[12] Although the unions had not achieved their specific pensions objectives, they had established the objective of bringing up to an acceptable — if not generous —

standard all pensions schemes: a minority of schemes already exceeded that standard, but many did not. The Working Party on Voluntary Redundancy similarly reached agreement only slightly behind schedule. In the initial note of November 1975 the unions recognized the need to reduce manning levels in the industry, to be achieved without compulsory redundancy; the financial impact of redundancy was to be limited by severance payments, either in a lump sum or in the form of guaranteed income maintenance. Workers accepting severance payments were to give up their union membership cards and leave the industry. The employers' objective throughout was the establishment of 'reasonable' manning levels, achieved through voluntary redundancy, no automatic replacement, restriction on future entry into Fleet Street, no future sharing of savings, and reform of the casual and permit system.

To encourage workers to leave the industry, the unions proposed two alternative schemes. Under option A workers leaving the industry would receive a lump-sum payment varying with age: 65+, one week's average earnings per year of continuous service, with a minimum equivalent to six months' earnings, payment in lieu of notice as per contract, and outstanding holiday entitlements; 60-65, two weeks' average earnings per year of continuous service, with a ceiling of 50 per cent of what the employee would have earned up to the age of 65½, with other conditions as for 65+; under 60, four weeks' earnings per year of continuous service, with other conditions as for 65+. Alternatively, under option B, workers would receive a minimum income guarantee for five years. The employers accepted option A, subject to amendments on the provisions for the 60-65 group, and concern about the estimated cost of £40m, but had difficulty in making a realistic estimate of the costs of option B. Accordingly, the employers offered to devise a scheme which would cost up to the financial commitments involved in option A, based upon a combination of the principles of options A and B: this would reduce the cash-flow problems which immediate implementation of option A would involve, especially for financially weaker houses, and limit the open-ended financial commitment involved in option B. Option C involved payment of a sum based upon age, length of service, and earnings. Individual gross entitlement would be based upon one week's gross pay for each year of age between the age of 16 and the time of leaving, half a week's gross pay for each completed year of service, and a number of weeks' pay graded according to gross weekly pay, ranging from two weeks' pay for workers earning £40 to fifty-two weeks' pay for workers earning £240 per week. The gross entitlement was to be paid in three parts: a lump sum equivalent to the appropriate government redundancy terms; net income guaranteed for five years, or until future earnings equal current net pay, or until gross entitlement was exhausted; settlement of the 'balance' at the end of five years in any way desired by the employee. The size of the gross entitlement was based upon recognition that obtaining new jobs or adjusting to new jobs once found became more difficult with age, that employees expected job property rights to increase with length of service, and therefore required increased compensation, and that workers with higher earnings would have greater difficulty in obtaining comparable jobs (a view-point expressed by NGA representatives). The three elements in the severance-pay entitlement were designed to incorporate all three major principles.

The scheme devised represented a compromise between the union desire for maximum flexibility for their members, and the employers' desire to minimize costs, consistent with obtaining union agreement. From the beginning the employers conceded that they would be obliged to accept 'full social responsibility' for workers wishing to leave the industry: they regarded union acceptance of voluntary redundancy as a major breakthrough, and were prepared to pay accordingly. The employers were prepared to pay up to £40m to secure union agreement, the estimated cost of option A. They initially hoped that at least part of the money would be provided by the government, as a once and for all payment which would not pose any permanent threat to press independence: the payment would be to establish the industry on a secure basis, similar to payments made in the docks industry. However, the Royal Commission on the Press did not recommend government funds in their report, a recommenda-

tion predictably accepted by the government: 'the publishers
will have to ensure that they can meet the terms on which
they agree from their own resources with such assistance by
way of loan as may be available under our recommendations.'[13] The Royal Commission recommended that the
industry should raise funds in the private sector, most appropriately from Finance for Industry. Where houses could
not meet FFI's condition the government should grant relief
of up to 4 per cent on the interest payable on loans for two
years, the loans to be used to finance redundancy compensation, decasualization, capital expenditure on new technology, and to meet problems of liquidity or debt structure.
The Royal Commission was fearful of government being
placed in such a position as to exercise 'partisan' influence
over newspapers, and of possible accusations of treating the
industry preferentially compared with other private industries.[14] Following rejection of any possibility of significant
government assistance, the employers recognized that funds
would have to be found from within the industry (except for
any financial assistance which might be made available by
the EEC, see below, pp. 197-8). Accordingly, the employers
were concerned to spread the cost over as long a period as
possible — hence the complex three-part arrangement for
payment. To meet the objection that the three-part scheme
constituted an enforced deferment of entitlement, the
employers agreed that where houses could face the financial
consequences of accepting option A forthwith, they would
have the option of doing so. Moreover, where houses were
already operating voluntary-redundancy schemes on different
principles from those agreed, those arrangements could continue. (The footnote heading refers to 'Better conditions',
but the text refers solely to 'different principles': it was presumably envisaged that the new agreement would automatically supersede 'worse' conditions.[15])

The employers' objective was to achieve a balanced run-
down in the labour force. They were therefore concerned
that the original 'option A' proposed by the unions favoured
the over-60s unduly, and did not provide sufficient incentive
for younger men to leave the industry, thus creating an
imbalance in the age structure in the future (although many

employers would have been pleased with such an outcome). They were also concerned that proposals for income maintenance would not be attractive to workers aged 60 or more, with fewer than five years to retirement. The problems involved in attempting to retain control of manpower levels whilst providing generous financial incentives for voluntary redundancy were well known from research in other industries, and had been brought home to Fleet Street management by the experience of the *Observer* in 1975. When the *Observer* was on the brink of closure in the summer of 1975 management negotiated a 30 per cent reduction in staff costs, to be achieved by redundancy: the chapels involved undertook to ensure that sufficient workers left to achieve the savings required. Although the terms were less generous than those suggested by the JSC more workers wished to leave than management desired, especially NATSOPA machine-room members. The *Observer* was therefore faced with severe problems of labour shortage in the autumn of 1975.[16]

On one major issue the employers gained a major concession in the agreement on voluntary redundancy: the agreement was not a minimum agreement, which could be improved upon by house- or chapel-level negotiations — in this respect it differed importantly from the pensions proposals. The agreement was not inflexible on the precise calculations to be used in assessing gross entitlement: houses could decide whether to follow option A or option C. However, it was specifically agreed that 'there is a preparedness in each office to go up to, but not exceed, the cost that would have been involved under the proposal originally put forward by the unions.'[17] In this respect, the agreement differed from the comments of the Royal Commission. After discussing the weaknesses of the Special Severance Scheme in the docks 1972–3, the Commission commented:

Circumstances differ among publishers and departments inside publishing houses in the same way as they differ among ports, and among port employers. These differences concern not only the amount of redundancy considered necessary, but also the age structure and composition of the labour force.

Such differences imply that a scheme which simply established terms to apply across the industry as a whole, and then left it to the individual worker to choose whether or not to accept them would not be satisfactory. We consider that one lesson of the [Special Severence Scheme] is that redundancies in the newspaper industry within an agreed national framework should be planned and agreed between employers and unions in the individual houses so as to produce a pre-dicted reduction in numbers.[18]

The employers rightly thought that the agreement would have to contain firm national-level limits to the extent of variation possible at house level, to prevent competitive bargaining between chapels. For this reason the agreement provided that reference would be made to the JSC when any 'difficulty' arose as to the 'formula to be adopted by individual offices'.[19]

Both the Pensions and the Voluntary Redundancy Working Parties reached agreement only slightly behind schedule. But this success was partly achieved by pushing all issues relating to the most intractable issue, decasualization, into the lap of the third Working Party, the Decasualisation Working Party. Hence the Pensions Agreement stated that it would not be possible to report on benefits for 'any con-tinuing casual workforce' until the Decasualisation Working Party had concluded its report, whilst the Voluntary Redundancy Agreement contained no mention of decasuali-zation,[20] which, not surprisingly, proved to be the major stumbling-block to the successful conclusion of the joint discussions. As in the docks, fluctuations in labour demand, due to variation in paging, in circulation, or in sickness and holiday needs, were met by the employment of approximately 2,200 casual workers — primarily NATSOPA members, mainly in the machine room, and SOGAT members in publishing areas, although some NGA stereo members were employed on a casual basis. In October 1975 25 per cent of casual shifts were worked in machine rooms, and 65 per cent in publishing rooms; just over half the shifts were worked on the popular daily newspapers, one-fifth on the popular Sundays and the bulk of the remainder in quality Sunday newspapers: comparatively few casual shifts were worked on quality daily newspapers.[21] As in the docks, both unions and managements agreed that casual working was undesirable: unions because of the uncertainties and worry experienced by their members and the potential threat which an institutionalized excess labour force posed to their regular workers or regular casuals; managements because they had long since lost the control over manning levels which casual working seemed to facilitate, and were unable to rely upon the quality of performance of casual workers. Accordingly, the joint statement published on 8 December contained an undertaking that employers would fulfil their social obligations to all employees in the industry, both regulars and casuals. It was to prove difficult to translate such general willingness into a specific agreement, since casuals could be identified only in the context of agreed manning levels. Establishing such levels, and therefore the extent of casual working, was at the heart of Fleet Street's problems, especially for houses using casuals extensively.

The unions proposed to achieve decasualization by jointly agreeing with the employers the existing pattern of casual working in the industry, and by NATSOPA and SOGAT, as the major unions concerned, identifying a corresponding number of individuals able to do the work. The workers would then either be given regular employment with one employer or allocated to a pool of labour supported by the industry. Workers in the pool would be hired out to particular houses, who would be charged a fee for their services. Casual workers, whether employed or in the pool, would be entitled to the same benefits as other workers. The employers accepted the unions' objective of eliminating casual working, and that the principles proposed were 'forward looking'. There was, however, a major difference between management and unions, which it was easy to bridge in general terms, but which was always likely to create difficulties in detail: the fixed quantity for the unions was the size of the labour force — work was to be found for the members involved; the fixed quantity for management was the work to be performed — members were to be adjusted to the amount of work available. The terms of reference for the working party were appropriately opaque: 'It is recognized that any recommendations would need to be phased in as and when optimum manning levels are agreed, and taking into account the agreed total staffs of regulars, Regular

Jobbers, and Casual casuals within the industry.' Management wished to link decasualization with new manning levels,
and thus a smaller decasualized labour force; the unions
wished to separate the two issues and decasualize the labour
force before agreement was reached on new manning levels.

Owing to this fundamental disagreement, progress in the
Working Party on Decasualisation was slow, and threatened
the viability of the whole JSC. For example, it proved
impossible to present an agreed report to the February Joint
Meeting of general secretaries and managing directors. The
union side maintained that, by linking decasualization to
agreed manning levels, agreement on decasualization would
be postponed for at least a year. Moreover, it was inappropriate to attempt to link the two together, since decasualization was linked to the national level, involving regularizing
the position of the Fleet Street labour force, whilst the
establishment of optimum manning levels was essentially a
house-level activity. After protracted discussion a strategy
for dealing with the issue of decasualization was agreed,
rather than a detailed set of proposals. Management and
unions agreed:

(i)   to the formulation of a register of *bona fide* casuals wholly
       employed on National Newspapers.
(ii)   to determine at Branch/Chapel/Management level the number
       of employees required to be registered in each office to accom-
       modate reviewed and subsequently agreed staffing levels.
(iii) when (i) and (ii) have been finalised this will establish the extent
       of the residual casual labour force.
(iv)   the total deal will then be capable of being costed and a com-
       prehensive proposal formulated for submission to the Joint
       Standing Committee, when decisions can be taken on the imple-
       mentation of these arrangements.[22]

The issue of how to achieve decasualization was postponed.
Employers conceded the principle of establishing a register,
leaving to the future detailed discussion of the numbers and
the names, involved. (Problems could arise in the future from
the London Central Branch of SOGAT's branch policy of
refusing to supply names, and it was recognized that there
might be an element of double counting.) The conditional
nature of the agreement was further underlined by the

second clause, which stated that future staffing levels would 'reviewed and subsequently agreed': it did not specify clearly by whom or how, nor was there any mention of optimum manning levels.

Throughout 1976 economic activity in the industry continued on a low level, with a continuing low level of advertising revenue, circulation drifting downwards, and the prospects of further increases in newsprint prices, due in August. It was feared that two or three newspapers would be in danger of closing, the evening papers being in an especially weak situation. There was therefore anxiety, both within the industry and outside, especially in the Government, about the apparent failure to capitalize upon the promise of the Joint Committee's evidence to the Royal Commission, especially the slow progress being made on decasualization, and the failure to place the Joint Committee on a firm footing. This lack of progress contributed to the initial failure of the application to the European Social Fund for £7.5m for vocational retraining. When the application was discussed in June the French Government representatives opposed the grant, on the grounds that the Joint Standing Committee was not an appropriate institution. A final decision was postponed until November, pending the British Government's provision of a full statement on the legal position of the Joint Standing Committee. Accordingly, in order to sustain the progress of the application for money to the European Social Fund, and in the expectation that the Decasualisation Working Party was about to reach agreement, the general secretaries and managing directors met to consider the future of the Joint Standing Committee on 16 July. The meeting elected W. H. Keys, who had been chairman hitherto, as chairman for twelve months, with M. J. Hussey, vice-chairman of the NPA, as vice-chairman, and decided that future meetings should be on a regular monthly basis.

From July the JSC took on a more formal existence.[23] The objectives of the committee were:

to secure the joint action of management, trade unions and employees to a common aim; the viability of the national newspaper industry, to maintain levels of employment compatible with a company's long-term viability with career opportunity and job security for all staff, to develop policies essential to the well-being of the industry and to provide a forum for dealing with problems of immediate urgency.

The committee comprised the general secretaries of SOGAT, NATSOPA, NGA, and NUJ and representatives of the EETPU and AUEW involved in national newspapers, together with the chief executives or their representatives of the eight NPA houses plus Mirror Group Newspapers Ltd. and Thomson Withy Grove Ltd. SLADE refused throughout to take any part in the Committee. The secretary of the TUC Printing Industries Committee, Kenneth Graham, and the director of the NPA, John Dixey, were jointly responsible for the administration of the committee, and were permanent members. Employer members were invited to submit man-power and technology Planning Proposals for the coming twelve months in detail, and for the two years following in outline. The Planning Proposals were to be considered by the JSC. The committee was charged with a number of specific responsibilities:

(a)   devise and establish a policy framework and procedures:
  — to enable staff to volunteer to leave the industry or retire before normal age;
  — to enable women over 60 and men over 65 to retire from employment in the industry;
  — to regularise all employment and ensure a wholly regular work force committed to a full normal working week or single shift appearance;
  — to establish minimum common scales of pension benefit.
  — to consider the implications of the introduction of new technology, and the co-ordination of plans for its introduction.
(b)   to represent the industry in discussions with Government and other authorities, where appropriate and mutually agreed.
(c)   to devise and monitor comprehensive procedures for the settlement of disputes.
(d)   to raise funds for, set up, monitor and ensure the completion of any training activity associated with the introduction of new technology.
(e)   to provide resources to advise staff leaving the industry on the use of financial benefits and on alternative employment possibilities. In co-ordination with the Department of Employment and Man-power Services Commission, to advise on Government training resources and organise retraining.
(f)   to examine demarcation issues arising from current production methods and new technology.

Decisions were to be by majority vote, except in matters of major principle, when any decision would be unanimous. The range of responsibilities was carefully graded, to make clear what responsibilities lay with the new committee, and what at house level: in the weakest category, it was only to 'examine' demarcation issues; more strongly, it was to 'consider the implications' of annual company manpower and technology proposals; yet more strongly, it was to 'devise and establish a policy framework and procedures' for voluntary redundancy, retirement, and pensions; yet more strongly still, it was to 'devise and monitor' comprehensive procedures for the settlement of disputes; finally it was to 'raise funds for, set up, monitor and ensure the completion of any training' associated with the new technology. The committee thus had limited 'executive' powers on training, but was restricted to devising procedures and exercising oversight in other areas, except where it was merely expected to record, and presumably comment upon, house-level proposals.

The distinctive position of training is worthy of comment, for it involved the JSC in an unusually active role. Training facilities for the new technology were of course provided by the companies at house level, to the limited extent permitted by unions before final agreement on the JSC, by the industry through the PPITB, and by public educational institutions like the London College of Printing. However, the JSC's application to the European Social Fund was for funds for vocational training, and to qualify for grants the JSC had to be charged with tasks in the public interest. It would therefore not have been sufficient for the JSC to supervise training, since that would have involved the JSC simply acting as a channel for EEC funds to other institutions, both public and private. The JSC was therefore charged with direct responsibility for training, which was financed by levies on employers, trade unions making a contribution towards administrative expenses. Provision was made for employers to carry out training on behalf of the JSC, and to obtain reimbursement from the JSC. Responsibility for scrutinizing and validating the training provided by the JSC was to lie with the PPITB. The extent to which the JSC would have been able to create an effective training function was never tested: its success would have depended heavily upon the co-operation of the PPITB. Since the Board had only a very small role in Fleet Street before the establishment of the JSC, the Board was eager to use its good influences to make the scheme effective. Whether the complex tripartite system of house, JSC, and PPITB involvement would have worked, or resulted in hopeless administrative confusion, it is impossible to say: at the very least it would have involved a quite major expansion in back-up facilities available to the JSC.

Both management and unions recognized that the JSC's success depended upon establishing effective joint institutions at house level. From the beginning it had been agreed that the introduction of new technology would be jointly supervised. However, the manner of that joint supervision was unclear. Since the constitution of the JSC provided only limited scope for JSC action, even greater importance became attached to establishing effective joint committees at house level. The extensive work required to launch such committees could only be undertaken after the principles underlying the JSC had been accepted by the unions and the companies, but a strategy for setting them up was required to provide credibility for the overall committee. *Programme for Action* proposed that Joint House Committees would consist of up to seven management representatives and two representatives from each union, except for NATSOPA, who would have three to ensure clerical representation: one representative from each union would be a chapel representative, whilst the other 'would be a nominee of the union', probably a full-time official.[24] In addition, each union would appoint liaison officers to liaise between the JSC and the JHCs, who would have the right to attend meetings. Employers initially hoped that full-time officials would play a more central role in the JHCs, possibly with the general secretaries attending the inaugural meetings of JHCs: but full-time officials were sensibly cautious about committing themselves fully to such involvement, since they accurately feared criticism for attempting to undermine chapel autonomy. The objectives of the Joint House Committees were:

(a)   To discuss and reach agreement on the more effective use of manpower in all areas, including new technology and consequent optimum manning levels.

(b)   To facilitate, under guidelines from the JSC, the introduction of voluntary redundancy, decasualisation, and minimum pension standards in line with the adopted recommendations of the appropriate working parties.

(c)   To consider and jointly co-operate in all steps necessary to facilitate the smooth introduction of new technology, including remuneration, selection and training.

(d)   To develop manpower and technology policies to ensure the future well-being of the Company and its employees, and to provide a regular forum for dealing with problems that arise.

The JHCs were thus charged with responsibility for supervising the introduction of new technology. *But*: 'Negotiations on specific matters will need to be conducted between management and union (or unions) and the chapels concerned. Regular reports should be made on these negotiations to JHCs.' Negotiations between management and unions would thus continue in the usual way on 'specific matters', which would be 'reported' to the JSC. The JSC would not have any authority over these negotiations, despite being charged with ensuring the smooth introduction of the new technology. It is difficult to conceive how specific matters could fail to fall within the remit of the JHC, nor how negotiations between management and chapels could fail to cut across the decisions of the JHCs.

Reflecting the employers' concern with the need for continuity in production, the JSC also devised a new disputes procedure for the industry, to replace the existing fourteen disputes procedures.[25] The procedure contained provision for the customary two stages — company level and industry level. Issues of dispute should initially be raised by the FOC with the departmental head; if unresolved, they should be referred to a meeting of the FOC, branch officers, departmental and senior managers. If unresolved at house level, the first stage of the industry level provided for a meeting between managers and union(s) concerned, including national or other full-time officials. If the national level meeting were to be unsuccessful, the parties involved were to refer the dispute to a JSC Disputes Committee of four members, drawn from JSC members not involved in the dispute. The parties involved were to agree the terms of reference for the JSC Disputes Committee; it could conciliate or arbitrate, and if it arbitrated it could make binding awards or not. Finally, if the JSC Disputes Committee failed either side could give twenty-eight days' notice of 'any action proposed'. Throughout the procedure the *status quo* prior to the difference was to be preserved and operations were to continue without disruption. To avoid delays, there were to be no more than five days between each stage, except where both sides agreed to a longer period. Importantly, the procedure explicitly excluded inter-union disputes, which were to be dealt with through procedures to be formulated by the members of the TUC Printing Industries Committee. The procedure agreement provides an important illustration of a number of general features of the JSCs' work. First, the procedure was commended to individual houses — it was not mandatory. It was thought desirable to establish a model agreement, which provided for relatively speedy resolution at house level, to avoid accusations of 'hiding behind procedure'. Secondly, it was decided that the JHC should not be involved in house-level disputes, as they might create difficulties for an institution which would, in any event, possibly have difficult early stages of development. Finally, it was recognized that the major problems in Fleet Street did not stem from inadequate procedures, but from failure to follow the procedures which existed. There are no precise figures available, but the majority of disputes in the industry were in breach of procedure. However, it was thought that a new procedural agreement, endorsed by the general secretaries, would provide an impetus for improved adherence in the future.

The terms of *Programme for Action* were agreed in October, before the meeting of the European Social Fund Committee to which the application for funds had been deferred in June. The meeting of the Social Committee provided a deadline; the application was likely to be deferred for a substantial period if it was not ready at the beginning of November, and delays would increase doubts about the appropriateness of the JSC as a joint institution. The application was successful, the Fund granting half of the funds requested.

More problematic was the reception to be accorded to the work of the JSC by members of the unions involved. It was recognized that a major effort would be required to 'sell' the JSC to union members. It was therefore decided to launch a new journal, *New Era*, to indicate the progress being made in joint consultation, but the launching was deferred until after union members had expressed a view on the JSC. *Programme for Action*, containing the working party proposals for dealing with voluntary redundancies, pensions, and decasualization, together with agreed documents on Joint House Committees, Disputes Procedure, Training, Education and Counselling, and on the 'Procedure on Manpower and New Technology', was published on 2 December. The document was prefaced by a note from the general secretaries of NATSOPA, NGA, SOGAT, and the NUJ, and a representative from the EETPU: the AUEW representative on the JSC did not sign the note. The employers believed that a joint preface would be counter-productive. The union representatives commended the proposals to their members:

If . . . the provisional agreements are rejected, there will be no agreed overall framework through which the problems facing the industry can be dealt with, and the consequences of this could well, in our view, be extremely grave and have a serious affect on the viability of some titles in the industry, the maintenance of employment, and the continuation of a strong and effective trade union organization.[26]

The programme was rejected: all unions except the NUJ showed a clear majority against accepting the programme. The reasons for the rejection differed from union to union, some had little to do with the specific issue, and are explored elsewhere (above, pp. 108–9, 134). But the basic issue was simple: how serious were the difficulties facing the industry? If it was felt that the industry was facing severe difficulties, it is difficult to see what union members could have wanted that was not provided in *Programme for Action*. There was a guarantee against compulsory redundancy, very generous terms for voluntary redundancy, and considerable scope for bargaining over the basic issues of manning levels and demarcation lines. The agreement did not open the flood-gates to employers' proposals for new technology. Nor was there any prospect of alternative sources of funds: there was no possibility of extensive government help — the cautious report of the Royal Commission ruled this out, either to existing publishers or through the establishment of a new national publishing company. On the other hand, if it was believed that the industry was not in serious economic difficulties, that the employers were simply crying 'wolf', as they had done before, and that either the economic situation would improve or that new financial resources would be brought into the industry, there was little incentive to accept *Programme for Action*. Judgements of the industry's economic prospects were difficult to make. The situation had improved significantly between 1975 and late 1976 — by the winter of 1976 advertising revenues were rising again, and the purchase of the *Observer* by Atlantic-Richfield had reinforced the confidence that the prestige of Fleet Street was such that 'something would always turn up.' Moreover, there was the view that if the industry was going to contract, the unions would 'go down fighting.'

The *Programme for Action* was put to union members as a comprehensive policy: it was a 'package deal', and ballots were not taken on individual items. Following its rejection, there was therefore the formal possibility of splitting the proposals, and developing each section in turn. However, this option was not pursued: the rejection had been too complete. The reputations of the general secretaries had been so damaged that they were not prepared to continue with a policy disapproved of by a clear majority of their membership. Nor were employers eager to proceed with the attempt to obtain joint agreement at national level: the collapse of *Programme for Action* naturally left employers free to attempt to negotiate agreements on new technology at house level, as MGN and TNL attempted to do. The collapse of the programme also had the effect of further discrediting the NPA, who had played a major role in setting up the programme, liaising closely with TUC officials who serviced the TUC Printing Industries Committee, and servicing the JSC from the employers' side. If the programme had been successful it would have given the NPA a greatly expanded role, beyond that of providing an industrial relations 'fire-fighting' service. The failure of the programme did not simply mean that a prosperous future did not materialize: it meant that the prestige invested in getting the JSC off the ground was lost. The employers' sectionalism and preference for house-level agreements were reinforced.

Although the JSC proposals were rejected, the European Social Fund application had been successful: the JSC therefore had to decide upon arrangements for training. Since it was expected that individual houses would proceed with the new technology, it was believed that the fund could be used to support such training. However, the rejection of the JSC meant that union officials were not in a position to state what unions would be willing to agree to on training. No joint institutions were set up, and therefore no grant from the Social Fund was received. It was decided that the JSC would remain in being, and meet on an *ad hoc* basis in future: but no meetings have been held and no reference to a possible role for the JSC has been made in the extensive discussions on industrial relations in 1978 and 1979. The JSC has simply faded away, as the Joint Board did before it.

ii

The history of joint institutions, whether of consultation or participation, in British industrial relations as a whole, not simply in Fleet Street, has not been encouraging: although joint institutions have been successfully established, their practical effects have been limited. The extensive discussions between major employers and the TUC following the Mond-Turner initiative in 1928 and the continued survival of the National Economic Development Office and its attendant 'little Neddies' indicate the continuing attraction of joint institutions for industrial statesmen.[27] Lower-level joint institutions, dealing with more detailed issues, have succeeded only in limited areas such as training, or working as industry pressure groups to reduce 'unfair competition' from overseas. Except for a very small minority of firms with a principled commitment to joint institutions, the scope of joint decision-making at company and plant level has been narrowly re-

stricted, usually to welfare and safety issues. In short, the
more specific the issue the lower the chances of success for
joint institutions. The reasons for this situation lie beyond
the scope of this study, in both the institutions of British
industrial relations and the assumption of participants. The
historical development of British trade unionism has involved
the establishment of more securely based collective-bargaining
arrangements, formal and informal, at plant level than in
other industrialized countries, thus limiting the potential for
joint institutions — although this is more to restate the
problem than to explain it. A further element may be the
pervasive assumption amongst active trade unionists that the
interests of workers and management are fundamentally
opposed — a feeling especially likely where managers stress
the importance of unity and question the legitimacy of trade-
union activity.[28] Whatever the explanation for the generally
limited success of joint institutions throughout British
industry, it is possible to pin-point specific problems in the
development of Fleet Street's Joint Standing Committee
which shed light on the general issue. The major relevant
issues are the relationship between joint institutions and
collective bargaining, the appropriate scope of national-level
agreements, the pressures making for unity and division
amongst employers and unions as well as between both
groups, and the appropriate administrative arrangements
for joint institutions once established on a permanent basis.

    Whether the joint institution is legislative, executive, or
consultative, the most difficult issue to resolve is the relationship with collective-bargaining machinery. Trade unionists
have seen joint institutions as a threat to union effectiveness
in collective bargaining, even when participation has involved
an extension of trade-union influence, either through providing
a rival system of representation or by placing individual
workers' representatives in a situation of irreconcilable role
conflict. As the most forthright opponents of worker representation on company Boards of Directors, the EETPU,
argued in their evidence to the Bullock Commission:

First, there is the institutional impossibility of separating the boardroom consultation from the potential negotiating implications behind
the issues under discussion. Second, there is the irreconcilable split

loyalties of the worker directors themselves. They will find it immensely difficult to separate their boardroom responsibilities dictated by business priorities from their representative functions derived from their relationship with the workforce.[29]

Proponents of joint institutions have argued that joint institutions would not damage existing arrangements for collective bargaining — might even improve them by extending their scope to new levels (the company) or over new issues (long-term investment decisions) — not that damage to collective-bargaining institutions would be unimportant, or possibly even desirable. Hence the Bullock Commission commented:

We see no necessary contradiction between board level representation and collective bargaining. Rather, we believe that they are similar and complementary processes. Both contain elements of cooperation and conflict, harmony and discord. Both by their very natures involve the mutal dependence of union and management. Perhaps most important, both have the same basic objective: to enable employees to participate in decision-making in the enterprise in which they work. And hence both involve 'participation' in 'management' . . . in the sense of participating in the formulation of [strategic] policies.[30]

Worker participation in company Boards of Directors of course raises wider issues beyond those involved in the establishment of a Joint Standing Committee for National Newspapers, most obviously the restriction upon shareholders' established rights: but the assumptions about the relationship between joint machinery and collective bargaining are similar. During the discussions of the Joint Standing Committee it was assumed that collective bargaining would continue as before. But the belief that collective bargaining could continue unaffected by the establishment of joint institutions was unrealistic. At the simplest level, participation in joint machinery provides access to information likely to be helpful in collective bargaining, even if confidentiality rules restricting the disclosure of information are respected. More fundamentally, the wider the range of issues covered by the joint institution, the more likely it is either to take specific issues out of the scope of collective bargaining altogether or to change the arena in which bargaining occurs. Even if only a more limited development takes place, it is likely to change the 'rules of the game'. On Fleet Street, the establishment of a joint committee whose objectives included 'to regularise all employment and ensure a wholly regular workforce committed to a full normal working week or single shift appearance' could hardly leave collective bargaining unaffected: at the very least, the scope of chapel bargaining would have been limited. Bargaining would, of course, have continued within the joint committee. But the need to co-cordinate bargaining with other unions or employers, and the desire to avoid the public odium which would be incurred by insisting upon group interest to the point of destroying the committee, as well as commitment to the institution itself, would have provided considerable pressure for successfully resolving differences without public confrontation.

In his study of trade unions under collective bargaining Hugh Clegg attaches primary importance to the level at which bargaining takes place, and the extent and depth of bargaining.[31] Similar factors influence the development of joint institutions. Running through discussions of the JSC was the issue of the appropriate scope of industry-level agreements (an issue which had, of course, been of funda-mental importance in the development of collective bargaining in the industry). The employers widened their conception of what might appropriately be covered by national agree-ments, under pressure of public expectations and with the realization that union leaders were more moderate than had been initially expected. Throughout, the employers' preference was for only limited industry-wide agreements: the national joint committee's role was to be one of agreeing principles and establishing parameters for negotiations at house level and monitoring agreements made at house level: national-level agreements were to be enabling and indicative rather than prescriptive. The language of the final agreement was that of devising policy frameworks and procedures. Yet, despite employers' preconceptions and the widely differing financial resources available to different houses, *Programme for Action* contained detailed agreed terms for voluntary redundancy, specific targets for pensions, and an 'agreed strategy' for dealing with decasualization. The seriousness of the industry's economic situation, the prospect of substantial financial assistance from the European Social Fund, and the union leaders' willingness to compromise encouraged publishers to make more substantial commitments at national level than had been expected a year earlier.

Programme for Action was both wider in scope and more detailed in provisions than generally anticipated when joint discussions began in December 1975. Yet the signature of the agreement establishing the JSC had not resolved the issue of the relationship between industry-level and house-level agreements: the rejection of *Programme for Action* meant that the appropriateness of the 'framework' was never tested. The statement of the JSC's objective on new technology read: 'to consider the implications of annual company manpower and technology planning proposals and the co-ordination and development of training and staff requirements.'[32] It was envisaged that individual houses would submit detailed proposals for new technology, together with manning requirements, to the JSC before beginning 'in-house' discussions. Even the presentation of proposals to the committee posed problems, since some employers felt that they would be disclosing commercially valuable information to their competitors: it was therefore decided to make detailed information available to union members of the JSC on a confidential basis, not to be disclosed to other employers. More substantial problems were likely over what the JSC would do with the information provided. Should the JSC endorse the proposals, give endorsement on conditions, and ask for their revision if the committee felt the proposals were unreasonable (for example, because of unrealistic manpower projections), or simply take note of them? Either endorsing the proposals or asking for their revision implied that the JSC had some authority over individual houses and the technical resources available to reach informed decisions: but the JSC did not have such authority, and individual houses had far more technical resources available. However, simply 'taking note' could prove a meaningless exercise, scarcely likely to bolster the credibility of the JSC, as the unions pointed out. Although MGN, the Financial Times, and TNL were ready to submit their proposals to the JSC, the rejection of *Programme for Action* meant that no submissions were ever made: in the light of later events, it is likely that the submission from TNL, which was expected to be the first, would have raised the issue of the JSC's authority at once.

Successful industry-level discussions or negotiations involve maintaining unity amongst employers and amongst unions. As has been shown elsewhere (above, pp. 44–5, Chapters 3 and 4), both employers and unions had different and often divergent interests in general. Individual employers and unions also differed in what they hoped for from the JSC. Amongst employers, there were differences in the financial resources available to individual newspapers, and therefore in the provision which could be made for financing pensions improvements or for severance payments above statutory levels: financial arrangements acceptable to MGN constituted a serious problem for the *Guardian*. There were also differences in the severity of the short-term economic pressures upon different houses, and therefore differences in the importance attached to inserting conditions into guarantees against compulsory redundancy. There were also differences between houses in their interest in new technology: there were no proposals for new technology for the *Sun*, and News International had therefore little interest in severance payments although it would be very much involved in decasualization and likely to be involved over pensions. Finally, there were differences amongst employers over the speed at which joint discussions should proceed. The divergent attitudes amongst employers towards the JSC partly reflected basic features of the industry. Such differences were reinforced by one feature of the competitive structure of the industry, the central importance of variations in labour costs. Agreement amongst employers on labour costs is most likely where agreement is required to rule out labour costs as a source of competitive advantage, enabling competitive pressure to focus upon other items, as in the engineering industry in the inter-war period. However, since there was little difference between newspapers in raw-material costs, and no competition between them on delivery times, because distribution arrangements were shared, the major scope for obtaining a competitive advantage on the production side lay in reducing unit labour costs: indeed, Beaverbrook explicitly followed a policy of 'bidding up' the price of labour during the 1940s, as a means of increasing pressure upon his competitors.[33] Despite such divergent interests and attitudes, Fleet Street employers achieved a surprisingly united strategy in their joint discussions with the unions.

Competitive pressures, of a different kind, existed amongst unions. There was little competition for members amongst production workers, owing to the precise system of job control and the pre-entry closed shop, although there was competition for some clerical workers. However, there was of course competitive wage-bargaining and awareness that levels of earnings varied widely between chapels, both within and between newspapers. Such competitiveness was especially strongly felt by disadvantaged chapels, whether against members of their own union (for example the resentment of time-hands against linotype operators in the NGA) or more strongly against members of other unions (especially NATSOPA machine assistants against NGA machine managers). More importantly, there was rivalry over the allocation of jobs under new technology proposals, especially between NATSOPA and NGA chapels. NATSOPA leaders believed that new technology would expand job opportunities for their members by rendering traditional demarcation lines irrelevant; NGA leaders believed that new technology would be introduced only within existing demarcation lines. It is therefore hardly surprising that NATSOPA and NGA leaders differed in their attitudes towards the JSC, as they differed in their attitudes towards new technology proposals at house level.

Like the employers, the unions in national newspapers thus had very different interests and different degrees of involvement in the Joint Standing Committee. W. H. Keys was the prime mover on the union side, as chairman of the TUC Printing Industries Committee and of the JSC itself. He was strongly supported by the general secretary of NATSOPA, Owen O'Brien. The NUJ general secretary, Ken Morgan, was also fully committed to the JSC, although he regarded his union as only tangentially involved, as his members were unlikely to be redundant, their pensions were more generous than those of production workers, and there was no suggestion that freelance journalists, the analogue of casual production workers, would be placed on a permanent basis. The special interests of the NUJ were recognized in that there was no requirement that NUJ members who left Fleet Street under voluntary redundancy provisions would be required to leave the industry. The NGA general secretary's attitude appears to have been ambivalent: he recognized that the JSC provided a possible solution to his members' long-term problems, but his Fleet Street members were not convinced. Accordingly, after having suggested that the NPA should take the initiative and call a meeting of both sides, the Association did not participate in the inaugural meeting. Throughout, the NGA representatives were obliged to look over their shoulders, unwilling either to commit themselves or to allow the JSC to proceed without them. Hence the NGA representative was willing to 'accept' the recommendations of the Pensions Working Party, but not to 'endorse' them. Similarly, NGA representatives had reservations about the terms of the redundancy proposals, but were willing to accept them without commitment. Nevertheless the NGA general secretary did commend *Programme for Action* to NGA members, a courageous action in view of the opposition to the talks which was already known to exist among his Fleet Street members. The AUEW representative was similarly cautious about involvement, not taking part in the initial meeting, frequently failing to attend meetings he was supposed to attend, and limiting the union's role to that of holding a 'watching brief' on developments. Contrariwise, the EETPU representative was more fully involved, unsurprisingly so, since the extended use of electronics would be to the advantage of his members: in the 1970s Electricians steadily increased their earnings levels compared with the Engineers. In maintaining commitment amongst union representatives a key role was played by the TUC, especially the secretary to the TUC Printing Industries Committee, Kenneth Graham. The TUC performed the essential staff work for the union side and provided the machinery for the initial approach. In addition to practical advantages, this avoided appearing to identify the initiative with any particular union, although inevitably Keys and O'Brien were more involved than other union representatives. However, even the TUC signally failed in one respect — despite employers' hopes SLADE refused throughout to take any part in the discussions.

Agreement amongst employers or amongst unions could be generated from within, or from without. For reasons outlined, pressure from within was limited. The customary pressure from without was from 'the other side', during industrial conflict. However, the level of industrial conflict was comparatively low in the industry during 1975-6, partly of course because of the JSC itself, partly because of the economic pressures which made the JSC necessary, and partly because of the operation of Phase I of the Social Contract: at worst, wage conflict was submerged. The alternative source of pressure for unity would have come from above, from Government. This was partially expected, as the Royal Commission on the Press (1975-7) was then sitting. The Royal Commission gave considerable encouragement to the JSC in its *Interim Report*, published in January 1976, and was extremely critical of print-union members for rejecting *Programme for Action* in its final report, published in July 1977.[34] The ACAS research team was similarly very favourably disposed towards the JSC:

> The third and most important reason for optimism that industrial relations changes will be forthcoming is that the parties have shown that they want them. The emergence of the J.S.C. and the wide range of questions being tackled by the Committee is a symbol of the wish of at least the leaders of the industry to seek a way out of many of its difficulties.

> The J.S.C. is potentially an important vehicle for change in the industry.[35]

However, as we have seen, the Royal Commission recommended only very limited financial assistance for the industry in its *Interim Report*, and, whether because the reaction to its initial report was so lukewarm or because it never intended to in any case, the Royal Commission's *Final Report* did not contain any further financial recommendations: 'We have rejected all the proposals for Government assistance which have been put to us.'[36] ACAS was not, of course, in a position to make any recommendations. The Government accepted the Royal Commission's view that no 'general subsidy' was necessary for the industry, and that the major expenses involved in rationalization and demanning could be met from loans raised privately, since a basic principle of the JSC's schemes was that costs should be met from savings within a comparatively brief period.[37] The Government did not commit itself on the Royal Commission's relatively modest proposal for short-term help for newspapers in special difficulty, instead showing a considerable disregard for the industrial relations situation in the industry by calling for specific agreed figures on demanning and compensation by the end of June 1976, before making a decision. The figures could not, of course, be provided. The Government thus did not provide the JSC with any resources to sustain cohesion. There was no likelihood of the Government imposing any sanctions upon the industry for its failure to maintain the momentum of the JSC, since to do so would have been a major interference in the independence of the press (even if the obvious sanctions available, like an end to zero-rating for VAT or the ending of favoured postal charges, had been politically acceptable).

The major outside pressure sustaining the JSC was the prospect of the grant from the European Social Fund and the conditions attached thereto. The Government could have used the Social Fund grant as a means of exerting pressure, since under EEC rules the application had to be forwarded through the government, but it used its influence solely to speed up the operation of the JSC, not to influence its decisions. Paradoxically, the French Government exercised the major influence by challenging the legal status of the JSC when the Advisory Committee considered the industry's application. To give the JSC even initial credibility — much less to satisfy French taste for codification — it was necessary to place it upon a firmer basis than it had when the application was first submitted. Accordingly, it was formally agreed to establish the JSC before the Decasualisation Working Party had reached agreement, to meet the exigencies of the European Social Fund timetable. But it was perhaps predictable that the carrot of up to £7.5m for vocational retraining would be more attractive to employers and to union leaders than to union members, and the European Social Fund grant made little difference to their evaluation of *Programme for Action.*

Since the JSC was never established on a permanent basis no firm decisions were taken about the committee's future administrative staff. However, basic issues relating to the provision of services for the joint institution were under initial consideration, for the resources to be allocated obviously indicated the priority the industry accorded to the committee, as well as determining its capacity to carry out its functions: if the industry was unwilling to provide adequate finance for the JSC the committee was obviously weakened, both practically and symbolically. Should the committee have its own staff, draw upon the staff of its constituent members, or rely upon the services of the TUC and the NPA? If the committee were to have its own staff and premises, should they be financed by employers, by both employers and unions, or by outside funds? If by both sides, should employers make the major contribution, as they possessed more financial resources than trade unions? Should the size of union contribution be a fixed sum or proportional to the number of members in the industry? The JSC was to be housed at the offices of the NPA, but to be financed by a levy upon both employers and unions and audited by the TUC auditors: no statement was made about the level of contributions, except that the levy 'may be calculated upon different bases with respect to trade union members and publisher members.' The committee did not have complete discretion over its funding, since the European Social Fund's rules for joint social institutions required that funds be provided by employers and unions, and of course obtaining a major grant required compliance with such rules, especially with the vigilance of French government representatives. In practice, union general secretaries were willing to accept some financial responsibility for the JSC, but obviously could not commit their unions to major expenditures until *Programme for Action* had been agreed by union members.

iii

In retrospect, as in prospect, it is hardly surprising that the JSC proved abortive, succumbing to problems similar to those of the Joint Board of 1964–7. It was established rapidly, at a time of crisis within the industry, with widespread good-will from outside the industry, but subject to considerable pressure from within. The fear that closures were imminent led union leaders, especially W. H. Keys and Owen O'Brien (through the TUC Printing Industries Committee) and Joe Wade (independently), to take the initiative in approaching the employers for joint discussions. The employers' own fears for the industry's economic position, their hope that union attitudes were changing, and their desire to appear reasonable before the Royal Commission, together with the attractive possibility of substantial outside financial assistance with the costs of the retraining in which newspapers already committed to new technology would be involved, led them to respond favourably. But the enthusiasm of Keys and O'Brien was not shared by other members of their own unions, and NGA leaders, although seeing the need for a joint approach, were suspicious that anything enthusiastically supported by Keys and O'Brien would be a threat to their own interests. On the employers' side, initial scepticism in some houses was never fully quietened. The rejection of *Programme for Action* inevitably confirmed such scepticism.

Union members' rejection of *Programme for Action* reduces the likelihood that the industry will respond in a similar way to future crises like that of 1975–6. Union leaders will obviously be reluctant to risk their reputations in embarking on discussions with employers on their own initiative, whilst prior consultation with Fleet Street members would inevitably provoke opposition. On one reading of the Fleet Street situation the ruling out of this option would not be undesirable. According to this view, national-level discussions are of very limited value because of the central importance of considerations specific to individual houses: product markets, the structure of labour costs, and the financial resources available differ so widely that national-level discussions cannot hope to produce more than platitudes. The effect of the JSC experiment was simply to complicate, delay, and obstruct house-level planning for new technology. However, this is to exaggerate the extent to which individual houses can act in isolation. Fleet Street is a distinct world, whose separation from the conventional routines of industrial life reinforces unity within it. The industry's economic difficulties have reinforced union members' solidarity throughout the industry — threats to NGA members at The Times are self-evidently threats to the interests of NGA members elsewhere. Both formal and informal contacts are so close that knowledge of developments in individual houses cannot be restricted. Therefore the possibility of individual employers concluding successful agreements involving changes of principle at house level is remote; and significant changes in manning levels to accommodate new technology raise issues of principle. It is impossible to transfer the assumption made by some employers in regional newspapers that it is possible to 'buy' jobs from individual chapels to Fleet Street — events are too visible. For employers there is therefore no effective alternative to establishing principles at industry level and negotiating their application to specific circumstances at house level. For unions, of course, there is: the major pressure upon unions to negotiate national agreements on new technology in the fear that without them some titles will close. The continued survival of the *Observer* indicates the difficulty in sustaining that belief. Detailed examination of events at house level largely confirms this assessment of the necessity of national-level agreement for the successful introduction of new technology in the industry.

Chapter 6

The Financial Times Ltd. and New Technology

Previous chapters have been concerned with events at industry level — the general crisis in Fleet Street in 1975, the structure of industrial relations, including the development of policy on new technology in the NGA and NATSOPA, and the joint union–management approach to new technology represented by *Programme for Action*. However, the initiative for the introduction of new technology came, of course, from individual managements, and the locus of responsibility for management decision-making remained with the individual house throughout, even during the period of greatest optimism about the JSC, when individual houses allowed their negotiations to lapse into limbo pending the successful negotiation of an industry-level framework agreement. The rejection of *Programme for Action* returned the initiative to individual houses to act independently. This and the following two chapters therefore examine in detail events at three companies, the Financial Times Ltd., TNL, and MGN. For each house the company background is outlined, the development of management thinking on new technology traced, and its industrial relations consequences examined.

i

The FT is part of the Cowdray interests, and its economic situation in 1975 has to be interpreted in the context of the experience of the group as a whole. The newspaper is a wholly owned subsidiary of Pearson Longman Ltd., alongside the Westminster Press Ltd. and Penguin Longman Ltd: as one of the largest publishers in Britain, Pearson Longman Ltd. publishes the *Northern Echo*, ten evening newspapers (including the *Oxford Mail*), over ninety weekly newspapers, nine sports newspapers, and thirteen periodicals, as well as the *Financial Times*. In 1974 FT interests contributed 19 per cent of the trading profit to the group, provincial and regional newspapers 44 per cent and book publishing 37 per cent. Pearson Longman Ltd. is, in turn, controlled by Pearson (S) & Son Ltd., who in 1974 owned 63 per cent of the Company's ordinary shares: Pearson (S) & Son Ltd. is a holding company whose interests cover merchant banking (Lazard Brothers), investment trusts (Whitehall Securities Corporation Ltd.), manufacturing industry (Doulton & Co. Ltd.), and French and American firms, as well as publishing. Although only one of many interests, newspapers and publishing accounted for 40 per cent of Pearson (S) & Son Ltd.'s profit in 1973, compared with 25 per cent banking and financial, 23½ per cent industrial and commercial, and other activities 11½ per cent. Pearson (S) & Son Ltd., which only went public in 1969, is controlled by Cowdray family trusts. The FT is linked with the Cowdray empire at Board level through a number of interlocking directorates: in 1974 the chairman of the FT Board was also chairman of Pearson Longman Ltd., executive deputy chairman of Pearson (S) & Son Ltd., and a director of the Cowdray Trust; three other directors were on the Board of Pearson Longman Ltd. and other companies within the group, both inside and outside publishing.[1]

The economic importance of the FT to the wider group is difficult to estimate for separate information about the FT is no longer published. Moreover, any assessment of the capital value of the company would be heavily influenced by the valuation placed upon the company's very valuable building, directly opposite St. Paul's (and the Bank of America) and upon 'goodwill' (the capital valuation of 'goodwill' for Pearson Longman Ltd. as a whole in December 1974 was £30m.). However, in 1970 the capital valuation of the FT was £7,864,000, compared with a total capitalization of £43,240,000 for Pearson Longman Ltd., and £119,270,000 for Pearson (S) & Son Ltd. — just under 7 per cent of the capital value of the holding company (although the subsequent acquisition of Penguin Books Ltd. by Pearson Longman Ltd. diminished the relative importance of the FT.).[2] The importance of newspapers and publishing to the overall economic position of the group was not, of course, necessarily directly proportional to the capital invested:

in 1973 and 1974 newspapers and publishing contributed more than proportionately to the profits of the Pearson group.

Table 6.1

				1973		1974
Pearson Longman	(a)	Turnover	£m	76.60	£m	92.80
	(b)	Net profit		7.80		5.65
	(b)	as percentage of (a)		10.2%		6.0%
Pearson:	(a)	Turnover		158.5		184.55
	(b)	Net profit		9.18		6.42
	(b)	as percentage of (a)		5.8%		3.4%

Neither Pearson Longman Ltd. nor the Pearson group regarded 1974 as a satisfactory year, but the economic performance of the group as a whole was significantly worse than that of its publishing subsidiary: a net profit of £6.42m on a turnover of £184.55m represented a very unsatisfactory return.

The significant drop in the profitability of both Pearson Longman Ltd. and Pearson (S) & Son Ltd. was, not surprisingly, reflected in trends in their share prices. Although 1974 was a poor year for shares in general, with the *FT* index touching a low of 150 in December 1974, it was an even worse year for Pearson Longman Ltd. and for Pearson (S) & Son Ltd. In 1973 Pearson Longman Ltd. shares fluctuated between a high of 209p and a low of 104p, those of Pearson (S) & Son Ltd. between 248p and a low of 138p; at the end of December 1974 Pearson Longmans stood at 41p, Pearsons at 45p.[3] Although the share prices recovered early in 1975, they turned down again before reaching 1973 levels.

The FT is thus part of an extensive group of companies, and developments there were affected by economic trends outside the national newspaper industry: the economic fortunes of Pearson (S) & Son Ltd. and of Pearson Longman Ltd. naturally influenced their attitudes towards their subsidiary. Hence the economic constraints faced by the Pearson group in 1974 paralleled and reinforced economic pressures upon the whole of Fleet Street — the pressures upon the whole group meant that the newspaper's economic problems could not be regarded with the indulgence traditionally granted to newspapers, at least by other proprietors and groups. Since the FT is not a publicly quoted company in its own right it is possible to give only a limited view of the newspaper's situation in 1974 and 1975. Although the *FT*'s financial situation compared favourably with that of other quality dailies in 1974 (the *Daily Telegraph, The Times*, and the *Guardian* lost over £2.5m between them in 1974), it compared badly with its own previous record, and therefore with what the group might have expected. In 1974 the *FT* made a profit of £1.1m, compared with £2.1m in 1973 and £2.2m in 1972; between 1973 and 1974 the *FT* pre-tax profit, as a percentage of turnover, dropped from 14 to 7 per cent. At the time of the announcement of the development plan in July 1975 estimates for the year varied 'almost daily', but a further reduction was expected, and it was anticipated that by 1978 there would be an annual deficit of £1.5m unless protective measures were taken (although it was recognized that such projections were subject to a large margin of error, and they proved to be totally inaccurate).[4]

The reasons for the *FT*'s economic difficulties were similar to those affecting other newspapers, often more sharply — inability to increase revenue sufficiently to match rising costs. Despite the alleged inelasticity of demand for the *FT* and its comparative lack of price sensitivity, its circulation began to drop in the winter of 1974–5, from an audited circulation of 194,000 in early 1974 to 188,000 over the period October 1974 to March 1975, a drop of 3.10 per cent. (Over the same period the circulation of *The Times* dropped from 345,000 to 335,000 (2.90 per cent), of the *Guardian* from 360,000 to 346,000 (3.89 per cent), and of the *Daily Telegraph* from 1,406,000 to 1,367,000 (2.77 per cent)). The slight drop in circulation was not, in itself, a major source of concern: even the lower figure represented a significant increase over the 1971 circulation, 171,000, and sales revenue made only a relatively small contribution to total revenue — £3.0m in 1974, compared with £11.2m by advertising. Moreover, readership was more important than circulation, especially readership amongst 'key influentials' in the business and political world, the main target for the extensive company advertising carried by the *FT*, and there was no evidence of a significant drop in readership. However, as FT manage-ment pointed out in July 1975, 'clearly, at some point, a further fall might jeopardize our standing with advertisers.' Moreover, trends in advertising revenues were more worrying than circulation figures. Over the whole period 1970-4 advertising revenue increased from £6.3m in 1970 to £11.2m in 1974. However, a significant part of this increase was due to increased prices rather than to increased output – for example, advertising rates increased by 28.5 per cent in 1974: over the period 1972-4 the number of advertising columns published dropped, from 397,000 in 1972 to 382,000 in 1974. The effects of customer resistance to increased adver-tising rates, as well as the reduction in advertising expenditure normally expected during economic recession, began to appear in 1974: despite the increase in rates revenue rose by only £.1m in 1974. This pressure on advertising revenues continued in 1975, with advertising volumes 8.5 per cent down in July 1975 compared with July 1974.

Thus by early 1975 both the *FT*'s major sources of revenue, sales and advertising revenue, were being squeezed: circula-tion was beginning to drop, partly as a result of increased cover prices (although the long-term price differential between the *FT* and the other quality dailies had narrowed), adver-tising revenues had reached a plateau (or were beginning to fall if allowance is made for inflation), and advertising volumes were beginning to fall. At the same time both fixed and variable costs were rising. Fixed costs, including promo-tions, commission, contributions, travel, telephone, etc. rose from £1,875,000 in 1970 to £3,671,000 in 1974, a rise of 96 per cent; such costs did not vary with output, and provided little scope for savings. The first major item of variable costs, newsprint and ink, was largely determined by market forces outside the control of the newspaper, although of course influenced by changes in circulation and in the size of the newspapers. By the 1970s the newsprint glut of the early 1960s, when newsprint actually dropped in price, had disappeared and prices rose steeply, especially in 1974, as shown in chapter 1, pp. 000-0. These changes were naturally reflected in the *FT*'s costs: variable costs rose from £1.5m in 1970 to £1.6m in 1971, £2.1m in 1972, £2.5m in 1973, and £3.1m in 1974. Further increases in newsprint costs were expected in 1975, an expectation which events confirmed: by January 1977 newsprint had risen to £248 per metric tonne. Early in 1975 newsprint costs, which accounted for £3.1m out of the *FT*'s £13.1m costs, were rising, with no immediate prospect of stabilization, and no long-term prospect of reduction: as the authors of the ACAS report, *Industrial Relations in the National Newspaper Industry* commented gloomily at the end of 1976, newsprint 'must be regarded to all intents and purposes as a fixed cost.'[5] Trends in the other major item in the company's budget, labour costs, were more satisfactory and offered more scope for further reductions: wage settlements in the industry were restrained by incomes policies in 1973 and 1974 and the *FT*'s labour costs rose by only 88 per cent between 1970 and 1974 (compared with 100 per cent for variable costs). Nevertheless, labour costs were the largest single item in the company's expenditure, and rose substantially in absolute terms over the period: from £3.4m in 1970 to £4.0m in 1971, £4.8m in 1972, £5.6m in 1973, and £6.4m in 1974. Moreover, no long-term reliance could be placed upon national incomes policies, nor the negotiation of below-average settlements. Since neither increasing revenues nor controlling raw material costs were possible solutions to the FT's economic problems attention naturally focussed upon labour costs: the results of this attention were determined by concurrent changes in technology, discussed in chapter 1, and in the company's management personnel.

Economic pressures on Fleet Street, and on the Pearson Longman group, made it necessary for 'something to be done' about the newspaper's labour costs; technological changes, outlined in chapter 1, made it possible to do something. However, the industry's economic difficulties were long-standing, and technological improvements which would have aided, although not solved, the company's difficulties, had long been available; mechanical publishing room equipment had been available since the late 1950s, but no major changes had taken place in publishing room manning levels. Major attempts to use new technology at the newspaper would not have occurred without major changes in the FT management in the early 1970s. The conservatism of Fleet Street management has been heavily criticized. Even the EIU report commented cautiously: 'Although we formed strong impressions about the quality of management in the various organisations, it would be unwise to formulate opinions about individuals on the strength of a brief survey. [However] the quality of management is uneven and the industry is short of professionally trained managers.'[6] The ambivalent caution of the judgement is more apparent than real; the authors clearly felt that newspaper management was unsatisfactory. Similar cautiously expressed views were echoed by ACAS a decade later.[7] At the FT major changes were already occurring, before the major crisis of 1975, in the direction pointed by ACAS: the management structure was elaborated and formalized, industrial relations were incorporated within overall planning, and new personnel were recruited from outside. Management changes to facilitate effective adjustment to economic pressure and technological opportunities were already underway.

In the mid 1960s the FT's top management structure was simple, and the number of personnel involved very small. The managing director (Lord Drogheda) and the general manager were the only executive members of the Board, and shared executive responsibility for the paper. The managing director held final responsibility, whilst the general manager was responsible for day-to-day administration, including decisions about purchasing, the size of the newspaper, and the ratio of editorial to advertising matter; the editor (Sir) Gordon Newton, had complete control over the editorial function, although he was not a member of the Board. Four non-executive directors completed the top management team. Inevitably, with the small size of the organization, and the long experience of the men involved (Lord Drogheda became managing director in 1945), 'great reliance [was] placed on the experience and personal control of the two executive directors.'[8]

By the mid 1970s both the structure and the personnel involved had changed substantially. The size of the Board increased, the management structure became more elaborate, and new men held most of the major positions. The seven-man Board of 1966 had become a ten-man Board by 1976, with the addition of more executive members: the editor, the chief executive, both joint general managers as well as the finance director and company secretary were all members of the Board. Below Board level the management structure also became more elaborate: the role of managing director had become that of chief executive and managing director, there were two joint general managers in place of one, and two totally new divisions, origination services and manpower services, were set up. The two new divisions were central to the development plan, since the major technological changes were to be in the origination area and the general responsibility for the social and industrial relations problems anticipated from the technological changes lay with Manpower Services. At the same time, the responsibilities for industrial relations at the St. Clement's Press, an independent company whose sole job was the printing of the *FT,* were brought within the sphere of the FT industrial relations executive, as part of a long-term plan to merge the operations of the SCP with the FT. The resulting management structure is outlined in Fig. 5.

Changes in structure were accompanied by changes in personnel at Board level and within both editorial and production management. At Board level, the major change in personnel was Lord Gibson's accession to the chair. Lord Drogheda ceased being managing director of the FT in 1970, and became chairman the following year. However, he retired from the chair in 1974, to be succeeded by Lord Gibson, who had been a non-executive director of the FT since 1957. Apart from Lord Gibson's personal judgement and skill, the change in chairman had two consequences. Firstly, the link between the FT and its controlling interests was strengthened: as chairman of Pearson Longman Ltd., deputy chairman of Pearson (S) & Son Ltd. and a close personal colleague of Lord Cowdray he could obviously view the FT's interests within the context of the whole group, and had access to extensive capital resources. Secondly, the position of the executive directors was inevitably strengthened: Lord Gibson had never had the close involvement with the FT of his predecessor, and therefore lacked detailed knowledge of its operations. Moreover, he

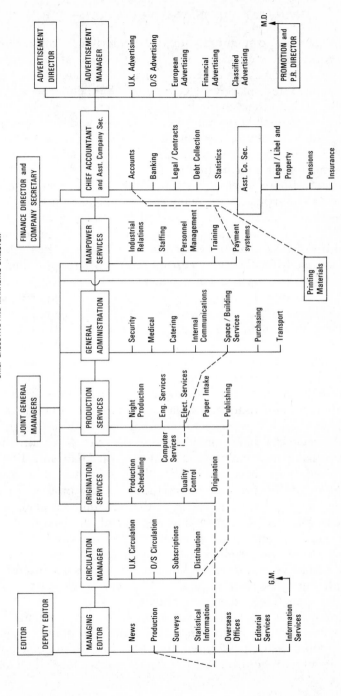

Fig. 5. Financial Times management structure, 1 October 1976. *Source:* The Financial Times Ltd.

had less time to spend on the job. In addition to his business interests he was chairman of the Arts Council, of the Council for the Preservation of Rural England, of the Redundant Churches Fund, of Covent Garden, of Glyndebourne, as well as active in other charitable organizations. This obviously made it impossible for him to exercise any detailed over-sight over the company, even if he had wished to do so. No other non-executive member of the Board was able to do what the chairman had no inclination to do.

Below Board level, the FT top management were also all new to their posts, and many had experience outside Fleet Street. A. V. Hare was appointed as managing director in 1971, and became chief executive in 1976: the major part of his previous career had been in the Foreign Office, which he left in 1963. The new editor, M. H. Fisher, appointed in 1973, had been with the newspaper since 1957, after working in the research division of the Foreign Office. The new joint general manager, a particularly important figure in the development plan, had only been with the FT since 1971, after previous work as a lecturer in industrial relations, and an adviser at the British Federation of Master Printers. At the next level down the managerial hierarchy, the head of Manpower Services had only been recruited recently from the Commission of Industrial Relations; the head of Origination Services had just been recruited to management, although he had previously been employed by the FT as a journalist, specializing in technological subjects; the Managing Editor had only just been apointed, although in this case more conventionally from amongst the FT's editorial staff. In short, during the early phases of the development plan, only one of the two joint general managers had followed the 'conventional' Fleet Street promotion path — from machine room to senior production — and had long experience of the company: and even he had become especially interested in the new technology and took a very active part in the initial launching of the development plan.

Even in a large organization such extensive changes in personnel are likely to herald major shifts in policy, if only as generational self-assertion, a means of establishing collective identity and control. Such changes were especially likely to produce new policies in a relatively small organization like the FT, where the top management team ('the Sixth Floor') were in frequent touch with each other, and the limitations imposed by the logic of large-scale organization negotiable. The extent of the personnel changes and the small size of the senior management group maximized the impact of particular individuals, making it possible to formulate radically new comprehensive policies without the political compromises enforced by large-scale organization. At the same time, the absence of well-informed and influential criticism available in a larger organization of course increased the risks of 'going over-board' on a particular policy.

ii

The FT's development plan was foreshadowed in the evidence of the newspaper's general manager, A. G. Cox, to the Royal Commission on the Press in January 1975, when he outlined the potential savings which could be gained from computerization. His paper and accompanying letter spelled out the logic of a computerized newspaper-production system and the savings which could be made, especially if the new technology was accompanied by the multiple use of production facilities, as in the United States.[9] However, the evidence was presented only in general terms, and throughout early 1975 discussions on a specific plan for the *FT* were confined to senior management within the newspaper. The first semi-public announcement of a specific plan was to a meeting of trade-union representatives at Bracken House on 11 July 1975.[10] The development plan was presented as a radical means of securing the long-term future of the paper by making substantial savings on production costs. FT management recognized that the paper's financial situation was better than that of many other papers, but 'our problems in current circumstances are no less severe, and in some ways more critical, than those of other newspapers, and . . . the survival and development of the newspaper depends on the plan we will be discussing with you.' Unless substantial savings could be made, management believed that the newspaper would experience successive cycles of boom and slump, the down-turns becoming deeper as the real income derived from advertising dropped. Immediately following the presentation FT management representatives undertook a series of informal discussions with national union officials. Before substantial progress was made these discussions were subsumed under the general discussions between the NPA and the TUC Printing Industries Committee on the new technology in the autumn, discussed in chapter 5. Simultaneously, FT management established a network of working parties to examine the detailed technical requirements of the development plan.

The development plan comprised two sections, the first on the proposed technology, the second on its social implications. The distinctive feature of the technology proposed was its comprehensiveness. Although the imagery of wheeling out the old and wheeling in the new overnight adopted by some opponents was exaggerated, it was anticipated that the paper's production system would be radically transformed within eighteen months. The plan involved a 'totally integrated computer system embracing both the typesetting and the commercial requirements of the company'.[11] The new type-setting system was to comprise central computers, with associated disc storage devices, and a 'front-end' computer for controlling editing and correction terminals; the commercial system was to use an identical computer, linked to the typesetting process by a communications link. The paper was to be totally converted to photocomposition by the end of 1976, with plates produced from photopolymers. Facilities were to be provided for direct input into the computerized production system by journalists and, eventually, by the wire services. No major changes were envisaged in the printing and distribution systems. The basic logic of the new system envisaged is set out in a simplified flow-chart for the type-setting system (Fig. 6).

The general manager responsible for the technical sections of the development plan had visited the United States, and the scale of the plan echoed American practice. By 1975 the majority of major American metropolitan newspapers, including the *New York Times*, had announced comprehensive plans for the introduction of new technology, although the

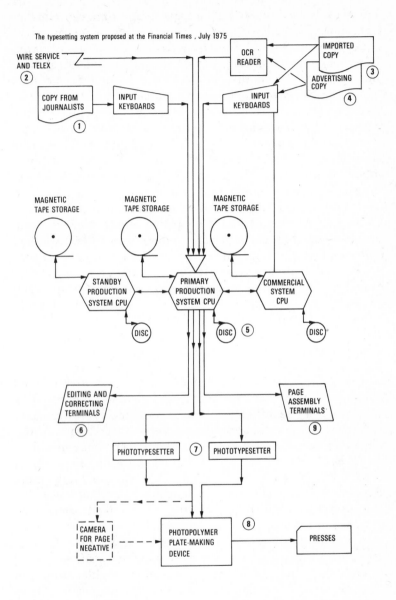

The typesetting system proposed at the Financial Times , July 1975

Fig. 6. The typesetting system proposed at the Financial Times, July 1975.

actual users of the new technology at that time were smaller newspapers, outside or on the fringes of major metropolitan areas, like the Long Island *Newsday* or the Baltimore *Sun*. However, the technology outlined was not identical with that widely used in the United States, as neither the FT's editorial nor its production requirements were the same as other newspapers. For example, the FT normally rewrote agency wire material more extensively than most major American newspapers did, and would thus require more facilities for rewriting; the FT's production schedule was much shorter and tighter than that of many American newspapers, which either ran morning and evening papers on the same presses or produced editions round the clock. The distinctive feature of the FT's plan was the reliance upon a single 'main-frame' computer rather upon than a linked system of smaller machines. The decision to opt for a very large central processing unit had a number of important technical and economic advantages, especially in the then existing state of computer technology: large machines could cope with the very sophisticated programmes required, were fast, and could handle a massive data base. However, there were also technical disadvantages: a centralized system was less flexible, there was less relevant proven experience, and editorial pressures at peak times (between 5.30 p.m. and 8.0 p.m.) might lead to over-load, queuing, and resulting frustration and inefficiency, unless so much excess capacity was provided that the intallation became uneconomic. Above all, there was the problem of back-up: very large machines naturally required very substantial back-up in case of mechanical or electronic failure. This was obviously more expensive than back-up for smaller machines. There was the possibility of using spare capacity in the linked commercial system at times of peak pressure in the production system; but this obviously required very elaborate software development and, in any case, depended upon the two peaks occurring at different times, which was fortunately probable. Moreover, the relatively centralized system had less margin for error, as American experience was to show. For economic reasons managements wish to buy the cheapest — in practice the smallest — suitable machines. However, machine capacity is related to the number of peripheral devices (including VDTs.) which can be supported. If the number of input devices is miscalculated and more are required for editorial reasons than can be sustained by the computer, there are obvious difficulties: editorial frustration, production complications, and further expenditure. A system of linked smaller machines would have required very sophisticated systems design, and might have been slower in operation; but it would have required simpler programmes, been easier to supplement, and have involved less risk. The FT management was opting for the most complex and the most risky technology.

The objective of the plan was to increase productivity by using the new technology to achieve lower manning levels. The major reduction in manpower was to be amongst NGA members: the number of linotype operators was to be reduced from 67 to 35, of case piece hands from 26 to 3, of stab hands from 57 to 16, and of readers (excluding overseers and deputies) from 33 to 8. To use the NGA general secretary's term, the effect was to 'decimate' the composing room.[12] There were also to be large savings in the foundry and in the machine room. In the foundry, plate-makers were to be reduced from 30 to 10; in the machine room the number of machine minders was to be reduced from 14 to 9. But, although the major focus of attention was upon reductions in NGA members, large reductions were also envisaged for NATSOPA members. In the NATSOPA machine branch the number of night-machine assistants was to be reduced from the equivalent of 62.6 X 5 nights to 30 X 5 nights, and of day assistants from 10 to 6. The NATSOPA RIRMA branch was to lose 75 jobs: the jobs of linotype assistants, copy-holders, revisers, and runners were to be eliminated, the number of cleaners reduced by 2, and the number of miscellaneous workers from 38 to 20. In the third NATSOPA branch, covering clerical and other workers, 128 jobs were to disappear. There were minimal changes in the distribution system, the major reductions in SOGAT members being the loss of 19 drivers' jobs, and the elimination of proof-pullers. Amongst engineering workers, the new technology involved a shift from mechanical engineering to electronics, with the elimination of 7 linotype engineers, and the expansion of the work area of electrical mechanics. Over all, the number of jobs likely to disappear amounted to 533, out of a non-editorial staff of approximately 900.

The major objective of the scheme was to reduce costs, without changing the quality of the final product. Whether the changes would improve, or damage the final product, or have no effect at all, was not examined explicitly: the assumption made was that they would have little effect. However, some American managements stressed the improvements in editorial quality made possible by the new technology, providing more editorial flexibility, and later deadlines; this was the view of journalists on the *Chicago Tribune*, which had experience of a prototype Hendrix 3400 system. Journalists at the FT were more sceptical, believing that the new technology was desirable for production reasons only: 'editorial in-put systems . . . are *not* designed for the journalists' benefit, and their installation is *not* done out of considerations of improving the job of the journalists or the quality of his individual or collective product. Such in-put systems are for the benefit of the *production* departments and arise from *production* requirements.' Paper was seen as being cheap, flexible, easy to reproduce for reading by others and discussion, and in practice rarely lost, VDTs as more complex to operate, less flexible, and less suitable for consultation with others. For example, it was suggested that if journalists wished to consult colleagues about a story they had written, it was easy to pick up the piece of paper, walk over to the relevant desk, and have the article checked. If the story were on a screen the story would have to be transferred to the second journalist's screen, which would be possible only if the screen had been wiped clean. The example cited is not, in itself, convincing: under the existing system, there is a high probability that the required journalist would not be at his desk, and therefore a prior telephone call would be necessary to avoid waste of time: the new system would simply involve asking the second journalist to come over to the first's desk, rather than the other way round. However, the problem it illustrates is that the technology does introduce significant changes in working practices, which could be disadvantageous, at least in the short run. Yet, the emphasis upon the difficulties the new technology would involve for journalists was misleading: journalists were being asked to contemplate a number of changes in working practices, involving possible short-term difficulties, in exchange for a fundamental increase in editorial control over the production process. At the very least, this represented a major accession of collective bargaining power. Nevertheless, there were good grounds for believing that the new technology would not improve the quality of the *FT*, despite saving labour costs.

The Company stated its assumption that arrangements for handling the technical and manpower changes would be subject to discussion. But, at the least as a means of providing a basis for discussion, management outlined the basic principles it planned to adopt: early retirement for workers aged over 60, no automatic replacement, and compensation significantly beyond that provided for in the Redundancy Payments Act. In early discussions with union officials at national level the principles of such compensation were clarified and elaborated, and made public at the end of October.[13] The major feature of the scheme finally adopted was the company's recognition of its 'radical and fundamental obligation to all its employees to preserve net income', as defined at 11 July 1975. Employees leaving as a result of demanning would benefit from 'an independent objective and professional study of their own future career interests and their potential skill; a personal training programme to equip them to a predetermined standard with agreed new skills; their placement in employment outside the Company in a job which would combine the best secure net income in the light of their own career interests and potential as determined [above].' The company guaranteed to maintain earnings in any future job, chosen under the agreed arrangements, until the gap between such earnings and earnings at the FT on 11 July 1975 had disappeared. 'By this means . . . the Company not only removes the stigma, insecurity, and monetary impact of redundancy but also ensures that individuals obtain training which can equip them both in terms of personal interest and general industrial and commercial opportunity for a new future career.' Employees aged 60 or over, of whom there were 93, were to choose either the retraining package or the special retirement provisions: employees over 65 were to receive one week's average earnings per year of continuous service to 65, employees aged 62-64 two weeks average earnings per year of service up to 64, and employees aged 60-62 three weeks on the same basis. In all cases there was to be an upper limit of £5,000. Workers aged 65 or over were to receive immediate pension, according to entitlement; 62-64 deferred or immediate pension according to entitlement.

The proposals represented a major advance in thinking about redundancy, in industry in general, not simply the newspaper industry — a serious attempt to avoid the personal as well as the economic difficulties of redundancy. The principles outlined provided a firm basis for discussion, leaving considerable room for negotiation on financial terms, and clarification of practical details. The concept of 'net earnings' obviously offered scope for discussion. How far would overtime and special bonuses be regarded as an integral part of net earnings? How should the average be obtained – by averaging the previous six months, the best three weeks in the previous year, or on some other principle? In what circumstances would the company invoke its explicitly reserved right to discontinue the scheme, owing to financial pressures? How far could the individual employee disagree with the occupational guidance provided by the 'independent and professional' outside experts, without prejudicing his entitlement? Had the balance between age and earnings levels been correctly drawn in the early retirement proposals? For example, on what grounds was it justifiable that employees retiring at 62 should receive three weeks average earnings per year of continuous service, whilst workers aged 63 should receive two weeks? Could earnings be linked to future expected earnings at the FT, rather than to actual earnings on 11 July 1975? Should employees be given the alternative of taking a lump sum, instead of being obliged to accept the earnings maintenance package? These and other questions occurred to employees contemplating the scheme. However, before detailed conclusions relating specifically to the FT had been reached with national officials, and before any significant progress could be made at house level, discussions on the impact of the new technology had begun at national level, and the FT's proposals had been taken aboard the higher-level discussions (see chapter 5 above). As events turned out, there was in fact to be no detailed discussion of the proposals with FT chapel officials.

The introduction of the new technology was seen as a way of reducing labour costs by reducing the number of employees, and by reorganizing the remaining labour force. The basic objectives of the reorganization were increased flexibility in allocating labour and in working arrangements, and the abolition of piece-work payments systems. Such changes naturally involved the abolition of existing lines of demarcation: as FT management claimed in July, the new technology 'so changes job relationships that existing demarcations will no longer be distinguishable.'[14] Individuals were to be selected for specific jobs 'on the basis of the objectively assessed suitability of the individual for each defined job within the new technology area. In particular, the allocation should be without regard to the traditional territorial concepts which any union would otherwise advance when extending into areas of new technology.' The anticipated hostility of some unions (especially the NGA) to the destruction of existing demarcation lines was to be partially met by the establishment of a novel, multi-union joint technology section, which would coexist alongside the existing unions. 'Every union involved would receive union subscriptions as if all employees in the total joint technology area were members of that union, but employees in the area would only pay the subscription, via the joint technology section, which they paid to the union of which they were originally members.' The new joint technology section was to negotiate jointly with the company over the distribution of jobs and over the new payment system.

The new payments system was to be based upon job evaluation, not upon piece-work payments. In July management stated:

It is our belief that the [new] technology renders inappropriate our wages structure. We wish to enter into discussions with you on the design of mutually acceptable payment and rewards systems around a socially just and logical base. Clearly a piecework payment system can have no role in the structure. When the piecework payment system ends, therefore, it will have been replaced by mutually acceptable 'flat-rate' remuneration linked to reasonable performance targets . . . provided we progress towards our goal of improved efficiency through new technology, we do not propose to reduce the total remuneration now received by those who remain with us.

The company's views on the basic way of achieving a more rational payments system were clarified over the summer. The existing payments system was to be replaced by a job evaluation scheme, in which remuneration would be based 'solely on the relative skill, responsibility, and effort content of each function within the new technology area, irrespective of the background of the individual allocated to that function'. Where job evaluation led to lower earnings for specific workers, the gap between those earnings and earnings on 11 July 1975 would be made up 'for such time as the difference existed'.

The FT management had a clear conception of its objectives, but recognized that achieving them would require union co-operation at national and house level. Accordingly, management suggested that the implementation of the 'social implications' section of the development plan should be supervised by a Joint Supervisory Board, consisting of two FT directors and a national officer of one of the printing unions, and chaired by the chairman of the TUC Printing Industries Committee. Four subcommittees, covering technology, remuneration, selection and training, and financial support, were to be established, consisting of branch and chapel officials, management representatives, and specialist advisers, and were to report to the Supervisory Board. In return, the unions were to undertake to accept the management's timetable for the introduction of the new technology, to agree to a disputes procedure terminating at the Joint Supervisory Committee, and to co-operate in the assessment and placing of workers, inside and outside the company.

The attention paid to demarcation lines and the wage-payment system reflected management's belief that it needed to regain control of its production system. The FT shared many problems with other newspapers: rigid demarcation lines, confused payments systems, fragmented and unco-ordinated bargaining, and inter-chapel rivalry. The negotiation of comprehensive agreements with individual chapels between 1967 and 1973 had not resolved local industrial relations problems: the negotiation of comprehensive agreements clarified the confusion, but in doing so heightened the rivalry between chapels, as well as fostering resentment by seeming to reward earlier unco-operativeness by 'buying out' restrictive working practices. The solution to demarcation problems most popular among both proprietors and trade unions was the formation of a single trade union for the printing industry. FT management supported the idea in general terms, but correctly saw that they could have little influence upon current moves towards unification, and in any case doubted its effectiveness at house level, owing to inter-chapel rivalry. The joint technology section was seen as a more accessible, and possibly more effective, alternative. Although complicated, the great merits of the scheme were that it guaranteed the financial interests of all of the unions involved, on the most generous terms, and that it could provide a locally effective umbrella for joint discussion of the new technology. It could be seen as a logical extension — over a long distance, admittedly — of the already existing co-ordination between NGA chapels symbolized in the NGA's Imperial Composing FOC. The ACAS research team were well disposed towards the proposed joint technology section, seeing it as one way of securing effective working arrangements between chapels, to which they attached high priority.[15] However, even within particular unions at the FT joint arrangements were incomplete: the NGA Imperial father had no responsibilities for the machine managers' or the stereotypers' Chapels. There was no institutionalized co-operation between chapels in other unions and no co-ordination between chapels in different unions. Moreover, the relationship between the new section and existing union structures was unclear and would require careful specification. How were negotiations between representatives of the new section to be 'cleared' with existing union representatives? It was also claimed that the new section was simply an embryonic 'house' union and therefore completely unacceptable to the unions involved. Such complete hostility was not universal. More common was the view that some form of joint working arrangement between chapels at house level, probably less structured and more conventional than the proposed joint technology section, was desirable, but that the difficulties involved in establishing such arrangements were insurmountable.

The preliminary discussions leading up to the announcement of the plan had been confidential, and its announcement in July 1975, not surprisingly, made considerable impact. After initial shock and fear, especially among NGA members, reactions settled into a predictable pattern, with NGA members critical, and NATSOPA members adopting a more flexible attitude. The NGA regarded the proposals as attempting to go too far too fast: as Joe Wade put it,

With their revolutionary scheme they appeared to cure all the past evils of the years in Fleet Street overnight.

What frightens me is the way in which some national newspapers are rushing into new technology with all the verve and suicidal tendencies of a kamikaze pilot . . . If unions and their members are to accept changes in technology — and I agree they have no alternative — the employers must equally accept the social costs involved.[16]

As indicated earlier, for the NGA leadership the only possible way of installing the new technology successfully was on the basis of existing demarcation lines, and the retention of more staff than required:

Those people who see new technology as an oportunity to sweep away at a stroke all the existing demarcation lines, they really are living in cloud-cuckoo land. The only realistic way in which new technology can get off the ground is to introduce it, at this stage anyway, on the basis of existing demarcation lines so far as practicable. Unless that is understood and accepted, the rest can be forgotten.

Wade was equally sceptical about the proposed joint technology section:

. . . what the F.T. are proposing to do is pretty analogous to what happened when two unions in the printing industry (NUPBP and NATSOPA] decided to amalgamate and said: 'We will throw our problems into the melting pot and we will sort them out once we are amalgamated'. What happens, of course, is that the merger came apart at the seams. It seems to me that that is the sort of thing which could happen if the ideas of the F.T. were to prove generally acceptable.[17]

Neither Wade — nor the FOCs at the FT — opposed re-organizing production at the FT in itself: they were opposed to any change in demarcation. Nevertheless, despite this opposition, Wade and NGA FOCs regarded the FT social-implications proposals as a basis for discussion, although they did not go far enough, were prepared to countenance 'no automatic replacement' arrangements, and recognized that existing demarcations lines could, in unspecified circum-stances, become 'impractical'.[18] NATSOPA were more favourably disposed to the plan than the NGA was. The Executive had no reservation in principle against co-operating with the FT over the introduction of new technology, and regarded the social implications proposals as 'progressive', if not without difficulties.[19] Feelings at chapel level were more reserved and more fearful: the extent of co-operation management could hope to achieve was unpredictable. Nevertheless, there were good grounds for management feeling that NATSOPA members would co-operate: the scheme offered improved promotion prospects both within the machine room and elsewhere in exchange for fewer jobs. The NGA and NATSOPA were the unions most directly involved in the FT proposals: other unions viewed them with less concern, although members of all unions would be involved eventually. The NUJ, for example, paid little atten-tion to the proposals at Executive level, but at house level pressed strongly for full consultation over the proposals. The need for consultation was also emphasized by SOGAT. The Executives of SLADE, AUEW, and EETPU took little interest in the events: SLADE because it had few members at the FT, and their jobs were not at risk; the two engineering unions were too preoccupied with events elsewhere to pay close attention to the special needs of a section of their respective press branches whose interests were different from those of the majority of their members.

The FT's proposals created immediate concern amongst affected groups, and a meeting was held with SOGAT at which precise figures were given. But before significant progress could be made in discussions on the social impli-cations at house level the proposals were subsumed under the umbrella of the Joint Standing Committee discussions.

Members of FT management were heavily involved in the NPA's discussions with the PIC over the establishment of the Joint Standing Committee. The general view at the FT was that their announcement in July 1975 stimulated action on new technology at the national level, and that it was appropriate that the major effort on the social-implications front should henceforth be expended on pressing for agreement, at least on general terms, at the national level before any attempt to reach agreement at house level. FT management therefore concentrated on technical issues at house level, whilst awaiting the outcome of the national discussions on wider, social, issues.

The twin elements in the July 1975 development plan, new technology and industrial relations, led to two sets of developments which ought to have been linked, but were in fact separate. The obvious line of development would have involved carefully co-ordinated progress on the working out of technical details and on the implementation of the social proposals in the July plan: the two should have developed *pari passu*. In fact this did not happen. Considerable progress was made in clarifying technical alternatives and in drawing up detailed specifications: in view of the complexity of the task, the technical working parties achieved considerable success, with the completion, in ten months, of the System Requirements Specifications, extending to ten large volumes. However, no similar progress was made in implementing the social proposals. After two years no formal or informal discussions had taken place with chapels in-house on the social proposals: following the initial announcement full reliance was placed upon the achievement of agreement at national level, successive failures to meet anticipated deadlines resulting in little more than exasperation and frustration at house level. The purpose of this section is to chronicle this discrepancy between technical progress and social stalemate.

In the autumn of 1975 FT management signed a development contract with ICL for the design phase of the proposed installation, without any precise agreement on the eventual placing of a final installation contract, and appointed a computer expert from IPC to act as project manager. The new man, whose original academic background was in physics but who had spent a considerable amount of time in computers, most recently at IPC, was hired to provide the advanced technical knowledge required to oversee the systems design and to liaise with ICL, existing personnel having a detailed knowledge of printing technology (including computerized printing technology), but no extensive knowledge of computers. Simultaneously, a Steering Committee consisting of seven members was set up under the joint chairmanship of the joint general managers, including representatives from editorial, advertising, business enterprises, and production, as well as the project manager. The Steering Committee was directly responsible for the implementation of the development plan. Seven working parties were set up, to examine the detailed application of the new technology in specific areas, to report to the project manager on a day-to-day basis, but to be under the authority of the Steering Committee.

The Steering Committee working-party structure provided an effective administrative framework for detailed technological planning. The working parties explored the detailed implications of the overall concept for particular sections, whilst the Steering Group meetings provided an opportunity for responsible senior management to be informed of progress, and to make arrangements for joint meetings where the interests of the different working parties overlapped — for example, between the editorial and the production working parties. Smooth working arrangements were made with ICL, three professionally qualified staff being allocated to the project by the computer company, eager to establish a lead in winning the final installation contract by doing an effective job on the development work. Even if the FT contract was not to prove profitable in itself, the experience and the prestige involved in establishing the system were seen as a valuable means of winning other contracts, especially overseas. Relations between the FT and ICL were therefore close and effective. However, the problems which were to bedevil the whole exercise were inherent in the initial arrangements. Owing to continuing lack of progress on the social-implications discussions at national level and the anticipated hostility of house chapels to technological change until national-level agreement was reached, the working parties had only very limited access to the production process. The production working party contained only relatively senior production management, production chapels not being informed of the details under discussion, much less having direct representation through FOCs on the working party: the working party thus inevitably lacked very detailed knowledge of the precise workings of the production process, and was obliged to work, to some degree, up in the air. Pending agreement at national level this isolation may have been necessary. But it inevitably resulted in considerable suspicion amongst production workers of management's intentions, and a refusal to accept that the pensions, early retirement, and income-maintenance schemes 'changed the rules of the game', as the joint general manager claimed. The working parties were thus seriously out of balance, arrangements working effectively in the advertising area, reasonably effectively on editorial, but least effectively on production. This basic imbalance was linked with personal, organizational, and technical problems.

The position of project manager for a development plan is a very difficult one, requiring political and diplomatic, as well as technical, skills: technological change substantially alters the distribution of power and authority, not simply the processes of production, and thus requires a sensitivity to personal and political interests. This sensitivity is especially important where the project manager is an employee of the company, with at least a medium-term commitment: if the project manager is working for outside consultants he may be able to disregard internal politics to some degree, or if he is too insensitive he can be replaced. Unfortunately, such personal skills are not necessarily associated with technical virtuosity and commitment to scientific rationality. As the success of systems design rests upon the precise application of carefully worked out principles, it was likely that a project manager recruited on the basis of technical expertise and systems-design experience and insensitive to purely customary working practices would clash with existing staff. This could be avoided only by extreme skill at personal relations, a clear edict from the highest authority that the project manager's authority was total, or, possibly, the creation of a twin-headed team, in which the project manager would work *alongside* a well-established and skilful member of the management team. None of these conditions was met. Because of the particular conditions of the national newspaper industry, the project manager could not be given complete authority, even if the chief executive wished to give it to him – it was not his to give. Nor was he made to work alongside an established manager. Instead, his difficulties were increased by his being required to report to both joint general managers, one responsible for the FT, the other responsible for the St. Clement's Press (the company directly responsible for physically producing the paper). The joint general managers, despite their agreement on the basic need for a new technology, naturally had different views in detail – all the more so as one of the general managers had been responsible for the basic concept of the original plan and did not always agree with the technical opinions of the project manager. Moreover, a structure of joint general managers is itself inherently unstable, especially where their backgrounds and personal approaches differed sharply.

The confusing effects of this administrative situation were reinforced by a lack of clarity on basic technical issues. In July management announced a clear technical decision, to adopt a relatively centralized computer configuration, involving three large computers. However, the project manager naturally believed that since he was responsible for installing the new system, he should have some say in its basic logic. Or, failing that, he should be told very clearly the parameters within which he was to work and absolved from responsibility if those parameters resulted in an unduly expensive or otherwise unsuitable system. His own view was that a number of linked mini-computers might be more effective and was at least worth exploring; but if that was impossible, he was willing to go along with the decision. His reservations were shared by other members of the working parties and reinforced by the conclusions of the editorial working party which visited a number of computerized newspapers in the United States in February 1976. This uncertainty was gradually removed and, despite a feeling that the system might prove unnecessarily expensive and difficult to set up, the System Requirements were drawn up on the basis of the July logic.

Regardless of the eventual system design chosen, the drawing up of specifications required a very detailed examination of existing working practices. The working parties carried out this task in the first seven months of 1976. Unfortunately, the working parties varied in effectiveness, mainly because of the limited involvement on the production side. Despite difficulties, the editorial working parties worked effectively: the FOC was fully involved (from March 1976) and the minutes of the working parties were made generally available on the editorial floor. It was impossible to pursue a similar policy on the production side: involvement in the working parties was restricted to management, the FOCs were not involved, and there was no generally available information. ICL representatives were frequently to be seen on the editorial floor; they were unable to go onto the production floor. Since effective systems design rests upon very precise and accurate details about production processes and working practices, there was a feeling of uneasiness about a system designed on the basis of such information. Even on the editorial side there was a feeling that the information might not be totally reliable; for example, members of the working party were being asked to estimate various word counts in the final stages of the design phase. As one well-informed journalist commented at the time: 'Because so many people (some of whom have now left) have been involved in this work, because it was done in piecemeal fashion, because (perhaps inevitably at that stage) the right questions were not asked and because the agencies do not have all the data we require there are gaps in the figures and those that we have are no more than estimates.' Whether his foreboding was justified was never to be tested.

The technical difficulties involved in drawing up the System Requirement Specifications were surmounted, and the detailed specifications were available by the end of July 1976: it was arranged that ICL should make a detailed presentation to management at the end of the following month. It was estimated that a new system could be installed within nine months of a firm contract being signed with ICL. However, a significant change of course occurred before the ICL presentation could take place: the logic of the July 1975 presentation was replaced. Early in August ICL was told to stop work, at the end of the month the project manager was released (on generous terms), and early the following month management announced to a meeting of trade unionists, and subsequently to all employees, a modified development plan. The idea of a comprehensive, one-off, change to the new technology was replaced by a phased change-over:

In the current situation of the industry . . . we shall make progress faster by introducing a plan on a phased basis rather than attempting to introduce the whole system over-night. We shall be ready to proceed with each subsequent phase as soon as the previous phase is completed, until we reach the position that all those processes have been computerised which can produce useful savings.[20]

It was announced that a pilot scheme would be set up covering the survey pages. This would involve extending the existing computer system used for the Stock Exchange pages to include material prepared directly by journalists: input would be handled by NUJ and NGA members, with NATSOPA members handling advertising input. The pilot scheme would involve 'the same flexibility of labour that we will ultimately be seeking in the complete Development Plan', but, as surveys did not involve time-sensitive material, it would 'allow sufficient time for staffs to become familiar with the new equipment.' The Steering Group was to remain in being to study the phased introduction, but the seven working parties were to be disbanded and the position of project manager scrapped. Responsibility for new technology was to be part of the responsibilities of the head of Origination Services; responsibility for manpower issues was consolidated under the head of Manpower Services, whose position was strengthened by the merging of the manpower responsibilities of the FT and St. Clement's Press.

The major reason given for the new approach was the need to avoid putting the newspaper at risk:

We originally intended to change from the conventional technology to the new technology in one move. However, having now measured the size of the task involved, we consider this phased approach is most

242 FINANCIAL TIMES AND NEW TECHNOLOGY

likely to ensure that at no stage during the introduction of the new technology would the newspaper be at risk, and that in this way personnel in all areas of the Company, will have the best opportunity to retrain in the new technologies in advance.

Moreover, now that the FT had stimulated the NPA into action and was taking an active part in NPA decisions on the new technology, it was felt that it would be appropriate for the major initiatives to come from industry level, especially in view of the hope that an announcement of agreement on the Joint Standing Committee would soon be made, enabling house-level negotiations to begin.

However, the situation was, naturally, more complex than stated, and reflected a loss of confidence in the July strategy. Retraining was not in practice a major problem if the conditions were right, and the possibility of agreement on the Joint Standing Committee might have been expected to stimulate action on the original course rather than a change of direction. From the beginning some members of staff had thought that the comprehensive change-over was unrealistic: that the technology was not available and that to attempt a massive change-over would be disastrous. However, whether the technology was available or not was irrelevant: with existing or with new technology the design phase for a computer installation of the size proposed by the FT would take several months. The only way it would have been possible to carry out a rapid change-over involved the design phase preceding the July announcement. But it would have been impossible to complete the design phase without the FT's plans becoming known, with disastrous results. Since the design phase had to follow the July announcement it was inevitable that the momentum of the plan would seem to have been lost, resulting in serious local industrial relations problems. The only prospect for the acceptability of the comprehensive plan at house level involved rapid implementation in a crisis situation. Once momentum was lost, as it inevitably was, the development plan was likely to be bogged down in the fragmented bargaining system. The effect of this loss of momentum was reinforced by an improvement in the FT's financial situation: over the winter of 1975-6 the paper's advertising revenues began to rise, and management publicly stated in September that its economic situation was healthier than it had been six months earlier. In one respect, the decision to change course in August 1976 was a final public recognition of what had slowly become clear over the preceding months, namely, that once a situation of urgency and crisis had passed, a gradualist approach was inevitable.

The change of course rendered a considerable portion of the work on the System Requirements Specifications redundant: the concept of a pilot scheme only made sense if the pilot was used in order to try out strategies, involving the possibility of modifying the overall scheme. The change also involved a change in the relationship with ICL: there was no longer the expectation that the company would receive the final implementation contract, involving ICL in loss of face as well as money, since development work is less profitable than installation work, even where companies resist the temptation to under-charge for development work in order to obtain the installation contract. The seven working parties were replaced by a single Surveys Working Party, charged with responsibility for a detailed analysis of the survey operation, both on the editorial and the production sides. Surveys were regarded as a particularly suitable area for a pilot scheme, as they involved the basic principles of direct journalist input, and computerized typesetting, but were not a vital ingredient in the paper's editorial success and involved very few production workers. Whether it was the technically most desirable area to experiment in was an open question: the marginality of surveys meant that the system would not be tested *in extremis*. However, it was envisaged that the new approach would involve a four-stage process: a possibly long stage during which the principle of editorial input would be established by the surveys experiment, and then shorter stages involving, in sequence, regular columns not necessarily set up on the day of use, news, and a management control system. Even if the survey pages would not be a particularly valuable technical test, they would be a good opportunity to establish the basic principle of editorial input.

Despite inevitably lower morale, work on the systems design for surveys continued over the winter, with the technical focus largely upon the choice of VDU screen for journalists. Although the choice of screen had implications for the total system in any circumstances, lack of progress elsewhere and continued editorial interest made it likely that the large irresolvable issues would be pushed towards a solution by this specific decision. The editorial feeling was that the ICL experimental screen was not satisfactory, that ICL lacked specific experience in computerized printing systems, especially in preparing soft-ware, and that in any event relations with ICL were soured by experience over the development phase. Instead, the choice was seen as being between two American systems (despite the dollar costs involved): a Harris system, similar to the one being installed in the *New York Times*, and an ATEX system, customized to the FT's requirements. Doubts about the viability of ATEX were calmed by Pearson Longman Ltd.'s experience with the company over the installation of an ATEX system at *The Economist,* and by US experience. The Surveys Working Party favoured an ATEX screen and therefore an ATEX system. The screen was more flexible than available alternatives and, though its key-board was relatively complex, it provided more all-round flexibility. In the spring of 1977 the working party's advice was accepted, and it was decided to purchase an ATEX system for the Surveys Pilot Schme.

However, by the time the detailed evaluation of alternative systems had been completed, the decision had been overtaken by developments elsewhere. The ballot on the Joint Standing Committee's proposals *Programme for Action* had been rejected. This absence of agreement at national level meant that there were no guidelines for in-house developments and no external union pressure on chapels to adopt a favourable attitude towards the new technology. In this new situation houses were faced with the prospect of 'going it alone'. This had, of course, been an initial possibility early in 1975 and a recurrent reaction throughout to the frustrating delays in reaching agreement on the Joint Standing Committee. However, the situation throughout the industry, and at the FT in particular, was different in 1977 from that of 1975: 'going it alone' looked less attractive. The crisis of 1975 had passed; the FT was making very satisfactory profits; there was a realistic appreciation of the technical problems associated with the new technology; and chapel reactions to the development plan had been as hostile as management had expected. Management therefore had the choice of pressing ahead with the pilot scheme or publicly postponing the whole exercise. It was decided to announce a postponement for an indefinite period. The potential rewards for continuing with the limited scheme were not thought worth the effort: since the basic principle of journalist in-put was at stake it was unrealistic to see it as a 'suck-it-and-see' policy, and it could not be sold to chapel officials on that basis. If the basic principle of editorial in-put was not adopted and a computerized system was used merely as a means of enabling subeditors to recall typeset material for further subbing and revising, it would not justify the expense. It was therefore announced:

We have regretfully come to the conclusion that we can make no progress with the Development Plan until all the Unions are ready to respond to the principles contained in our original proposals.

The main reason for this conclusion is the problem of jurisdiction. *The Financial Times* newspaper unlike other national newspaper companies cannot justify investment in the new technology without an agreement from the outset to the principle of direct inputting into the system from all sources of news and advertising and until this is agreed by all Unions we should be wasting money and distorting the wage structure in attempting to reach agreements piecemeal. As soon as this problem is overcome . . . we will be able to move forward quickly to implement the Plan.[21]

On this note the hopes of the July 1975 development plan finally foundered: whether they would be revised in six months, or five years, was not then known. In the immediate future, instead of proceeding with plans for large-scale computerized photocomposition, FT management devoted its attention to the launching of a European edition, printed in Germany from text originated in London, and transmitted by facsimile transmission. The first edition was successfully printed in Frankfurt in January 1979. The issue of computerized typesetting and photocomposition was to re-emerge in November 1980, when the FT announced that it was to buy a computerized system from Linotype-Paul, to be installed between late 1981 and the beginning of 1984.

The company did not propose to introduce single key-boarding, NGA members alone operating the equipment, as at MGN. The new system was initially to replace the existing computer-assisted photocomposition system, used to produce the paper's statistical material, but to be extended in phases to special surveys, features, and news coverage. The FT's proposals in 1980 were very different from those put forward in 1975, and closer to those of MGN in 1975 (see below, chapter 8).[22]

In the two years between July 1975 and June 1977 the FT development plan evolved through two distinct phases: between 1975 and the summer of 1976 the comprehensive aspirations survived, although with growing doubts about their outcome. Between August 1976 and June 1977 the company was committed to the gradual introduction of new technology, but with diminishing enthusiasm and commitment. This phase ended with the announcement of the postponement of the plan in June 1977. Considerable progress was made in evaluating alternative technologies, and a small group of employees acquired a highly sophisticated understanding of the new technology. But the amount of positive progress made was small. No new electronic equipment was brought in-house, and little progress made towards familiarizing employees with the new equipment, as a necessary preliminary to retraining. No progress was made in persuading production chapels of the need for the new technology (although some employees at least were well disposed at the beginning, believing that some change was inevitable) and the progress made in persuading the NUJ Chapel of the advantage of the new system was largely lost by the decision to suspend the whole plan. The proposals for dealing with early retirement and voluntary redundancy had received wide support and provided the basis for FT management policy throughout. They were also well received by the ACAS team, the Royal Commission on the Press, and, most importantly, by the Joint Standing Committee. But they played little role in-house, as discussions with the chapels on the proposals did not get under way. Had such discussions got under way, it is likely that such proposals would have provided a viable basis for negotiation.

What, then, emerges from this account? Does it merely indicate that newspapers are better at telling others what to do than at putting their own house in order, illustrating the distasteful edict 'do as I say, not as I do'? Does it seriously damage the 'credibility' of the FT and Pearson Longman Boards, as a resolution passed by the NUJ Chapel on the announcement of the postponement in June 1977 alleged? Was it, as one participant argued, an exercise in how not to implement technological change?

iii

The fundamental decision FT management had to make was whether to put forward a development plan at all. There were compelling pressures leading towards such a plan: it was seen as the only way of securing the long-term future of the newspaper, which seemed to be under serious threat if the economic trends of late 1974 were to continue. Once the decision to put forward a plan had been taken, the basic alternatives were between a gradual, phased plan, and a comprehensive, total, one-off change. Other newspaper companies, most notably at that stage MGN, had announced plans for introducing new technology on a phased basis and within existing demarcation lines. TNL subsequently announced a similar phased plan, but not within existing demarcation lines. However, the FT had different objectives from those of MGN and a different working situation from that of TNL. In view of the size of the composing room and its level of earnings, the FT's major — though not sole — savings could be made in the composing area. Moreover, this could not be done with existing technology, for the composing room was not significantly over-manned for large (48-page) newspapers — it was only over-manned for smaller newspapers, and it was impossible to predict what future advertising levels, and therefore future pagination, would be. It had to be assumed that 48-page papers, although rare early in 1975, would return. Changes would therefore be required in the technology of the composing room. One solution would have been to invest in new machinery within existing demarcation lines — for example, with the use of typesetting machines with computerized hyphenation and justification.

However, the productivity improvements to be expected from such partial changes were small and, on the basis of past experience, would be unlikely to involve major savings in labour costs: the negotiation of previous marginal manning changes had simply involved spreading savings amongst remaining employees, resulting in further industrial relations problems as relativities were disrupted. A root-and-branch solution was therefore necessary. The success of American newspapers using direct editorial input suggested that such a solution was available. The need for a comprehensive system was reinforced by industrial relations requirements. Any attempt at a piecemeal solution would involve the plan in being bogged down in bargaining with individual chapels, making overall progress slow. Moreover, experience over the negotiation of 'comprehensive' agreements indicated that piecemeal productivity bargaining could be expensive, as well frustrating. Events were to show that the comprehensive solution involved more difficulties than were anticipated: but that is not to argue that the comprehensive proposals were inappropriate.

Following the July announcement, FT management were caught in a cleft stick. Even on the most optimistic assumptions the detailed work of computer systems design would take several months, and the writing of the software several more: there was thus likely to be a delay of several months, even if the hardware was available 'off the shelf'. The most comparable newspapers in the United States took several years to implement computerized systems, even with the wide availability of computer expertise, the existence of local printing system companies, and, in the case of the *New York Times*, very large financial resources. However, the industrial relations logic involved maintaining a sense of urgency: initial reaction among NGA members was one of shock and a willingness, at least among older members, at least to contemplate accepting voluntary redundancy. The longer events seemed to take, the more opponents began to think that FT management had simply been making a tactical move in making the July announcement: NGA reactions therefore hardened. The London regional secretary commented on the waning sense of urgency amongst newspaper owners early in 1976, singling out the FT.[23] However, systems design and analysis could not be rushed if the system was to work effectively, and it was impossible to maintain a sense of crisis over several months, especially when the newspaper's financial situation was known to be improving. There was thus a tension between technical logic and industrial relations logic at house level, without taking into account the frustrations stemming from developments at national level.

Lack of obvious progress on either the technical or the social front may have been one factor in the decision to change course in August 1976 and adopt a piecemeal approach. This made sense in one way. The July 1975 plan had pointed in a very specific direction and had indicated what turned out to be an unrealistic timetable. The August 1976 decision was presented as simply a rephasing, suggesting that the eventual destination would be the same, but that a more realistic timetable was being adopted. However, as one of the participants involved argued at the time, the new policy involved movement in a particular direction, not towards a particular place; it was unrealistic to have a detailed comprehensive plan when the economic situation and the technology available were changing rapidly. It was therefore disingenuous to argue that the change was simply a change in phasing, making explicit the timetable which had already come to be accepted in practice. If the new phasing merely represented a public acceptance of what had privately become recognized as inevitable, it is surprising that it was associated with such extensive consequences as the scrapping of the working parties, the release of the project manager, the ending of the special relationship with ICL, and the collapse of the morale of many of the employees most involved in the project. It is difficult to believe that it was not recognized that the partial, piece-by-piece approach was not on – at the very least, the NGA's opposition to the principle of direct editorial input made clear that any attempt at editorial input, even on a partial, trial basis, would be strongly resisted. NGA members were well aware of the threat posed to the 'principle' of NGA monopoly over composing, and FT management of NGA determination to resist the 'take-over of the composing function by any other union'.[24] The abortive experiment on the survey pages indicated clearly that FT management had no alternative to a comprehensive strategy.

FT management's policy over the 1975 development plan thus involved a sequence of U-turns, as the NUJ Chapel complained. Such changes inevitably raise questions about managerial credibility. One reaction to such criticism is to make a moral virtue of necessity: newspapers are vulnerable, newspaper managements are fearful and weak, but, in Lord Goodman's words, 'some of the greatest moral courage displayed by newspapers has been a readiness to capitulate.'[25] Such casuistry – black is not merely grey, but white – is hardly convincing. However, changing direction indicated flexibility, rather than moral vice or virtue: a willingness to recognize that the balance of forces which had made one strategy look right in 1975 had disappeared the following year. The evaporation of the sense of crisis in Fleet Street in general between 1975 and 1976 was remarkable; it had more justification at the FT than elsewhere, owing to the FT's especially favourable financial situation. This improvement, the necessarily slow technical progress of the working parties, and the stalemate on the Joint Standing Committee undermined the 'big-bang' strategy. By July 1976 FT management were bound to lose face, as the original timetable had disappeared. One reaction would have been to allow the timetable to disappear silently. However, the initial interest created by the July announcement, the concern in-house, and the continuing discussions on the Joint Standing Committee, made it impossible for the plan to disappear unobtrusively. It was therefore necessary to make a public announcement, with the consequent loss of face involved. The remodelling of the development plan to incorporate the Surveys Pilot Scheme was a means of maintaining impetus, without committing extensive resources, pending clarification of the national situation. Once it had become clear that national developments were hostile to the new technology, managment was faced with the dilemma of continuing the pilot, which could not any longer be a pilot, returning to the original strategy, or abandoning the plan. The fact that worthwhile labour savings could be made only by a comprehensive plan, rather than the inherent character of the technology itself, made small-scale innovations inappropriate. However, a comprehensive plan could not be implemented by a single newspaper acting alone, without very considerable difficulties, as indicated by the experience of The Times and MGN, discussed in the following two chapters. If the FT acted independently, other newspapers would increase production to win circulation, or, if agreement between proprietors or union pressures made this impossible, large resources would be required to sustain a long dispute. The unions involved, especially the NGA, would naturally regard the FT as a test case and provide extensive financial support and pressure on other houses. FT management feared they would be 'taken to the cleaners', in the widely used phrase. Subsequent events at other houses suggested they were probably right.

The evolution of FT management's policy reflected a flexible response to a changing situation: subsequent events largely confirmed the substantive decisions produced by management's growing scepticism. However, criticism focused upon the mode in which decisions were made, as much as upon their content, especially the lack of consultation.

The development plan emphasized the need for consultation and openness in the discussions. One aspect of this openness was a willingness to show FOCs the firm's accounts on a regular basis, and to discuss the firm's financial situation (even when it was doing well and such knowlege helped chapel bargaining); another was the willingness to allow an outsider access for research. However, throughout the two years a major complaint was the lack of consultation, whether with individuals in specific instances or with representatives in general. This lack of consultation was expected by production FOCs: until agreement was reached in the Joint Standing Committee on the framework for house-level consultations there was no structure for the discussions, and when it finally became clear that *Programme for Action* was a dead letter, management did put forward proposals for a Joint House Committee. There was no question of any workers other than FOCs taking part in the production working party, and there was no likelihood of FOCs' agreeing to participate on terms acceptable to management. There was no attempt to discuss the new technology with FOCs, even during the balloting of the Joint Standing Committee proposals, as it was thought likely to be counter-productive and would, in addition, serve to undermine the national officials who had signed the document. However, editorial workers took a different view. Opinions varied among journalists on the merits of the new technology and on the extent to which financial compensation ought to be sought for new working arrangements; but there was little opposition in principle to a change which would enhance editorial power. No journalists' jobs were at stake. Nevertheless, despite the involvement of the NUJ FOC in the editorial working party and the wide availability of relevant documentation (including the ten fat volumes of System Requirements Specifications, for the curious), there were complaints about lack of consultation on crucial decisions and an occasionally expressed feeling that the 'sixth floor' did not understand life on the second, editorial, floor. Hence the NUJ Chapel passed motions criticizing the lack of consultation on the part of higher management both at the beginning of the exercise and at the end. Such feelings were to be expected, but, except in individual cases, scarcely justified. There was adequate provision for consultation on routine decisions, the level of involvement far exceeding that of American houses, even houses in which journalists were unionized, and management stated categorically that the department's specified needs would be met. However, the complaints related to more specific major decisions, about which there was minimal consultation, on generally recognized grounds of personal embarrassment or commercial confidentiality.

In view of the traditions of the industry, the lack of consultation with production FOCs and the slowness in getting the house-level joint committees first mooted in the July 1975 plan off the ground were predictable. There was no house-level tradition of co-ordination between chapels, much less between management and chapels; any attempt to develop joint institutions before agreement at national level ran the risk of being accused of attempting to set up a house union and of undermining union solidarity. Nevertheless, the absence of consultation had important consequences:

management could only guess at shop-floor reactions, and the shop floor could only suspect the worst of management. In such circumstances it is not surprising that the Imperial FOC of the NGA caused a one-day stoppage in October 1975 over management's refusal to give a definite guarantee that there would be no compulsory redundancies, although the whole assumption of management strategy was that there would be no need for compulsory redundancies.[26] Similarly, suspicions developed that FT management was attempting to 'do a deal' with national-level officials and then use that agreement to secure acceptance of management plans at house level. The speedy creation of joint institutions at house level, had that been possible, would not have avoided industrial tension, but might have alleviated it. Moreover, in a situation in which the possibility of Fleet Street proprietors' – or even simply 'quality' proprietors' – acting in concert was remote, the only hope of achieving the installation of the necessary new technology lay in enlisting as near wholehearted support as possible at house level. In such circumstances joint institutuions, even if only supported by the journalists, were a prime necessity.

Chapter 7

Times Newspapers Ltd.
and Technological Change

In 1974-5 The Times faced problems similar to those faced
by the FT, in a more acute form. The small losses experienced
by the group in the early 1970s turned into substantial
losses in 1974 and 1975, revenue from the *Sunday Times*
being insufficient to cover *The Times*'s continuing substantial
losses. Increased cover prices maintained circulation revenue,
but circulation was falling (especially of *The Times*) and
advertising revenue was beginning to fall. The overall problems
and solutions were similar to those of the FT, although the
details differed. The TNL Board was considering the scope
for major savings in production costs through computerization at the same time as the FT Board, and was fully aware
of FT thinking, both through the NPA and through direct
informal contacts. It was therefore hardly surprising that in
May 1976 The Times publicly announced plans for new
technology similar in overall conception to those announced
by FT management the preceding July. However, as is well
known, events developed differently in the two houses;
Times management pressed ahead with its proposals for new
technology despite the collapse of *Programme for Action*,
the decision of FT management to suspend its development
plan indefinitely, and opposition from its employees. The
suspension of publication in November 1978 was not the
direct result of new technology, but the uncertainty about
new technology contributed to the frequent interruptions to
production which led to management's determination to
attempt to reassert control; without new technology the
disruption might have been less and it might have proved
easier to negotiate agreements on new disputes procedures
and continuity of production. This chapter does not attempt
a detailed history of industrial relations at TNL in 1978-9
or the course of events which led to TTO's decision to sell

the newspapers in 1980. Instead, it is a general examination of the development of new technology at The Times, in the context of overall trends in Fleet Street.

Times management publicly announced its plans for new technology, 'Opportunity for Success', in *The Times* on 28 May 1976.[1] 'Our intention is to introduce, in the most practical and precisely phased way, a computerised photo-composition system, linked closely with the production, advertisement, editorial and accounting departments.' Despite an initial ambitious plan to install the first phase of the new system by January 1977, the process of implementation was slower, both for technical and for industrial relations reasons. Industrial relations at the group deteriorated in 1977 and 1978, partly for reasons independent of new technology, and management became more committed to new technology as a means to achieving a major once-for-all transformation in the company's industrial relations, with an assertion of management's authority. In April 1978 management threatened the suspension of publication unless new agreements covering guaranteed continuity of production, a new disputes procedure, new manning levels, and new technology were concluded by 30 November 1978. Very little progress was made in the negotiations before the deadline, and despite last-minute government intervention, resulting in extension of the deadline for the conclusion of the agreements until 13 December, the papers ceased publication for eleven and a half months. Not surprisingly, for Times management the struggle became symbolic of the problems facing British industry, with Times management accepting a challenge evaded by other less courageous managements.

This dispute is in some ways a symbol of a national crisis . . . These major historic themes — that unofficial strikes are a mortal danger to effective trade unionism, that new technology is the inevitable future of the printing industry and is already the present of the printing industry in the United States, that the battle for higher productivity means concern for higher real pay and not higher paper wages — are what the negotiation in Times Newspapers is concerned with.[2]

Union reactions to Times management's proposals grew predictably more hostile: readiness to discuss new technology within the normal context of collective bargaining gave way to determination to resist 'duress'. The suspension of publication lasted longer than either management or unions expected, resolution of the conflict becoming possible only when management recognized that agreement on new technology could not be achieved before the resumption of publication. Following the resumption of publication, new manning levels were negotiated in some sectors, and training upon new machinery began. However, no major changes in demarcation lines were negotiated, and major issues remained unresolved when Thomson British Holdings Ltd. announced on 22 October 1980 that it intended to sell, or close, Times Newspapers Ltd. within six months.

This chapter examines the sequence of events in four sections: section i deals with the economic background and with the place of Times Newspapers in the Thomson Organisation; section ii outlines management's thinking on new technology and the process of implementation; section iii covers the industrial relations situation at TNL, especially during the suspension in 1978-9; and section iv deals with the significance of developments at The Times.

i

Like the FT, TNL is a small part of a large multinational conglomerate corporation, ultimately controlled by family trusts: also like the FT, its financial contribution to the overall fortunes of the group is insignificant.[3] Yet Times Newspapers Ltd. played a disproportionate role in the Thomson group's thinking. Traditionally, owners of The Times have regarded it as a national institution. To the irritation of other newspapers, this claim to be more than simply a daily newspaper is widely accepted: publication in The Times is accorded an authoritative status not accorded to publication elsewhere. Although the second Lord Thomson did not appear to enjoy the same relish in the ownership of a national institution as his father, filial piety and the desire to avoid needlessly offending a government whose goodwill was required for the most profitable exploitation of North Sea oil rights ensured a level of financial support unjustifiable on financial grounds alone. The Sunday Times and the three supplements do not possess the distinctive status of The

Times; nor do they usually lose money. Times Newspapers Ltd. thus had access to the very substantial capital resources of a major multi-national corporation without being subject to strict financial control: it thus had considerable scope for initiative in developing its technological and industrial relations policies. But the price of this indulgence was occasional and decisive intervention from outside.

After outlining the corporate structure of the Thomson group, the following section examines the significance of the links between TNL and the Thomson Organization.

Before entering British newspapers, Roy Thomson was a major newspaper proprietor in North America, whose fortune was based upon paper manufacturing as well as on publishing: his attitude towards newspapers was essentially an entrepreneurial one, with an ostentatious disinterest in editorial policy.[4] His first British purchase was the *Scotsman*, acquired in 1955; he acquired the *Sunday Times* and the rest of the Kemsley empire from Lord Kemsley in 1960, and in 1966 *The Times* and its supplements from the Astor family. After detailed investigation by the Monopolies Commission the unprofitable *Times* was merged with the *Sunday Times* to form Times Newspapers Limited. From 1967 onwards Times Newspapers Limited was a subsidiary of the Thomson Organisation, which owned 85 per cent of its shares, the remainder belonging to Astor family interests. Between 1967 and 1978 the Thomson Organisation was owned by Thomson Scottish Associates (65.9 per cent), Thomson British Holdings (13.9 per cent), and independent investors. In 1978 the International Thomson Organisation was set up in Canada, as a 'shadow' company for Thomson British Holdings, all shares in the former being related to the latter, and the interrelations between the companies involved were reorganized.[5] The International Thomson Organisation and its British shadow are both controlled by Thomson Equitable Corporation Limited, which owns 81.3 per cent of their shares: the latter company is wholly owned by Thomson family interests. Fig. 7 summarizes the group's corporate structure following the 1978 reorganization.

The objective of the restructuring of the Thomson Organisation in 1978 was to facilitate the merger of the Thomson

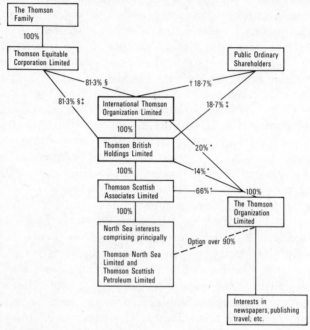

* approximate percentages
† including 1,460,451 shares (1·0 per cent.) owned by the Thomson family.
‡ all shares in International Thomson Organization Limited will have related to them shares
  in Thomson British Holdings Limited.
§ including 4,000,000 shares (2·87 per cent.) to be transferred by Thomson Equitable Corporation
  Limited to the Thomson family immediately after the Scheme becomes affective.

All the above companies are incorporated in the United Kingdom except for Thomson Equitable
Corporation Limited and International Thomson Organization Limited which are incorporated in
Canada.

Fig. 7. The organization of the Thomson Group after 1978
Source: The Financial Times

family interests in North Sea oil with the interests of the
Thomson Organisation.[6] To reduce risks to TTO the initial
costs of Thomson's North Sea oil exploration were financed
directly by loans raised by Thomson family interests, The
Thomson Organisation being given an option to acquire 90
per cent of the oil interests for a nominal amount: the reorganization involved the exercise of the option. However, to
reduce UK tax liabilities and to widen the range of investment options, the new International Thomson Organisation

was established in Canada, where there were no exchange controls: this avoided the danger of the British TTO accumulating cash from the Piper and Claymore North Sea oilfields, then beginning to reach peak production, without being able to find profitable outlets for new investments. Monopoly legislation inhibited investment in areas of likely interest in Britain, especially in publishing, and the system of exchange control then operating inhibited investment abroad. The aims of the reorganization had little to do with TNL. However, the expansion of North Sea oil output and the resultant reorganization had three effects on TNL. The increased financial strength of the Thomson group inevitably made it economically feasible for the group to sustain heavy losses at TNL without substantially damaging the group as a whole, providing grounds for critics to allege that Times Newspapers were using North Sea oil to break the power of the Fleet Street unions: it may thus have contributed to the unexpected duration of the suspension. It also reduced the financial significance of TNL to the group. Finally, although TTO remained based in London, the creation of the shadow ITO based in Toronto inevitably reduced the group's long-term commitment to the United Kingdom. The group announced that it intended to become 'a leading international publishing, communications and information business with strong interests in leisure and natural resources'. Although the company emphasized its continuing commitment to the United Kingdom, the first major purchase made was the American textbook publisher Wadsworth (from Thomson family interests), and subsequent investments have been mainly in North America.

A second major financial restructuring of 1978 involved TNL more directly, the taking over of financial responsibility for TNL by the Thomson Organisation directly. Although TNL had been part of TTO since 1966, its finances had been sustained directly by the Thomson family, with the family retaining the option to transfer the financial responsibility at six months' notice. The option was exercised in 1978. Although it had no immediate effect, for the long term it symbolized the evolution of TNL away from its special status towards a more conventional relationship with its holding company. In the long term this may have resulted in the application of conventional financial criteria to TNL, leading to the eventual decision to sell.

As an almost wholly owned subsidiary, TNL is linked into the Thomson Organisation by overlapping boards of directors. In 1978 the main Thomson Board comprised: Lord Thomson, G. C. Brunton (managing director), W. C. Golding (deputy managing director), Sir Denis Hamilton, Lord Thomas of Remenham (chairman, Chesham Investments), J. A. Tory, W. M. Brown, G. B. Parrack (managing director, Thomson Publications), and J. Evans (secretary). The main board of TNL comprised Sir Denis Hamilton (chairman and editor-in-chief), M. J. Hussey (managing director and chief executive), G. C. Brunton, T. D. P. Emblem (representing Lord Astor), H. M. Evans (editor of the *Sunday Times*), Lord Greene of Harrow Weald, Sir Kenneth Keith (subsequently Lord Keith of Castleacre), M. Mander, D. Nisbet-Smith, W. Rees-Mogg, Lord Robens of Woldingham, Lord Roll of Ipsden, J. A. Tory, and Professor Hugh Trevor-Roper (subsequently Lord Dacre of Glanton). The TNL Board comprised three major groups: public service directors appointed to ensure the maintenance of *The Times*'s traditional public service role; executives of the Thomson Organisation, with no special interest in national newspapers; and national newspaper executives. The public service directors probably had the smallest role to play in management decisions on industrial relations – Greene, Keith, Robens, Roll, and Trevor-Roper. The major formal links with the Thomson Organisation were provided by the second group, those who were members of the boards of both companies, namely J. A. Tory, Q. C., J. Evans (secretary of TTO), Sir Dennis Hamilton, and especially G. C. Brunton, the managing director of the Thomson Organisation. The third group comprised newspaper executives, who also belonged to TNL's Executive Board: M. J. Hussey (chairman), H. M. Evans, M. Mander, D. Nisbet-Smith, W. Rees-Mogg. The Executive Board also included D. Cruickshank, D. F. Heritage, and D. Jewell, who were newspaper executives.

It is impossible to obtain accurate information on the significance of the overlapping directorates and the level at which specific decisions were reached: the proceedings of the

Boards involved remain confidential, and conflicting views have been expressed on the degrees of involvement of different institutions and persons in different decisions on new technology. However, it is noteworthy that no member of the Times Executive Board was also a member of the main board of the Thomson Organisation, suggesting a relatively low degree of group integration (or the marginality of The Times to the overall interests of the group). Opinions were therefore conveyed through a system of indirect representation. This increased the importance of personal links between the participants and of the ability of representatives from lower boards to represent accurately their own board's decisions and to obtain higher authority's support. The main focus of decision was the Board of Times Newspapers Ltd. advised on a detailed basis by the executive directors who were also members of the Executive Board; the two members of the TNL Board who were also on the TTO Board presumably spoke for the views of the one to the other when required. This *may* have influenced decisions at a crucial stage, during Lord Thomson's visit from Canada in July 1979, when the Thomson's Board was involved in the management decision to accept reinstatement without prior commitment to the principle of direct input by non-NGA members; Sir Dennis Hamilton was thought to be a 'dove' rather than a 'hawk'. But it is more likely to have simply made the process of decision-making less predictable and less smooth than in a more integrated group. Throughout, the emphasis was upon the direct responsibility of the TNL Board, and more particularly the Times executives on it, for decisions about TNL: there is no evidence of dictation from North America, although North American experience was of course regarded as relevant, and on specific occasions North American influence was important (especially over the decision to employ Systems Development Corporation).

Since the senior management group at TNL was relatively small, personalities and personal relations were important. This may have been given further imporance by the limited institutional links between The Times and TTO. Hence the special importance of the role of G. C. Brunton, chief executive and managing director of TTO, and M. J. Hussey, managing director and chief executive of TNL. Before becoming chief executive at TTO, Brunton had had a varied career in printing and publishing, both within the Thomson Organisation and outside it. He had been managing director of Tower Press Group from 1958 until 1961, director at Odhams in 1961, before joining the Thomson Organisation and becoming managing director of Thomson Publications Ltd. in 1961. In addition to his work in TTO, Brunton was active in the PPITB, the Periodical Publishers' Association, and other trade bodies. On a wider stage, he had an extensive interest in management education, being an active member of the Council of the Oxford Centre for Management Studies. M. J. Hussey was a more traditional establishment figure than Brunton, educated at Rugby and Trinity College, Oxford, whereas Brunton had been to Cranleigh and the London School of Economics; military service in the Grenadier Guards compared with the Royal Artillery. Most of his working life was spent at Associated Newspapers, under Rothermere; he joined Harmsworth Publications as managing director in 1967, but left after only three years to join Thomson's. He was appointed to Thomson's Executive Board in 1971. Following Hussey's appointment, a number of changes occurred lower down the management hierarchy. Most importantly, John Dixey, who had been Production Services Director and who had implemented cost reduction exercises and introduced computerization and phototype-setting of Stock Market pages at *The Times* in 1968-9, left to work directly with Brunton, and subsequently to become director of the Newspaper Publishers' Association. Geoffrey Rowett, who had been director and general manager of TNL since its formation in 1966, left and subsequently became chief executive of the Charterhouse group. Rowett was succeeded by Harvey Thompson, formerly with MGN and the *Guardian*, who played a central role in developing thinking about new technology at TNL, and choosing the system. His early death in 1978, due to a heart attack, seriously disrupted the project. He was succeeded by Dugal Nisbet-Smith, the manager responsible for successfully negotiating the installation of new technology at MGN's Glasgow *Daily Record*, and a member of the MGN Board.

TNL's membership of TTO gave the company access to extensive financial resources, especially following the coming on stream of the Piper and Claymore North Sea oilfields. But the financial links were not associated with close organizational integration: TTO directors and senior executives were not newspapermen, and allowed TNL Executives to follow their own policies. (It was reported that some members of the TTO Board first learned of the date of the suspension of publication of Times Newspapers from newspaper reports.)[7] TTO was a holding company, with few central resources, and none suitable for providing management direction for the implementation of new technology in national newspapers. Thomson Regional Newspapers had acquired extensive experience of computerization in provincial newspapers: Thomson's Reading *Evening Post*, using computerized type-setting, photocomposition, and web-offset printing was launched as long ago as 1965, and at the time was claimed to be the most technically advanced newspaper in the world.[8] But it was believed that the technical and other requirements of provincial publications and Fleet Street were different, and that only the most general lessons of the one were applicable to the other: hence there was no attempt to transfer technically qualified personnel from Thomson's Regional Newspapers. Organizational independence from TTO was not simply a practical issue; it was justified on the hallowed grounds of editorial independence — the fundamental value of editorial independence overrode any practical advantages organizational interdependence might have had. From the newspaper point of view independence had considerable advantages. But it also meant that when TNL suspended publication no other group within TTO was clamouring that its interests were being damaged. There was therefore less pressure from other companies within the group for a rapid settlement.

The EIU commented on *The Times* under the Astors that the Board 'probably regarded [the newspaper] as a national institution, rather than as a commercial business.'[9] The tradition was maintained by the Thomsons. The function of TNL within the Thomson group was felt to be as a cultural flag-ship, transforming the organization from an anonymous multi-national conglomerate into a national institution. Identification with British national interests was thought to be especially important for a foreign-based company, as TTO had largely become with the establishment of the International Thomson Organisation in 1978, making very substantial profits from exploitation of a national resource — perhaps comparable to multi-national sponsorship of native culture in the Third World. This special status was symbolized by the presence of 'public interest' directors on the Board. Ownership of TNL was thus a prestige symbol for the Thomson group. However, prestige was not regarded as priceless, and may indeed have been tarnished by the extensive publicity, not always favourable, given to the newspapers' industrial relations problems in 1978–9. Moreover, during the suspension the British establishment was subject to inconvenience, but hardly to paralysis, suggesting that other newspapers could, if convinced of the long-term absence of *The Times*, attempt to fill *The Times*'s traditional role. Throughout the suspension TTO maintained that *The Times* was not for sale, and that eventual republication, under existing ownership, was assured. But the future maintenance of the publications was to be conditional upon the prospect of breaking even financially, and of avoiding spectacular industrial relations crises: the conditions were not to be met.

The function of Times Newspapers within the Thomson Organisation may have been symbolic; but the group was not totally insensitive to TNL's finances. TNL is a comparatively small part of a Canadian based multi-national corporation, whose major interests are in North Sea oil, travel, and publishing, including regional newspapers and books as well as national newspapers. In 1976 TTO had a turnover of £284,541,000 and an overall net profit (after payments to minority interests and extra-ordinary debits) of £5,475,000: a pre-tax profit of £15,184,000 was derived from £7,304,000 from travel, £5,584,000 from regional newspapers, £6,559,000 from other publications, £447,000 from general activities, and a loss of £1,470,000 by TNL.[10] TNL's financial results in 1976 were not unusual: losses were also made in 1974 and 1975. *The Times* itself has lost money every year since

it was acquired by Lord Thomson in 1966. In publicly
announcing the development plan in May 1976 TNL provided a gloomy analysis of its financial position.[11] *The Times*
itself continued to lose money, whilst even the *Sunday Times*
lost money in 1974 and 1975. For the group as a whole,
circulation revenue rose from £6m in 1970 to £13,300,000 in
1975 but this was due to increases in cover prices, not to
increases in circulation. The price of *The Times* rose from
8*d* (3.03p) in 1970 to 12p in 1976, that of the *Sunday Times*
from 1*s*.3*d* (6p) to 18p over the same period, faster than the
rate of increase in the general level of prices. *The Times*
reached its highest level of circulation in 1970 (388,000) and
by 1976 had dropped back to 310,000, although one reason
for the reduction was reduced marketing effort, since the
marginal increase in circulation did not justify in increased
advertising revenues the increased costs of production. The
Sunday Times peaked in 1973, at 1,517,000 and by 1976
had dropped back to 1,382,000. Advertising revenue rose in
the early 1970s, but the rate of increase tailed off in 1973–4;
in 1975 it declined in absolute terms from the level achieved
in 1974 (£27,800,000 in 1975, compared with £28,300,000
in 1974), at a time when inflation was running above 20 per
cent a year. TNL expected the rate of decline in advertising
revenue to increase, in real if not in money terms, as economic
recession worsened: both *The Times* and the *Sunday Times*
included large numbers of small advertisements, which were
thought to be highly sensitive to the level of economic
activity. Recession was thought to be especially disadvantageous to *The Times*'s revenues from small advertisements
because the newspaper published large numbers of job
advertisements, especially sensitive to economic recession.
The Thomson Organisation did not regard TNL as a 'major
profit centre'; instead, it wanted the newspaper to be 'self-
sufficient'. In 1978 it was publicly stated that the holding
company would not take any profits from TNL over the next
five years — although on the basis of past experience this
self-denial was hardly necessary.[12] The group was not seriously
concerned about occasional losses. But it was concerned that
TNL should be established on a secure financial basis for
the long term. As *The Times* commented editorially in March

1976: 'One of the conditions for a free and independent press is that it should be commercially viable over a period of years. Most newspapers, like other organizations, should be able to take a few bad years in their stride, but a state of chronic and mounting deficit is quite another matter.' By 1978 the Thomson family had lost over £16,000,000 in attempting to bring *The Times* into profit, and the support provided by the *Sunday Times* was weakening. Large-scale action was necessary to prevent the continuation of 'chronic and mounting' financial deficits.[13]

Like other newspaper managements, TNL management was pessimistic about the prospects for expansion in either readership or advertising revenues. This reflected partly long-term assessments, and partly the recession of 1974–5. In its editorial on 'A Press that makes losses' *The Times* commented, 'there is no prospect of demand from either readers or advertisers being such as to offer the hope of salvation through higher revenue in time to save a number of publications.' Instead, 'the only hope lies in cutting costs.' One of the largest costs was newsprint, but there was little scope for savings on newsprint because its price was determined by world markets and the level of the pound. Therefore, 'savings on the necessary scale can be obtained . . . only by cutting production costs and the developement of new technology presents a last chance for some papers and the opportunity for all of getting on to a more secure commercial foundation than for a great many years.'[14] The major savings could be made in the composing room, and would therefore most benefit newspapers with large amounts of print to set, but low circulation, like *The Times*. But savings could also be made by lower manning levels elsewhere.

In view of this analysis, the announcement of TNL's development plan ten days later was hardly surprising.

ii

Both elements in the 1976 development plan had existed for some years at TNL — systematic reductions in manpower, and computerization. Serious attempts to reduce labour costs at TNL had been under way at least since 1969, when the cost-reduction programme was put into operation. Reductions were achieved amongst clerical workers, in the machine room, in the stereo department, and in the publishing room. In the machine and publishing area the number of folders was reduced from six to four, with a consequent reduction in the number of casual staff: this was seen as the first phase of a comprehensive review of manning levels. It was agreed in 1970 that joint management–union working parties would be set up, consisting of an overseer and a chapel representative. Throughout the early 1970s reductions in staff were achieved in all major production areas, although on a much smaller scale than envisaged in the 1976 development plan. The most ambitious attempt to reduce costs through rationalization was the movement of *The Times* from Printing House Square to Grays Inn Rd., providing the opportunity for major savings. Computer-aided composition was also well established at the newspaper, the Stock Market page having been set by computerized methods since 1968.

Although reductions in manning and the use of computers were achieved in the late 1960s, the seriousness of the economic situation in 1975 led to a heightened sense of urgency. At the same time, the presentation of the joint union–NPA evidence to the Royal Commission, and the progress towards the establishment of the Joint Standing Committee, suggested the very real possibility of union co-operation in attempting to place the newspaper on a sound economic footing: at the very least, it would be possible to use the commitments of national trade-union leaders to exert pressure on individual chapels. The TNL plan announced in May 1976 was therefore ambitious in conception and comprehensive in scope.[15] The technological centrepiece was the establishment of a computerized photocomposition system, which was to be linked, by computer, with the production, advertising, editorial, and accounting departments. As at the FT, 'because computers are an integral part of these new systems, it will no longer always be possible to separate traditional departmental functions.' The new system was to be developed gradually, but from the beginning would be directed towards eliminating dual key-boarding: 'the build-up must be logical from the start . . . our final requirements . . . are to eliminate duplicate key-stroking and to speed up and improve many ancillary operations.' The improvement was to involve substantial savings in manpower. The operation was to proceed in phases, beginning with the three supplements, the *Times Educational Supplement*, the *Times Higher Education Supplement*, and the *Times Literary Supplement*. In the first phase, brought-in material – the bulk of both editorial and advertising copy for the supplements – was to be keyed into the system from a new electronic composing room. During the second phase phoned-in tele-sales copy was to be entered directly into the system by the advertising department. Eventually, 'at an appropriate stage', in-house editorial copy was to be directly entered into the system. It was planned to begin by composing one of the supplements on both the old and new systems, to phase in the new system, and to transfer the production of the supplements to the new system in stages. Only after the supplements had been totally converted to production by the new system was it planned to turn to *The Times* and *Sunday Times*, beginning with the advertisement sections.

The conversion of the editorial copy of *The Times* and *The Sunday Times* to computerized photocomposition is a matter of timing, dependent partly at least upon the rate of staff reduction within certain areas. The company has no intention of bringing in systems faster than they can be absorbed by the people who have to make them work, or of involving itself in heavy capital expenditure without any cost benefits, or of installing systems and hardware which have not been fully tested.

The major benefits expected from the new system were economic – lower production costs. But it was also hoped that the new systems would have operational benefits. For editorial staff, the new system would be faster, more accurate, and more flexible. The editor of the *Sunday Times*, Harold Evans, was critical of American newspapers – 'among the worst edited in the world' – and of the way in which American newspapers had introduced new technology, especially where they had adopted dual key-boarding.[16] However, he believed that electronically based systems would have advantages, both editorially and in production. Editorially, electronic data processing would improve investigative reporting and graphics; on the production side, there would be fewer errors, as well as lower costs. As a member of the TNL Board his views inevitably carried weight. For advertising staff, computerization would increase the speed and accuracy of assessment of costs, and the checking of financial status.

The new system was to be phased in gradually, both for industrial relations and for technological reasons. The company hoped to negotiate agreement 'within the frame-work and spirit of the National Joint talks and the three joint statements of 5th December 1975, 16th January 1976 and 13th February 1976 issued by the Newspaper Publishers Association and the printing unions.'[17] The company suggested that the appropriate mechanism for house-level discussions would be through a company level Joint Standing Committee, as suggested by the National Joint Standing Committee, but expressed willingness to listen to different views on procedure from the trade unions. The principles of no compulsory redundancy, phasing at a speed determined by the rate of voluntary staff reductions, adequate training, and nationally agreed redundancy and pensions proposals were accepted. Potentially more contentious was the company's final proposition:

We cannot be responsible for people not currently employed by us; but we intend to undertake our responsibilities for our staff and any additional casuals we agree to employ under the decasualization scheme. The proposals are therefore based on the principle of no compulsory redundancy and non-replacement of those staff in areas where staff reductions are necessary.

The trade-union view was that companies — like the unions themselves — had a commitment to workers in the whole industry, and not simply to their own employees — all the more so because of the convenience to management of casual working. Mindful of past experience, the company statement warned: 'We will not succeed in the present challenge if there is a negative approach from any minority or if there are wildcat disputes. That will undermine the future of every-one in the company.'

At the time of the public announcement of the development plan TNL was on the point of signing contracts for the supply of equipment for the first stage of the project. The company had drawn up the initial specification for a new system in-house, drawing upon experience acquired in the computerization of the Stock Market page. Estimates and detailed proposals were then obtained from five possible suppliers, and more detailed specifications drawn up, based largely upon the presentations made by the potential suppliers. Assessment was then made on the basis of the ability of the companies to meet the specification. Among the criteria taken into account in choosing a supplier were experience of the printing industry, especially newspapers, presence in Britain, and price. Different groups within the organization evaluated different potential suppliers differently – editorial preferred Harris, largely because of the key-board, production preferred Linotype-Paul because of the experience in print, and commercial and advertising preferred Systems Development Corporation because of their established reputation in the installation of accounting and commercial systems. In view of the differences of opinion and the impossibility of establishing appropriate comprehensive criteria, the Project Working Party made no specific recommendation to the Board, the Board deciding to purchase from the Systems Development Corporation of Santa Monica. The company had experience in newspapers in California, and was already installing systems in the Philadelphia *Inquirer*, the Toronto *Star*, and the Baltimore *Sun*. However, the agreement did not work satisfactorily, partly for reasons outside the control of The Times. The systems being installed in North America were not performing to specification, and companies were holding up progress payments. The result was financial difficulty for the firm. As a response to the difficulties Systems Development Corporation reorganized its Newspaper Systems Division, and concentrated its resources on fulfilling existing contracts, if necessary in less ambitious form.[18] One consequence of the firm's difficulties was that, following delay, SDC successfully sought renegotiation of the contract with TNL, providing for the installation of a less ambitious system than had been initially envisaged, or contracted for.

The difficulties encountered by TNL in its relations with its supplier were of course unanticipated. TNL were victims, like other newspapers, of extravagant hopes about the extent to which computers could be used in newspaper production — there was a large gap between technical feasibility and operational effectiveness. This was reinforced by the very rapid expansion of work in the area, resulting in a high level of turnover in staff and in inflated salaries. Since companies such as SDC were small and heavily dependent for their survival upon highly qualified professional staff much in demand, they suffered badly from high staff turnover. The failure to achieve promised specifications increased the resources the company was required to devote to fulfilling existing commitments, and produced cash-flow problems. Notwithstanding the prestige of the Times contract, the firm was not in a position, either in terms of personnel or finance, to expand successfully into a major new market in Britain. Moreover, some difficulties could have been antici-pated in dealing with a software company rather than directly with a manufacturer. Software companies were not in as favourable a position to provide for up-dating machinery, which manufacturers were willing to do, nor to provide full guarantees on maintenance. If TNL had possessed very substantial computer expertise in-house such difficulties might not have been serious; lacking such depth in expertise, they were.

Installation of a major computer system is conventionally seen by management consultants as a five-stage process: systems planning; project definition; preliminary systems design; systems installation; and production systems support. The process in conveniently summarized in Fig. 8. In practice, events do not always follow the neat sequences of the pre-scriptive charts of management consultants: business objec-tives, and information needs, change; equipment evaluations grow out of date as new equipment becomes available or as experience reveals unexpected weaknesses in existing equip-ment; detailed software development reveals inadequacies in the initial specification of information needs. In techno-logical terms, the system-planning chart remains an aspiration, but an indispensable one, since it provides the basic sequencing of operations: changes at a late stage to items falling early in the sequence cause very significant extra expenses as well as delay. If alterations are made late in the sequence, without

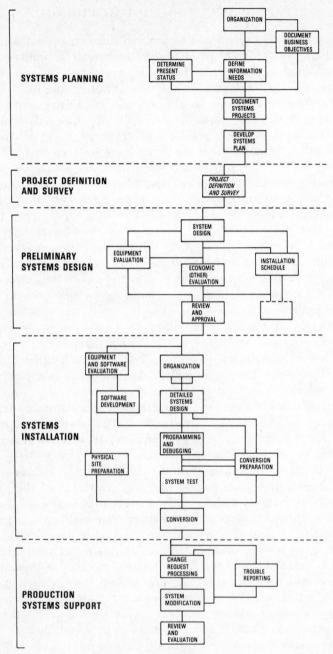

Fig. 8. A systems planning chart
Reproduced by permission of Arthur Andersen & Co.

retracing steps, sub-optimal systems result. This constituted one aspect of the problem of new technology at TNL. Closely linked to this was the predictable problem of employee relations. As a working necessity, planning charts assume a predictable environment — the parameters of change permitted are built into the system. Predictable assumptions may be justified during installation of an accounting system in a commercial organization, with weak trade unions (or none at all), and employees committed to the installation of the system; they are inappropriate in attempting to install a production system in a highly unionized industry facing economic uncertainty.

Even without SDC's financial difficulties the development of a computerized photocomposition system on the model presented in May 1976 would have posed considerable technical difficulties. *The Times* shared with the *FT* the problems of complex layout and a large number of editions; the *Sunday Times* presented the additional difficulty of very long print-runs. Some of the difficulties related to the capacity of the Hewlett-Packard hardware; but the extensive use of mini-computers reduced the significance of the problem of computing capacity, at the expense of elaborate programming problems. As in many other systems projects, the development of the software provided more serious problems. Considerable delays were experienced in developing programmes capable of elaborate layouts; it was alleged in November 1978 that the programmes could not identify which subeditor or executive had been responsible for specific revisions; nor could they mix classified and display advertisements on the same page.[19] Frequent reference was made — possibly apochryphal — to the problems stemming from using the American *Webster's Dictionary* instead of the *Oxford English Dictionary*. Although the extent to which the technical difficulties were overcome never became clear, since the system was never operated, with time the technical problems could doubtless have been surmounted: the industrial relations problems associated with the project were less tractable.

In the late 1960s Times management had successfully negotiated the use of work study techniques with the unions, including the NGA. The cost-reduction programme had also been lauched with the co-operation of chapel officials. It was also hoped that the new technology programme would be implemented with union co-operation – hence the reference in the May 1976 announcement to the establishment of a house-level Joint Standing Committee. However, little progress was made towards involving house-level union representatives in the new technology project. There were no chapel representatives on the working parties which drew up the system specifications, and although references were made to the need for joint responsibility no joint institutions were established. Chapel officials were kept informed of the progress of events, but not significantly involved. This was an explicit management philosophy, in line with the conception of new technology as the occasion for the reassertion of managerial authority. In February 1976 the *Times* NUJ Chapel had suggested to management that an independent outside assessment of the newspaper's proposals should be made on behalf of the unions, the initial expense of paying for preparation of a brief to be financed by the chapel.[20] But the proposal was rejected, mainly on the grounds that other unions would make similar requests, resulting in expense, delay, and confusion. According to the NUJ, the rejection of the proposal 'effectively closed any constructive exchange on management's part with us on New Technology.' Nor was there any consultation with other chapels involved. Significantly, the letter from Times management to the general secretaries in April 1978 outlining the proposals management wished to see accepted made no mention of house-level consultation on new technology: following the collapse of *Programme for Action*, which appeared to leave house-level negotiations as the only means of progress, Times management did not embark on a programme of discussion with chapel representatives.

Times management were closely identified with the negotiations over *Programme for Action*, with Hussey, as vice-chairman of the NPA, leader on behalf of the employers. With the collapse of *Programme for Action* in the spring of 1977 further progress could only be achieved through house-level negotiations. However, the new technology project was beset by technical difficulties; the initial target date for the operation of the first phase, January 1977, had passed with the only progress being the installation of some of the hardware (a mixed blessing, since the rate of technical change in the industry rapidly rendered hardware out of date). Rumours about the precise form of the new technology and about the timetable for its introduction inevitably created uncertainty. This was further increased by the machine-cleaning dispute with NATSOPA in March 1977, resulting in the complete cessation of publication for ten days, and a number of smaller disputes: in January 1977, for example, publication was prevented by the NATSOPA Machine Chapel over the proposed publication of an article by David Astor, former editor of the *Observer*, on 'censorship' by Fleet Street unions.[21] Major management effort was required to maintain continuity of production during such uncertainty.

In summary, The Times's new technology proposals were launched in 1976 as a means of establishing the newspapers on a sound long-term commercial basis by making major savings on labour costs. It was planned to make major capital investment in the immediate future, with a view to bringing in a phased programme beginning in January 1977. The national-level negotiations on the Joint Standing Committee were seen as clearing the ground by providing a framework of nationally agreed principles within which the house-level negotiations could be conducted. However, neither the technological nor the industrial relations elements in the programme worked out as anticipated. The firm appointed to carry out the installation of the new equipment proved unable to carry out their contractual commitments, and the contract had to be renegotiated. The installation of the new system did not progress according to schedule, taking considerably longer than expected, and the performance obtained from the system during trials did not match the promised specification. The national negotiations were not brought to a successful conclusion; the national framework for house-level negotiations did not materialize. Indeed, the rejection of *Programme for Action* made it more difficult to achieve agreement at house level than if the programme had never been launched: union policy became established, and proposals perhaps acceptable in themselves to some chapel officials became tarnished as attempts to introduce *Programme for Action* through the back door. Times management did not pursue a policy of house-level consultation on new technology, partly because of their commitment to a 'national' strategy, and more substantially because of the state of industrial relations at the company in 1976–8.

iii

The industrial relations system at TNL was similar in structure to that in other houses. The company was a member of the NPA and relatively heavily involved in its workings, M. J. Hussey being vice-chairman from 1972 until 1979. In addition to national agreements, negotiated through the NPA, the newspaper negotiated house-level agreements with individual chapels. As in other houses, these had become increasingly formalized as 'comprehensive' agreements in the late 1960s and early 1970s, replacing previous verbal agreements. In the early 1970s the industrial relations function was in the process of becoming professionalized, with the production services director John Dixey's appointment of industrial relations staff, organized in a Production Services Department, which, working alongside a Personnel Department, provided industrial relations advice to line management, and conducted negotiations (where they involved more than one chapel). Fifty-four chapels were recognized by the company. However, TNL's problems were more complex than those of the FT, since the company produced five publications, with overlapping production systems, rather than one: just as the technical requirements of the new system were considerably more complex than the requirements of other houses, so were the industrial relations problems. The five publications employed different sets of editorial and clerical staff and two sets of production staff, for *The Times* and the *Sunday Times*, who worked on two sets of presses in buildings almost a mile apart, until *The Times*'s move to New Printing House Square in 1974.

Workers on *The Times* and the *Sunday Times* were members of different chapels, even when employed on the same jobs: with the development of new technology, some areas acquired three chapels. The rivalries which might have been expected to emerge from this situation were made all the more likely by the circumstances surrounding the development of production facilities in Grays Inn Road. *The Times* was moved from Printing House Square to New Printing House Square in 1974 as a means of rationalizing production facilities as well as of realizing a valuable property asset; the overall concept was to integrate the operations of *The Times* and the *Sunday Times* more closely, and to print *The Times* on *Sunday Times* presses; spare capacity on the *Sunday Times* presses was already used to print the London print-run of the *Guardian* under contract. The rationalization proved more difficult to achieve and less financially beneficial than expected, owing to the differentials which existed between employees of *The Times* and those of the *Sunday Times* — *Times* workers were less well paid than *Sunday Times* employees. *Sunday Times* chapels also had a reputation for militancy, which *Times* chapels did not. The new proximity of the two publications inevitably stimulated rivalry at a time when management would have had difficulty in meeting *Times* employees' expectations, even if it had wished to do so, owing to government incomes policy. Since there were substantial differences between week-night and Saturday-night working, the rivalry between production chapels was held in check (although the 1977 machine-cleaning dispute had its origins in the 1974 move, see above, pp. 142–5); but there was also considerable rivalry between NUJ chapels, where such recognized differences did not exist. Regardless of any other events, the move of *The Times* to New Printing House Square was likely to produce industrial relations difficulties; as it was, the unresolved problems raised by the move provided an unsatisfactory background for attempts to deal with the consequences for industrial relations of trying to introduce new technology.

In the mid 1970s the number of copies lost by TNL through house-level industrial action was less than in many other houses: in 1975, for example, the *Sunday Times* lost only 320,000 copies out of a total of 25 million Sunday papers lost on Fleet Street as a whole.[22] Whether this was

due to Times management paying 'over the odds' to its
employees is impossible to say, since the earnings of workers
employed at particular houses are not publicly available.
However, it is unlikely to have been so: workers at TNL have
consistently claimed to be amongst the lowest paid in Fleet
Street, and although this claim is unlikely to be true for all
workers, management has not publicly disputed it. In view
of the intense conflict surrounding relativities in the industry,
more accurate evidence is unobtainable. By 1978 the industrial
relations situation at TNL had changed significantly for the
worse, as measured by the number of copies lost through
industrial action. Some of TNL's difficulties stemmed from
the uncertainties surrounding the new technology project and
associated proposals for changing manning levels, some from
the effects of successive pay policies.

Many print-union officials were sceptical of the value of
pay policies. Nevertheless, despite reservations, especially in
the NGA because of their affects upon differentials, the
print unions attempted to follow TUC policy, namely to
accept the Labour Government's policies from 1975 until
1977, but not to do so in 1978. The pay policy had of course
a direct impact upon negotiations between the print unions
and the NPA, and settlements in 1975, 1976, and 1977 were
in accord with the terms of the social contract, providing
for £6 in 1975-6, and £2·50-£4·00 in 1976-7; the informal
guidelines of 1977-8 had little impact. However, the relationship between NPA-negotiated rates and earnings was, as
indicated earlier, variable: house-level agreements and overtime boosted average earnings to approximately three times
the national minimum rates (see above, pp. 000-0). The
extent to which pay policy effectively limited the rise in
earnings therefore depended on the extent to which individual houses attempted to carry out the policy. At The Times
both management and employees claimed that TNL had
attempted to carry out the policy more rigorously than other
houses, for example by being unwilling to grant payment for
notional overtime. The result was to widen the differentials
between employees at TNL and those at other Fleet Street
houses.

Uncertainty over new technology, the perceived invidiousness of the effects of pay policy, and personal differences led to increased difficulties at The Times in late 1977 and 1978.[23] Although 1977 was 'easily the best year Times Newspapers has ever had' in financial terms, there were a number of unofficial disputes, involving SOGAT and the NGA as well as NATSOPA.[24] The number of copies lost through industrial action increased in 1978, according to Times management reaching 7.7 million copies in the first quarter.[25] Times management saw the continuing lost copies and the uncertainties as damaging both to readership and to advertisers. 'The Company itself cannot survive under these circumstances and the point of irreparable damage is very rapidly being reached.' *The Times* had fallen back from approaching profitability, and the *Sunday Times*'s expansion plans had been suspended. Accordingly, in April Times management arranged a secret meeting with the print-union general secretaries in Birmingham and, following a second meeting, wrote to them in the following terms:

1. The common purposes will be the absolute continuity of production. All arbitrary restrictions will be lifted. No unofficial action will be taken. Dispute procedures and current agreements will be honoured. Overtime will be worked as necessary to maintain full and uninterrupted production.
2. We negotiate a fast-acting and effective disputes procedure.
3. We negotiate, in consultation with Union representatives, a general wage restructuring. This will be based on new technology and systems, and on efficient manning levels in all departments. A considerable improvement in earnings and conditions could accrue, but only on an agreed basis of savings shared between the staff and the Company. Special attention during this exercise will be devoted to the particular concerns of the lower paid.
4. . . . no compulsory redundancy will arise from the introduction of new technology systems.
5. All these negotiations shall be concluded by 30 November 1978.

. . . if it is not possible to negotiate a joint approach to resolve these problems and if disruption continues, publication of all our newspapers will be suspended.[26]

In Fleet Street terms, Times management was asking for the moon, in seven months: the introduction of new technology, new manning levels, wage restructuring, the abolition of restrictions on production, the ending of unofficial action, and the negotiation of a new disputes procedure constituted a programme no print union could accept. Some of the demands could be negotiated without major difficulty, notably a new disputes procedure. The advantage of a new procedure for management was that it would bring full-time officials into the house more rapidly than the existing one, thus perhaps increasing union discipline. But the major problem with the existing procedure was not that it was unsuitable, but that it was disregarded. Other demands could be negotiated gradually, on a piecemeal basis with national officials and chapel representatives — notably wage restructuring, the introduction of new technology, and possibly new manning levels. Yet others could never be met in any circumstances — absolute continuity of production, no unofficial action, and the ending of 'arbitrary restrictions' on work. Even if chapel officials agreed to a formal guarantee, there were major problems in defining 'arbitrary restrictions' and unofficial action: reel breaks could be interpreted as either accidental or intentional sabotage, as the controversy over David Astor's article on 'Censorship' indicated; was the systematic provision of inexperienced casual hands in the machine room simply accidental or a means of restricting production?; was the refusal to work overtime simply the avoidance of excessive hours of work, or blackmail?

It was unclear how far Times management's proposals were negotiable or capable of being treated separately. Part of the statement referred to the achievement of a 'joint approach' to the solution of the problems, another to acceptance of the proposals as a matter of urgency; the programme was presented as a whole, but throughout there remained uncertainty about the commitment to new technology. Predictably, no print union accepted the proposals, although no union rejected them out of hand. Initially, the general secretaries of SOGAT, NATSOPA, and the NUJ, and the president of the NGA expressed their willingness to discuss the proposals: Keys (SOGAT), the chairman of the TUC Printing Industries Committee, commented: 'there is no doubt that the industry cannot support the losses much longer and there is a dangerous challenge from other media. I welcome this move by the Times Newspapers if it is a catalyst to bring order into Fleet Street.'[27] The Executives of SOGAT,

NATSOPA, and the NUJ concurred with the general secretaries, and expressed a willing ness to meet Times management: the NATSOPA Executive expressed resentment at negotiating under duress, but suggested an initial meeting at national level. But the NGA Executive responded differently, and refused to negotiate until the threat of suspension was removed.[28] Despite attempts by Keys to arrange a meeting between all print unions, the NGA kept to its policy; the union was opposed both to the methods being adopted by TNL management, and to the content of the proposals, especially, and unsurprisingly, to the use of journalists to in-put material into the computer system as envisaged in the new technology proposals.

The reason for Times management's threat of suspension in April was anxiety about the effects of the continuing high level of losses under existing methods of production; the issue of new technology was secondary, and as late as September new technology represented a 'grey area' in management thinking.[29] The threat did not have any effect upon the level of lost production: in the seven months before the suspension the number of copies lost though unofficial action increased, as might have been expected. Loss of copies was particularly severe on the *Sunday Times*. Simply to list occasions on which 200,000 or more copies were lost: on 16 July 390,000 copies were lost, owing to disputes in the machine room and mechanical problems; on 6 August 239,000 copies were lost owing to a late start by SOGAT members in the publishing room; on 13 August 384,000 copies were lost for the same reason; on 8 October 430,000 copies were lost owing to disputes in the composing room and the machine room; on 15 October 290,000 copies were lost owing to difficulties with the NATSOPA Machine Chapel; on 5 November 329,000 copies were lost as the NATSOPA Machine Chapel refused to work overtime; on 12 November 341,000 copies were lost owing to action by the *Sunday Times* NATSOPA clerical staff and by NATSOPA refusal of overtime; on 26 November 568,000 copies were lost owing to NGA and NATSOPA Machine Chapel meetings, slow running, and NATSOPA refusal of overtime. The major source of difficulty on *The Times* was the refusal of overtime by NGA machine minders.

Between April and September there was a delay, whilst Times management prepared detailed chapel by chapel proposals for new agreements covering work organization, manning levels, and pay, and attempted to arrange a meeting with national-level representatives of all the unions involved. Eventually, a meeting was arranged on 18 September, at which Times management gave formal notice of its intention to dismiss employees rendered redundant when publication was suspended; under the Employment Protection Act employers were required to give at least ninety days' notice to the unions involved and to the Department of Employment, when proposing to dismiss 100 or more employees as redundant. 'In the event of agreement not being reached, notices of termination of contracts of employment will be issued to staff on November 30, to take effect from December 18 onwards, depending on the terms of individual contracts.'[30] The length of notice required varied between two and twelve weeks. No notices were to be issued before November 30, and no notices were to be issued to executives and senior managers, or 'to any member of any union that has reached agreement with the company, except in the event that agreement cannot be reached in a reasonable time.' The meeting was the occasion for Times management to present its document to the appropriate unions, not a negotiating session. It had the effect of crystallizing the situation and persuading union representatives that Times management intended to carry out its threatened suspension: Keys stated: 'I have no illusion at all that the firm means what it says and will close unless there is an agreement.' Although the NGA refused to negotiate under duress, the NGA general secretary attended the meeting on the explicit understanding that the meeting was for discussion, not for negotiation, and would not be concerned with the question of new technology.[31]

Following the meeting on 18 September Times management held meetings with national officials of the unions concerned who were willing to meet them — NATSOPA, NUJ, SOGAT, and SLADE. The NGA subsequently decided to meet Times management to discuss new technology, but not to discuss possible means of ensuring continuity of production. According to Wade,

We are not prepared to attempt to meet the November 30 deadline. They [Times management] know, and everybody knows, that there is no way that I or anybody else could give a guarantee of continuous production. The only way to stop unofficial action is for management to get the goodwill of the people on the shop floor, and they are not going to get that by hanging threats over the workers' heads.

The union declared its willingness to negotiate if the threat of suspension was lifted.[32] The effect of the meetings at national level was to clear the way for meetings with individual chapels and the presentation of detailed proposals on a chapel-by-chapel basis. The company aimed to negotiate at full-time officer level on the terms of Section 2 of the proposed Agreements, and at chapel level on matters specific to individual chapels. Section 2 broadly covered conditions of employment (length of notice, holidays, sick pay, deductions for lost time), procedures (disciplinary, individual grievance, and disputes), and the length of the agreement. The company proposed improved pensions, sick pay (52 weeks' full pay in any 18 months), holidays (6 weeks for all), and pay (depending on job).[33]

The discussions on the establishment of new disputes procedures with national-level union officials proceeded smoothly; before the deadline agreement was reached in negotiations with national leaders of all the unions involved except the NGA. However, the procedure agreement had not been put to chapels by the date of the suspension, and Times management did not believe that agreement on disputes procedures at national level alone constituted sufficient grounds to lift the suspension. Less progress was made with the more detailed proposals presented to individual chapels; some chapels were willing to negotiate, others, notably the NGA chapels, were not. The first chapel to reach agreement was the small SOGAT Circulation Representatives' Chapel with fifty-three members; by the date of the suspension it was reported that only two chapels had signed agreements, the second being the *Sunday Times* NUJ Chapel.[34] On the day of the suspension two further chapels signed, the Engineers (150 members) and UCATT (17 members). A notable failure was the failure to reach agreement with the *Times* NUJ Chapel, which had traditionally adopted a moderate stance

and accepted a new disputes procedure, but rejected management proposals by 124 votes to 94 at a meeting on 30
November: in addition to its concern over new technology,
and management's tactics, it was concerned to establish
'parity' with the *Sunday Times* NUJ Chapel.[35] The *Times*
NUJ Chapel became the eighteenth group to sign when, on
18 December, it reached an interim 'working agreement',
which protected them from dismissal: the working agreement
provided for improved pay — bringing them closer to *Sunday
Times* journalists — and for further talks on pay and conditions
related to the introduction of new technology.[36]

At the time of the suspension the Labour Government felt
that it could do little. The NATSOPA general secretary asked
the Government to intervene by asking the company to lift
the threat of suspension, but neither the minister directly
concerned, Albert Booth, nor the prime minister, who was
kept directly informed, felt that the Government could act
unless both sides wished to negotiate. An emergency debate
was held in the Commons on 30 November, in which the
minister briefly summarized the dispute in general terms.
He promised: 'I stand ready to respond to any invitation
from any of the parties to the dispute to do anything that I
or my Department can do to help' — hardly the basis for
positive action.[37] James Prior, the Opposition spokesman,
asked for a gesture from management and a reciprocal
response from the unions: 'I appeal to the management to
make some positive gesture to create a better climate in
which these negotiations make [*sic*] take place. I appeal to
the unions to accept that gesture and to make one themselves by all agreeing to get on with the negotiations.'[38]
Despite his statement that he could do nothing, Booth
appealed to the parties to reopen negotiations. Management
responded to the request for a gesture and announced that it
would not proceed with issuing notices of dismissal for two
weeks, although it would carry out the suspension on schedule.
It was hoped that the two weeks would provide the opportunity for negotiations.

The two weeks did not see the beginning of 'meaningful
negotiations'. Despite the efforts of Albert Booth to convene
'round table discussions' without preconditions, which

appeared to promise hopes of success in bringing the NGA into discussions alongside the other print unions, no full-scale meeting was held. Agreement was reached on the procedure for conducting discussions at a meeting chaired by the minister on 13 December, but the NGA was willing to take part only if the notices were withdrawn. Times management refused to withdraw the notices until agreements were concluded.[39] Attempts by the NGA to involve Lord Thomson directly in discussions also proved abortive. Lord Thomson stated:

I have no intention of intervening in any way with the negotiations which are currently being conducted. I understand that Mr. Wade . . . has stated that he would like to talk to me. I take encouragement from this but would respectfully suggest that any such meeting should be held with the management of Times Newspapers who are directly responsible for the negotiations.[40]

Accordingly, notices issued on 14 December to members of the thirty-seven chapels which had not concluded agreements, including over 3,000 employees, began to take effect two weeks later; thereafter, workers left the paper at the rate of approximately 100 per week. There was not great concern about the immediate financial position of members leaving, since NATSOPA members were confident of finding alternative work in Fleet Street and NGA members were given substantial financial assistance by their union, partly through a special levy on other Fleet Street NGA members. According to Les Dixon, NGA president, 'they will be very little worse off, if they are worse off at all.'[41] Although NATSOPA members were found alternative work, they remained members of Times and Sunday Times NATSOPA chapels, the alternative work being regarded as only temporary.

Throughout the early weeks of the suspension unions mobilized resistance through the branch and chapel inter-union liaison committees, and won wide support for their cause throughout the trade-union movement. The first issue of the Times Challenger was published in January — two further issues were to be published in March and May. In addition to support from unions and chapels in the printing industry, the publication received public support from the Scottish TUC, the South East Regional TUC, ACTT, FTAT,

T&G (Wales Region), CPSA, NUM (Scotland), NUM (Kent), NACODS (Kent), AUEW-TASS, FBU, Tobacco Workers, NUR, and the Upper Clyde Shipbuilders' Joint Shop Stewards' Committee.[42] The effect of the dismissals was to unite national union opinion against discussions until the notices had been lifted. Despite this opposition, discussions proceeded with chapels, although very little progress was made. In March Times management claimed that agreement had been reached with twenty groups, but seventeen of these had been concluded by the beginning of December: the largest groups involved were the Printing Machine Branch of SOGAT, and twelve of the fourteen sections of NATSOPA RIRMA.

At Mr Booth's initiative, meetings between the minister, management, and unions in March resulted in a formula being agreed whereby dismissed workers would be re-engaged until 17 April: employees would receive 50 per cent of their lost earnings as compensation, the remainder of the earnings forgone being made up when publication was resumed on 17 April. Discussions during the period of re-engagement would cover the issues raised by Times management — a new disputes procedure, 'efficient working arrangements', a time-table for new technology, and a timetable for agreement on new manning levels — but would be without preconditions. Issues unresolved by 7 April would be referred to ACAS. The formula was agreed by the general secretaries and subsequently endorsed by the Executives of NATSOPA, NGA, SOGAT, and SLADE.[43] Most importantly, the NGA believed that it had achieved its major objective, reinstatement. Although the re-engagement period enabled discussions to proceed and agreement at office and branch level was achieved with SLADE, no progress was made on the central issue of new technology with the NGA.[44] According to Times manage-ment, the NGA were insisting on 'an inefficient and impractical monopoly of the new system', despite more money, generous voluntary-redundancy payments, consultation, reviews, and a long period of phasing in. According to the NGA, Times management was expecting the union to surrender a funda-mental principle, on which compromise was impossible: the union therefore rejected both the Times proposals, and arbitration by ACAS. Little progress was made in discussions

concerning the NATSOPA chapels which had not ;
reached agreement. Times management therefore decided to
continue payment of workers re-engaged only until the end
of the week in which 17 April fell, and thereafter to suspend
publication indefinitely. According to Times management,
'We are certainly no further forward than before we started
these last five weeks of negotiation. Certainly the picture
is grim.'[45]

Following the failure of the Booth initiative, Times
management went ahead with arrangements to print an overseas issue of *The Times*. Although Times management stressed
that the publication would not circulate in Britain, and could
therefore not be regarded as provocation, the unions saw
the move as an escalation of the conflict. Attempts to print
in Germany were abandoned when police stated that they
could not guarantee the safety of the workers employed at
the Tehrdruckerei plant in Zappenheim near Frankfurt,
a Turkish language house publishing a right-wing newspaper
for circulation amongst immigrant workers in Germany.[46]

Although relations between management and unions
deteriorated following the failure of re-engagement and the
attempt to print the 'Eurotimes' in Frankfurt, informal
contact through intermediaries was maintained. Most importantly, in June the editor-in-chief, Sir Denis Hamilton, who
was reputed to be a 'dove' in management circles, met the
all-union chapel liaison committee for the first time. The
decision by Times management to attend a meeting of the
chapel liaison committee represented an important change
in management policy, which had hitherto relied on negotiations at national level as a method of approach: the failure
of the Booth initiative indicated the very limited value of
agreements negotiated at national level. A major change in
management policy became publicly known on 27 June,
when Lord Thomson suggested that the realization of the full
potential of the new equipment was TNL's 'ultimate' aim.
TNL management agreed with the NGA that the issue of
direct input should 'no longer be an obstacle' to negotiated
republication of the titles. Instead, the issue of direct input
should be negotiated over a twelve-month period, initially
with the NGA and subsequently with NUJ and NATSOPA.[47]

Following this agreement, the way was open for negotiation on other items with the other unions involved, and on 5 July Times management presented its proposals, *Republication and Return to Work at Times Newspapers*. TNL's terms for republication were: agreement on a new common disputes procedure, guarantee of continuous production, including overtime, acceptance of 'essential new and replacement equipment', including a new commercial computer and publishing-room equipment, operation of a new composing room, on 'back-end' principles, unrestricted publication of 80-page *Sunday Times* issues and colour supplements without restrictions on size, and equalization of machine- and press-room working hours.[48] The paper was not insisting on the principle of direct in-put but it was retaining the other major demands of April 1978, and rectification of the major causes of unofficial disputes in 1978 (especially in the publishing room). Once new operating agreements, based on the conditions, had been negotiated with individual chapels, members of the chapels concerned would be reinstated at old wages plus the 1 October 1978 increases plus 5 per cent; once agreement had been reached with all chapels, and republication begun, the new agreed pay rates would be back-dated to the date of re-engagement. On resumption of publication, £200 would be paid to all workers wholly unemployed between 24 April, the end of the Booth re-engagement payments, and re-engagement. Existing manning levels would not be made up with new recruitment or casuals before republication. If full operating agreements had not been reached on republication, payment would be at the 're-engagement' rate. If full agreement had not been reached within six months of the date of re-engagement, the parties in disagreement would go to arbitration by an independent chairman, assisted by two assessors from each side.

The new proposals were rejected by the general secretaries and alternative proposals were put forward on 17 July. According to the NGA the management proposals did not reflect the 'helpful' attitude shown by Lord Thomson and Sir Denis Hamilton, but the long-standing aggressive attitudes of Times management.[49] Following the impasse, G. C. Brunton agreed to the general secretaries' request for a meeting which produced agreement subject to ratification by chapels: the agreement provided for a new disputes procedure, guarantees of continuous production, including overtime where necessary, and the phased introduction of computerized photocomposition. Management and unions committed themselves to republication of *The Times* and the *Sunday Times* within four weeks of re-engagement, and of the supplements within six weeks.[50] All former employees were re-instated, with continuity of service, pension rights made up, and holiday entitlements accruing during the suspension recognized; there was to be no victimization by the company or by the unions, although, as it turned out for a small number of people significantly, 'it is recognized that there can be no interference with the correct operation of union rules.'[51] The company agreed to pay £500 to each full-time regular employee, regardless of length of time out of work. The company also committed itself to annual direct negotiations with the unions, outside the framework of the NPA. The agreement claimed to cover basic principles, leaving the details to be negotiated later.

The Company, Chapels, and Unions acknowledge that the first essential requirement for reinstatement and republication is agreement on matters of principle, and these are contained within this agreement. In many cases matters of detail may require detailed and protracted negotiations, but in the spirit of the agreement the conditions and undertakings set out . . . should not preclude Times Newspapers Limited from reinstatement and republication of all their titles.[52]

Reinstatement was to be on the terms prevailing at the suspension, plus the 10 per cent granted by the NPA on 1 October 1978 plus 10 per cent 'on account'. Manning levels were also to be as before, but with the full utilization of specified equipment already installed; the company explicitly recognized that the maximum size of the *Sunday Times* would be 72 pages (not the 80 originally hoped for). Following reinstatement, management, unions, and chapels were to undertake joint discussions on new technology (excluding front end systems), 'staffing, new all-in rates, buy-out provisions, hours and holidays, sickness and pension provisions and other operating matters, to provide the basis of new agreements.' If any issues remained unsettled after six months the parties were to appoint an independent chairman to 'resolve' the problem, with the assistance of one representative from each side; this committee was 'to conciliate, advise, and guide the parties in disagreement', but not to arbitrate. In exchange for reinstatement and generous financial terms, the unions had made general commitments to the 'absolute necessity' of full production, but no specific commitments on manning levels in the medium and long term: work was to resume without any significant resolution of the major problems which had led to the suspension. Dugal Nisbet-Smith claimed that The Times had negotiated 'one of the best new technology agreements in the country'.[53] But the company had made the elementary bargaining error of surrendering their major weapon, the suspension of publication, in exchange for only general commitments, leaving the more important specific details, relating to manning levels and money, to be negotiated subsequently; as the unions recognized, management could not realistically contemplate further suspension and could be 'taken to the cleaners' at leisure.

The agreement was accepted by the print unions and the NUJ at national level, and recommended to the chapels. SLADE chapels were the first to sign new operating agreements, followed by the Sunday Times SOGAT Publishing Chapel. NGA members at The Times also accepted the proposals.[54] However, despite NATSOPA Executive's acceptance, the Sunday Times Clerical and Machine NATSOPA Chapels rejected it, both rejecting the proposals on new technology and demanding higher pay. The resistance by NATSOPA members was successful: Times management conceded increases of more than 50 per cent over two years to the NATSOPA Sunday Times Machine Room Chapel, disrupting the traditional differential of 12½–25 per cent between NATSOPA and NGA members in the machine room. Sunday Times NATSOPA clerical members also held out, eventually reaching agreement whereby republication would begin before all clerical jobs were filled at the Sunday Times – reversing the usual tactic, the Sunday Times Clerical Chapel correctly realizing that TNL would have difficulty recruiting clerical workers and believing that it would be possible to exert greater pressure once resumption had made management aware of the difficulties of operating below strength, or of recruiting to get up to strength. In retaliation against the NATSOPA *Sunday Times* machine-room settlement NGA machine managers reopened discussion, claiming reduced hours (32 instead of 37½), longer holidays (8 weeks instead of 6), and increased staffing in the *Sunday Times* machine room, as well as restoration of the differential.[55]

The suspension ended in the atmosphere of brinkmanship with which it had begun. TNL set a deadline of midnight on 17 October for conclusion of talks between the NGA and TNL management aimed at restoring the machine-room differential over NATSOPA members; the deadline was not met. TNL were due to announce their decision whether to close the newspaper or not on Friday, 19 October. However, NGA leaders asked for a 48-hour reprieve, and the TUC Printing Industries Committee arranged a meeting with Times management at Congress House. Times management agreed to the reprieve, the new deadline being 4.00 p.m. on Sunday, 21 October. Following continuous negotiations from Friday through to Sunday morning between Times management and the NGA agreement was reached at 11.30 on the Sunday. The agreement provided for substantial pay increases – a comprehensive craft rate of £217 per week in the composing room (compared with £185 offered in April for work on the new technology) – and for substantial changes in working practices and in manning levels, including 'total flexibility in working practices'. There was no agreement on manning levels in the machine room, where changes in manning levels were seen as the best means of re-establishing NGA differentials over NATSOPA members: it was agreed to go to binding arbitration by ACAS chairman, Jim Mortimer, assisted by a panel of three representatives from the Times management and three representatives from the NGA.[56]

The Times reappeared on 13 November 1979; the *Sunday Times* on 18 November, the *Times Education Supplement* on 16 November, and the *Times Higher Education* and *Times Literary* supplements on 23 November. TNL succeeded in securing agreement to the installation of new technology at Times Newspapers on the basis of existing demarcation lines – like MGN, or the *Daily Express*. For Times management this represented a partial advance: new arrangements were negotiated covering, for example, the increased use of computers in commercial and advertising departments, including access by NATSOPA members to the computers for information and credit checking, but not for in-putting material: 'header' processing, whereby NATSOPA tele-ad girls entered coded information into the computer, was permitted on the VDTs in the advertising and advertising accounts departments. More significantly for the long run, the NGA was thought to have agreed to secondary editing by the NUJ members. The relevant NGA chapels also agreed to the buying out of the London Scale of Prices, on the model of the *Mirror* agreement: linotype operators and piece case hands were to receive lump sums of £16,000 at the *Sunday Times* and £14,000 at The Times, and subsequently to receive the composing-room rate alongside other NGA composing-room staff. Significantly, the lump sum was not related to age, length of service, or anticipated future employment. Considerable flexibility was achieved in the composing room, workers being involved in reading, cut-and-paste, as well as keying-in. However, the production system envisaged as operating following the settlement was a 'back-end' system, in which all input was to be by NGA members – the system earlier severely criticized by the *Sunday Times* editor.[57] Times management hoped that by integrating the work of NGA and NUJ members, allowing NGA members to perform work previously done by NUJ members, as well as the converse, it would prove possible to secure agreement within the twelve months period agreed on the resumption of publication. More substantial changes occurred in the operation of existing technology and in obtaining greater continuity of production – although the guarantees of continuous production were to prove ineffective after a short honeymoon period, at least until the announcement of the impending sale of TNL by TTO in October 1980. According to Times management in January 1980, the settlement represented the achievement of 70 per cent of their initial objectives: but no TNL newspapers composed in the new 'cold-type' composing room had then been published. No publication appeared composed in the new composing room whilst TNL remained in Thomson hands.

iv

According to a *Times* editorial on 24 November 1978, three themes led to the threat of suspension of *The Times*.[58] The first was the collapse of internal discipline in trade unions, which was seen as a product of the 1960s (misleadingly, since chapel separatism was inherent in the structure of printing trade unionism). The second was the revolutionary change from mechanized to electronically based means of communication. The third was the need to raise British productivity to European and American levels.

Low productivity is our central economic failure. It can only be overcome by strong managements dealing with strong trade unions. A strong management is one which is prepared to shoulder its responsibility and take initiatives, even of a very difficult kind, to raise the efficiency of its own business. A strong trade union is one which recognizes that trade unionism depends equally on its cooperative and its adversary relationship with management. The cooperative relationship requires that trade unions should accept the role of management in increasing the efficiency of the business. The adversary relationship consists in seeing that trade unionists get their fair share of the improvements in productivity that higher efficiency will create. It is management's job to take the initiative in introducing measures to increase productivity; it is the union's role to secure the maximum rewards for its members from the higher productivity achieved.

The Times's editorial represented management's view of the issues involved in industrial relations in Fleet Street and the role of new technology in increasing productivity. The theme of the need for union discipline was a recurrent one in speeches made by Times management and in editorials. In an editorial on 'The Collapse of Discipline' *The Times* stressed that the restoration of discipline in Fleet Street was partly a management responsibility, but even more a trade-union responsibility: 'the greater responsibility for restoration of discipline rests with the trade unions . . . partly because they are the principal agents of its collapse and partly because they now have the greater purchase on their members.'[59] Perhaps significantly, the editorial was published very shortly before Hussey's letter to the general secretaries threatening the suspension of publication. The editorial ignored the fundamental point of Allan Flanders's classic paper on 'What are Trade Unions For?'.

The essence of this view [of 'responsible' trade unionism] is that trade unions are there to act as a kind of social police force — to keep the chaps in order and the wheels of industry turning. To this there is only one answer. The first and over-riding responsibility of all trade unions is to the welfare of their [own] members . . . not to a firm, not to an industry, not to the nation. A union collects its members' contributions and demands their loyalty specifically for the purpose of protecting their interests as they see them, not their alleged 'true' or 'best' interests as defined by others.[60]

Flanders ignored the difficulty of conflicting expressions of view within unions, the problems of reconciling the views of minorities directly involved with majorities not directly involved inherent in the internal politics of print unions, the majority of whose members were not employed in Fleet Street. But his criticisms of the inappropriateness of the concept of 'responsible' trade unionism remain as relevant as when they were first published in 1968. It was naïve to think that the authority which union leaders acquired by serving their members' conceptions of their interests could be used to oppose those conceptions, without damaging the authority itself. Moreover, on a political level, the prospects of the organization responsible for the collapse of discipline being capable of reasserting it were slight, unless the factors which facilitated the collapse of discipline changed.

Yet there was an ambivalence in management's attitude towards union discipline. As William Rees-Mogg stated, the NGA is 'basically a good trade union. It is well organized, it has an intelligent and capable leadership, both nationally and at branch and house levels, and it commands the loyalty of a high proportion of its members. It does not have the problem of anarchy which exists in some chapels of some of the other Fleet Street unions.'[61] Yet management also saw the NGA's obduracy as at the centre of the newspaper's problems, with the union adopting an unyielding opposition to other unions' members sharing in typesetting. The NGA was not damaging to Times Newspapers because of its lack of discipline, but because of its discipline; it was able to prevent Times workers from surrendering the principle of monopoly control over the key-board to other unions, even if they wished to do so on the grounds that little was involved at The Times, because the NGA leadership was concerned about the repercussions surrendering the principle would have elsewhere in the industry. The NATSOPA leadership had less control over its members at TNL, and Times management had considerable difficulty with its NATSOPA members; but the managements of other newspapers had fewer difficulties with NATSOPA members, establishing closer rapport with NATSOPA chapel officials than had been achieved at Times Newspapers. Perhaps not surprisingly, Times management was critical of unions for their lack of discipline, and for their excess of discipline when mobilized against Times management.

Times management showed a limited appreciation of the NGA's position by pointing to its obduracy: the attention paid to a further problem at The Times, that of fragmentation, was more justified. In a speech to the Engineering Employers' Federation in February Rees-Mogg summarized the problem picturesquely:

[Fleet Street negotiation] is a process which offers at every stage the opportunity to say 'No', regardless of the policy of the Government, regardless of the policy of the trade union movement, regardless of the wishes of the members, and regardless of the interests of the members. Our position on *The Times* is like that of a man at the end of a wind-swept pier in some cold and out-of-season seaside resort — perhaps Scarborough in late November. We are confronted with a set of seven rusty and ancient fruit machines. To reach agreements we have to line up three strawberries on each of the fruit machines at the same time. Somehow — heavens knows how — we have managed to line up three of the strawberries on two machines, and we have a couple of strawberries registered on a third. Of the others, some reject the coin that is put in — however large — while one has a lemon and another has a raspberry rusted permanently in place on the centre of the dial.[62]

The speech was doubtless well recived at the EEF — especially as the AUEW was one of the fruit machines. The problem of fragmentation was a serious one. But in suggesting that chapels were acting regardless of the wishes of their members Rees-Mogg was being misleading: chapel fragmentation and sectionalism were important because they accorded with the wishes of chapel members — it was not a case of chapel members being led astray by false leaders.

The second historic theme was seen as being the replacement of mechanical by electronically based media of communication, the first major technological innovation in newspapers since the development of reel-fed presses and linotype machines in the late nineteenth century — and with considerably wider implications. Electronically based equipment was faster, more flexible, cheaper, and easier to use than mechanically based equipment. Times management's proposals did possess important potential. However, the widest implications were not involved — for example, there was no plan to distribute data acquired and stored electronically by any means other than through newspapers. The company was making major changes in the early stages of its production system, with major consequences for the social organization of labour and industrial relations: but the wider consequences of the transition from mechanical to electronically based systems were not at stake. The transformation from mechanical to electronic means of reproduction had revolutionary potential, but Times management was preoccupied with the short-term issue of profitability, not the long-run issue of new methods of disseminating information.

More relevant was the third major historic theme, productivity. Measurement of productivity in newspapers is both primitive and controversial, even within a single house. This is especially so when attempting to assess the productivity of specific groups of workers, since the interdependent process of production meant that problems encountered in one section had knock-on effects in another section — slow output of pages from the composing room inevitably meant excessive waiting time in the machine room and publishing room, with apparent low productivity. Similarly, major difficulties stemmed from the quality of the equipment and variations in the quality of the raw material, notably the newsprint: reel breaks might be due to careless methods of working or to variability in newsprint quality. However, comparison of the total labour input with other types of newspapers and with similar newspapers in North America suggested that productivity was low, at least partly owing to inefficient working practices. In the composing area specifically, the linotype machine operators achieved a rate of about 3,500 characters per hour: the NGA promised 7,000 characters per hour on electronically based equipment, and Times management sought 10,000; Times management claimed that operators setting the 'Euro-Times' in Frankfurt achieved 12,500 characters, in a foreign language.[63] The comparison ought not to be regarded as precise: the rates represent averages, and are affected by, for example, the rate of flow of copy, the quality of the copy, the frequency of interruptions, as well as the efficiency of the machinery. Nevertheless, a major problem at TNL was low productivity, and new technology offered a means of raising it.

The issue of productivity was linked to a fourth historic theme, not mentioned by *The Times*, profitability. The Thomson family and the Thomson Organisation had lost £16m by 1978 in attempting to make *The Times* profitable, without success. The introduction of new technology was seen as a once for all attempt to establish the TNL newspapers on a profitable footing, partly through the savings directly attributable to the new technology, and partly through savings made through simultaneous changes in other departments. For both technical and industrial relations reasons the introduction of new technology did not proceed smoothly. At the same time, the newspapers' normal operations suffered disruption. Despite industrial relations problems, TNL made a small profit in 1977. However, the size of the industrial relations problems increased in 1978, ending the short-term prospects for even minimal profitability: some of the problems were long-standing restrictions on flexibility in the use of labour, which management decided would no longer be accepted, and others derived from management's exasperation with chapel tactics in pursuit of collective bargaining objectives. Accordingly, in an attempt to gain the industrial relations initiative, in April 1978 TNL management presented the printing unions with demands for the negotiation of new disputes procedures, guaranteed continuity of production, new manning levels, and the introduction of new technology, before 30 November 1978. It was hoped to resolve current problems and to achieve the introduction of new technology with one bold, or foolhardy, stroke. The negotiations were not successful, and publication was suspended for eleven and a half months.

The effect of the suspension of publication on short-term profitability was disastrous. By the date of republication it was estimated that the dispute had cost the company £27m, an estimate subsequently revised to £39.3m; in 1980 it was reported that TNL had borrowed £10m from its parent company to maintain operations and was still running at a loss: TNL lost £6.4m in the first six months of the 1980 financial year, compared with £17.3m during the same period in 1979, when the papers were suspended.[64] It is of course impossible to speculate on the effects of the suspension on the medium- and long-term profitability of the company, since the company is not to survive beyond March 1981 in its present form. In the industrial relations sphere, the official guarantee of continuous production and the new disputes procedure could conceivably have resulted in greater stability in the long run, increasing the confidence of advertisers, readers (and distributors). But, after a brief lull, in the short run the suspension was followed by industrial unrest among groups which had not previously been to the forefront in major conflicts, including the *Sunday Times* clerical workers and *The Times* journalists, as well as among traditionally disputatious groups like the NATSOPA Machine Chapel. The changes in working practices negotiated, especially the merging of *The Times* and the *Sunday Times* composing rooms, might have eventually resulted in substantial recurring savings. But there was to be no medium or long term. Even in the short term, there were major unanticipated costs in implementing the changes, and savings were slow to appear. Moreover, the suspension had a direct ratchet effect upon overall earnings in Fleet Street, including The Times. The growth in circulation and pagination at the *Guardian, Daily Telegraph*, and *Observer* during the suspension led to higher earnings through piecework and bonuses, which TNL was obliged to match at the end of the suspension; following resumption, *Times* earnings were believed to have become the highest in Fleet Street. (Paradoxically, in the medium term the *Guardian* and *Observer* were major losers from the suspension of *The Times*, since their expansion and subsequent contraction led to considerable financial and industrial relations difficulties.) Much of the equipment specified as 'already installed' in the July agreement was made operational, including the ICL 2903 commercial

computer. But the phased introduction of compute
photocomposition proceeded very slowly, and alth
extensive familiarization and training programmes were
undertaken, no newspaper or supplement was produced on
the new equipment whilst TNL was under Thomson ownership, successive datelines being postponed. No progress at
all was made towards the achievement of single key-boarding,
the NGA successfully resisting pressure to go further than it
had already gone at MGN. Following the resumption of work
after the suspension, management claimed that it had achieved
70 per cent of its objectives, the unions that they had won
a historic victory. If the general principles of the July agreement had been followed by successful negotiations on
specific issues, including appropriate manning levels for new
technolgy, management's claim might have been justified.
Major reductions in manning levels were achieved, for example
in the machine room, but no major progress was made in
the areas most affected by new technology. Agreement on
general principles did not lead to such detailed agreements,
and major issues unresolved on the resumption were still
unresolved twelve months later, confirming doubts about
the value of the initial agreement, and its lack of 'penalty'
clauses.

In confirmation of this scepticism, TNL announced a
major reorganization of the company structure in June 1980,
to be effective from 1 July. The new structure involved
the creation of a new holding company, Times Newspaper
Holdings Ltd., under the chairmanship of Sir Denis Hamilton,
including M. J. Hussey as vice-chairman and the independent
directors of TNL; the holding company was to be concerned
with long-term strategy and the protection of the independence of the newspapers. The TNL Board itself was reconsti-
tuted as the major operating board, comprising only executive
directors, under the chairmanship of James Evans, joint
deputy managing director of Thomson British Holdings Ltd.;
Dugal Nisbet-Smith succeeded Hussey as managing director.
Two new Executive Committees, one for *The Times* and its
supplements, chaired by William Rees-Mogg, and one for
the *Sunday Times*, chaired by Harold Evans, were also set
up, with overall responsibility for their respective publications,

excluding editorial policy. The effect of the changes was two-fold. M. J. Hussey, who had been centrally identified with TNL management policy during the suspension, was removed from day-to-day management responsibility to a senior ad-visory and diplomatic position; 'specifically he will be concen-trating on the long term strategy and development of the newspapers. We want him to travel round the world finding out what the other quality newspaper groups have been up to and, more important, what they are *planning* [italic in the original], and advise us accordingly.'[65] Equally importantly, senior managers from other companies within TTO were brought into TNL, questioning the assumption that Fleet Street had to be regarded as special; in addition to James Evans, Jack Bryers, formerly personnel director of Thomson Publica-ions, was appointed to the Board of TNL, as personnel director. Similar changes were introduced lower down the management hierarchy, especially in the industrial relations area.

Although Times management suffered major set-backs in 1978–9, and did not achieve the major objectives outlined in its statement 'Opportunity for Success' published in May 1976, the victory of the print unions was not unequivocal. Union solidarity was exemplary, at both official and un-official level; Times management succeeded in creating unity between previously antagonistic groups, whether in the same union, as in NATSOPA, or between unions, as between the NUJ and the NGA. Both the official and the unofficial liaison committees worked effectively, despite the differences between chapels that had signed agreements with the company and those that had not. However, the suspension created further difficulties for union leaders already in trouble with their Fleet Street members. Effective control of the conduct of the dispute lay with the Chapel Liaison Committee, chaired by the NATSOPA clerical FOC, B. A. Fitzpatrick, and it was only after contact had been established directly between the management and his committee that the way opened for a settlement (although of course other factors were also involved in the achievement of the breakthrough). Moreover, the uncertainties surrounding the eventual settlement, which was almost thwarted by the disagreement between the NATSOPA and the NGA Machine Room Chapels, indicated the continuing fragmentation of chapel interests. Nevertheless, despite the organizational problems presented by the suspension for the print unions, the successful prevention of the implementation of The Times's plans for technological change represented a major victory for the print unions, especially for the NGA. The power of Fleet Street trade unions was enhanced, rather than weakened, by the suspension of publication of Times newspapers.

The limited character of the trade-union 'victory' became clear in October 1980, when TTO announced 'their intention of withdrawing from the publication of *The Times, The Sunday Times*, and their associated publications.'[66] The company proposed to sell the publications or to close them if no sale had been agreed before 15 March 1981. In explaining their decision, Thomson British Holdings Ltd. pointed to the failure of TNL to achieve financial viability:

In the current financial year Times Newspapers Limited is expected to incur a pre-tax loss of some £15 million and to borrow from TBH £22 million. Since the formation of Times Newspapers in 1967 more than £70 million has been advanced from Thomson sources and used for investment, working capital and losses incurred . . . if the present situation is allowed to continue it will threaten the development of and the future security of the Organisation as a whole.

TTO attributed the major reason for TNL's financial difficulties to poor industrial relations:

The major reason behind this decision is the continuing troubled history of industrial relations which goes back over many years. This includes the eleven month suspension of publication in 1978–9 in the attempt to introduce disputes procedures, guarantees of continuous production, a new wage structure, more realistic manning levels and the introduction of new technology.

Management referred specifically to the failure to implement agreements made on the resumption of publication. It is impossible to say whether TTO would have eventually decided that TNL was not financially viable in the long term, regardless of the state of industrial relations in the company; but, at the very least, the company's failure to introduce new technology, primarily for industrial relations reasons, provided a major, publicly acceptable, justification for action which could have been justified on commercial grounds years earlier.

Chapter 8

Mirror Group Newspapers Ltd.
and Technological Change

In 1966 the Economist Intelligence Unit reported that

Daily Mirror Newspapers Ltd. . . . . must be considered a successful company by any yardstick. The circulation of both the *Daily* and *Sunday Mirror* is continuing to rise with a publicity budget which is proportionately much less than most of its competitors. This indicates that it has found a formula which is attractive to a large section of the population. The circulation of the *Daily* and *Sunday Mirror* newspapers is similar and this allows the productive equipment to operate at a high utilisation rate throughout the seven days of the week. The company operates as a business throughout, with a high degree of cost consciousness and a well-developed desire for efficiency.[1]

The professional approach to management survived into the 1970s, but to less effect. The circulation of the *Daily Mirror* was 5,132,000 in 1966; in 1970 it had dropped to 4,570,000; and in 1976 to 3,851,000. In the same years the circulation of the *Sunday Mirror* dropped from 5,219,000 in 1966, to 4,826,000 in 1970, and to 4,101,000 in 1976. Whereas in 1966 the *Daily Mirror* had a circulation lead over its nearest rival, the *Daily Express*, of 1,154,000, by 1976 its lead over its nearest rival, the *Sun*, had dropped to 143,000, although the decline was arrested the following year.[2] The *Sunday Mirror* maintained its circulation more successfully, not facing competition from the *Sun*: it rose from having the third largest weekly circulation, behind the *News of the World* and the *People* in 1966, to having the second largest, behind the *News of the World*, in 1976, despite the absolute decline in its circulation — a dubious advantage to MGN, since it also published the *People*. The financial fortunes of MGN varied more directly with changes in circulation than those of TNL, since the proportion of revenue derived from cover prices was greater. For the first time in decades, the MGN lost money in 1973-4.[3]

Equally worryingly, the rate of decline in circulation increased in in 1974–5.

Like the FT and TNL, MGN anticipated serious economic difficulties in 1975: increases in revenue were not keeping pace with increases in costs. Concern was all the greater because Reed International regarded MGN as a significant source of profits (or, at worst, a generator of cash). In the immediate past MGN newspapers, especially the *Daily Mirror*, had been both commercial and editorial successes, with the reputation of profitable, lively, and in some circumstances politically serious, popular newspapers. With continuing competition from the *Sun*, the scope for re-establishing the group's fortunes by expansion were limited; the group anticipated, at best, a period of stability in circulation.[4] The scope for reducing costs through lower raw-material costs was also limited, although some savings could be made by using lower-quality newsprint. Newsprint represented a relatively high proportion of production costs for popular newspapers (36 per cent in 1975), and MGN was therefore disproportionately disadvantaged by the rise in newsprint prices in 1974–5; although the group was part of a major paper-manufacturing multi-national and could therefore have been partially protected from the effects of newsprint price rises, Reed International's Canadian newsprint manufacturers were experiencing difficulties, and in any event attempts to aid MGN by holding down newsprint costs would hardly help Reed International's financial performance.[5] MGN management's attention was therefore inevitably focused upon reducing labour costs, both by reducing manning levels on existing technology and by introducing new technology. Since MGN's cost structure differed from that of the FT and TNL, the emphasis in its cost-reduction programme differed: the savings to be obtained from reducing linotype operators' earnings were lower, those to be made in the make-up and publishing areas were greater. Nevertheless, MGN management's proposals were similar in concept to those discussed earlier: computerized photocomposition, with electronic page make-up, was to be introduced, and the composing room was to be reorganized. In addition, editorial and composing work in Manchester were to cease. However, unlike the FT or TNL, MGN did not propose direct editorial or clerical input into the system: the NGA jurisdiction over key-boarding was to be protected. As events were to show, MGN encountered considerable technical and industrial relations difficulties in attempting to introduce new technology, and by the end of 1979 had achieved only very partial success.

The structure of this chapter follows the pattern of the preceding two. In the first section the corporate structure of the Mirror Group is outlined, together with the financial problems the company faced in the mid 1970s. The second section outlines the company's thinking on new technology and technological developments between the announcement of the first phase of the development plan in June 1975 and December 1979. The third section examines the manpower implications of the new technology, and the industrial relations problems which accompanied its implementation. The fourth briefly summarizes the significance of developments at MGN.

i

Like the *FT* and *The Times* the Mirror newspapers were the visible standard-bearers of a major international corporation, in this case Reed International. The Mirror newspapers were acquired by Reed in 1970, when the company took over the International Publishing Corporation, and retained the name IPC Newspapers Ltd. until 1975, when Reed International was reorganized.[6] Unlike Pearson (S) and Son Ltd. and TTO, Reed International was not controlled by family trusts - there was no equivalent to the Cowdray or Thomson families (although according to senior managers, Cecil King acted like a proprietor): according to company reports, no shareholder was known to own more than 5 per cent of the company's shares.[7] The company's interests were originally in paper and board, but throughout the 1960s and especially the 1970s the company diversified vertically, both up and downstream. Major acquisitions were made in pulp and lumber, in packaging, in decorative and building products, in stationery, and in publishing, both in Britain and abroad, in Europe, Canada, South Africa and the Far East. In 1974–5

Reed International's United Kingdom operations contributed 54.33 per cent of company pre-tax profits (£46.4m out of £85.4m). The company believed that international diversification provided the safest means of maintaining growth, overseas earnings balancing domestic difficulties, and vice versa — although the company's difficulties in 1977–8 indicated that internationalization did not guarantee stability, difficulties occurring simultaneously in Canada, South Africa, the Far East, and the United Kingdom.

Although Reed International's structure changed in the 1970s in detail, the outline remained as it had been established with the merger of Reed and IPC in 1970. In Britain, and the European mainland, there were five operating divisions: MGN Ltd., IPC Ltd., Reed Group Ltd., The Wall Paper Manufacturers Ltd., and Reed Building Products Ltd. Abroad, the company operated through Reed Consolidated Industries Ltd. (Australia), Reed Paper Ltd. (Canada), and Reed Finance (Pty) Ltd. (South Africa). MGN itself comprised five principal subsidiaries — Daily Mirror Newspapers Ltd., Odhams Newspapers Ltd. (the *Sporting Life*, the *Sunday People*), Reveille Newspapers Ltd., Scottish Daily Record and Sunday Mail Ltd., and West of England Newspapers Ltd. In addition, MGN had very substantial shares in Associated Television Co. Ltd., the parent company of ATV (13.9 per cent voting shares), and similar shares in Westward TV, Radio Clyde, and Plymouth Sound. The second operating arm, IPC, covered the printing and publishing of periodicals, directories, and books, together with contract printing. Its interests included IPC Magazines Ltd., IPC Business Press Ltd., (ABC Travel Guides, Kelly's Directories, etc.), Butterworth & Co. (Publishers) Ltd. (major law publishers), the Hamlyn Publishing Group Ltd, IPC Printers Ltd. and Odhams (Watford) Ltd., major magazine printers. IPC also held major shareholdings in Associated Television Co. Ltd. The Reed Group operated a number of companies involved in the manufacture of paper, paper packaging, and office supplies, including Spicers Ltd. and Bogden Data Paper Ltd.; the operations of the remaining divisions are indicated by their titles.[8]

Reed International expanded rapidly in the 1970s as Table 8.1 shows.

Table 8.1 Reed International: Financial Data 1968–1977

Year ending 31 March	Ordinary shareholders' funds	Loan capital	Total capital	% growth	Loan capital as % total capital
1968	154	84	258		32.56
69	155	94	270	4.65	34.81
70	162	96	281	4.07	34.16
71	239	142	404	43.77	35.15
72	251	138	415	2.72	33.25
73	298	169	493	18.80	34.28
74	331	191	558	13.18	34.23
75	351	221	627	12.37	35.25
76	355	300	737	17.54	40.71
77	408	399	916	24.29	43.56

Source Reed International Ltd: *Annual Report 1978, p.6.*

Year-on-year growth in capital employed rose from 4.65 per cent in 1968–9 to an exceptional peak of 43.77 per cent in 1970–1, but throughout the 1970s continued well above the level of the 1960s.[9] Initially, the growth was sustained by capital raised from the market: it was subsequently based on loan capital. The financial years 1975–6 and 1976–7 saw a sharp increase in the company's reliance upon loan capital, permitted by a change in the company's articles of association in 1975, raising the borrowing limit from the aggregate of issued share capital plus consolidated reserves to one and a half times share capital plus consolidated reserves.[10]

Reed International's economic fortunes declined sharply in the mid 1970s. In his first address as chief executive in 1975 Alex Jarratt, who had succeeded Lord Ryder as chief executive in December 1974, drew attention to the serious financial problems the company faced in 1974–5:

The problems of the three-day week, considered so traumatic at the time, appear in retrospect fairly simple compared with those of running a business in conditions of massive inflation, high taxation, and stagnant demand, with little evidence up till now that the seriousness of the situation has been fully comprehended and, least of all, is being acted upon.[11]

Only the Reed Group increased its profits in Britain over 1973-4 levels and overall profits in the United Kingdom dropped from £46.5m to £46.4m: if adjustments had been made for inflation the deterioration would have been even more substantial. At home, the group faced major industrial relations problems at IPC, with a long dispute at Odhams (Watford) Ltd. in July 1974, as well as at MGN. The decline in the demand for paper and pulp in the last quarter of 1974 severely hit Reed's finances, both in Britain and especially in Canada. The situation did not improve the following year, 1975-6: overall profits slumped from £88m in 1974-5 to £50m in 1975-6. The company's performance in Britain improved: the industrial relations situation at Odhams (Watford) Ltd. improved, with consequent benefit to the financial results at IPC; the closure of the Alex Cowan Mill at Penycuik in Scotland reduced the losses in the Reed Group; and the success of the Scottish *Daily Record* bolstered the financial performance of MGN. But the gradual improvements in Britain were offset by very poor performance abroad, in the Far East, in South Africa, and especially in Canada. The company experienced major strikes in British Columbia and Quebec, exacerbating the effects of the weak market for pulp and paper.[12] Dividends per share dropped from 12½p in 1970-1 to 9.1875p in 1972-3, and then rose gradually to 9.398p in 1973-4, 10.283p in 1974-5, and 11.0775p in 1975-6: separate financial results for IPCN and MGN are not publicly available.

The company's expansion in the 1970s reduced the financial significant of MGN to Reed International in profit terms (although its favourable cash flow was of central importance). By 1975-6 printing and publishing contributed 24.1 per cent to the group's turnover, and 19.9 per cent to the group's profits; printing and publishing included the IPC as well as MGN.[13] Despite the reduced financial importance of printing and publishing, financial pressures on the whole group meant that all operating divisions were subject to central pressure to improve performance. This was especially so in MGN and IPC where performance had deteriorated significantly since the 1960s. Reed International's move 'down stream', away from primary products, might have been expected to have resulted in an increased rate of return on capital invested, especially since the company acquired constituted a 'market leader'. However, events had not turned out as expected; far from providing financial strength, by 1975–6 printing and publishing were a source of weakness.

MGN's membership of Reed International provided access to the holding company's financial resources; the funds for the development plan were provided by Reed International. There is no evidence of close supervision by the parent company of MGN, and this would have been unlikely: both Lord Ryder and Alex Jarratt played major roles in national economic policy, and faced serious problems in the operation of the group as a whole – they had little time, even if they had the interest, to oversee MGN. The main board of Reed International in 1976 did not contain a single director of MGN, and there was no interchange of management personnel or expertise. The links between the two organizations were financial – MGN's financial planning was of course integrated into the financial planning of the whole group – and indirect, through the election of directors. The financial resources of Reed International made it possible for MGN to contemplate major capital investment, but the parent company's financial difficulties made it necessary for the investment to make a relatively rapid return: hence Reed were willing to provide £15m for the MGN development plan, but it was publicly justified on the grounds that it would produce a return of £4.8m in 1976–7 – an optimistic estimate which proved in retrospect wildly extravagant.[14]

MGN's operating links with Reed International were not close. However, MGN operated more self-consciously as a company than other companies which covered both national and provincial newspapers. Hence the experience of the Scottish *Daily Record* and *Sunday Mail* at Anderston Quay was explicitly drawn upon in the London and Manchester development plan, although it was not expected that Anderston Quay would be replicated. Similarly, the plans for the printing of the western editions of Mirror newspapers at Plymouth were integrated into those of the group's provincial newspaper company, West of England Newspapers Ltd., based in Plymouth: a new offset plant, rebuilt from the bomb-damaged Belfast plant, was erected, to print both West of England newspapers and West Country editions of the *Daily Mirror*. No similar links existed between the FT and the Westminster Press, although of course the FT's small circulation and concentration in the south-east made the specific issue of regional printing irrelevant. Most relevantly, MGN was concerned to establish a fully 'professional' approach to management, which would be effective throughout the group. This selfconscious professionalism was especially apparent in the manpower and industrial relations areas. Unusually, both for newspapers and for British industry in general, the Manpower Function had explicit representation at Board level in MGN. Reporting to the Manpower Services Director, R. Wooliscroft, were seven specialist departments: labour relations; education and training; productivity services; personnel services; manpower planning; executive controller; safety and welfare. Corporate objectives were laid down for industrial relations and manpower, as for other functions in the company.[15]

In summary, as at Pearson Longman Ltd. and TTO, the immediate background to the launching of MGN's development plan was a deterioration in the financial performance of the controlling corporation, which reinforced the financial pressures already operating in Fleet Street. MGN was less hit by declining advertising in 1975 than either the *FT* or *The Times*, since it carried fewer column inches, and its rates were lower per thousand readers (although not lower than *The Times* per column inch): it was more concerned with income from sales. Since sales proved more resilient than advertising revenue in 1975, the financial results of MGN were better than those of the FT or TNL: for the year 1 April 1975–31 March 1976 profit amounted to £3m — substantially better than any newspaper except the *Sun*, but derisory in relation to the level of turnover or the level of profitability achieved in the 1960s; Reed International's publishing and printing activities generated a trading profit of only £9.0m on turnover of £275.3m in that year.[16] The group was further especially seriously hit by the rise in the price of newsprint in 1974–5: by 1976 nearly 50 per cent of the costs of production were due to newsprint.[17] Although the effect of high newsprint prices upon MGN might normally have been expected to be balanced by their contribution to the financial results of other Reed International companies, production difficulties, industrial disputes, and controversies over pollution involving Reed International's Canadian subsidiary limited the company's ability to take advantage of a favourable world-market situation.

The availability of new technology therefore provided the obvious means for making a very substantial improvement in MGN's financial position.

ii

MGN's assessment of the economic prospects for national newspapers was as pessimistic as that of the FT and The Times. According to the MGN chief executive, Percy Roberts: 'There is no way, in the present economic climate and in the environment in which we will be operating for the next few years, in which we can achieve substantial improvements in revenue. During the next few years we cannot expect advertising revenue to increase substantially in real terms.'[18] The future survival of MGN required substantial savings in costs, especially in labour costs: there was little prospect of making substantial savings on raw materials — the major raw material, newsprint, was rapidly increasing in price. Accordingly, MGN management announced the first stage of its development plan 'Blueprint for Survival' in June 1975; the second stage was announced the following October. The plan comprised three phases: the concentration of production of the *Mirror, Sunday Mirror,* and *Sunday People* in Holborn, with the subsequent closure of the Stamford Street plant; the installation of computerized photocomposition in Holborn for all four national titles; and the rationalization of production at Manchester.[19] The major rationalization involved in Manchester was the ending of composition at both Withy Grove and Northprint, and the closure of Manchester as an editorial centre: pages were to be transmitted from London to Manchester by page-facsimile transmission, for printing in Manchester. Although it was planned to introduce computerized photocomposition, there was no intention of challenging NGA control over key-boarding:

it was therefore correctly hoped that NGA opposition would not be as great as it was to prove at The Times. Despite major achievements, the introduction of new technology at MGN has not realized management's initial hopes. By the end of 1979 cold-type methods of composing were being used for approximately two-thirds of the group's output. But the costs and difficulties of achieving the change were greater than had been anticipated and the quality of the final product worse. As at TNL, although for different reasons, technical and industrial relations problems combined to produce a confused situation, in which major managerial groups came to doubt the wisdom of the initial decision to proceed with new technology before it had been fully tested. The company's major success was the ending of editorial and composing work in Manchester, a change which could have been achieved without major technological change in London.

Unlike those of the FT or TNL, MGN's plans for new technology in London and Manchester built directly upon earlier experience in the company. Both facsimile transmission and computerized photocomposition had been used earlier in the group, at least partly as conscious experiments; facsimile transmission had operated between Manchester and Belfast from 1966 to 1971, when the Belfast plant had been destroyed by IRA bombs; and computerized photocomposition at the Scottish *Daily Record* and *Sunday Mail* in Anderston Quay, Glasgow, since 1971. Personnel involved in the earlier innovations were involved in the changes in London and Manchester: Joseph May, the man responsible both for the Belfast facsimile operation and for Anderston Quay, became the development editor for MGN, whilst the man responsible for management of the introduction of new technology at Anderston Quay, Dugal Nisbet-Smith, became a member of the Board of Directors of MGN (and was of course to play a central role at The Times). The experience of Belfast and Anderston Quay was thus directly relevant to the plans for London and Manchester.

Between 1966 and 1972 Irish editions of the *Daily Mirror* and the *Sunday Mirror* were printed in Belfast, with plates made from pages transmitted by facsimile transmission from

Manchester.[20] The technology to be used in facsimile transmission from London to Manchester was basically the same
as that used in the earlier project, and was to be obtained
from the same manufacturer, Muirheads. The technology was
thought to have worked effectively in 1966–71. Although
transmission was comparatively slow, no edition had been
lost, no major breakdown had occurred, and clarity of
definition in the final product had been acceptable. But the
operation was not a total success and no attempt was made
to rebuild the plant following its destruction by the IRA in
1971. One reason for the failure was the political and
economic instability in Ulster, which began in 1969. A second
was the plant's continuing industrial relations problems:
many problems which existed on the opening of the plant
in March 1966 were still unresolved when it closed five years
later. From the beginning, MGN attempted to obtain what it
described as 'realistic' manning levels, resulting in conflict
with all print unions on manning levels. In addition, there
were three major areas of demarcation dispute: in the process
area, where the company eventually agreed to employ SLADE
members on the automatic developer, although it had hoped
to simplify industrial relations at the plant by using NGA
rather than SLADE members, keeping SLADE completely
out of the plant; in the plate-making area between ASLP and
NSES; and in the press room between NGA and NATSOPA.
The experience of printing in Belfast showed that decentralized printing from a central composing room, with facsimile
transmission of fully composed pages, and large-scale web-
offset printing, including the use of colour, was technically
possible. But it also showed that a policy of decentralized
printing would not necessarily simplify production operations nor necessarily result in improved industrial relations.

MGN also had direct experience of the successful intro-
duction of computerized photocomposition at Anderston
Quay in Glasgow, where MGN's Scottish *Daily Record* and
Sunday Mail were produced by computerized photocomposi-
tion and printed on web-offset presses from July 1971 on.[21]
As envisaged at Holborn, composing continued to be done by
(Scottish) Graphical Association members at Anderston
Quay, retrained to use an electronic key-board; the key-

board used was modelled on the traditional linotype key-board, although new staff were to be trained on key-boards modelled on typewriter key-boards. However, the technology represented a 'first-generation' computerized system, with the use of computers to increase vastly the speed of an existing operation, not to transform the operation. For example, hard copy continued to be used. Compositors selected type-face, size, and column width, and typed material onto machine-readable paper-type; simultaneously, operators received a hard-copy of the material in-put, which could be used for alterations and corrections. Both the original edited typescripts and the hard copy print-out were passed to readers for correction. After correction, the operator released the material, in the form of paper tape, into the photo-composing room. The paper tape was then processed through a photocomposition camera (the Linotron 505 C) which produced a photocopy of the text to be seen eventually in the newspaper. Page make-up continued to be done by cut-and-paste methods. Thereafter, production proceeded on conventional photocomposition and web-offset methods of production. Anderston Quay thus provided some experience of the technology of computerized photocomposition, but only a limited amount: it represented a transition phase between hard-metal and electronic methods of composing, and, although among the most sophisticated systems extant in 1971, had been significantly superseded (in theory) by 1975. The number of characters composed per second had increased from 0.9 to 2.2 on average, or to 7,200 per hour, the organization and physical appearance of the composing room had been transformed, but the electronics were essentially being used to speed up an existing process, not to transform it.

Anderston Quay was an important 'green field' project for MGN, involving the expenditure of £7m: 'It gave the company an opportunity to rationalise manning levels, to sweep away traditional demarcation, to streamline the production flow and to create a new generation of young and expert management.' In the composing room, a composing-room rate was negotiated to cover all employees there (except SOGAT copy-readers), in place of the existing three-level arrangement, and flexibility between operations was obtained; the number of employees dropped from 126 to 109 by 1974. In the process area the number of operatives was reduced from 19 to 15, in plate-making from 29 to 19, and similar reductions were obtained elsewhere by a process of attrition. The attempt to negotiate increased flexibility succeeded: in the machine room all press crew were given craft status and pay, although 50 per cent were NATSOPA members — helped by the fact that the machine managers were members of the Scottish Graphical Association, not of the NGA. The major problems arose with SLADE, both over jurisdiction over cutting and assembling the bromides, plate-making, and redundancies: SLADE eventually agreed to share jurisdiction. In addition to industrial relations problems, the new system experienced technical difficulties. The amount of computing capacity required was underestimated, and instead of being kept as a back-up the second computer had to be used to store operator output, to avoid 'store-full' condition being reached before stories were completed. Similarly, development work continued to be required in the plate-making area. In 1974 the company was still running at a loss. Nevertheless, by 1975 MGN management were convinced that the Anderston Quay operation had been successful; computerized composition and web-offset printing had been installed; colour printing was being effectively achieved; circulation was increased. By 1979 MGN management were claiming that the Anderston Quay operation represented a major success, both in production and in economic terms — with pre-tax profits of £2.5m in the year ending April 1979.

MGN considered two alternative basic strategies for development in the 1970s. Following from the Belfast experiment, there was the possibility of increasing regionalization and using satellite presses linked to London. Editorial and composing would continue in London, but printing would be done in regional centres. Facsimile transmission would be used to transmit composed pages from London to perhaps nine regional centres. This would have been compatible with reducing editorial and composing in Manchester. MGN's announcement in June 1975 that the West of England edition would be printed in Plymouth suggested that regional-ization was likely. This would inevitably have involved long-term reductions in the print-run in London, with associated reductions in employment and space requirements. However, MGN management explicitly denied that the decision to print in Plymouth was part of a regional strategy: it was regarded as a one-off project, made possible by the ownership of spare printing capacity, and made desirable by the very early dead-lines required to meet the 12.30 from Paddington, which served newspaper distributors in the West of England.[22] Regionalization was technically feasible, and made desirable by MGN's continuing dissatisfaction with the NPA agreed distribution system. But it was rejected in favour of main-taining existing production levels in London, primarily because of the very high level of capital investment which the acquisi-tion of new presses would have involved − although the industrial relations difficulties to be anticipated from attemp-ting such a strategy were also daunting.

Following the rejection of the regionalization alternative, there remained the possiblity of repeating Anderston Quay in London, with the acquisition of a 'green-field' site and the establishment of a new factory (similar to IPC's disastrous development at Southwark Offset or News International's current development in the East End). However, there was no equivalent 'green-field' site, and too much capital already sunk in existing buildings and equipment; the company could not contemplate an investment equivalent to £7m at 1971 prices (although computer hardware had actually dropped in price since 1971, so the expenditure might not have proved as large as feared). Nor were there any plans to introduce web-offset printing at Holborn − the existing rotary presses had only been bought in the 1960s. Instead, the closure of Manchester as an editorial and composing centre and the introduction of new technology and manning levels in London were seen as the minimal defensive measures necessary to arrest a decline in productivity brought about by a decline in circulation, without a corresponding reduction in capital or labour employed. Even more than for the FT or TNL, for MGN new technology was less a demonstration of confidence in the future than a means of achieving savings

which could, in a different situation, have been achieved
without new technology at all.

New technology at MGN did not involve any change in
the journalistic function (although it did cause considerable
unrest amongst journalists). However, the composing room
was transformed, with the installation of Linotype-Paul's
'System 5'. The system comprised four computers (although
two were originally envisaged) and twelve minicomputers:
in addition to thirty-two input key-boards (some based on
linotype key-boards, the majority QUERTY), there were
twenty linoscreen key-boards, and twelve page-view terminals.[23] Since the newspaper comprised far fewer characters
than *The Times* or the *FT* far fewer input key-boards were
needed. There was also less computer power. The key-boards
also differed in detail. The physical layout of the composing
room also differed from that at TNL: at TNL key-board
operators were grouped in fours, whilst at MGN operators
were arranged in lines. On the other hand, the facility for
electronic page make-up was more important than for *The
Times*, owing to a heavy production emphasis on lay-out and
design. In theory, the page-composition terminal provided
the facility for three alternative methods of full-page composition.

The first method involves the simultaneous retrieving of all material
scheduled for inclusion in a page and having it automatically placed
in the position determined by the 'Pageset' commands . . . Under the
second method, the retrieving and positioning processes are carried
out in blocks with the aid of column lines which appear on the screen,
while with the third method the 'Pageset' commands are suppressed
in favour of the interactive positioning.

When completed the make-up operator released the page for
exposure. In practice, the system had difficulty in exposing
illustrations along with the text, proved very complex and
slow to operate, and has not operated as originally envisaged
(see below, pp. 317–18).

The page-facsimile system comprised two scanners
(Muirhead 1243) and one data compressor at the trans-
mitting end, with two recorders and a data reconstructor at
the receiving office. Two complete systems were installed.
The data compressor was used to reduce the cost of the Post

Office wideband transmission line required, without sacrificing speed in transmission. The speed of transmission was approximately 3 minutes per page, but could be up to 4½ minutes if extensive pictures were used. The role of the operator (NGA TAE) was limited to loading either film or proof onto a drum, a delicate task since accuracy was essential and the drum circulated at very high speed. Transmission and reception were automatic, the receiver being controlled via the communication link, as was error checking. The major problems encountered were in proof reproduction, especially in the reproduction of half-tone graphics, where data compression caused distortion. By October 1979 144 pages per week were published by facsimile, out of a weekly total of up to 384 pages per week.

Despite the problems in ensuring clarity with half-tone graphics, MGN's facsimile transmission system worked satisfactorily. Changes at Holborn were less successful. The increases in speed of operating expected from the use of computerized composing were slow to materialize: it therefore proved impossible to achieve the savings in manpower expected in the composing room. More importantly, if predictably, it proved impossible to obtain adequate performance standards from the page-composition terminal: it proved impossible to make electronic full-page make-up work. The performance achieved by the new system proved either too slow, or otherwise inadequate, owing to difficulties in programming. Accordingly, cut-and-past methods of page make-up were retained, resulting in a substantial hiccough in the system.

The new technology introduced at MGN has suffered from technical problems: the system is not, at the time of writing (January 1980) operating as had been envisaged in 1975. As at TNL, legal proceedings against the suppliers of the equipment were considered, but not proceeded with. According to MGN, the equipment had failed seriously to live up to the specifications promised: although it could be made to work, the operations were so complex that the error rate was high and the system very slow. According to the manufacturers, MGN's initial specifications were inadequate, and the labour used to operate the equipment inadequately trained. Doubtless both sides could justify their viewpoints. As in other situations, inadequate systems analysis created programming difficulties, which only revealed themselves fully once the equipment was operating; inadequate computing expertise was available to remedy the technical problems encountered; and the computer expertise available was not fully aware of the newspaper world. Technical difficulties thus led to the abandonment of the planned phasing of the change over to cold-type, making the industrial relations problems MGN were already encountering even more difficult.

iii

As mentioned earlier, MGN established its manpower function in 1969, with a Board-level appointment (R. Wooliscroft) — unusually for national newspapers.[24] The function was organized in seven divisions: labour relations; education and training; productivity services; personnel services; manpower planning; executive controller; and safety and welfare. The day-to-day conduct of industrial relations was thus separated from long-term planning, which was the responsibility of the manpower-planning section. MGN thus had a more elaborately developed manpower strategy than other news-papers had, outlined by the company in its evidence to the Royal Commission in 1974. In general terms, the objective was to create a more profitable organization, with a more flexible labour force, but without damaging 'good industrial relations'. Unfortunately, there was considerable tension between the different objectives of the strategy; the desire to increase profitability inevitably conflicted with employees' conceptions of good industrial relations. According to MGN management, employees identified with the chapel rather than with the employer and rejected 'the concept of reason-able demands on skill and knowledge during agreed work periods'. The objective was a smaller, more committed, labour force. Unfortunately, attempting to break down chapel loyalties and increase identification with the company at the same time as attempting to introduce new technology and lower manning levels was an impossible task. All unions were involved in disputes at MGN during the 1970s.

MGN management correctly saw that the core of their industrial relations problems lay in their relations with their chapels: 'recognising [the destructive power of the chapels] our relationships with chapels must be the first priority in our dealings with trade unions.' Management saw the chapel organization as a barrier to effective use of labour, fragmentation and inter-chapel rivalry preventing the allocation of work on the basis of production requirements. They saw the chapels as solely concerned with maximizing wages and conditions, with the single exception of the NGA Composing Room Chapel Technical Committee. To reduce fragmentation management wished to foster inter-chapel co-operation — hence the major importance attached to achieving a single composing room chapel — although management attempts to influence chapel organization could be counter-productive. MGN management were also concerned to establish direct contact with their employees, seeing chapel officials as a barrier to effective communication. Hence, in April 1974 management proposed a consultative council, but the proposal was not acceptable to the chapels. More success was achieved with the 'Windsor' concept, a series of joint management-union meetings on 'neutral' ground, St. George's Chapel, Windsor, and the establishment of Joint Committees on Health and Safety. But the most significant achievement was the establishment of a Joint Clerical Committee, through which a job evaluated wages structure was established and administered for clerical workers. However, management attempts to establish direct contacts with chapel members ran counter to the basic principles of chapel organization, especially in the NGA. Attempts to increase awareness of management policies through the publication of a house newspaper, *Mirror Group News*, and a special 'dial-a-phone' system, had only limited success.

MGN believed that the chapels were the central industrial relations issue faced. But they were only one level: in addition to agreements with individual chapels and with groups of chapels, MGN also negotiated directly with national-level trade-union officials (over general wage awards), and indirectly through the NPA. (Although MGN had withdrawn from the NPA for labour purposes in April 1974, agreements negotiated with the NPA operated until the negotiation of new MGN agreements in 1975.) Although MGN was very critical of the NPA, like the other houses it believed that national-level negotiations were the best means of achieving agreement on general principles, which would then be applied on a house basis. It was then hoped that national union officials would be able to persuade, or exert pressure upon, individual chapels to transform general agreed principles into effective working agreements. Not surprisingly, 'this policy is meeting with resistance.'

The company was mainly concerned to establish what it regarded as an appropriate structure for 'good industrial relations', modelled upon the pluralist conception of progressive professional management: effective collective bargaining over wages and conditions, close consultation over welfare and related issues, and acceptance of managerial authority in matters of work organization. Good industrial relations necessarily involved acceptance of agreed procedures, and the use of strike action (or equally disruptive alternatives like mandatory chapel meetings, which were less costly to the workers involved) only when procedures had been exhausted. Although no figures were provided for the number of disputes in the company, industrial disputes in the industry were 'as bad as can be found in any other industry'. Accordingly, the MGN Board announced that 'the company placed a high value on acceptance of procedures', and intended to cease paying for working hours lost through industrial action. During the period 1975–9 the company showed a readiness to hold workers involved in unofficial action in breach of contract and to issue protective notices to other employees, as they did over the dispute with SOGAT in April 1975 and with the journalists over their claim for a £3,000 increase in November 1977. As part of its attempt to establish a coherent industrial relations policy, the company also hoped to negotiate a more orderly pay structure, including a narrowing of differentials, notably in the composing room, through a reduction in what Percy Roberts called the 'obscene' level of earnings of linotype operators.

Even before the announcement of its proposals for new

technology the company attempted to secure agreement on 'no automatic replacement'. On 1 October 1974 Percy Roberts announced that the company would be attempting to negotiate no automatic replacement agreements during the impending pay negotiations: 'If the unions could be persuaded . . . to accept a policy of no automatic replacement and retirement at 65, then within twelve months savings within the industry could be — very conservatively — at the rate of £5m. on its wage bill at current rates.'[25] The company proposed no automatic replacement as a means of achieving new minimum manning levels.

The minimum manning levels are the levels required by the Company in order to assist in achieving the long-term security of the business and its employees. These minimum manning levels are those required by the Company to operate the equipment needed to produce the paper by present methods and techniques or such new methods and techniques or such new methods and equipment as may be introduced . . . Reductions in current manning levels imply that the traditional manning agreement, both national and local, will be amended.[26]

The company insisted that they were not attempting to establish a no-replacement clause. It was proposed that regular six-monthly meetings would be arranged with individual chapels, to which other union officials could be invited, to review the operation of NAR principles, and to discuss anticipated retirements. The proposed agreement ended with the optimistic clause, 'this agreement is conditional upon acceptance in total by all printing and maintenance unions involved.' In exchange, MGN offered 14 per cent w.e.f. 1 October 1974, with a minimum of £7·00 guaranteed on departmental average earnings for a five-shift working week: the percentage to apply to basic rates (with consequential knock-on increases).

The 'non-automatic replacement' policy was one aspect of the attempt to reduce labour costs. The broad outlines of the new policy were made explicit in an announcement by MGN management in January 1975: no money was to be made available to finance payments above nationally agreed levels except in the context of reduced manning levels. Any savings from reduced manning levels were to be apportioned between management and men by negotiation — but the

principle of 50/50 (or even 60/40) was not regarded as sacro-
sanct. Any future reductions in labour requirements, whether
because of reduced pagination or reduced circulation, would
be accompanied by reduced staffing.

No automatic replacement was seen as the most appealing
method of achieving reduced manning levels, since it involved
a guarantee of no compulsory redundancy and was accompanied by a very substantial (by 1974 standards) pay increase.
However, it was not a principle the print unions were willing
to accept automatically: the print unions naturally wished to
obtain the increase without conceding the principle. Resistance was encountered even from NATSOPA clerical chapels,
with whom management's relations were unusually good:
since clerical chapels had high rates of turnover, no automatic replacement would affect them first. As a result of
disruptions to production caused by mandatory chapel
meetings on Wednesday, 15 January, MGN management
stopped printing and issued protective notices.

The NGA eventually reached agreement with MGN on the
acceptance of no automatic replacement in exchange for
10 per cent back-dated to 1 October 1974, and 7.5 per cent
from 1 April 1975, although there was substantial opposition
to the deal from some chapel members: voting was reported
as being 561 to 315 for acceptance.[27] The NUJ accepted
a similar offer, after a one-day dispute. SOGAT chapels
rejected the proposals, instead asking for the agreement
negotiated with the NPA (7 per cent in two stages) to be
translated to MGN. When MGN refused SOGAT members
struck (in April 1975) resulting in the dismissal of SOGAT
members and the issuing of protective notices to other
employees. The SOGAT Executive instigated arbitration
proceedings (at ACAS), against the wishes of MGN SOGAT
members. An eleven-days-long dispute ended, after fifteen
hours of talks between SOGAT national officials and MGN,
with agreement on 'no further recruitment' in place of 'no
automatic replacement', in exchange for 10 per cent from
1 October 1974 and 7.5 per cent from 1 April 1975. Recruitment was to be suspended, pending agreement with chapels
on new manning levels. The existing mechanization and
productivity agreement was to continue, whereby labour

savings resulting from new investment were to be shared 60/40; no payment was to be made to chapels for men attrited; but 25 per cent of the savings from voluntary retirement under the 65+ scheme were to be shared by the chapels concerned, and an additional week's holiday was to be paid for.[28]

At the expense of 17.5 per cent over eighteen months, and the loss of two weeks' publication and several interruptions to production, MGN secured acceptance of the principle of no automatic replacement without conceding any principles on the proportion of the savings to be paid to the chapels concerned. However, the effectiveness of the agreement depended upon the negotiation of new lower manning levels with the chapels, as recognized in the agreement with SOGAT. 'No automatic replacement' could simply mean repeated arguments over specific vacancies, which might or might not result in replacement, depending upon the industrial relations situation at the time. According to MGN management in evidence to the Royal Commission in August 1975, it was impossible to say 'in quantitative terms' what effect the agreement had had. But 'the Unions and Chapels now know exactly how management will react in a dispute situation.'[29] The principle gained was unlikely to have had a major impact upon labour costs at MGN: any significant effect would only become apparent over a long-period, and before a long period could elapse MGN management had announced their 'Blueprint for Survival'.

Following the announcement of 'Blueprint for Survival' in two stages in 1975 MGN undertook negotiations with the print unions on the general terms of the manpower changes which would be required and on the application of the proposals to individual chapels. Although it was initially hoped that the new system would begin at least partial operation in October 1976, no deadline was set for the conclusion of the negotiations, and it was recognized that negotiations would be prolonged. Like other houses, MGN was simultaneously involved in discussions with the print unions through the Joint Standing Committee. Little progress had been made at house level by the time MGN management gave oral evidence to the Royal Commission on the Press, in March 1976, although negotiations were under way, especially with representatives of the NUJ and the NGA, whose members would be most immediately effected by the prospect of fewer jobs.

The first major element in 'Blueprint for Survival' was the ending of editorial and composing work in Manchester. MGN's decision to consolidate editorial and composing in London, leaving only a small editorial sub-office in Manchester in the long run, was in some ways surprising. The *Daily Mirror*'s reputation was as the spokesman for the northern working-man, a reputation reflected in the regional concentration of its circulation as well as the imagery of Andy Capp; MGN's profit was alleged to be largely derived from its northern circulation. Moreover, regional newspapers were expanding, whilst the circulation of national dailies was contracting; concentration of editorial staff in London would inevitably reduce the 'regional flavour' to the level of the publication of accounts of different football matches. Finally, labour costs and the level of industrial disputes were lower in Manchester than in London; labour costs in the composing room in Manchester were especially significantly lower than in London, owing to the absence of piece-work. In Manchester all composing-room employees were covered by a single agreement and paid a single basic rate, an objective which Fleet Street managements were trying very hard to achieve. Working relationships between the unions were also closer than in Fleet Street; for example, NATSOPA agreed to members of other unions doing Saturday night casual work within their jurisdiction when NATSOPA members were not available.[30] Moreover, MGN had contracted with Thomson Withy Grove for the production of the Mirror Northern editions until 1981, and any disentangling would involve obtaining the co-operation of TWG. In short, newspapers had already obtained in Manchester many of the objectives they were hoping to achieve in London without much prospect of success, including the sharing of production facilities.

The proposal to run down editorial and composing staff in Manchester over a three-year period inevitably aroused opposition from the workers involved. The Manchester

Mirror NUJ Chapel sought a delay in implementation, and the extension of the period of run-down. The NUJ lobbied northern MPs about the MGN's disregard for regional interests, both culturally and economically, and Alan Fitch, the Labour MP for Wigan, publicly criticized MGN's centralization plans.[31] Following journalists' pressure, a joint management–NUJ working party was set up to consider the proposals. The working party accepted the logic of MGN's planning, but suggested that the period of the run-down should be increased from three to five years. This was accepted by the Manchester journalists. Since 1976 MGN's editorial staff have been considerably reduced, some journalists being transferred to London and others leaving the company: by 1981 the northern editorial staff will be restricted to that required to provide an adequate coverage of northern affairs, not to publish a distinctively northern edition. The subsequent publication of the *Star* from Manchester, not anticipated at the time of MGN's decision, has since further weakened the *Mirror*'s position in the northern market, both directly, and indirectly through its effects upon Manchester wage rates. MGN's plans also involved the ending of composing in Manchester. Since composing was done by Thomson Withy Grove, under contract from MGN, and the contract was due to run until 1981, the run-down in composing could be only gradual, and with the full co-operation of TWG management. NGA eventually negotiated a gradual run-down in Manchester composing, phased over a five-year period until 1982; there was to be no compulsory redundancy, and workers who did not die, retire, or choose to accept voluntary redundancy were to be guaranteed lifetime employment (on the American model) (see above, p. 109).

Although the MGN's proposals had more profound consequences for Manchester than for Holborn, opposition continued for longer in Holborn than in Manchester. MGN's proposals in London involved a reduction from 267 to 170 in the size of the composing room, a reduction in space requirements, the introduction of a seven-day rotating shift system, the buying out of the London Scale of Prices, and increased flexibility in the use of labour in the composing room. Although the NGA control of key-boarding remained, the changes in working practices, manning levels, earnings levels, and union structures proposed were extensive. For MGN management the aim was to establish a unified composing-room labour force, preferably within a single chapel, in place of the existing twenty-four in three composing rooms, with flexibility between linotype operators, time-hands, and readers, and with the allocation of tasks between NATSOPA and NGA members as required by management. A single composing-room rate would be paid, covering all three groups, in place of the existing wide scatter of earnings between the three groups, and between linotype operators. In exchange for the new technology and associated changes, management were offering substantially enhanced earnings (on average, but not for the majority of linotype operators), shorter hours, and longer holidays. Management allocated £8m for redundancy pay, and £4½m for the purchase of equipment.

Negotiations between MGN management and the NGA lasted for twenty months. The final agreement was not signed until two years after the announcement of the second stage of 'Blueprint for Survival', on 10 November 1977; even after the agreement was signed, the company had considerable difficulty in making it work.[32] As MGN management antici-pated, acceptance of the principle of NGA control of key-boarding was highly attractive to NGA national officials, since it involved acceptance of the NGA's basic approach to new technology. However, the offer was less attractive to MGN NGA chapels, less concerned with the broad principles of union policy and more with the specific price to be obtained for selling jobs. There was therefore a basic contrast in the reactions to MGN's proposals by the NGA nationally, and at chapel level. In any circumstances the opinion of chapel officials would have been important, but they were especially so at MGN since the FOCs organized themselves into a Provisional Negotiating Committee, to watch over both MGN management and NGA national officials. Manage-ment's initial offer was a composing-room rate of £126 together with reduced hours and improved holidays: the NGA was looking for £200. During negotiations MGN increased their offer to £170, for a four-day week, with six weeks' holiday. NGA President Les Dixon agreed to re-commend acceptance of the agreement, but the agreement was rejected by the MGN FOCs. Accordingly, Dixon decided to appeal over the heads of the FOC Committee to the mass membership of the NGA at a meeting in London Central YMCA on 27 March 1977: the meeting was claimed to be a reporting back by the President, but was clearly designed to assess the strength of feeling behind the FOCs' rejection. Following the meeting negotiations reopened with MGN, which resulted in 'no change'. After the failure of the president to persuade the Provisional Committee to accept £170, he succeeded in persuading MGN to add a £4 increase, due under a regular NPA formula on 1 April 1977 and initially included in the £170, as an additional element. This was initially rejected by the Provisional Committee, but the Executive decided to proceed to ballot the chapels involved. When it became clear that the president was willing to accept the deal and the Executive to take it to ballot, the Provisional Committee agreed to recommend acceptance. The ballot showed a 2 to 1 majority in favour of accepting the agreement.

The agreement negotiated between MGN and the NGA provided for an NGA composing-room rate of £174, with provision for increases of 10 per cent or the NPA national increase, whichever was the larger, over the succeeding three years. Workers were to work 34 hours a week, in four shifts, with six weeks' holidays plus Bank Holidays. A joint referral committee was to be established to assess the implementation of the agreement; no unofficial action would be taken until the committee had acted. The London Scale of Prices was to be bought out at a cost varying between 'a few hundreds' and £12,000 per worker, depending upon earnings the previous year: the average entitlement was reported as being £6,000. It was initially doubted whether the agreement would be accepted by the Department of Employment, since the increase in earnings considerably exceeded the increase permitted under the pay policy prevailing, but it was accepted as being justified by a completely new system of production.

Successful conclusion of the agreement was only the first step towards implementing the new system. In view of the opposition to the agreement from chapel officials it was hardly surprising that the company had considerable difficulty in implementing the agreement. The first stage in the transfer to the new system was to be the use of computerized photo-composition on *Reveille*, which was initially scheduled to go 'on-stream' on 24 January 1978. However, a last-minute dispute over management's reallocation of responsibility for the collation of copy for proof-reading from NGA to NATSOPA led to non-publication, although NGA national officials had accepted the reallocation. The new system was first used three weeks later.[33] In April unofficial action by NGA machine managers over a 'self-financing' productivity deal, involving reduction in the manning level from 21 to 18 per shift, and the chapel's claim for a shift rate of £39·65, led to further losses.[34] The first four months of *Reveille*'s production on the new system were marked by frequent disputes, both in the composing room and 'down-stream', where differentials were inevitably disturbed by the composing-room rate and existing production methods disrupted by the technical difficulties encountered with the new production methods. The new system also created difficulties for the company with the journalists. Owing to management's preoccupation with the NGA, little attention had been paid to the effects of new technology on journalists − their consent was taken for granted. However, MGN had historically had more industrial relations problems with journalists than other newspapers − the occasion for the break between MGN and the NPA was a journalists' dispute in 1974 − and NUJ members were already concerned over the editorial run-down in Manchester. The effect of the agreement with the NGA was to disrupt completely differentials between the composing-room average and journalists' rates: whereas very high earnings for a minority of linotype operators were tolerable, the very high rates agreed for all composing room staff were not. Accordingly, NUJ members demanded a £60-per-week increase: management offered an immediate increase of £1,533 a year, plus an editor's merit review, £225 p.a. for training, and unspecified extra payments for special responsibility and skill.[35] However, the journalists did not accept the offer, which was subsequently withdrawn following objections from the Department of Employment on the grounds that it was outside the pay guide-lines. Following disruption of production by a series of mandatory meetings, the journalists involved were dismissed, and the *Mirror* ceased publication for thirteen days. In view of the dispute's effect on their members, Keys, O'Brien, and NGA officials intervened; the NUJ chapels accepted a return-to-work formula providing that the NUJ would pursue their demand through normal channels, MGN would withdraw dismissal notices, and a joint committee would be set up to consider payment during the period of dismissal. No indication was given of the likely outcome of the discussions on the substantive issue of the financial compensation to be provided for the new technology. Agreement was eventually reached on terms similar to management's initial offer, which was relatively generous since the changes in working practices for journalists were slight.

The new composing-room rate also disturbed differentials between the composing and the machine rooms. For example, as indicated earlier, *Reveille* was delayed by three weeks and subsequently experienced frequent disruptions to production, primarily in the machine room. The magazine was already in financial difficulties, as its market had contracted (or disintegrated, according to MGN management): its average circulation in the six-months period October 1975 to March 1976 was 7.26 per cent lower than its average circulation in the six-months period October 1974 to March 1975 (551,994 compared with 595,227) and thereafter continued to drift downwards.[36] MGN management had hesitated to stop publication, although industrial relations difficulties had led to threatened liquidation in 1977: stoppages in the machine room led to renewed threats to cease publication in August 1979. When the stoppages continued, MGN management told print-union leaders that publication would cease unless they used their authority to ensure adherence to agreed procedures. The print-union leaders did not act, and, to the surprise of union leaders involved, MGN carried out the threatened closure. The repercussions of the closure were less than expected: since the labour was predominantly casual and redundancy payments in accordance with the 1977 agreement were made, existing employees did not suffer major financial hardship — although long-term-earnings opportunities were obviously lost. *Reveille* was already in difficulties before the introduction of new technology: but the industrial relations difficulties associated with the new system sealed the fate of a journal already under threat.

The process of transferring other publications to computerized photocomposition encountered major technical difficulties, as indicated above. With the continuation of a mixed production system labour costs in the composing room increased. Although the London Scale of Prices had been bought out for workers on new technology, it continued for workers operating traditional technology: to encourage workers to transfer from the traditional to the new, a complex pooling system was devised, to share the earnings generated by the London Scale of Prices. Additional employees were hired to cover new and traditional technology and the training programme. Elsewhere in the organization the attempt to reduce manning by natural wastage achieved some success, notably in the NATSOPA clerical and RIRMA areas: there was little change in the publishing area.

The introduction of new technology at MGN did not achieve management's industrial relations objectives: it did not create a more unified and flexible labour force. Management succeeded in establishing a composing-room rate, but the effects of this were undermined by technological failures. A new layer of conflict had been superimposed upon existing layers, between workers involved with the new technology and those employed on the old. Labour costs had not been significantly reduced in the short run. However, the reorganization of the composing room reduced the significance of competitive sectionalism in that area. Moreover, the negotiation of a three-year agreement in 1977 resulted in management maintaining partial control over the rate of increase in earnings during a period of rapid inflation — as trade unionists pointed out. The introduction of the new system also significantly reduced the company's space requirements. But the changes had been introduced at the price of considerable industrial conflict, reduced productivity in the short term, and, according to some, an inferior product. MGN management were more successful in achieving the running down of editorial and composing work in Manchester, which was proceeding according to the revised schedule at the time of writing.

iv

In the mid 1970s MGN were well placed to take advantage of the opportunities for reducing labour costs provided by new technology. The group had the organization and personnel to develop a long-term technology and labour-relations strategy, and, through access to the resources of Reed International, the financial backing to carry the strategy through. Under the impetus of acquisition by Reed the company had established a long-term Corporate Plan (on a revolving five-year basis), and a short-term business plan: through the Manpower Planning section of the manpower function the company had undertaken detailed feasibility studies of future developments. The claim by Percy Roberts, then MGN managing director and chief executive, that MGN possessed the depths of management skill required to undertake major initiatives was largely justified. The decision to leave the NPA in 1974 meant that the company was unconstrained by the need to co-ordinate policies with the NPA, although the group took part in the *Programme for Action* discussions, and linked its industrial relations policies to those of the NPA when it seemed convenient to do so (see above, p. 000). Reed International were willing to provide £15m in 1975 to cover the cost of acquiring plant and machinery, redundancy compensation, and pay restructuring, on terms which in retrospect appear generous. Moreover, the group had direct experience of new technology at Anderston Quay in Glasgow, and of facsimile transmission with the Manchester–Belfast transmissions of 1966–71, and had already acquired experience of both the technological and industrial relations problems involved.

    As in other houses, MGN planned to make major savings both in areas directly affected by new technology and elsewhere: indeed, as Percy Roberts stressed, the major savings could be made in areas where it was not proposed to install new technology. The basic technology of the cold-type system to be installed was similar to that at TNL. But the mode of working planned, and the strategy for implementation, differed, as would have been expected in view of the differences in the final product. MGN newspapers had fewer words and fewer small advertisements than TNL newspapers: there was therefore less concern with avoiding dual key-boarding and less concern with direct access to the system by journalists and tele-ad staff. However, there was greater concern with sub-editorial rewriting and with design and lay-out: the potential savings on full-page electronic page make-up were therefore centrally important. The basic strategy for implementation therefore differed from that of TNL, notably in the willingness to concede to the NGA the right to retain control of key-stroking, at least for the forseeable future.

Following the announcement of 'Blueprint for Survival' in two stages in June and October 1975, MGN management embarked on a series of detailed discussions with national and chapel officials over the implications of the proposals for individual chapels: no targets for new manning levels were publicly specified, and according to management there were no specific targets at the outset — the final levels to be achieved would be determined by negotiation. The proposals were, not surprisingly, greeted with opposition, especially from the groups most directly affected by them — the NUJ in Manchester and the NGA in both Manchester and London. The major focus of opposition was to the loss of jobs involved; even with guarantees against compulsory redundancy and of lifetime contracts for workers no longer required, at a minimum future opportunities would be lost. Additionally, for Manchester journalists MGN's decision represented a betrayal of their conception of the newspaper as the nearest approach provided by the mass media to a popular expression of northern working-class opinion — a view endorsed by the Northern Group of Labour MPs. However, the opposition to the run-down in Manchester was only partially successful, with the extension of the period of run-down until 1982; the attempt to maintain the regional character of the paper failed. The opposition to the development plan in London met with more success, aided by the unexpected technical problems experienced.

The original plan for the installation of new technology involved the introduction of the new system for *Reveille*, followed by *Sporting Life*, the two Sunday papers, and finally the *Daily Mirror*. The technology appeared to work reasonably successfully with the weekly *Reveille*, although there were serious industrial relations difficulties which delayed going on-stream, led to frequent disputes about manning levels once the new system had been introduced, and contributed to the final closure of the publication in September 1979. However, the system encountered insuperable problems when introduced at the daily *Sporting Life*; the system was unable to cope with the amount of material and speed of through-put required for even a slim, specialized daily newspaper. According to MGN management, a major reason for the failure was technological — the simple inability of the system to live up to the performance promised; according to the manufacturers, the major problem was the inability of the labour, retrained NGA members, to operate the system effectively. The problem was especially severe with *Sporting Life* because of the elaborate sign language which had developed over the years between sub-editors and compositors: the terminology was gibberish to the non-racing men operating the new system. Regardless of the responsibility, MGN were obliged to change their strategy. Instead of changing to the new system completely for particular papers a gradual switch to the new system was required, on a page-by-page basis. Beginning in November 1978, a gradual change to the new system occurred. By the end of 1979 approximately two-thirds of the *Daily Mirror* was being produced by the new system, as well as complete editions of the *Sunday Mirror, Sunday People*, and *Sporting Life*. The most time-sensitive pages were still being produced by traditional hot-metal methods of composition. Moreover, the attempt to work electronic full-page make-up was given up in July 1979, make-up continuing with traditional cut-and-paste methods. According to journalists, the mixed production system resulted in less flexibility (fewer edition changes, earlier deadlines, greater difficulty in carrying though late changes), and a lower-quality product.

Even before the new system went on-stream in February 1978 MGN management had been forced to concede higher earnings levels than initially envisaged. At the beginning of the negotiations with the NGA it had been hoped to establish a composing-room rate of £125 per week; eventual agreement was reached on £174 per week, rising to £230 over three years, a considerable increase even allowing for 'normal' increases in earnings over the twenty-month period of negotiations. Perhaps even more importantly, the voluntary redundancies required to achieve the manning levels envisaged by MGN management and thus to justify the composing-room rate, were not achieved: at the end of 1979 manning levels were substantially as they had been in 1975 in the NGA area, although some reductions had been obtained in the NATSOPA area. The major reason for the lack of change in the NGA area was the difficulties encountered by the new technology. In any circumstances the early stages of introducing new technology would have involved man-power difficulties, to cover the retraining of staff for the new technology. However, the technical difficulties encountered by the new system meant that three groups of staff were required: to operate the traditional hot-metal system, to retrain for the cold-type system, and to operate the new cold-type system. Estimates of the extra labour costs involved have varied from £750,000 to £3m. Moreover, the bottle-necks and confusion resulting from the mixed system inevitably increased industrial relations problems, both within the NGA area and further down the production system, where operations were disturbed by difficulties in the composing and reprographic areas.

MGN's introduction of computerized photocomposition has not been successful in either financial or production terms. The short-run costs involved have been greater, and the gains in efficiency less, than had been anticipated in 1975. Major industrial disputes have occurred with all the major unions involved, at different times, including the NUJ. In the short term, the production of the newspaper has become less efficient, with increased labour costs and less flexibility. The group has been obliged to call upon the financial resources of the holding company, not only for money to cover new investment, but also to cover the unexpected difficulties encountered in attempting to implement the system. The financial results of the group were better in 1976-7 under the old system than they were to be in 1977-8 and 1978-9, although of course far more factors were involved than the development plan.[37] However, the project was not without even its short-term successes: a single composing-room rate was established; the London Scale of Prices was bought out; the composing-room chapels were reorganized; manning reductions were achieved; production was consolidated in Holborn, with the closure of Stamford Street, the ending of composing in Manchester, and the run-down of editorial staff in Manchester; the introduction of cold-type computerized photocomposition was achieved, albeit with difficulties.[38]

Inevitably, the senior management responsible for the development plan were held at least partly responsible for its difficulties. The MGN chief executive and chairman since 1977, Percy Roberts, retired at the end of 1979, shortly before his sixtieth birthday — although his retirement had been specifically agreed in 1977, on his appointment as chairman, and before the difficulties involved in new technology had become clear; the technical director at MGN, directly responsible for the project throughout, including the drawing up of the original specifications, retired at the same time. Yet, as experience at the FT and The Times showed, the problems encountered at MGN were not peculiar to the company — the difficulties encountered at MGN were shared by the other houses with major projects in the new technology area. MGN management, like others, were attempting to resolve the major problems of the industry in a single major initiative, making the introduction of new technology the opportunity to seize the industrial relations initiative which management had lost in the preceding twenty years. In 1975 the industry's economic difficulties and the printing unions' fears about the future of the industry appeared to provide an ideal opportunity to reassert managerial authority. In some areas the assertion succeeded: the journalists, for example, did not gain the financial rewards they demanded in exchange for co-operation with new technology — although the terms they obtained were hardly miserly. But in the major production areas no major change in the frontier of control occurred. In the conditions of 1975 it had been reasonable to think that new technology would provide the opportunity to achieve long-term benefits in exchange for a short-term cost in both the production and the industrial relations systems. And once the development plan had been launched it was difficult to withdraw — although not impossible, since the FT did so at the expense of considerable loss of face, staff morale, and money. Unfortunately for MGN, the short-term costs proved heavier than anticipated, and at the end of 1979 the long-term benefits had still to show themselves.

Chapter 9

Fleet Street and New Technology

In 1975 the endemic economic difficulties of Fleet Street were becoming acute. In September the Labour Government requested the Royal Commission on the Press, which it had set up in July 1975, to produce an interim report on the industry's economic position as quickly as possible. The Commission reported six months later, in March 1976:

(i)   the financial position of the industry is poor and in particular the cash-flow of a number of houses, including most of the quality newspapers, is becoming critical;

(ii)   there is no immediate prospect of increasing revenue sufficiently to change this position for the better;

(iii)   the only adequate means of cost-saving is to secure higher productivity through reductions in manpower and the introduction of new technology;

(iv)   these changes can only be made quickly and effectively if socially acceptable terms can be agreed;

(v)   there is a genuine will in the industry to reach agreement on a wide range of hitherto intractable matters;

(vi)   the prospective Joint Standing Committee . . . offers the best opportunity of achieving the necessary changes;

(vii)   the changes required should be put in hand forthwith;

(viii)   the estimated cost to the publishers of redundancy is between £30 and £35 million, and for investment, some £20 million;

(ix)   some financial help from outside the industry is necessary but not by way of a general subsidy.[1]

The Royal Commission recommended that the funds required should be sought from Finance for Industry, the organization set up by a group of banks to provide funds for investment in British industry; the government was recommended to grant up to 4 per cent relief on the loan interest, with the possibility of further relief 'in cases of proven need'. The Commission was eager to assist financial stability in the industry, but anxious to avoid direct government involvement — hence the attractiveness of FFI, which had access to the capital required but no links with the government.

The situation outlined by the Royal Commission was not new: the market for national newspapers was contracting, and the cyclical decline in advertising revenues combined with the unprecedented rise in newsprint prices after 1973 to bring to a head financial difficulties which had existed at least since the ending of newsprint rationing in 1955. Nor were the Commission's prescriptions, lower labour costs and new technology, new. Even before the severe economic pressures of 1975 Fleet Street proprietors were investigating the potentialities of computerized photocomposition; in view of recent heavy investment in traditional rotary presses there was little interest in web-offset printing, despite its extensive use in provincial newspapers. However, the industry's difficulties in 1975 gave urgency to the investigations, and within the space of eighteen months the *Daily Express*, Financial Times, MGN, and TNL all announced major changes in their methods of production. From being a technologically conservative industry, whose production methods had remained relatively stable since the late-nineteenth century, Fleet Street was proposing to become one of the most technologically sophisticated industries, with a high reliance upon computers.

The introduction of new technology to reduce labour costs was recognized as having a major impact on industrial relations. Since several houses were facing similar economic difficulties, proposing broadly similar plans and anticipating similar difficulties, it was inevitable that proprietors should attempt to co-ordinate their policies, most conveniently through the NPA. In view of the seriousness of the industry's economic position and the threat to their members' interests, print union leaders agreed that an industry-wide approach was desirable to prevent 'chaos' in the industry. Accordingly, discussions between the NPA and the TUC Printing Industries Committee in the winter of 1975–6 resulted in the presentation of an agreed joint statement to the Royal Commission, the establishment of a Joint Standing Committee, and the signature of a joint agreement, *Programme for Action*, in November 1976. The agreement provided for major improve-

ments in pensions, procedures and financial terms for voluntary redundancy, and an 'agreed strategy' for abolishing
casual labour. The agreement was submitted to a ballot of
the union members involved early in 1977, with a recommendation from the general secretaries for acceptance. The
agreement was rejected by a majority of members involved,
except in the NUJ.

The rejection of *Programme for Action* ended the attempt
to negotiate an industry-wide approach to the introduction
of new technology; the Royal Commission's hopes that the
Joint Standing Committee would provide the basis for a new
approach to industrial relations in the industry were disappointed. Individual companies were therefore obliged to
adapt their strategies to their own circumstances, without
the benefit of a national framework or the assistance of often
sympathetic national union officials: the outcome of house-
level negotiations came to rest almost wholly upon the
attitudes adopted by individual chapels, with consequently
varied outcomes. The FT suspended its development plan
indefinitely, channelling its energies into the more modest,
but potentially highly profitable, launching of its Frankfurt
edition, which was successfully accomplished in January
1979. The Times continued with its original proposals, after
considerable delay, in the face of extensive opposition,
culminating in the suspension of publication between
November 1978 and November 1979 and the decision in
October 1980 by TTO to sell the newspapers; management
failed to secure chapel agreement to its basic strategy. MGN
proposed less radical changes in working practices than either
the FT or The Times, and successfully negotiated agreements
on new technology; but the company failed to achieve the
expected financial benefits. In short, the optimistic statements of the Royal Commission proved premature; the spirit
of co-operation between unions and management proved
short-lived, and the Joint Standing Committee abortive. The
new technology of computerized photocomposition,
developed mainly in the United States and widely adopted
in the British provincial press, has not been generally transferred to Fleet Street. Issues which had previously been
intractable remained so. The reasons for this depressing

conclusion are partly economic, partly technological, and partly industrial relations.

The economic fears of 1975 were not realized; even between the government's request for an urgent interim report and publication of the report six months later the financial position improved significantly. By 1977 the industry had substantially recovered from the difficulties of 1975. The Thomson Organisation had its best ever results from national newspapers in 1977, reporting a profit of £1.9m (a negligible return of 3.04 per cent on a turnover of £62.6m).[2] As the financial crisis in Fleet Street receded, the sense of urgency on new technology evaporated. The improvement in the industry's finances reduced the immediate pressure upon management to achieve agreement and increased the ability and readiness of union members to resist management changes. This readiness was notably strengthened by the rescue of the financially most marginal newspaper, the *Observer*, by the Atlantic-Richfield Corporation in November 1976, and by the purchase of Beaverbrook Newspapers by Trafalgar House, apparently confirming Fleet Street's own assessment of its unique role as a major cultural institution and a source of prestige to its owners. This resilience is shown in the surprising employment stability in the industry, which negated the PPITB's pessimistic forecasts of 1975: in 1976–7 the industry employed 36,402, in 1977–8 36,361, and in 1978–9 36,369. The number of compositors, the group whose demise was anticipated, increased from 4,010 in 1976–7 to 4,202 in 1978–9.[3] Whether the industry's improvement would continue could not be foreseen; but experience suggested that the industry could successfully accommodate to a succession of alternating periods of expansion and contraction in the future, as it had in the past. Indeed, the difficulties of 1975 could be seen as exceptional, with the normal recession-induced decline in advertising revenues being exacerbated by the exceptional rise in world newsprint prices and the weakening of sterling. If the industry could recover from the difficulties of 1975 within three years it was more resilient than had been feared, and fears of permanent damage could be dismissed as alarmist or as predictable management cries of 'wolf'. At the end of 1979

Fleet Street's economic future looked considerably brighter than it had four years earlier, at least for the short term, despite continuing industrial relations difficulties.

If the economic fears of 1975 had been disappointed, so had the technological hopes; new technology had not lived up to the predictions of its supporters. Some of the difficulties were purely technological; although the technology of computerized photocomposition developed rapidly in the 1970s, it could not yet successfully meet the demands of the Fleet Street timetable. However, the failure was not primarily technological: the new technology has worked effectively in the United States and in regional and local newspapers in Britain. More fundamentally, the introduction of new technology failed to provide the means for significantly reducing labour costs in Fleet Street. The failure to meet financial targets has been partly due to the maintenance of higher manning levels than planned, to cope with practical operating difficulties — for example to cover for men training on the new machinery. But manning levels have remained generally substantially higher than management planned mainly because the improvement in the industry's economic fortunes reduced the fearfulness of union members, ennabling groups opposed to the introduction of new technology to use the multiple opportunities provided by the industry's industrial relations system to oppose management, without apparently threatening the long-term viability of the industry. In the NGA and NATSOPA the chapels centrally involved were thus able to disagree with their national officials and to see their opposition increase in effectiveness, as shown in chapters 3 and 4: in both unions attitudes towards new technology were more hostile in 1979 than they had been five years earlier. But the change in attitude was most evident in the NUJ, the only union to support *Programme for Action* in 1977.

The NUJ general secretary, Ken Morgan, was fully involved in the discussions about the Joint Standing Committee, and the NUJ members in national newspapers accepted *Programme for Action*, although by only a small majority. However, many members of the union, especially in regional and local newspapers, were unhappy with the NUJ leadership's apparent willingness to co-operate with employers without securing adequate financial rewards. The 1977 Annual Delegate Meeting of the union accordingly passed a resolution criticizing the Executive for failing to inform the membership about negotiations on new technology; the conference elected a special committee to consider the union's policy on new technology and to report back to the ADM, not to the Executive: '. . . in the mean-time . . . the Union will not cooperate with the introduction of any new systems which involve direct input by journalists, or any other system in which journalists are expected to absorb the jobs of another union.'[4] The committee, chaired by Bill Robertson of MGN's Scottish *Daily Record* and consisting primarily of local and regional journalists, was strongly critical of *Programme for Action*, '[which] was rejected by the ordinary members of practically every union involved. In our view it deserved to be rejected.'[5] Instead, the committee recommended that the NUJ should declare that it had no intention of seeking to 'extend journalistic work into the field of production at present covered by the other print unions.' The Executive should seek 'comprehensive national inter-union agreements on demarcation and new technology'; in default of new agreements, NUJ chapels 'should negotiate on direct input (or other facets of new technology which absorb work traditionally carried out by another print union) only if that other union has reached agreement to abandon that field of work.' Further, 'NUJ members will share in the economic benefits of new technology, and . . . no chapel will work with new systems for wages and conditions inferior to those enjoyed by other departments.'[6] The 1978 ADM accepted the recommendations of the committee, which thereafter formed the basis for NUJ policy in Fleet Street. The policy of 'no inferior wages or conditions' proved of considerable importance to NUJ policy at MGN. Although Fleet Street chapels could disregard national NUJ policy, they were naturally less willing to defy policy than to ignore the probable wishes of a majority of union members lacking constitutional authority, as some had done in 1976. This reluctance was reinforced by experience during The Times dispute, which brought NUJ members into close association with the production chapels, and by subsequent discussions with the NGA about demarcation issues.

The industrial relations reforms, which had been hoped for in 1975 and would have facilitated the introduction of new technology, did not occur; at the end of 1979 industrial relations were more similar to those of a decade earlier than had appeared likely in 1975. Moves towards greater co-ordination, among both management and unions, made slower progress than anticipated. In their report, *Industrial Relations in the National Newspaper Industry*, ACAS stressed the need for more effective joint procedures at national level and more comprehensive agreements at house level.[7] But there was no significant progress towards improved co-ordination at national level amongst employers. National-level co-ordination amongst trade unions had improved, with substantial discussions on possible amalgamations between the NGA and NATSOPA, the NGA and SLADE, the NGA and SOGAT, the NATSOPA and SOGAT, and the growth of joint working arrangements, including arrangements in the composing area between the NGA and the NUJ. But progress towards amalgamation proved slower than was initially expected, and no major amalgamations have occurred. Moreover, disagreement between NATSOPA and NGA/SLADE over the 'Fair' List and competitive recruitment amongst clerical workers indicated the limitations of joint working arrangements. At house level, unity between chapels increased, especially where managements proposed the introduction of new technology: events at TNL significantly increased co-operation between chapels, especially between the previously distant NUJ and NGA chapels. But the fragmentation which had been characteristic of industrial relations in 1975 remained predominant in 1979. Greater co-ordination between employers and unions would not have guaranteed the successful introduction of new technology; but the lack of co-ordination made substantial progress impossible, except at the price of very substantial increases in labour costs, which would have defeated management's objectives.

Fleet Street employers failed to introduce new technology on the terms and conditions desired. Despite initial optimism, events followed a similar pattern to previous attempts at reform in the industry: management loss of initiative and failure to maintain momentum in the face of effective chapel bargaining power. Part of the difficulty lay in the specific situation in Fleet Street, especially its industrial relations system, and the particular circumstances of the late 1970s. But a major part of the problem lay in the inherent difficulties of transferring technology developed in one country, with particular institutions and values, to another. The final section of this study turns very briefly to the question of the relevance of American experience to Fleet Street.

ii

The impetus for management's desire to introduce new technology urgently came from the industry's economic difficulties. But the direction was pointed by developments in the United States, where computerized photocomposition was already in widespread use by 1975, although the major metropolitan newspapers had announced, but not implemented, their plans. The nearest American equivalent to the British quality press, both in self-image and in production problems, the *New York Times*, was fully committed to the introduction of a computerized 'cold-type' system and involved in extensive discussions with the Harris Intertype Corporation on systems design and implementation. Major metropolitan tabloid newspapers, like the Chicago *Daily News* and the Chicago *Tribune*, were also engaged in major systems developments. Research into the technology of full-page electronic page make-up was also well developed, mainly at the Research Centre of the American Newspaper Publishers' Association in Easton, Pennsylvania. Executives of the major British newspapers contemplating introducing new systems paid frequent visits to the United States and held extensive discussions with American newspaper publishers and potential equipment suppliers. British trade unionists were also very aware of developments in the United States, the NGA having especially close links with the headquarters of the International Typographical Union in Colorado Springs. The Royal Commission was also very aware of American experience, helping to finance a visit to the United States by Rex Winsbury, an *FT* journalist especially concerned with new technology, and publishing his report, *New Technology and the Press: A Study of experience in the United States.*[8] In short, American experience explicitly provided a model for Fleet Street proprietors.

But how relevant was the experience? There were obvious contrasts in the structure of the market for newspapers in the two countries, which were recognized by Fleet Street proprietors.[9] American newspapers were regionalized, often comprising local monopolies — more comparable to British regional dailies than to national newspapers. The technologically most sophisticated newspapers, like the Long Island *Newsday* which was visited by FT executives, were established in expanding suburban areas, with a growing demand for newspapers: increased productivity was required to satisfy growing demand, not simply to reduce costs through the loss of jobs. Other innovations were in areas where trade unions were weak, such as Florida. Because circulations were smaller and regionalized, distribution problems were less severe and dead-lines less constricting than in Fleet Street. The extensive use of syndicated and wire-service copy, which could be transmitted, stored, and processed electronically, helped to simplify production systems and increased the economic benefits which could be derived from new technology. Moreover, senior British journalists argued that American newspaper readers accepted a lower-quality product than would be acceptable in Britain, tolerating poorly designed and messily laid out newspapers: high standards were regarded as unnecessary since newspapers were essentially throw-away products. In short, the American newspaper market was significantly different from Fleet Street's, and American newspaper publishers faced different, and more tractable, problems.

There were also significant differences in the industrial relations systems in the two countries, which helped newspaper proprietors determined to introduce new technology. The density of union membership was lower and the legal immunities of trade unions less in the United States than in Britain, although the precise position varied from state to state, determined by state as well as federal legislation — there were important differences between New York and

Virginia, which directly affected negotiations on new technology. Nevertheless, it would be easy to exaggerate the
differences between industrial relations in the industry in the
two countries. In both countries the industry was relatively
heavily unionized, the ITU being regarded as the strongest
traditional craft union in the United States. The ITU had
jurisdiction over the composing room, and, like the NGA,
controlled the supply of labour; through the operation of the
seniority system it directly determined recruitment. However,
as in Britain, trade unionism in the industry was fragmented
between the journalists and the production workers and
among production workers between the ITU and the rest,
most importantly the Pressmen, who organized the machine
room. Although discussions were held on the possibility of
amalgamation between the American Guild of Journalists
and the ITU in the early 1970s, relationships between the
two at local level were often distant, in part because of the
low level of membership of the Guild: the Guild had not
established a bargaining position comparable to that achieved
by the NUJ. Moreover, there was considerable tension between the ITU and the Pressmen, comparable to the tensions
between the NGA and NATSOPA, deriving from the same
sentiments of exclusiveness and resentment. Finally, the
tensions between national and local officials revealed in the
NGA were also evident in the ITU; the New York Local 6,
with nearly 2,000 compositors, comprised an independent
group within the union, and acted independently of Colorado
Springs in negotiations over new technology. The ITU's
policy on new technology was similar to that of the NGA
national officials: defence of the jurisdiction over key-
boarding, but reluctant acceptance of no automatic replacement and early retirement incentives, combined with lifetime guarantees for existing employees.

However, the ITU was less successful than the NGA, as
both unions recognized. The monopoly over key-boarding
was not maintained; compositors' jobs disappeared rapidly or
failed to materialize in areas where newspapers were expanding. The union's fortunes varied between regions even
more sharply than did those of the NGA. In Florida, following
disputes at the *Miami Herald*, and in Virginia, following major

disputes at local newspapers owned by the Media General Corporation, the ITU was effectively destroyed. In Chicago the ITU local achieved more success; in exchange for conceding direct clerical and editorial input the ITU obtained lifetime job guarantees for a list of named members during negotiations with the Chicago *Tribune* and the Chicago *Sun-Times/Daily News*. In New York there were major disputes between the union and the employers, which eventually reduced the number of newspapers from eight to three (although the disputes were not the sole reason for the financial difficulties of the newspapers that disappeared). In 1974 a major agreement was negotiated between the proprietors of the *New York Times, New York Post,* and *New York Daily News* whereby existing workers and named regular casuals were guaranteed jobs until the age of 65, with regular cost-of-living and wage increases built in; in addition, provision was made for six months' sabbatical leave for employees during the life of the contract, and incentives provided for early retirement. In exchange the ITU agreed to mobility of labour in the composing room, the use of new technology, and no replacement of members who left. The contract was to last for eleven years. In 1974 the ITU did not concede direct editorial in-put in New York. However, following the major disputes in 1978, the principle of direct in-put was conceded. Even the strongest locals believed that total rejection of new technology was impossible, and were prepared to negotiate away future jobs in exchange for guarantees for existing members. This was especially so in New York, where the high average age of compositors limited interest in the long-term future of the industry.

Although the ITU's objectives were similar to those of the NGA, it had less success in achieving them: the NGA succeeded where the ITU had failed. The reasons for the contrasting outcomes lie partly in the organization of the industry in the two countries: in the United States it was more dispersed and competition between titles was less intense. Trade unions were weaker, both nationally and locally, and solidarity limited. However, the major direct contrast was in the policies of the employers. Even where titles were in direct competition employers effectively combined for union negotiations.

In Chicago, for example, despite the rivalry between the Chicago *Tribune* and the Chicago *Daily News*, negotiations with the ITU were conducted jointly. In New York, the *New York Times, New York Post*, and *New York Daily News* negotiated jointly, until the defection of Rupert Murdoch, the proprietor of the *Daily News*, from the alliance during the 1978 dispute, following Fleet Street traditions. In contrast, the unity amongst Fleet Street proprietors was fragile, even during the discussions on the Joint Standing Committee: with the collapse of *Programme for Action* employers followed totally independent courses of action on new technology, regardless of their effects upon simultaneous negotiations in other houses. Whereas Fleet Street proprietors were less united than their American counterparts, the NGA was more united: the principle of control over key-boarding was regarded as central to the survival of the union, and resistance to management attempts to undermine it was strongly supported by all groups within the union, even where not directly involved – as was shown by the effective support for NGA members locked out during the dispute at The Times.

However, the short-sightedness of Fleet Street proprietors and the exaggerated importance attached to proprietorial autonomy are not sufficient explanations for the contrasting outcomes of the attempt to introduce new technology. Major problems stemmed from the technical difficulties experienced in developing the new systems and from the lack of resources available in Britain to cope with the difficulties experienced. The American computing industry was by far the largest in the world in 1975; the depth of computing experience available in the United States was unmatched elsewhere. Moreover, companies specializing in the application of computers to manufacturing processes were well established, including, for instance, Harris Intertype and Hendrix in printing. The American computing industry, because of its size and heterogeneity, contained the resources to deal quickly and knowledgeably with the technical problems posed by the use of computerized photocomposition in exceptional circumstances. In contrast, the much smaller computing industry in Britain suffered from a shortage of experienced staff and non-specialized employees had only limited acquaintance with computers, especially in their application to manufacturing industry. The shortage of technical personnel resulted in high rates of turnover in staff, exceptionally high salaries, and tension in relations between technical and non-technical personnel. More specifically, there was only limited experience in Britain in developing the software required for the application of computers to newspaper manufacture. Hence reliance had to be placed upon American expertise. However, the rapid expansion of computerized photocomposition systems in the United States meant that even the American computing industry was experiencing difficulty in coping with the level of demand, for software if not for hardware. The British market was inevitably seen as marginal, despite the attractiveness of prestige projects like the FT or Times development plans. In both countries, but especially in Britain, financial pressures led newspapers to press for the rapid installation of new systems. Speed could be achieved by standardization. However, although standardization may have been possible in the United States, it was impossible in Fleet Street. Consequently, the pressure for rapid completion led to hasty systems analysis, inadequate data, and faulty programming; operating problems were inevitable. When the inevitable technical difficulties appeared during installation and implementation there were insufficient back-up resources available, resulting in further operating difficulties. There was an especial lack of in-house computing expertise available to Fleet Street managements, resulting in heavy dependence upon the technical resources of the installing companies, or upon outside consultants inevitably lacking detailed knowledge of the operating problems of newspapers. Even MGN, which had unusual experience in new technology and sophisticated management, allowed its computing resources to run down once the installation of the new system was under way: supervision of the work of the manufacturers and outside consultants was inevitably weakened. The reliance of newspaper managements upon the newspaper industry for its management recruits meant inevitably that there was only limited knowledge available within the industry of technical developments elsewhere. Limited experience and knowledge led to exaggerated expectations about the speed with which new systems could be introduced and to underestimation of the difficulties involved in their operation: experience of substantial difficulties inevitably led to disillusion and to scepticism about the value of the new systems.

The hopes of the Royal Commission for a substantial change in Fleet Street were disappointed. The policies devised for new technology in 1975–6 were not carried through: the elaborate plans for improved pensions, voluntary redundancies, and decasualization proved abortive. But the ideas developed in response to the 1975 crisis provide the basis for future policy. The principles put forward by the FT for dealing with the social implications of technological change remain relevant: guaranteed lifetime earnings for employees leaving the industry remains the most effective basis for securing union agreement to reductions in manning levels. Similarly, the proposals for Joint Standing Committees, at both industry and house levels, provide a basis for negotiated acceptance of new technology. Although there remain significant problems, even in conception, with the proposals, as discussed earlier, they provide a framework for further negotiations when the next economic crisis appears on Fleet Street. The economic difficulties of 1975 disappeared relatively quickly. But the cycle of boom and slump is likely to continue in the future, with the booms reaching lower peaks and the slumps lower troughs as the secular decline for newspapers, both as sources of information and as advertising media, continues. New technology is likely to remain the most effective means of achieving lower production costs, especially with the increased reliability and lower prices of computers that have occurred since 1975. The next crisis is likely to come with Fleet Street in a weaker position than in 1975, with continued competition from commercial television and radio for advertising revenue, the expansion of regional and local newspapers, and the growth of electronic data-transmission systems for the provision of up-to-date news and information. It is to be hoped that similar attempts to achieve a joint approach to new technology do not prove similarly abortive.

Notes

Chapter 1.

1. For television ownership see *Social Trends, 1974* (HMSO, 1974) p. 110: 15,900,000 TV licences were issued in 1970, 17,400,000 in 1974.
2. Royal Commission on the Press: *Interim Report* (Cmnd. 6433, 1976), Appendix E, Table E 1, p. 92 (henceforth *Interim*); Royal Commission on the Press, *Final Report: Appendices* (Cmnd. 6810-1, 1977), Table C 1, p. 105 (henceforth *Appendices*).
3. See p. 15. According to the Royal Commission, the IBA regard press ownership of television shares as 'valuable'; Royal Commission on the Press: *Final Report*, 1977 (Cmnd. 6810, HMSO, 1977) p. 142 (henceforth, *Final Report*).
4. The BBC was the first to do so, in 1954: P. Seglow, *Trade Unionism in Television* (Farnborough: Saxon House, 1978), p. 28.
5. Royal Commission on the Press, *Oral Evidence*, 9 OE 1, p. 3 (MGN).
6. *Interim*, p. 99 (expanded).
7. Economist Intelligence Unit, *The National Newspaper Industry: A Survey* (EIU, 1966), Table 36.
8. *Interim*, p. 37.
9. *Bank of England Quarterly Bulletin*, December 1978, p. 516.
10. Although the report by the Labour Research Department *National Newspaper Industry* (Printing and Kindred Trades Federation, 1972) contains much useful information.
11. *The Stock Exchange Official Year Book, 1979-80* (East Grinstead: Thomas Skinner & Co., 1980) p. 1238.
12. *Appendices*, p. 35.
13. *The Stock Exchange Official Year Book, 1979-80*, p. 692; *The Stock Exchange Official Year Book*, 1975-6, p. 1201.
14. *Interim*, p. 99.
15. *Social Trends*, 1977 (HMSO, 1977) p. 51.
16. *Interim*, p. 92 (adapted).
17. *Interim*, p. 96.
18. *Interim*, p. 33.
19. *Final Report*, p. 38; see also *Appendices*, Appendix E, Advertising and the Press, pp. 125-36; *Financial Times*, 13 Sept. 1979, p. 11.
20. *Interim*, p. 34.
21. *Interim*, p. 25.
22. Calculated from Economist Intelligence Unit, op. cit., Table 8.
23. *Interim*, p. 27.
24. *Final Report*, p. 39.
25. G. Cleverley, *The Fleet Street disaster: British national newspapers as a case study in mismanagement* (Constable, 1976), p. 46.
26. *Final Report*, p. 57.
27. *Ibid.*, p. 42.

28. Ibid, p. 57.
29. *Hansard Parliamentary Debates, House of Commons, 1974*, Vol. 873, col. 1165.
30. Royal Commission on the Press, *Oral Evidence*, 9 OE, MGN.
31. *Appendices*, Appendix B.
32. *Hansard Parliamentary Debates, House of Commons, 1974*, Vol. 873, col. 1227.
33. Ibid., col. 1180.
34. Ibid., cols. 1122–1240.
35. Labour Party, *People and the Media* (Labour Party, 1974).
36. *Labour Party Annual Conference Report*, 1975, p. 331.
37. *Hansard Parliamentary Debates, House of Commons 1974*, Vol. 873, cols. 1171 (Edelman), 1210 (Bedwell), 1205 (Evans).
38. Ibid., cols. 1158 (Freud), 1166 (Grimond).
39. Royal Commission on the Press, *Written Evidence*, 84 E 1, Liberal Party.
40. *Hansard Parliamentary Debates, House of Commons*, Vol. 872 (1974), col. 1322.
41. Royal Commission on the Press, *Final Report*, p. 1.
42. *Hansard Parliamentary Debates, House of Commons 1974*, Vol. 873, col. 1169; *Labour Party Annual Conference Report, 1975*, p. 331.
43. *Final Report*, p. 3.
44. *United Kingdom Press Gazette*, 27 May 1974, p. 22.
45. The establishment of the Royal Commission on the Future of Broadcasting was announced in April 1974, together with the name of its chairman: its membership was announced in July 1974.
46. See the comments in the *United Kingdom Press Gazette*, 1 July 1974, p. 3.
47. D. E. Butler and D. Kavanagh, *The British General Election of 1974* (Macmillan, 1974), for the press's treatment of the election campaign of February 1974.
48. *Hansard Parliamentary Debates, House of Commons, 1974*, Vol. 873, col. 1146.
49. For a clear account of newspaper-production technology see The Open University, P. 881, Unit 4, *Press, Papers, and Print: A Case Study* (The Open University Press, 1976), pp. 13–19; K. Sisson, *Industrial Relations in Fleet Street*, (Basil Blackwell, 1975) pp. 8–12.
50. D. C. Hunter, G. L. Reid, D. Boddy, *Labour Problems of Technological Change*, (George Allen & Unwin Ltd., 1970) Part II.
51. Ibid., p. 55.
52. R. Winsbury, *New Technology and the Press* (HMSO, 1975), provides a brief general discussion of new technology.

Chapter 2.

1. G. Cleverley, op. cit.: see especially R. Winsbury's 'Preface' p. 12.
2. For a fuller account see ACAS, *Industrial Relations in the National Newspaper Industry* (HMSO, 1976), pp. 70–80, 115. Henceforth ACAS.
3. Advisory, Conciliation, and Arbitration Service, *Industrial Relations in the Provincial Newspaper and Periodical Industry*, Cmnd. 6810-2 (HMSO 1977), p. 100.
4. ACAS, pp. 252–7.
5. Adapted from ACAS, Appendix 5, Table 7, p. 256.
6. H. A. Clegg, *The Changing System of Industrial Relations in Great Britain* (Basil Blackwell, 1979), p. 66.
7. ACAS, Appendix 5, Table 1, p. 248.

8. Quoted in K. Sisson, op. cit., p. 163.
9. For a fuller account of the distribution system see Royal Commission on the Press, *Appendices*, pp. 137–43. The United Kingdom Newsprint Users' Association was also administered by the NPA, to co-ordinate newsprint purchases.
10. Royal Commission on the Press, *Oral Evidence*, 9 OE 1, p. 15 (MGN).
11. *Appendices*, Appendix E, p. 135.
12. Royal Commission on the Press, *Final Report*, p. 251; *Oral Evidence*, 9 OE 1, p. 16 (MGN).
13. Ibid., 28 OE 1, p. 1 (NPA).
14. Ibid., 9 OE 1, p. 1 (MGN).
15. ACAS, pp. 71, 269.
16. *Final Report*, p. 224.
17. Beaverbrook had specifically followed a policy of pushing up wages in order to exert pressure on his financially weaker competitors.
18. S. Jenkins, *Newspapers: The Power and the Money* (Faber & Faber, 1979).
19. Royal Commission on the Press, *Written Evidence*, Mirror Group Newspapers Sector 5, p. 6.
20. ACAS, Appendix 6, Table 7, p. 267.
21. Ibid., pp. 46–8.
22. Ibid., Appendix 6, Table 2, p. 264.
23. C. Gill, R. Morris, J. Eaton, *Industrial Relations in the Chemical Industry* (Teakfield: Saxon House, 1978), chapter 2.
24. *TUC Report, 1973*, pp. 103–5.
25. See above, pp. 328–9.
26. H. A. Turner, *Trade Union Growth, Structure, and Policy: A Comparative Study of the Cotton Unions* (George Allen & Unwin, 1962), p. 291.
27. ACAS, Appendix 9, Table 1, p. 282.
28. Calculated from ACAS, pp. 249, 257.
29. Calculated from ACAS, pp. 283–4.
30. For SLADE's activities in advertising, see *Report of Inquiry into certain trade union recruitment activities* (HMSO, 1979); *Financial Times*, 18 Oct. 1979, p. 1.
31. K. Sisson, op. cit., p. 103.
32. *Final Report*, p. 225; ACAS, pp. 186–8.
33. Calculated from ACAS, pp. 248, 257.
34. *Department of Employment Gazette*, September 1972, p. 857, for paper, printing, and publishing.
35. ACAS, p. 284 (modified).
36. ACAS, p. 232.
37. Data supplied by PPITB, March 1976.
38. ACAS, p. 249.
39. J. T. Dunlop, *Industrial Relations Systems*, 2nd edition (Southern Illinois University Press, 1970), p. 7.
40. Ibid., p. 9.

Chapter 3

1. *Print*, April 1967, p. 86; June 1977, p. 14.
2. ACAS, *Industrial Relations in the Provincial Newspaper and Periodical Industries*, p. 99.

3. British Printing Industries Federation, *The Economy and the Printing Industry,* February 1979, p. 74.
4. ACAS, *Industrial Reltions in the Provincial Newspaper and the Periodical Industries*, Appendix 6, Table 5, p. 113.
5. Ibid., Appendix 6, Table 4, p. 112.
6. National Graphical Association, *Rules*, 1973 edition, p. 7.
7. National Graphical Association, *Model [Chapel] Rules*, 1975, pp. 1-8.
8. *Print*, February 1979, p. 17.
9. A. J. M. Sykes, 'Trade Union Workshop organization in the printing industry – the Chapel', *Human Relations*, Vol. 13, 1960, p. 63.
10. NGA, *F.O.C.'s Handbook*, Section 1, p. 1.
11. A. J. M. Sykes, 'The Cohesion of a Trade Union Workshop Organization', *Sociology*, Vol. 1, 1967, p. 159.
12. ACAS, Appendix 8, Tables 3 and 4, pp. 274-5. The figures are incomplete, since ACAS was unable to obtain full information from four houses.
13. ACAS, *Industrial Relations in the Provincial and Periodical Press,* Appendix 5, Table 1, p. 106.
14. ACAS, Appendix 8, Table 1, p. 272.
15. *Print*, February 1979, p. 17.
16. NGA, *F.O.C.'s Handbook*, Section 4, p. 9.
17. *Print*, April 1978, p. 4.
18. For the NGA's financial situation see *Print*, August 1975, p. 20.
19. NGA *Rules*, p.8.
20. *Print*, April 1976, p. 11.
21. ACAS, p. 291.
22. *Print*, April 1977, p. 7.
23. *Print*, December 1976, pp. 7-8.
24. *Print*, December 1978, p. 4.
25. *Print*, October 1977, p. 5.
26. *Graphical Journal*, 1967, p. 111.
27. *Print*, March 1978, p. 4: see also letters, ibid., pp. 6-7.
28. Calculated from the detailed results, published in *Print, passim*.
29. *Print*, December 1976, pp. 7-8.
30. *Print*, August 1978, p. 6.
31. *Print*, September 1977, p. 3.
32. *Print*, July 1978, pp. 8-9.
33. NGA, *Rules*, Rule 8 5, p. 11.
34. Ibid., p. 11.
35. Ibid., p. 19.
36. Ibid., p. 11.
37. *Print*, July 1978, p. 19.
38. NGA *Rules*, p. 18.
39. *Print*, July 1976, pp. 8, 12, 6.
40. *Print*, July 1978, pp. 12, 16, 13.
41. *Print*, July 1978, p. 13.
42. *Print*, March 1978, p. 7 for criticism of concentration on MGN.
43. e.g. in *Print*, April 1976, p. 4.
44. *Print*, February 1979, p. 25.
45. *Print*, January 1976, p. 4.
46. Published in *Print*, February 1979, pp. 8-12.
47. *Print*, July 1976, p. 20.
48. *Print*, April 1976, p. 12.
49. *Print*, July 1976, p. 12.

50. ACAS, *Industrial Relations in the Provincial Newspaper and Periodical Industries,* pp. 10–12.
51. Ibid., p. 42.
52. Royal Commission on the Press. Evidence of National Graphical Association, 4 Mar. 1976, p. 5.
53. *Print,* July 1976, p. 16.
54. *Print,* October 1977, p. 5.
55. *Print,* May 1977, p. 1.
56. *Printing Industries,* Vol. 74, no. 11, November 1975, p. 178.
57. *Print,* July 1976, p. 14.
58. *Printing Industries,* Vol. 76, no. 1, January 1977, p. 18.
59. *Print,* January 1977, p. 5.
60. *Print,* February 1979, pp. 13–16.
61. P. J. Kalis, 'Inter-union Membership Disputes and their Resolution by the Disputes Committee of the T.U.C.' (Unpublished D. Phil. thesis, University of Oxford, 1976), pp. 272–3.
62. *Print,* February 1979, p. 14.
63. *TUC Report,* 1979, pp. 72–3.
64. Kalis, op. cit., p. 347.
65. *Print,* November 1976, p. 4.
66. *Print,* April 1977, p. 4.
67. *Print,* April 1978, p. 4.
68. *Print,* June 1978, p. 1.
69. *Print,* July 1978, p. 11.
70. *Print,* July 1977, p. 4.
71. A. Dubbins, *Print,* December 1977, p. 12.

Chapter 4

1. Until 1970 named National Society of Operative Printers and Assistants, it is still generally known as NATSOPA.
2. K. Sisson, op. cit., p. 32.
3. NATSOPA, *Journal and Graphical Review,* January 1976, p. 1; henceforth *NATSOPA Journal.*
4. ACAS, Appendix 9, Table 2, p. 283. For the merger with SOGAT, see above, p. 000.
5. Ibid., Appendix 9, Table 3, p. 284.
6. For the constitution and organization of chapels see Rule 7, *Rules of the National Society of Operative Printers, Graphical and Media Personnel* (1973 edn.) pp. 26–30; henceforth *Rules.*
7. ACAS, Appendix 8, Table 3, pp. 274–5.
8. *Rules,* p. 182.
9. Ibid., rule 7, p. 29.
10. Ibid., rule 7, clause 12, p. 29.
11. Ibid., rule 22, clause 1, p. 91.
12. ACAS, p. 284.
13. *Rules,* rule 23, clause 2, p. 94.
14. Ibid, rule 18, clause 8, p. 78.
15. Ibid., rule 23, clause 12, pp. 96–7.
16. Ibid., rule 11a, clause 2, p. 58.
17. Ibid., rule 8, clause 6, p. 32.
18. Ibid., rule 11, pp. 48–58 for E. C. powers.

19. Ibid., rule 11, clause 22, p. 55.
20. *NATSOPA Journal*, July 1978, p. 7.
21. Ibid., July 1978, p. 8.
22. *Rules*, rule 10, clause 3, p. 44.
23. *NATSOPA Journal*, July 1978, p. 6.
24. *NATSOPA Journal*, August–September 1977, p. 1; November 1977, p. 9.
25. *Rules*, rule 13, clause 3, p. 59.
26. For Darlington NUJ disputes see *NATSOPA Journal*, August–September 1977, p. 11.
27. *Rules*, rule 13, clause 4, p. 60.
28. For Edwin Smith, see J. Moran, *NATSOPA: Seventy-Five Years*, (NATSOPA, 1964) p. 40; for Briginshaw and writs, the *Observer* 28 Oct. 1979.
29. Cf. J. D. Edelstein and M. Warner, *Union Democracy* (George Allen & Unwin, 1975) p. 153, for 1918–65.
30. *NATSOPA Journal*, June 1978, p. 3.
31. For an account of the accusations publicly available, see *NATSOPA Journal*, July 1978, p. 6, and the *Observer*, 25 Mar. 1979.
32. *Observer*, 25 Mar. 1979, *Guardian*, 28 Mar. 1979; *NATSOPA Journal* May 1979, p. 10.
33. *NATSOPA Journal*, May 1979, p. 1.
34. *NATSOPA Journal*, July 1978, p. 9.
35. *NATSOPA Journal*, October 1978, p. 10.
36. *Observer*, 25 Mar. 1979, p. 1.
37. Ibid.
38. *NATSOPA Journal*, May 1979, p. 1.
39. *NATSOPA Journal*, August–September 1978, pp. 6–7.
40. *NATSOPA Journal*, August–September 1979, p. 13.
41. *NATSOPA Journal*, January 1979, p. 10.
42. *NATSOPA Journal*, December 1979, p. 9.
43. *NATSOPA Journal*, May 1977, June 1977 and August–September 1977.
44. *NATSOPA Journal*, February 1977, p. 3.
45. *NATSOPA Journal*, January 1977, p. 9.
46. *NATSOPA Journal*, April 1977, p. 3.
47. *NATSOPA Journal*, June 1977, p. 9.
48. *NATSOPA Journal*, June 1976, p. 1. The theme of his article, 'New Technology Why?', was repeated in speeches at District Conferences throughout 1976.
49. For the difficulties involved, see above, pp. 189–91.
50. NATSOPA evidence submitted to the Royal Commission on the Press, 31 Dec. 1974.
51. *NATSOPA Journal*, June 1976, p. 1.
52. *NATSOPA Journal*, January 1976, pp. 6–7.
53. P. J. Sadler and B. A. Barry, *Organizational Development: case studies in the Printing Industry* (Longmans, 1970).
54. *NATSOPA Journal*, March 1979, p. 3.
54. A. Davis to the author, 7 Sept. 1976.
56. *NATSOPA Journal*, March 1978, p. 9.
57. *NATSOPA Journal*, May 1979, p. 10.
58. *NATSOPA Journal*, August–September 1979, p. 14; *T.U.C. Report.* 1979, pp. 539–40.
59. *NATSOPA Journal*, October 1979, p. 9.
60. *NATSOPA Journal*, November 1976, p. 9.
61. *NATSOPA Journal*, February 1976, p. 1.

62. See above, Chap. 8, for an account of events at MGN.
63. *NATSOPA Journal,* December 1979, p. 7.
64. *NATSOPA Journal,* April 1979, p. 8.
65. *NATSOPA Journal,* March 1979, p. 8.
66. *NATSOPA Journal,* May 1979, p. 8.
67. *NATSOPA Journal,* April 1979, p. 8.
68. *NATSOPA Journal,* May 1964, p. 30; *SOGAT Journal,* August–September 1968, p. 55.
69. *NATSOPA Journal,* May 1977, p. 9; October 1978, p. 10.
70. *NATSOPA Journal,* May 1977, p. 9; October 1978, p. 10.
71. *Financial Times,* 11 Mar. 1977, p. 11, *Daily Telegraph* 10 Mar. 1977, pp. 1, 3, 6; *The Times,* 11 Mar. 1977, pp. 1–2.
72. *NATSOPA Journal,* June 1977, p. 9.
73. Quoted in the *Daily Telegraph,* 10 Mar. 1977, p. 1.
74. *Financial Times,* 11 Mar. 1977, p. 11.
75. *NATSOPA Rules,* rule 20, clause 1 (a), p. 81.
76. *NATSOPA Journal,* January 1978, p. 8.
74. *NATSOPA Journal,* February 1978, p. 9.
78. *NATSOPA Journal,* November 1977, p. 3. December 1977, p. 10.
79. The terms of the reorganization were: The Thomson Publications Chapel was to be confined to production runs only, including all pre- and post-production work from 2.00 p.m. Saturday until 6.00 a.m. Sunday; the Times Newspapers Day Staff Chapel was to cover everything except production runs; but there was to be no loss of jobs or earnings, existing Saturday shift men continuing to participate in non-productive work on the Saturday–Sunday shift, under administrative control of the Day Chapel (*NATSOPA Journal,* January 1978, p. 9).
80. *Times Challenger,* May 1979, p. 1.
81. *NATSOPA Times Diary* (NATSOPA, 1978). The pamphlet contained copies of the correspondence between Times management and the unions.
82. *NATSOPA Journal,* July 1978, p. 9.
83. *NATSOPA Journal,* November 1978, p. 10.
84. *NATSOPA Times Dairy, passim.*
85. Ibid., p. 1.
86. *NATSOPA Journal,* December 1978, p. 1.
87. *Times Challenger,* January 1979, p. 10.
88. Ibid.
89. John Mitchell, London Machine Branch Secretary, *Times Challenger,* May 1979, p. 3.
90. *NATSOPA Journal,* December 1978, p. 3.
91. Ibid., p. 3.
92. *NATSOPA Journal,* April 1979, p. 3.
93. John Mitchell, *Times Challenger,* May 1979, p. 3.
94. *NATSOPA Journal,* December 1978, p. 1.
95. *NATSOPA Journal,* March 1979, p. 9.
96. *NATSOPA Journal,* January 1979, p. 10.
97. Owen O'Brien to M. J. Hussey, 15 May 1978, *NATSOPA Times Diary,* n.p.
98. *NATSOPA Journal,* May 1979, p. 9.
99. *NATSOPA Journal,* June 1979, p. 9.
100. *NATSOPA Journal,* March 1979, p. 9.
101. *NATSOPA Journal,* August–September, 1979, pp. 1, 14.
102. *Financial Times,* 2 Aug. 1979, p. 7; 3 Aug. p. 8.

103. *NATSOPA Journal*, December 1979, p. 9.
104. *NATSOPA Journal*, January 1979, p. 10.
105. For computers and clerical work in general see E. Mumford and O. Banks, *The Computer and the Clerk* (Routledge & Kegan Paul, 1967), although the research on which it was based is now seventeen years old; for a more recent comment see R. Crompton, 'Trade Unionism and the Insurance Clerk', *Sociology*, Vol. 13, no. 3, September 1979, pp. 414-17, and references.
106. Royal Commission on the Press, *Minutes of Evidence*, 25 OE 1, NATSOPA, p. 13.
107. Interview with Mr Ken Child, PPITB, 14 May 1976.
108. *NATSOPA Journal*, October 1979, p. 9.
109. *NATSOPA Journal*, March 1979, p. 8.
110. *NATSOPA Journal*, December 1979, p. 9.
111. Royal Commission on the Press, *Minutes of Evidence*, NATSOPA, p. 5.
112. *Times Challenger*, January 1979, p. 7.
113. *NATSOPA Journal*, April 1979, p. 8.
114. Royal Commission on the Press, *Minutes of Evidence*, NATSOPA, pp. 4, 9.
115. *NATSOPA Journal*, October 1977, p. 1.
116. *NATSOPA Journal*, July 1976, pp. 8-9.
117. *NATSOPA Journal*, February 1978, p. 9.
118. *NATSOPA Journal*, May 1978, p. 9.
119. *NATSOPA Journal*, August-September, 1979, p. 13, October 1979, p. 9.
120. *NATSOPA Journal*, August-September 1978, p. 1.
121. *NATSOPA Journal*, February 1977, p. 9.
122. *NATSOPA Journal*, July 1979, p. 1.
123. *NATSOPA Journal*, December 1979, p. 1 contains a strong statement on encroachment, by O. O'Brien.
124. *NATSOPA Journal*, December 1979, p. 1.
125. *NATSOPA Journal*, August-September 1979, p. 1.
126. *NATSOPA Journal*, January 1979, p. 9.
127. *NATSOPA Journal*, June 1979, p. 10.
128. *NATSOPA Journal*, August-September 1979, pp. 12-13.
129. *NATSOPA Journal*, November 1979, p. 9.
130. *NATSOPA Journal*, November 1978, p. 1.
131. *NATSOPA Journal*, May 1979, p. 3.

Chapter 5

1. *Report of the Royal Commission on the Press*, 1961-2 (Cmnd. 1811, HMSO, 1962) p. 115; cf. *Interim*, p. 86.
2. Economist Intelligence Unit, op. cit.; quoted in *Print*, May 1967, p. 102.
3. Sisson, op. cit., p. 160.
4. *U.K. Press Gazette*, 8 Sept. 1975, p. 5.
5. *The Times*, 25 Nov. 1975, p. 1.
6. *The Times*, 9 Dec. 1975, p. 2.
7. See p. 000.
8. Royal Commission, *Interim Report*, pp. 89-90.
9. Ibid., p. 89.
10. Ibid., pp. 68-73.
11. *Programme for Action*, p. 19.
12. Ibid., pp. 19-22.
13. Royal Commission, *Interim Report*, p. 66.

14. Ibid., pp. 11–12.
15. *Programme for Action*, p. 12.
16. *United Kingdom Press Gazette*, 23 June 1975, *et seq.*
17. *Programme for Action*, p. 12.
18. Royal Commission, *Interim Report*, p. 65.
19. *Programme for Action*, p. 13.
20. Ibid., p. 21.
21. ACAS, Appendix 4, Table 1, p. 235.
22. *Programme for Action*. p. 22.
23. Ibid., pp. 9–10.
24. Ibid., p. 27.
25. Ibid., pp. 28–30.
26. Ibid., p. 4.
27. For Mond-Turner see H. A. Clegg, *The Changing System of Industrial Relations in Great Britain* (Basil Blackwell, 1979) pp. 332–40.
28. See, e.g., the extensive sociological literature on working-class images of society cited in ed. M. Bulmer, *Working Class Images of Society* (Routledge & Kegan Paul, 1975).
29. Quoted in *Report of the Committee of Inquiry on Industrial Democracy* (Bullock), (Cmnd. 6706, HMSO, 1977) p. 39.
30. Ibid., pp. 124–5.
31. H. A. Clegg, *Trade Unionism under Collective Bargaining* (Basil Blackwell, 1976), p. 8.
32. *Programme for Action*, p. 10.
33. Jenkins, op. cit., p. 64.
34. Royal Commission, *Interim Report*, p. 13; *Final Report*, p. 226.
35. ACAS, pp. 182, 174.
36. Royal Commission, *Final Report*, p. 126.
37. *Hansard Parliamentary Debates, House of Commons*, Vol. 907, 17 Mar. 1976, cols. 1322–8.

Chapter 6

1. *The Stock Exchange Official Year Book, 1979–80*, pp. 1268–9 for recent financial history of Pearson Longman and Pearson (S) & Sons Ltd.; PKTF, op. cit., pp. 40–44; Pearson Longman Company Reports, 1970.
2. PKTF, op. cit., p. 43.
3. *The Times*, 13 Dec. 1974, p. 21; 31 Dec. 1975, p. 20.
4. The Financial Times Ltd., Statement on Development Plan, 11 July 1975, contains details on the *FT*'s economic situation.
5. ACAS, p. 68.
6. EIU, op. cit., pp. 55–6.
7. ACAS, p. 64.
8. EIU, op. cit., p. 46.
9. Royal Commission on the Press, Evidence, The Financial Times, January 1975, 3 OE 1–5.
10. Presentation to Trade Union Representatives at The Financial Times, Bracken House, regarding the future development of the newspaper, 11 July 1975.
11. Ibid.
12. *Print*, April 1976, p. 4.
13. Proposals for Implementation of The Financial Times Development Plan, n.d., 1975.

14. Presentation to Trade Union Representatives, 11 July 1975.
15. ACAS, p. 199.
16. *Print*, April 1976, p. 4.
17. Royal Commission on the Press, Oral Evidence, NGA, 24 OE 1, p. 9.
18. Interview with Mr J. Wade, BBC Radio 3.
19. Personal Communication, Mr A. Davis, 7 Sept. 1976.
20. Financial Times Development Plan, Progress Note, 2 Sept. 1976.
21. Statement on The Financial Times Development Plan, 13 June 1977.
22. *Financial Times*, 14 Nov. 1980, p. 8.
23. *Print*, April 1976, p. 9.
24. *Print*, January 1976, p. 4.
25. Royal Commission on the Press, Oral Evidence, 28 OE 1, p. 1 (Lord Goodman).
26. *Daily Worker*, 24 Oct. 1975, p. 1.

Chapter 7

1. *The Times*, 28 May 1976, p. 4.
2. *The Times*, 24 November 1978, p. 15.
3. See above, pp. 214–16.
4. For Lord Thomson's background and attitudes see R. Braddon, *Roy Thomson* (Collins, 1965), and Lord Thomson, *After I was Sixty* (Hamish Hamilton, 1975).
5. Proposals for the merger of The Thomson Organisation Ltd., and the North Sea Petroleum Interests of Thomson Scottish Associates Ltd., Scheme of Arrangement, 26 July 1978; *The Times*, 27 July 1978, p. 17.
6. *The Times*, 27 July, 1978, p. 11.
7. *New Statesman*, 3 Nov. 1978, p. 570.
8. See the report in the *New Statesman*, 2 Apr. 1965, pp. 521–2.
9. EIU, op. cit., p. 45.
10. The Thomson Organisation Ltd., *Report and Accounts 1976*.
11. *The Times*, 28 May 1976, p. 4.
12. Times Newspapers Limited, Statement to all Members of Staff, n.d. [1978].
13. *The Times*, 18 Mar. 1976, p. 17.
14. Ibid.
15. *The Times*, 28 May 1976, p. 4.
16. *United Kingdom Press Gazette*, 23 June 1975, p. 10.
17. *The Times*, 28 May 1976, p. 4.
18. *New Statesman*, 3 Nov. 1978, p. 569.
19. Ibid.
20. *Times Challenger*, May 1979, p. 3.
21. *The Times*, 14 Jan. 1977, pp. 1, 2; 19 Jan. 1977, p. 15.
22. *Sunday Times*, 14 Mar. 1976, p. 4.
23. For two of the personalities involved on the trade-union side see E. Jacobs, *Stop Press: the Inside Story of the Times Dispute* (André Deutsch, 1980), pp. 56–7.
24. TNL letter to the general secretaries, NATSOPA Times Diary.
25. Ibid.
26. Jacobs, op. cit., pp. 6–8; TNL letter to the general secretaries, NATSOPA Times Diary.
27. Reported in the *Sunday Times*, 7 May 1978, p. 3.
28. *Sunday Times*, 23 July 1978, p. 2; *Print*, October 1978, p. 1.
29. Jacobs, op. cit., p. 53.

30. *The Times*, 19 Sept. 1978, p. 1.
31. *The Times*, 15 Sept. 1978, p. 2; Jacobs, op. cit., p. 41.
32. *The Times*, 28 Sept. 1978, p. 2.
33. NATSOPA Times Diary.
34. *The Times*, 29 Nov. 1978, pp. 1, 2.
35. *Guardian*, 1 Dec. 1978, p. 1.
36. *Daily Telegraph*, 15 Dec. 1978, p. 1.
37. *Hansard, House of Commons Debates*, 30 Nov. 1978, Vol. 959, col. 732. The debate lasted for three hours, but did not raise new issues (cols. 715–77).
38. Ibid., cols. 774–5.
39. *Financial Times*, 16 Dec. 1978, p. 28.
40. *Financial Times*, 5 Dec. 1978, p. 36.
41. *Guardian*, 29 Dec. 1978, p. 24.
42. *Times Challenger*, January 1979.
43. *Financial Times*, 9 Mar. 1979, p. 1.
44. *Financial Times*, 14 Apr. 1979, p. 1.
45. *Daily Telegraph*, 19 Apr. 1979, pp. 1, 10.
46. A full account is provided in Jacobs, op. cit., ch. 7.
47. *Daily Telegraph*, 30 June 1979, p. 1.
48. *Daily Telegraph*, 7 July 1979, p. 19.
49. *Daily Telegraph*, 21 July 1979, p. 2.
50. *Daily Telegraph*, 31 July 1979, p. 6.
51. Agreement published in *U.K. Press Gazette*, 6 Aug. 1979, pp. 5–9.
52. Ibid.
53. *Financial Times*, 22 Oct. 1979, p. 1.
54. *Daily Telegraph*, 4 Aug. 1979, p. 2.
55. *Daily Telegraph*, 6 Oct. 1979, p. 2; accounts of the final stages of the dispute appeared in the *Daily Telegraph* daily until 25 Oct. 1979.
56. *Daily Telegraph*, 22 Oct. 1979, p. 10.
57. See above, p. 268.
58. *The Times*, 24 Nov. 1979, p. 15.
59. *The Times*, 3 Apr. 1978, p. 3.
60. A. Flanders, *Management and Unions* (Faber & Faber, 1970), p. 40.
61. *Daily Telegraph*, 1 June 1979, p. 18.
62. *Daily Telegraph*, 28 Feb. 1979, p. 2.
63. *Daily Telegraph*, 1 June 1979, p. 18.
64. *Financial Times*, 30 Aug. 1980, p. 16.
65. Public statement by Sir Denis Hamilton, *The Times*, 25 June 1980, p. 23.
66. Public statement by Mr Gordon Brunton, 22 Oct. 1980.

Chapter 8

1. EIU, op. cit., p. 10.
2. Circulation figures for 1966, 1970, and 1976 from Royal Commission on the Press, *Final Report*, p. 272.
3. Reed International Ltd., *Annual Report*, 1973–4; PKTF, op. cit., p. 50, for profits 1960–71, although differences in the coverage of the statistics make direct comparison impossible.
4. Percy Roberts, in MGN Manchester Development Plan, 28 Oct. 1975, p. 10.
5. Royal Commission on the Press, *Interim*, Appendix E, Table 11. p. 101; Reed International, *Annual Report*, 1974–5.
6. Reed International, *Annual Report*, 1975–6.

7. Reed International, *Annual Report*, 1974–5.
8. Royal Commission on the Press, *Appendices*, pp. 50–61.
9. Reed International, *Annual Reports, passim.*
10. Reed International, *Annual Report*, 1975–6.
11. Reed International, *Annual Report*, 1974–5.
12. Reed International, *Annual Report*, 1975–6.
13. Royal Commission on the Press, *Final Report, Appendices,* p. 51.
14. *Mirror Group News*, June 1975.
15. Royal Commission on the Press, Written Evidence, MGN, April 1975.
16. *The Times*, 29 June 1976, p. 23.
17. Royal Commission on the Press, Written Evidence, MGN, Sector 4.
18. *Mirror Group News*, 28 Oct. 1975, p. 10.
19. *U.K. Press Gazette*, 16 June 1975, pp. 5–6; *Mirror Group News*, 28 Oct. 1975.
20. Royal Commission on the Press, Written Evidence, MGN, Ancillary Document 9, on the Belfast Printing Plant.
21. Royal Commission on the Press, Written Evidence, MGN, Scottish Daily Record and Sunday Mail; see also *Tonight at Anderston Quay* (MGN, n.d.).
22. *United Kingdom Press Gazette*, 16 June 1975, p. 5.
23. Documentation kindly loaned by Dr Paul Willman, Imperial College of Science and Technology, University of London.
24. Royal Commission on the Press, Written Evidence, MGN, Sector 3, *passim*.
25. *The Times*, 17 Jan. 1975, p. 1; 18 Jan. 1975, p. 1; 22 Jan. 1975, p. 2; *United Kingdom Press Gazette*, 20 Jan. 1975, p. 6.
26. Royal Commission on the Press, Written Evidence, MGN, Ancillary Document no. 3.
27. *United Kingdom Press Gazette*, 17 Feb. 1975, p. 5; 24 Mar. 1975, p. 12.
28. Ibid., 7 Apr. 1975, p. 5.
29. Royal Commission on the Press, Written Evidence, MGN, August 1975: Answers to questions raised on initial evidence, p. 15.
30. ACAS, p. 152.
31. *United Kingdom Press Gazette*, 26 Jan. 1976, p. 3.
32. See S. Hardcastle, Revolution at the Mirror, *Listener*, 26 Jan. 1978.
33. *The Times*, 23 Jan. 1978; 24 Jan. 1978; 25 Jan. 1978.
34. *The Times*, 19 Apr. 1978.
35. *The Times*, 3 Dec. 1977.
36. ACAS, p. 231.
37. Reed International, *Company Reports*.
38. For a general discussion involving Percy Roberts see *Campaign*, 1 Mar. 1980.

Chapter 9

1. *Interim*, p. 13.
2. The Thomson Organisation Ltd., *Report and Accounts*, 1977.
3. From data kindly supplied by the PPITB, October 1980.
4. National Union of Journalists, Advisory Committee on Technology (NUJ 1978).
5. Ibid., p. 1.
6. Ibid., p. 4.
7. ACAS, p. 185.
8. R. Winsbury, op. cit.
9. For a general account see E. C. Hynds, *American Newspapers in the 1970s* (New York: Hastings House, 1975).

Index